WOMEN'S STUDIES
ENCYCLOPEDIA

WOMEN'S STUDIES ENCYCLOPEDIA

Revised and Expanded Edition

Q–Z

Edited by
Helen Tierney

Greenwood Press
Westport, Connecticut

Library of Congress Cataloging-in-Publication Data

Women's studies encyclopedia / edited by Helen Tierney.—Rev. and
expanded ed.
    p. cm.
    Includes bibliographical references and index.
    ISBN 0–313–29620–0 (alk. paper)
      1. Women—United States—Encyclopedias. 2. Women—Encyclopedias.
    3. Feminism—Encyclopedias. I. Tierney, Helen.
    HQ1115.W645   1999
    305.4'03—dc21   98–14236

British Library Cataloguing in Publication Data is available.

A CD-ROM version of *Women's Studies Encyclopedia:
Revised and Expanded Edition* is available from Greenwood
Press, an imprint of Greenwood Publishing Group, Inc.
(ISBN 0-313-31074-2).

Library of Congress Catalog Card Number: 98–14236
ISBN: 0–313–29620–0 (set)
ISBN: 0–313–31071–8 (A–F)
ISBN: 0–313–31072–6 (G–P)
ISBN: 0–313–31073–4 (Q–Z)

First published in 1999

Greenwood Press, 88 Post Road West, Westport, CT 06881
An imprint of Greenwood Publishing Group, Inc.
www.greenwood.com

Printed in the United States of America

∞™

The paper used in this book complies with the
Permanent Paper Standard issued by the National
Information Standards Organization (Z39.48–1984).

10 9 8 7 6 5 4 3 2 1

Contents

Acknowledgments

Our sister, Helen Tierney, the editor of this *Women's Studies Encyclopedia*, died on October 31, 1997, when the encyclopedia was almost complete, but before she had acknowledged the myriad of individuals who made this book possible. Helen worked on this edition, almost to the exclusion of everything else, for the better part of two and a half years because she considered the availability of information about women of the utmost importance—their contributions to literature, art, science, learning, philosophy, religion, and their place in history. Her family has taken the few remaining steps necessary to see this project to completion.

The encyclopedia is a collaborative effort of many women and men who have given generously of their time, experience, and expertise. Acknowledgment and special thanks are due to all those who contributed articles and to the consultants whose advice and counsel were essential in choosing topics, in recommending the professionals who wrote the articles, and in reviewing articles. Acknowledgment and thanks are due to Helen's colleagues in the Women's Studies Program and the History Department of the University of Wisconsin for their assistance and support, particularly Gloria Stephenson for her help with articles Helen was working on at the time of her death. We do not know all the names of the many individuals who provided their generous assistance along the way, but we would like to express our deepest appreciation to them on Helen's behalf.

The Family of Helen Tierney

Introduction

The *Women's Studies Encyclopedia* contains information about women from all fields and disciplines of study, written in nonspecialist language and in a style accessible to all readers. The idea for the encyclopedia grew out of the discovery, when I first began to organize a course in women's history, that to teach about women, information from beyond the confines of my own area of expertise was essential. Conversations with colleagues interested in offering introductory women's courses or courses in their own disciplines showed that we all shared the same problem: a need for knowledge outside our own fields of interest but with neither the time nor the training to find and understand the results of current research in disciplines other than our own.

Students discovering the then brand-new world of women's studies, male colleagues interested either in broadening their own courses to include something about the other half of humanity or at least in finding out "what the fuss was all about," and women in the "real world" of business and homemaking also evinced interest in a reference that would offer basic information with the latest research and reflection about women from a feminist perspective. The encyclopedia tries to meet these needs.

Since the publication of the first edition of the *Women's Studies Encyclopedia*, research on women has proceeded rapidly; feminist thought has grown and branched out; conditions for women have changed markedly in some areas of life, for good and for ill, and little in others; material conditions in various areas of the world have offered new opportunities or set back advances. Less than ten years after its publication, many articles in the *Encyclopedia* had become out-of-date. In fact, the rapid changes taking place in Eastern Europe a decade ago were making some articles obsolete even before the third volume was published.

Since the early 1980s there has been an increase in women's studies and feminist reference materials, but the need for a multidisciplinary reference tool that touches on all facets and aspects of the female condition is still needed. To better meet that need, the new edition of the *Encyclopedia* has been somewhat enlarged, but, of course, three volumes cannot do more than scratch the surface. There are new articles; some articles have been completely rewritten; many others have been revised or updated. Some omissions have been corrected, and the number of articles in some areas has increased. There is more complete coverage of violence against women, as well as additional materials on women in public life. There are also more articles on contemporary conditions for women in specific countries or regions, but it was impossible to cover every country and every region of the world.

The entries in the *Encyclopedia* are meant to convey information to an educated audience without expertise in the subject under discussion. The bibliographic apparatus is, therefore, limited. The references included at the end of many of the articles are meant primarily to direct readers to works from which they may obtain a fuller explanation, more detailed information, or different perspectives on a subject.

The focus, as in the first edition, is on the American experience. Although a wide array of articles deal with women in other areas of the world and other cultures or on women in general, unless otherwise specified articles deal with women in the United States.

The articles are not written from a single feminist perspective. One aim in inviting contributions was to incorporate as wide a variety of feminist approaches as possible, so that all shades of opinion, from those so conservative that some will deny they are feminist, to the most radical, are represented. They do not, therefore, necessarily represent or agree with my own perspective.

As in the first edition, uniformity of organization and structure for articles of such widely varying subjects was not feasible, but one feature, the omission of the word "women" from entry titles, is fairly consistent, since every article is about women.

This edition is arranged more simply than the last, in alphabetical order. In cases where it was thought that the grouping of entries would make locating them more convenient, individual entries will share a common heading (e.g., articles related to French women's history, such as the Code Napoleon, are listed under "France"; articles about dowry in Western Europe and in India are listed under "dowry").

Cross-references have been reduced to a minimum. When a word or phrase used as the heading of an entry appears as a noun in another entry, the cross-reference is indicated by an asterisk. When a major topic might be listed under several different headings, cross-references to the heading are given.

The names of the authors of entries follow the entries and are also listed under Consultants and Contributors. Those articles that are not signed were written by the editor.

Helen Tierney
October 1997

Q

QUERELLE DES FEMMES is debate about the social role of women in modern Western society that began in France at the beginning of the fifteenth century. The *querelle* was part of the larger literary debate of the Renaissance that was initiated by Petrarch and Boccaccio, who championed "classical" models of human behavior grounded in the misogynist platonic tradition. The *querelle* was women's rebuttal of the "humanistic" ideals that denigrated the role and nature of women. Though the debate was literary, its participants addressed all of the areas in which women were being excluded by the consolidation of postmedieval society: politics, economics, and religion.

Christine de Pisan (1364–1430?) was one of the earliest and best-known writers who defended women from the increasingly misogynist attacks levied against them by church polemicists and spokesmen for the modern European states that were forming as patriarchal monarchies. She was an Italian scholar who traveled to Paris when her father was appointed to a position in the French Valois court. Widowed at an early age, Christine de Pisan used her humanistic training to support herself and her family and set an important precedent for women's participation in public discourse.

Christine moved from writing courtly literature to the arena of Renaissance humanism when she entered the *querelle de la rose*, a debate about *The Romance of the Rose*, a thirteenth-century poem that had been reworked by Jean de Meun at the beginning of the fifteenth century. Jean de Meun's version scorned the medieval ideals of courtly love while glorifying realism and logic. In denying the power of heterosexual love, he ridiculed the qualities of women. Writing in the same rhetorical style as other Renaissance writers, Christine de Pisan rebutted his vision and presented her case to the queen of France, thereby introducing the role of women into both scholarly and political debates throughout Europe.

In her analysis of the *querelle* Joan Kelly identified the debate as "the vehicle through which most early feminist thinking evolved." According to Kelly, the nearly 400-year-long debate was essentially static in character, though texts were composed by writers throughout Europe at different times (see Kelly's notes for bibliography.) For women living under the cultural hegemony of patriarchal society, the *querelle* served as a vital public forum in which they could develop and share their literary talent. If the endless discussion of essential qualities such as reason by mythological and noble characters gives the *querelle* an ahistorical quality, it is because the *querelle* was the collective voice of the loyal opposition that resisted secular changes that threatened the welfare of women.

Though its title suggests that the *querelle* was exclusively about women, the debate was a correction of other transformations that were taking place in European society between the fourteenth and nineteenth centuries: the shift to centralized nation-states, religious dissent and the secularization of society, and the development of a market economy—all of which subordinated the social role of women.

The attack on women was part of the attack on nature that characterizes modern Western culture. Renaissance writers vilified female reproductive and nurturing capacities that seemed to be antithetical to the ideals of reason, logic, and the ostensible objectivity of science. By denying nature, men felt free to plunder the environment in search of material wealth and to subject other human beings to economic and political exploitation. This view of the natural world changed in the eighteenth century, when philosophers again saw a common nature in human beings and formulated a more egalitarian social doctrine based on natural rights. Although women were ironically excluded from the Enlightenment view of natural rights, they participated in the debate with the same vigor that characterized the *querelle*. Mary Wollstonecraft's *Vindication of the Rights of Women* (1792) generally marks the beginning of modern feminism, when the *querelle des femmes* moved from the rhetoric of moral allegory to the heated political argument that characterizes modern democratic society.

Reference. Joan Kelly, *Women, History and Theory* (Chicago, 1984), 66.

JANE CRISLER

R

RAPE. Since rape laws are written at the state, not the federal, level, there is no consensus on a legal definition of rape in the United States. As Patricia Searles and Ronald Berger point out, there is a continuum of legal definitions ranging from "the most traditional statutes, which call the offense rape and limit the crime to vaginal-penile intercourse, to the statutes most consistent with feminist goals, which call the offense sexual assault and define the crime more broadly to include sexual penetration generally (i.e., vaginal, oral, and anal) as well as touching of intimate parts of the body" (27–28).

It has taken years of feminist struggle to get most states to reform their rape laws to include marital rape, forced oral, anal, and digital penetration, and penetration by a foreign object. According to Searles and Berger, "Over half of the states continue to label the primary offense rape, and one-third of the states retain the most traditional definition (i.e., rape limited to sexual penetration). Less than one-fifth have adopted the most feminist conceptualization (i.e., sexual assault including both penetration and touching)" (28).

Statutory rape refers to the nonforceful sexual penetration of a female or male below the age of consent. This age varies from a low of 13 years to a high of 18 years. Sixteen years is the age of consent in most states (Searles and Berger, 29). It is unnecessary in cases of statutory rape for the victim to resist.

The *incidence* of rape refers to the number of new cases that occur within a specified period, usually a year. The *prevalence* of rape refers to the number of individuals who have been raped at a specific time.

In 1996 the Federal Bureau of Investigation (FBI) reported that 97,464 cases of forcible rape or attempted rape had been reported to law enforcement agencies throughout the nation during 1995. Eighty-seven percent of these cases were completed rapes. The estimated *rate* of rape was 72 per 100,000 females, or .072 percent.

However, these figures do not include the much larger number of unreported rapes. Estimates of the percentage of rapes reported to the police range from the National Crime Survey's high rate of approximately 60 percent to Mary Koss and Mary Harvey's low rate of 5 percent (25). Many rape survivors are unwilling to report their experiences to the police because they fear being blamed for their own victimization. In addition, the myth that women often "cry rape" falsely out of vengeance may be a factor in the police practice of "unfounding" (disqualifying) many cases of reported rape. Eight percent of the rape complaints made in 1995 were "unfounded" because the police considered them to be "false or baseless" (FBI, 24) compared to only 2 percent of the other index crimes (murder, robbery, aggravated assault, burglary, larceny-theft, motor vehicle theft, and arson). Rape also has the lowest apprehension and conviction rate of any violent crime.

In recognition of the fact that most crimes are never reported to the police, the federal government instituted the National Crime Surveys (NCS) in 1972 to augment the FBI's statistics on reported crimes, including rape. These surveys (now called the National Crime Victimization Surveys [NCVS]) are conducted yearly. Despite the long-overdue revision of their methodology in 1992, they remain so severely flawed that they continue to find very low incidence rates for rape, from which they draw the erroneous and dangerous conclusion that rape is a rare crime. Michael Rand, chief of the Victimization Statistics Unit at the Bureau of Justice Statistics (BJS— the body responsible for the NCVS), informed me that typically, the approximately 50,000 females who were/are regularly interviewed for the NCS and NCVS victimization surveys yield only from 60 to 100 actual rape cases of females aged 12 and over in the previous 12 months (personal communication, July 17, 1997).

In 1978, Diana Russell conducted the first study (and the only study to date) whose major objective was to assess the incidence and prevalence of rape and other forms of sexual assault. It was a federally funded survey based on in-person interviews with a probability sample of 930 adult female residents of San Francisco. Applying the very restricted legal definition of rape current in California and most other states at that time, 24 percent of the 930 women disclosed at least one experience of completed rape, and 44 percent disclosed an experience of attempted or completed rape (35). Half (22 percent) of the surveyed women who disclosed an experience of rape or attempted rape had been raped more than once by different perpetrators.

Russell's rape incidence in the 12 months prior to the interviews was 35 per 1,000 females. This was 7 times higher than the NCS incidence rate of 5.0 per 1,000 females residing in San Francisco in 1974 (the only NCS study of San Francisco) and 21 times higher than the NCS national incidence rate of 1.7 per 1,000 females in 1978.

In 1990, the National Women's Project undertook the first national study of the prevalence of rape in the United States (Kilpatrick, Edmunds, and Seymour). This study obtained a prevalence rate of 12.7 percent for completed rape and an incidence rate for completed rape of 7.0 per 1,000 females in 1990. The rate for completed rape is 7 times higher than the 1990 NCS incidence rate of 1.0 per 1,000 females for both completed and attempted rape.

A more recent national study conducted by the National Survey of Family Growth reported a prevalence of completed rape of 20.4 percent.

These three surveys reveal that the incidence and prevalence of rape are extremely high in the United States and many times higher than the federal government's sources routinely find.

Russell is the only researcher to date to examine the changes in the prevalence of rape over time. She found that the rape rates for the 930 San Francisco women rose significantly for each younger cohort. For example, 22 percent of the women 60 and older had been victimized by rape or attempted rape at some time in their lives, compared with 59 percent of women in their 30s and 53 percent of women aged 18 to 29 (Russell, 53). Since the youngest cohort still had the most years at risk, their 53 percent rape rate was the highest per number of years at risk.

These data suggest that the real rape rate, as opposed to the reported rate, is increasing dramatically. Although these findings apply to the years prior to 1978, it would be very surprising if these sizable, consistent, linear increases in the rape rates over several decades were suddenly to reverse themselves.

Thirty-five percent of the 930 women surveyed by Russell had been the victim of rape or attempted rape by an acquaintance, friend, date, boyfriend, unrelated authority figure, lover, or ex-lover—over three times more than had been victimized by a stranger (11 percent). Twelve percent of married, divorced, or separated women had been the victims of rape or attempted rape by a husband or ex-husband.

Studies conducted on student populations also report very high rates of rape and attempted rape, many of which are date rapes (e.g., Koss, Gidycz, and Wisniewski). Well over half of these attacks (57 percent) were date rapes.

It is widely believed that African American women are far more subject to rape than white women, although several studies have contradicted this belief (e.g., Russell; Wyatt). In addition, some studies found no significant relationship between rape and social class, whereas other studies report that poor women are subject to higher rape rates than middle-class women.

Difficult as it is to ascertain the prevalence of rape, it is more difficult still to determine the percentage of men in the population who perpetrate rape. Research has shown that males typically downplay the seriousness of their sexually abusive behavior. However, numerous studies reveal high percentages of male students with rape-supportive attitudes or self-reported desire to rape women. For example, Neil Malamuth found that, on average, 35 percent of several groups of male college students admitted there was some likelihood that they would rape a woman if they could be sure of getting away with it.

Half of the 432 high school males interviewed in another study believed it was acceptable "for a guy to hold a girl down and force her to have sexual intercourse" in situations such as when "she gets him sexually excited" or "she says she's going to have sex with him and then changes her mind" (Goodchilds and Zillman).

The high prevalence of rape and rape-supportive attitudes suggests the inadequacy of theories that stress psychopathology as the major causative factor in rape.

Research has repeatedly found rape to be associated with immediate and long-term damaging psychological effects, including sexual problems (e.g., aversion to sex, loss of sexual satisfaction, promiscuity), anxiety, depression, relationship difficulties, and physical symptoms (e.g., gynecological complaints and somatization). Rape victims are also thought to constitute the largest single group of PTSD (posttraumatic stress disorder) sufferers, who typically experience intrusive thoughts about danger, intense fears about future victimization, devastating panic, and vivid memories that manifest in nightmares, flashbacks, and intrusive thoughts (Koss and Harvey, 1991). Flashbacks of the rape "may not occur until months or years following the trauma when recollections are triggered by some actual or symbolic reminder" (p. 78). (See RAPE TRAUMA SYNDROME.)

Before feminists began writing and protesting about rape in the early 1970s, most clinicians and rape researchers blamed the victims. By recognizing the connections between sexism and rape, feminists have transformed contemporary thinking about this traumatic form of male aggression. In addition, the feminist movement has enabled survivors to start speaking out publicly about their experiences and the often devastating effects of rape on their lives without fear of being blamed.

Feminists set up rape crisis centers throughout the country to assist survivors. At the same time, feminists like Kate Millett, Susan Griffin, the New York Radical Feminists, Andra Medea and Kathleen Thompson, Diana Russell, Susan Brownmiller, Lorenne Clarke, Debra Lewis, and others started to write about rape and the role it plays in keeping women subservient to men. These writers also exploded many myths about rape, for example, that it is an infrequent crime perpetrated by strangers who are crazy, psychopathic deviants who have nothing in common with "normal" men or that most rape victims are to blame (for wearing provocative clothes, for being out late at night). Instead of separating men into the rapists and the nonrapists, Russell and others have conceptualized a continuum of sexist woman-abuse by males ranging from sexually harassing whistles, obscene calls, breast grabbing and bottom slapping, to rape.

Pointing to the fact that the vast majority of rapists are male, some feminist theorists have concluded that male sex role and sexual socialization are crucial to an understanding of why men rape. Lorenne Clark and Debra Lewis see rape as a consequence of the coercive sexual and nonsexual power males have over females in patriarchal cultures. They argue that rape cannot be eradicated without changing this power relationship. Susan Brownmiller and others have stressed that men as a gender benefit from rape because it keeps women fearful and dependent.

While some of these feminist writers and researchers have emphasized that most rape is perpetrated by men who are known to the survivors, only in the last few years has date rape* become the center of popular attention. Its ascendance into public awareness has coincided with a vicious backlash* by some male academics, supporters of the so-called men's movement, and the male-dominated media who have tried to discredit the empirical evidence of the high prevalence of rape and child sexual abuse (e.g., Neil Gilbert).

While rape victims often receive better treatment today than they did 20 years ago, feminists and others concerned about rape have been singularly ineffective in diminishing its prevalence. The fact that feminists now have to fight a backlash intent on turning the clock back to the good old days, when women did not talk about rape, is cause for militant protest and action.

References. Joyce Abma et al., "Fertility, Family Planning, and Women's Health, *Vital and Health Statistics* 23, 19 (1997); Pauline Bart, *Stopping Rape* (New York, 1985); Susan Brownmiller, *Against Our Will: Men, Women, and Rape* (New York, 1975); Lorenne Clark and Debra Lewis, *The Power of Coercive Sexuality* (Toronto, 1977); FBI *Uniform Crime Reports 1996* (1996), 24; Neil Gilbert, "The Phantom Epidemic of Sexual Assault," *Public Interest* 103 (Spring 1991): 54–65; Jacqueline Goodchilds and Gail Zillman, "Sexual Signaling and Sexual Aggression in Adolescent Relationships," in N. Malamuth and E. Donnerstein (eds.), *Pornography and Sexual Aggression* (New York, 1984); Dean Kilpatrick, Christine Edmunds, and Anne Seymour, *Rape in America: A Report to the Nation* (Charleston, S.C., 1992); Mary Koss, Christine Gidycz, and Nadine Wisniewski, "The Scope of Rape: Incidence and Prevalence of Sexual Aggression and Victimization in a National Sample of Higher Education Students," *Journal of Consulting and Clinical Psychology* 55 (1987): 162–170; Mary Koss and Mary Harvey, *The Rape Victim* (Newbury Park, Calif., 1991); Neil Malamuth, "Rape Proclivity among Men," *Journal of Social Issues* 37 (1981): 138–157; National Crime Survey, *Criminal Victimization in the United States, 1979* (Washington, D.C., 1981): 15; Andrea Parrot and Laurie Bechhofer (eds.), *Acquaintance Rape: The Hidden Crime* (New York, 1991); Diana E. H. Russell, *The Politics of Rape* (Chelsea, Mich., 1989); Diana E. H. Russell,

Rape in Marriage (Bloomington, Ind., 1990); Diana Russell, *Sexual Exploitation* (Beverly Hills, Calif., 1984); Peggy Sanday, *Fraternity Gang Rape* (New York, 1990); Diana Scully, *Understanding Sexual Violence: A Study of Convicted Rapists* (Cambridge, 1990); Patricia Searles and Ronald Berger, "The Current Status of Rape Reform Legislation: An Examination of State Statutes," *Women's Rights Law Reporter* 10 (1987); Gail Wyatt, "The Sociocultural Context of African American and White American Women's Rape," *Journal of Social Issues* 48 (1992).

Acknowledgment: I am grateful to Gayle Pitman for her editorial assistance with this entry.

DIANA E. H. RUSSELL

RAPE TRAUMA SYNDROME. Posttraumatic stress disorder (PTSD) has replaced rape trauma syndrome as the descriptive label for the aftermath of rape. Although the PTSD diagnosis was originally created to describe the symptoms induced by the traumatic experiences of war, many rape survivors experience the characteristic PTSD symptoms, including repeated daytime intrusive memories and/or nightmares that are so discomforting as to motivate them to go to great lengths to avoid reminders of the trauma. Ninety-four percent of rape survivors assessed immediately after an assault are now diagnosed with PTSD symptoms, and survivors are the largest single group of PTSD sufferers due to the high prevalence of rape combined with its high likelihood of induced symptoms.

Unfortunately, the PTSD diagnosis does not fully account for the varied symptoms that women may experience after a rape. Other critiques of the PTSD diagnosis assert that it medicalizes and individualizes a social problem of violence against women. One positive effect of the diagnosis, however, is that PTSD has been a unifying force drawing together the service providers and academics focused on a number of different life-threatening traumas.

Virtually all women are affected in some way by the experience of rape, but it is difficult to predict the magnitude of impact and the type of response specific individuals will have to sexual assault. Rape can affect a woman's emotions, cognitions, relationships, and physical health. Immediate responses following rape may include shock, intense fear, numbness, confusion, extreme helplessness, and/or disbelief. The most common long-term symptoms experienced by rape victims are fear and anxiety. Fear is often triggered by stimuli associated with the attack itself or situations that are perceived as reminders of rape. Generalized anxiety may lead to jumpiness, sleep disruptions, and/or a lack of concentration. Symptoms of depression are also common after rape. These symptoms include sleep and appetite disturbance, a loss of interest in normal activities, a decrease in the ability to concentrate, and/or feelings of alienation and loneliness. While some women actually develop severe depressive symptoms following the rape, others will experience only some of the symptoms and not for extended periods of time. One study found that almost one in five raped women in the community had attempted suicide. Rape victims are also more likely than nonvictims to receive several psychiatric diagnoses, including alcohol abuse/dependence and drug abuse/dependence even several years after the assault.

Feelings of guilt, shame, and self-blame are also common postrape experiences and may be a result of cultural myths about rape and unsupportive responses of their social support network. Women who blame themselves for the rape are more likely to experience greater distress and poorer adjustment. Thus, these negative feelings may be even worse in women who were raped by known partners. A woman's cognitive beliefs and schemas about safety, power, trust, esteem, and intimacy are also often affected after rape. Many women experience feelings of vulnerability and loss of control that often stem from no longer believing that they are secure in the world, that the world has order and meaning, and that they are worthy persons. While some may actually gain a more flexible belief system through such a destabilizing experience such as rape, others may suffer from pervasive negative beliefs that one is bad, evil, responsible, and untrustable. Some women also experience a fear of sex, arousal dysfunction, and/or decreased sexual interest, which may be the result of a lowered sexual self-esteem, negative feelings about men, and/or increased insecurities concerning sexual attractiveness due to the rape.

Women also experience a wide range of physical symptoms in the aftermath of rape. While discomfort from abrasions, bruising, and genital injuries add to the distress of the experience, the chronic somatic consequences of rape are more significant in terms of lost quality of life. Several medical diagnoses such as gastrointestinal syndromes, pelvic pain, chronic pain syndromes, and headaches are diagnosed disproportionately among women with a history of sexual assault.

Many women may not feel "recovered" within a few months or even years after an assault, and many never view the world the same. However, the majority of women continue to function in everyday life after experiencing a rape, and within four to six years most report that they feel they have healed. Research on rape-related PTSD has found that the negative effects of rape actually are often canceled by the healing effects of time and cognitive coping strategies. However, these findings suggest that the healing process may take longer than the previously stated four to six years.

References. R. N. Bell et al., *Violence against Women in the United States: A Comprehensive Background Paper* (New York, 1996); N. A. Crowell and A. W. Burgess (eds.), *Understanding Violence against Women* (Washington, D.C., 1996); L. Heise, J. Pitanguy, and A. Germain, *Violence against Women: The Hidden Health Burden* (Washington, D.C., 1993); R. Janoff-Bulman, *Shattered Assumptions: Towards a New Psychology of Trauma* (Toronto, 1992); M. P. Koss and L. Goodman, *No Safe Haven: Male Violence against Women at Home, at Work, and in the Community* (Washington, D.C., 1994).

MARY P. KOSS and LAURA BOESCHEN

REFORMATION. The Reformation deeply influenced the public attitude about morals, the role of women in society, and prostitution. The leaders of both the Reformation and the Counter-Reformation strongly defended the patriarchal concept and tried to keep women within the rigid framework of the family. However, marriage itself acquired a positive value as the Protestant clergy now entered matrimony. Martin Luther, in his *Vom ehelichen Leben* (1522, WA 10/2, 275–304), painted the novel ideal of woman as loving wife and mother. Katharina von Bora (1499–1550), Luther's wife, was an exemplum of this new ideal of women. Regulating marriage became an integral part of the church's administrative functions; the ceremony now had to be performed by a minister of the church. The ceremony replaced the traditional contract between the families as the basis for a marriage and thus established institutional power over the individual. The city of Zurich, for instance, in 1525 forbade all forms of concubinage in all strata of society. In other words, the people's sexuality per se became an object of social control.

Protestant and Catholic women alike took an active part in the Reformation. Protestant women, often in the role of ministers' wives, accumulated a significantly larger influence over family affairs and also spoke out publicly on religious questions. Katharina Zell (1487/1488–1562), a minister's wife in Strassburg, was one of the strongest supporters of the Reformation in that city. Argula von Grumbach (1429–1554[?]) gained great notoriety in Bavaria and south Germany for her public letters and pamphlets defending the Reformation. Elisabeth Cruciger (d. 1535) composed new and important liturgical songs for the Protestant Church service. A few women even succeeded in occupying an independent role within the church. One such woman was Margarethe Blarer (d. 1542), who organized a Protestant hospital in Constance.

Women were also active participants in the Catholic Reformation. As a reaction to the social and theological upheaval all over Europe, women such as Teresa of Ávila (1515–1582) sought the renewal of Christian belief in the form of Christ-oriented mysticism and in reforming and founding new monastic orders. Other women who established important new orders were Angela Merici (1474–1540), founder of the order of St. Ursula; Jeanne de Chantel (1572–1641), together with St. Francis de Sales, of the Visitation Order; and Mary Ward (1585/1586–1645/1646), creator of the Institute of Mary in England.

However, despite radical changes that the Protestant Reformation brought about in the sixteenth century, women did not experience a considerable improvement of their lives. Patriarchy gained a much stronger grip on married life, and peasant and bourgeois women particularly faced a considerably more limited lifestyle.

Both in the country and in the city women kept their double role as both mother/housewife and relatively independent worker earning her own money. (See MEDIEVAL WOMEN, Lives of Urban Women; MEDIEVAL WOMEN, Peasant Women.)

The freedom with which young people, especially in the country, made their choice of a marriage partner, however, was a remarkable aspect of sixteenth-century social life. Far-reaching equality existed between man and woman in this respect, although many theologians argued strictly against it.

There was a general tightening up of moral standards all over Europe. Police regulations in both Protestant and Catholic areas reduced widespread prostitution, concubinage, and the total number of brothels, thus helping to contain the devastating disease syphilis. Occasionally, however, guilds in such cities as Ulm in southern Germany requested the reopening of the brothels (1537) in order to ventilate tensions between the patricians holding the authority in the city and the large group of apprentices and journeymen who were not allowed to marry before they gained the rank of master.

In the cities there were still approximately 10 percent more women than men, although this rate could differ remarkably from region to region. The marriage age moved up to the mid-20s, thus reducing the total number of pregnancies. A continuously high mortality rate was partially compensated for by an increased life expectancy for women. The small-size family with only a few children and also few grandparents was not a development in the wake of the Industrial Revolution but rather is evident as early as the sixteenth century.

Some women managed to keep their positions in the crafts and guilds, but the relative professional freedom of the Middle Ages was increasingly reduced. A shortage of jobs imposed rigid limits on workingwomen. Whereas in the fifteenth century women still occupied a considerable role in local industries, the economic crisis of the turn of the century restricted their rights to employment except in the areas of nursing, health care, and textile manufacturing. Gradually, however, even the privileged work area of health care came under heavy attack from barber-surgeons, physicians, and apothecaries. By the end of the sixteenth century, many cities had issued regulations explicitly forbidding women from practicing medicine in any way, although they could never totally suppress women's medical activities altogether.

However, a distinctive feature of early modern times was that a man could not open a craftsman's workshop in a city unless he was married, and his widow was even able, to some extent, to preserve her role as head of the whole workshop. Nevertheless, the laws of the guilds certainly excluded women from learning their crafts. Only in the field of lace making could sixteenth-century women preserve a dominant position. For instance,

Barbara Uttmann, wife of a wealthy Annaberg patrician in the Erzgebirge (southern East Germany), introduced this art around 1560 in her area and thus established an expanding and profitable industry mostly employing women. Women also remained very active in the money trade and in other forms of trading, such as the cloth trade. Dutch women in particular appeared in the forefront of both types of business.

Noblewomen either married, thus continuing in their traditional role of representative of, and reproductive element for, the family, or they entered a nunnery. The latter choice was considerably reduced with the Reformation, since the Protestant Church forcibly closed most convents and transformed them into hospitals and homes for the poor and old members of society. The upper-class woman was often destined to a life as an aesthetic object, decorous and chaste, and thus participated even less in the public life than women of the lower classes.

However, there were a surprisingly large number of women rulers during the period. Mary I Tudor (1553–1558); Elizabeth I (1558–1603); Mary Stuart (1542–1567); Anna de Beaujeu (1483–1522); regent for Charles VIII of France; Catherine de Medici (1519–1589); Isabella I of Spain (1474–1504); and Isabella d'Este of Mantua (1490–1539) exercised independent rule over their countries. Many noblewomen also had a considerable say within their territories. The duchess Elisabeth von Rochlitz, when widowed, introduced the Reformation into Saxony in 1539 against her father-in-law Georg of Saxony's opposition; Katharina of Mecklenburg continued the Reformation in Mecklenburg and convinced her husband, Duke Henry of Freiburg, to follow the new belief. Renata di Francia (1510–1575), daughter of Louis XII of France, strongly supported the Huguenot (Protestant of Reformed communion) movement. Marguerite de Navarre (1492–1549), author of the *Heptamaeron* (1559), was an equally vocal defender of the new theology and also promoted the intellectual life at her court.

Married noblewomen of high rank emerged in the intellectual, artistic, and religious worlds. Vittoria Colonna (1492–1547), girlfriend of Michelangelo, and Charitas Pirkheimer, literata and abbess of the Nuremberg St. Claire convent, became the nuclei of highly reputable circles of poets and philosophers. Women such as Olympia Morata (1526–1555), a Ferrarese Greek and Latin scholar Catherine des Roches (1542–1587); Louise Labé (1525–1566), a Lyonese poet; Argula von Grumbach (c. 1492–1554); Cassandra Fedele (1465–1558); Gaspara Stampa (1523–1554); and Marguerite de Navarre (1492–1549) boldly proved that women could excel in intellectual subject matters.

Most women artists and intellectuals, however, were the offspring of upper-class artists, philosophers, and poets and were trained by their fathers. Sofonisba Anguissola (c. 1532–1625) became an important painter of portraits. She was limited to this subject because the study of nude male bodies, the basic object of study for all aspiring artists at that time, was not possible for her. Sofonisba provided a role model for other female artists such as Artemisia Gentileschi (1593– c. 1652), Lavinia Fontana (1552–1614), and Fede Galizia (1578–1630). Still-life painting developed as a special domain for women painters in the early 1600s because this genre did not require a particular training with a master of the arts. The most reputable women painters lived in the Flemish and Dutch areas, such as, for instance, Marie Bessemers (1520–1560).

Women also contributed to the religious literature of the Reformation period. Because they could not pursue an advanced education, they expressed themselves predominantly in emotional terms; they did not write systematic theology. Consequently, they did not theorize over the Bible's message but rather stressed that the Holy Spirit had provided them with an unmediated access to the true understanding of God's words. Although few members of any spiritual movement of that time dared to speak out against social injustices based on gender differences, some women such as the Franco-Bavarian Argula von Grumbach courageously defended women's case even against sharp male criticism. Women's education was furthered to some extent by the Protestant stress on the need for everyone, even women, to read God's word. Schools teaching minimal literacy were widespread, at least in Northern Europe, for girls of the upper classes.

At the same time, continuing misogyny coupled with a rapidly growing belief in witchcraft caused the intensification of the witch-hunt. In 1484 Pope Innocent VIII published his bull *Summis desiderantes affectibus*, and in 1487 Heinrich Institioris and Jacob Sprenger printed the notorious *Malleus malificarum*, the most popular and influential guidebook for witch-hunt. These texts became the principal cornerstones of the devastating witch craze of the later sixteenth and seventeenth centuries. (See WITCH-CRAFT CRAZE.) Women, especially those marginal to society, such as old widows and spinsters ("hags"), easily became the prime target. More women were killed during the entire period from 1480 to 1700 for this alleged crime than for all other crimes put together.

Much information about women's status during the period from the late fifteenth to the early seventeenth centuries can be gleaned from treatises on women, such as Sir Thomas Elyot's *Defense of Good Women*, published in 1540. These texts were written for both a popular and scholarly audience, that is, for scholars, married couples, teachers and the clergy.

Many male authors claimed authority in the field of female beauty and gave meticulous descriptions of what a beautiful woman was supposed to look like. In Agnolo Firenzuolo's (1492–1548) *Sopra la bellezza delle donne* from 1523 and Johann Fischart's (1546–1590) *Ehezuchtbüchlein* from 1578, those male concepts about femininity found some of their most eloquent expressions.

References. Albrecht Classen, "Frauen in der deutschen Reformation," in Paul Gerhard Schmidt (ed.), *Die Frau in der Renaissance* (Wiesbaden, 1994), 179–201;

Natalie Zemon Davis and Arlette Farge (eds.), *A History of Women in the West*: III, *Renaissance and Enlightenment Paradoxes* (Cambridge, Mass., and London, 1993); R. Kelso, *Doctrine for the Lady of the Renaissance* (Urbana, Ill., 1956); Hennelore Sachs, *The Renaissance Woman* (New York, 1971); Wendy Slatkin, *Women Artists in History: From Antiquity to the 20th Century* (Englewood Cliffs, N.J., 1985); Merry E. Wiesner, *Working Women in Renaissance Germany* (New Brunswick, N.J., 1986).

ALBRECHT CLASSEN

RELIGION, ANCIENT. Women were significantly involved in the religious activities of ancient cultures. Ordinary women held sacred office and participated in religious events. The office of priestess included various responsibilities encompassing religion, philosophy, prophecy, ethics, healing, ritual, writing and scribal duties, temple construction and maintenance, and, in later periods, raising money.

In the prehistory of the Mediterranean basin, the weight of archaeological evidence favors the importance of women as religious leaders in prepatriarchal, agrarian cultures. The sacred pantheon reflected a society often termed matriarchal and structured around the concept of the mother. Although there is no written documentation to support the contention that women were priestesses and religious leaders, the great abundance of art and artifacts indicates that this was surely the case, as do the conclusions of anthropology, comparative religion, and evidence from Minoan Crete, which reflects this early culture.

All Asia Minor worshiped a mother goddess, whose names were many. The goddess and her queen-priestesses, warrior-priestesses, and temple servants reigned long over the cultural life of the area. The priestess dressed to resemble the goddess she served and was called by the name of the goddess. The education of a priestess included music and dance, memorization and performance of ritual, the rites of purification, and medicine. As representatives of the protectress of animals, children, and seasonal vegetation, priestesses assured the continuance of life. This they did in two ways: by living the life of the goddess through her rituals and through their knowledge of medicine.

In Sumer and Babylon there is documentary as well as archaeological evidence for women's high status as priestesses. In the Old Babylonian period (second millennium B.C.E.), the daughters of kings and rulers were appointed as moon-priestesses, or priestess of Inanna/Ishtar (called *en* or *entu* priestesses). They wore distinctive clothing, which included the same insignia and garments worn by the ruler, and lived within the sacred shrine, having charge of temple management and affairs and performing ritual and ceremonial duties. They were usually unmarried. In ancient Sumer, priestesses (called *nin-dingir*) had a similar role; these women participated annually in the Sacred Marriage, representing their goddess and thus ensuring fertility and the continuance of life. It is most likely that the later idea of "temple prostitution" arose from the participation of high priestesses in the sacred marriage rituals; however, such participation rather represented an example of sacred sexual service. Enheduanna, daughter of King Sargon of Akkad (c. 2371–2316 B.C.E.), was a lifelong priestess of the goddess Inanna/Ishtar and the first known woman poet. *Naditum* priestesses were forbidden childbearing and served the male gods Marduk and Shamash. They were drawn from the upper levels of society and entered a temple-complex at an early age. The *naditum* priestesses brought to the temple rich dowries, which reverted to their families at their death. They were free to use these dowries for capital in business ventures, to lend money at interest, and to leave the temple to take care of their business dealings. Since they did not bear children, they often adopted daughters and could leave their property to female heiresses. There were many lesser female religious functionaries found in temple-complexes, which sometimes housed upward of several hundred women.

In the area of Syria-Palestine, the worship of Inanna/Ishtar survived in the worship of Asherah. She was a great mother goddess and was associated with the nurturance of infants. After the Hebrews conquered Canaan (c. 1200 B.C.E.), her importance continued. There is evidence that she was worshiped in the temple in Jerusalem as late as 586 B.C.E. *Asherahs*, wooden pillars, possibly symbolizing the goddess or painted to resemble her, were set up on hilltops. The power of the goddesses and their priestesses in daily life and in popular religion continued for centuries in the Near East.

In the religious life of Crete and its affiliated Greek Islands (2400–1400 B.C.E.) women were also of primary importance. A highly devout people who knew no fortifications or war, the people of Minoan Crete worshiped a mother goddess with many characteristics familiar to the eastern Mediterranean world: she was mistress of animals and vegetation, protectress of the young, and associated with the moon and rhythms of the sea. Women were moon-priestesses, and everywhere in Minoan art there are representations of them with their sacred articles. These include the snake, symbol of rebirth and the power of the earth; the double ax, symbol of the warrior aspect of the goddess and of the moon; the moon itself; and crescent-shaped horns that symbolized both the bovine aspect of the Egyptian goddesses Hathor and Isis and the moon. There is no evidence of patriarchal oppression on the islands during this period; the mythology associated with Theseus and the Minotaur refers to the period after the conquest of these people by the Mycenean Greeks during the Bronze Age.

We have much more written documentation for the classical period in Greece. In Corinth, women were devoted particularly to Aphrodite, who was originally a Near Eastern goddess equivalent to Inanna/Ishtar. Priestesses practiced sacred prostitution and were responsible for the assurance of good weather and calm seas, for this Aphrodite was also the goddess of the sea. In Sparta, the goddess Helen was worshiped for millennia despite the propaganda in the Helen stories associated with the Trojan War. During the classical period women in Sparta retained a high status, remaining essential for the continuing religious and social well-being of the country.

In Athens, religion was the major sphere of public life in which women participated. Religion was in the hands of men and was subordinate to, and an integral part of, the state. The patron goddess of Athens was Athena Polias; hereditary priestesses who presided over her festivals played an important role in the religious life of the community. Athenians celebrated the birthday of Athena, the Panathenea, annually, and every four years honored her with magnificence. During the festival the great statue of Athena in the Parthenon was presented with a new robe, woven by girls between the ages of 7 and 11 and "chaste matrons."

In the Eleusinian Mysteries, the most important personal religion in the Greco-Roman world, two priestesses, one representing Demeter and one Persephone, assisted the high priest, who was male. The high priestess of Demeter had prestige equivalent to that of the high priest. She was named Demeter and represented the goddess as a living woman. The Eleusinian Mysteries, which celebrated the abduction of Persephone, the mourning of her mother, Demeter, and the daughter's return, was a salvation religion that promised a happy eternity and reunion with loved ones. Women danced the sacred story during the rituals, with the priestess of Demeter acting the part of the goddess. Groups of priestesses sacred to Demeter, known as *melissae*, lived together in segregated complexes and had no contact with men. Their office was one of great antiquity, going back to prepatriarchal days when such sacred women possessed autonomy and great power.

The Thesmophoria was a celebration honoring Demeter and reserved only for women. It employed ancient rituals of the sowing of grain and involved fertility magic. The Thesmophoria was another survival from the matriarchal period when all religion was in the hands of women; the connection of women with fertility and birth was retained even in this most misogynous of polities.

The most important priestesses in the Mediterranean world were the Delphic oracles. For more than 2,000 years, the Delphic oracle, known as Pythia, Dragon Priestess of Earth, was the highest religious authority in the world. Although this is a most sacred shrine celebrating the sacred power of women, right of access was restricted to male citizens and priestesses in the classical period. This restriction seems to reflect the acknowledgment and fear of women's sacred power by the patriarchy, which nevertheless honored the sacred feminine in the person of the Delphic priestess. The priestesses were chosen from young girls who showed sacred potential. They remained priestesses all their lives, undergoing strict training and discipline as well as many levels of initiation. The Pythia conducted the oracular rituals herself, going into a trance and giving answers in verse that were communicated through a priest to the seekers who came to Delphi. (See GREEK GODDESSES.)

In Rome, cultivation of the heavenly powers was the province of women. There were two kinds of religion, native religions that supported the goals of the state and were supported by the state, and the Oriental religions, which included the Mystery religions of the great mother goddesses. The most important state religion was that associated with Vesta, goddess of the hearth. The hearth symbolized the continuity of family and community, and it was a serious affair to let the hearth fire go out. Virgin priestesses tended the fire in the Temple of Vesta, and any Vestal who allowed the fire to die was scourged. The Vestals were active in other aspects of Roman religion, especially in agricultural and fertility rites. Sacred to the unmarried goddess, they worked their sacred magic as virgin priestesses had from time immemorial. In the historical period, Vestals were chosen between the ages of 6 and 10 and served as priestesses for 30 years. Afterward, they were given dowries and were free to marry, although most did not. Those Vestals who did not retain their virginity were buried alive. When calamities happened to the Roman state, the Vestals were suspected and often persecuted. The Vestals were probably the most emancipated women in Rome, for they were under the guardianship of no man and had certain legal privileges other women did not. The religion of the Vestal virgins was disbanded in 394 C.E.

Isis was a national goddess of Egypt from at least 2500 B.C.E. As time went on, she was identified with many other Mediterranean goddesses, including Astarte (Ishtar), Demeter, Athena, Hestia (Vesta), and Artemis. She had magical powers, healed the sick, and promised a blessed afterlife. Isis was a wife and mother but had also been a whore; all women could identify with her. Egypt was a land in which women enjoyed high status; women and queens held the title of prophetess from the earliest period, and the priestess of the goddess was equal to, if not higher in status than, the priest. The High Priestess of Isis identified herself with the goddess and was considered her living embodiment. She was an oracle and a prophet, speaking with the voice of the goddess and interpreting her intent, as well as healing the sick and presiding over theological discussions. There were four sacred professions for women in Egypt: priestess, midwife, mourner, and temple dancer. All involved rigorous training and were held in the highest regard. (See EGYPT [ANCIENT].)

Isis reached the shores of Italy in the second century B.C.E. This was a time that coincided with the growing emancipation of women in the Roman Republic. In the Hellenistic and Roman worlds, the religion of Isis was of extreme importance, and wherever she went, she elevated the status of women. Equality with men was mentioned in her doctrines, and women held high positions within the Isiac religion, including the high office of priest (*sacerdos*).

With the religion of Isis, women's status as important participants in the religious life of their communities was temporarily restored. Women were spiritually integral prior to patriarchy; after its establishment, women continued their important sacred duties but were gradually stripped of religious office. In late antiquity, women lost their position in the religious life of the community, retaining only minimal status, and were silenced in their participation in religious matters. (See also ASCETICISM, In Western Antiquity.)

References. Ross S. Kraemer, *Maenads, Martyrs, Matrons, Monastics: A Sourcebook on Women's Religions in the Graeco-Roman World* (Philadelphia, 1988); Gerda Lerner, *The Creation of Patriarchy* (Oxford, England, 1986); Merlin Stone, *When God Was a Woman* (San Diego, 1976).

KRISTINA M. PASSMAN

RELIGION, WOMEN'S ROLES IN, have varied widely, as has religious life itself. In some traditions, women commonly hold specialist roles—that is to say, they become adept in tapping and channeling spiritual powers or pursuing intensive forms of religious discipline. Other people look to such specialists for leadership or expert help, much as Jews or Christians look to a rabbi, priest, or minister. In many of the world's religions, however, men have dominated most important functions; women's roles are mostly supporting or peripheral. Women more often lead in small-scale traditions whose beliefs and practices are principally carried by oral transmission. Women's roles become more peripheral in traditions with heavy emphasis on written and on complex legal or theological interpretation, probably because women have historically had poorer access than men to advanced literary training. However, even in traditions where their roles are habitually minor, women often claim some area of religious life as their own—some special type of service, festal role, or category of ritual.

Women of Calling. When women of traditional cultures take up special religious roles, they most often do so in response to involuntary and compelling experiences of "calling." That is to say, they do not choose their roles but instead are chosen by them. For example, ecstatic or "out-of-body" experiences, together with subsequent rigorous training, commonly qualified practitioners for the archaic role of shaman. The shaman, in trance, left her or his body to pursue wandering souls or to gain information from spiritual realms. Women have held shamanic roles interchangeably with men among many tribal groups of northern Siberia and the Americas; women shamans predominate throughout East Asia. Although the status of shamans who practice in East Asia today is low, women shamans of ancient China, Korea, and Japan were revered and powerful; no emperor of ancient Japan, for example, could take action without the advice of the combined shaman and priestess, who was called a *miko*. (See CHINESE RELIGION; JAPANESE RELIGION.)

The role of the *spirit-medium* inverts that of the shaman. Here the qualifying power is invasive; a divinity or ancestral spirit possesses the medium. Often the spirit-medium functions as a diviner and general-purpose counselor; the medium's possessing spirit advises the medium's clients about the causes of sickness, the fate and needs of the dead, locations of lost objects, methods of resolving family tensions, or prospects for contemplated projects. Women mediums are common among many tribal groups of Africa and their New World descendants; women mediums also predominate in Spiritualist churches of North America.

Women are sometimes found as well among the ranks of prophets—persons invaded by an all-powerful God for the purpose of delivering a divine message. Three of the known minor prophets of the ancient Jews were women: Deborah, Huldah, and Noadiah. However, women prophets are more often associated with the revivalist sects and "new religions" that have appeared in many regions of the world within the past two centuries. Miki Nakayama was the first of many women prophet/founders of "new religions" in Japan; perhaps the best-known prophet/founder in the West was Ann Lee, founder of the Shaker community of North America. (See SHAKERS.)

In fact, a striking feature of many "radical" Christian and quasi-Christian movements has been the prominence of many women preachers, who have been driven to speak by the conviction that some divine initiative has called them. Quaker women preachers testified to their inspiring "inner light," and nineteenth-century Methodist revivalists to compelling experiences of "conversion" and "sanctification." American Pentecostal women such as Aimee Semple McPherson sometimes became powerful revivalist speakers after being "slain by the Holy Spirit" and undergoing spiritual transformation.

Women as Ritualists. Women's ready access to inspired roles in religious traditions that value such roles highly is often contrasted with their frequent exclusion from professional priesthoods and roles of ritual leadership. Generally, some property of the female body is cited as disqualification—for example, periodic impurity resulting from bleeding during childbirth and menstruation.*

However, what disqualifies can also qualify; powers resident within the female body per se or resonances between a woman's body and other potent symbols and spiritual forces may require that women alone take up particular ritual functions. For example, female ritualists of the Bolivian Qollahuaya people specialize in driving away bad luck because of perceived resonances between the female body and natural forces that flow and erode and hence dispel unwanted qualities from the community. Women of the North American Iroquois led songs and rites associated with gardening because of special ties between femininity and powers associated with growing. Sometimes a particular condition of the woman's body is the qualifier for a special function: only virgin women could tend the sacred fire of Vesta in ancient Rome, and only a woman past the age of 50 could take up the role of the Pythia, priestess of the ancient Greek oracle at Delphi. (See RELIGION, ANCIENT.)

Women Renouncers. No transformative calling or physical qualification need summon a woman to a path of religious renunciation; she need only feel drawn to a life of intense spiritual discipline. Buddhism and Roman Catholic Christianity are the best known of the world's religions that maintain supportive communities and orders for women and men observing such discipline. Practitioners may live apart from homes and families and make use of only minimal possessions. They take new names to signify rejection of all "worldly" forms of identity; that this includes gender identity is shown by their frequent vows of celibacy, shapeless and unadorned clothing, and occasional practice of shaving or closely cropping their hair. Some women observing such spiritual renunciation spend their lives in service to the sick and poor, as do the many orders of Roman Catholic sisters or the *sannyasinis*, "female renouncers" of the contemporary Hindu Sharada Mission. Others may live in contemplative seclusion, as do cloistered Roman Catholic nuns. Occasionally, women renouncers, like men, may take the still more radical step of living as hermits, apart from any organized forms of supportive community. Both the Tantric traditions of Hindu India and Christian medieval Europe knew examples of such female "spiritual loners." (See ASCETICISM, Ascetics, Recluses, and Mystics [Early and Medieval Christian]; ASCETICISM, In India; ASCETICISM, In Western Antiquity.)

Women in Support. Religious vocations for women are not necessarily contradictory to family living—female shamans and medium/diviners are often married; in fact, income from their practice may support their households. However, religious options in most of the world's major religious traditions are usually more limited for women who also have roles as wives and mothers. Such women most commonly perform religious tasks that support more conspicuous and prestigious functions maintained by males. In the combination of worship and community life provided by Christian churches, women frequently prepare the sanctuary for services, sing in choirs, organize fund-raising projects, cook for church suppers, and tend and train smaller children in Sunday school classes. In Buddhism, whose renunciant communities were supported only by lay donations, housewives' offerings of food, small requisites, and cloth for robes were often essential to such communities' survival. In Jewish communities of Europe, women supported their husbands' study of the Torah not only by rearing children, doing housework, and maintaining kosher kitchens but also often by marketing and working outside their homes to meet their families' living expenses. In India and East Asia, where home is usually the main locus of religious life, and maintaining family shrines or altars is very important, often a household's women clean and care for the family shrines and maintain their ordinary, everyday offerings. Throughout the world, women cook, clean, and mobilize resources for family-centered feasts and festivals; often women preserve the oral lore that contains the guidelines for such periodical practice.

Women's Special Niches. Finally, ordinary women of many traditions have taken up small religious functions that then come to be considered women's special province. In Hindu India, for example, women organize and carry out optional ritual sequences called *vratas* (vows) to achieve a specific result, usually the well-being of a family member. Middle Eastern women also carry out vows on behalf of their families, but these feasts or pilgrimages to the tomb of some saint are enacted only if the goal for which the vow was made has successfully come to fruition. Women of many cultures specialize in preparation of the dead and mourning; older women of Black Carib cultures in Central America take charge of a complex sequence of memorial festivals. Women commonly also preside over rites associated with birth and menstruation.

References. Nancy A. Falk and Rita M. Gross (eds.), *Unspoken Worlds: Women's Religious Lives in Nonwestern Cultures* (San Francisco, 1980); Rosemary Ruether and Eleanor McLaughlin (eds.), *Women of Spirit: Female Leadership in the Jewish and Christian Traditions* (New York, 1979); Arvind Sharma (ed.), *Women in World Religions* (Albany, N.Y., 1987).

NANCY ELLEN AUER FALK

RELIGIOUS DISSENT IN COLONIAL NEW ENGLAND began with the first generation of settlers, who believed they had left controversy back in England only to find that they had brought the seeds of their discontent along with them. Governor John Winthrop and other Puritan founders of the Massachusetts Bay Colony did not wish to share the religious liberty they had obtained for themselves but rather tried to create a theocracy, a state ruled by God, with themselves, ministers and magistrates, in charge as the sole interpreters of God's word. By exercising strict control, they hoped to prevent the devil from insinuating himself into the new colony.

Two women were the focus of religious dissent: Anne Hutchinson and, some years later, Mary Dyer. The Antinomian Controversy, which swirled around Hutchinson, was an intense eruption that lasted from October 1636 to March 1638; it involved virtually all of the ministers and most of the magistrates and church members of the Massachusetts Bay Colony. The colony's extreme reaction showed that much more was at stake than an obscure doctrinal point.

In 1634 Anne Hutchinson of Lincolnshire, aged 43 and deeply rooted in Elizabethan Puritanism, sailed from England on *The Griffin* with her husband, William, and their children to the Massachusetts Bay Colony. She was following her pastor and religious mentor, John Cotton, whose dissenting views had forced him to flee England. After being admitted to the First Church of Boston, where Cotton was teacher, she began to conduct weekly meetings in her Boston home to instruct women on Scripture by interpreting Cotton's sermons. These meetings grew to include men, among them leading merchants and the young governor Henry Vane. Questions of Hutchinson's orthodoxy and her right to conduct religious meetings arose, especially when it was said that she accused many Massachusetts Bay clergymen of not being able ministers of the Gospels. She preached, as did Cotton, the covenant of grace, also called the doctrine of free grace, by which she meant that the Holy Spirit may dispense grace to believers irrespective of good works or merit obtained through good works. An individual could thus gain salvation through a direct experience of God's grace, rather than through the mediating offices of church authority. The potential political ramifications of this doctrine, in its inevitable weakening of church authority, alarmed ministers and magistrates alike. Moreover, the fact that Hutchinson was a woman giving public lectures was regarded as dangerously disruptive by the male establishment. In a social storm that prefigured the Salem witch trials more than half a century later, Hutchinson was twice brought to trial. In November 1637, with Governor Winthrop presiding (newly restored to power after Vane's ouster), the General Court convicted her of heresy and sentenced her to imprisonment, then exile. A church trial in March 1638, declared her excommunicated and anathema.

Scholars have not reached a consensus as to whether or not Hutchinson actually held heretical doctrinal views. The trial transcripts suggest that her positions never differed from those of Cotton, who was himself interrogated by his fellow ministers but managed to pass muster with them. The theological idea that the covenant of grace exempts the elect from moral accountability to church law has a long history that can be traced back to Paul's epistles. In New England, antinomianism became an issue completely intertwined with Hutchinson's refusal to submit to Massachusetts Bay authorities; it denoted the conflict between man's works, regarded as synonymous with church authority, and the saving grace dispensed by the Holy Spirit. Hutchinson denied that she was an antinomian, since to her, as to most Puritans, the term implied licentious behavior and religious heterodoxy. In her trials she argued brilliantly for her orthodoxy, citing Scriptures that supported her interpretations. She was at first upheld by Cotton, but he turned against her later, possibly out of fear for his own position. Many passages in the record show that Hutchinson was on trial not only for her doctrinal views but for being a disturber of the peace, a woman who refused to submit to church authority and to confine herself to a conventional female domestic role. Hutchinson did not make her gender an issue, but her male accusers did.

With Hutchinson's exile in 1638, the authority of Puritan magistrates and ministers was restored. After she left Boston, Hutchinson helped to establish the first democracy in North America, the Aquidneck colony in Rhode Island, where she resumed her public lectures and created such a stir in the Massachusetts Bay Colony that a delegation of ministers was sent to try to silence her, in which mission they failed. After her husband died in 1642, Hutchinson left Rhode Island and moved to a Dutch settlement on Pelham Bay in New York, where she and five of her children who had accompanied her were massacred in an Indian raid in late summer 1643. Her youngest daughter, Susannah, was taken hostage by the Indians.

Hutchinson created a paradigm for women's religious rights through her insistence on defying church authority in order to speak publicly on doctrine in accordance with her own conscience. Her purpose was not to free herself from male religious authority, for she was an avid supporter of Cotton and of the minister John Wheelwright, her brother-in-law and fellow exile. She did not define herself essentially through her relationship to men but was rather primarily focused on fulfilling her spiritual aspirations as an independent human being. Her essential identity lay in her sense of herself, from which center she related directly to her Maker. Through her understanding of the covenant of grace, she developed a spirituality based on individual intuition and the gift of prophecy, both of which she grounded on scriptural texts.

The Massachusetts Bay authorities knew that in the covenant of grace as propounded by Hutchinson they were faced with an alternative conception of the self and, by implication at least, a radically different order of society. The certain knowledge resulting from the influx of grace to the soul would authorize the individual to act without reference to external authority. The Antinomian Controversy thus had implications well beyond the realm of church structure to society at large. It articulated a tension in American culture between private and public realms.

Although Hutchinson's departure from the mainstream of New England Puritanism was forced upon her rather than sought by her, she was nonetheless a forerunner of more radical religious dissenters, the Quakers. Her link to them was through her friend Mary Dyer. In 1635, a bride of 18, Dyer accompanied her Separatist husband William from England to Boston, where she became a member of Cotton's First Church and a friend and supporter of Hutchinson, incurring the wrath of Governor Winthrop, who considered the Dyers as troublesome as Hutchinson herself. When Hutchinson was banished, the Dyers followed the Hutchinsons to Aquidneck, where they settled to raise a large family. Dyer returned with her family in 1652 to England for a visit with her aged mother. While there, she joined the Quakers, or Society of Friends, a group newly founded by George Fox in the north of England. They based themselves on the belief that there is that of God in every one, which is to say that every person is worthy of reverence and has within themselves a seed which can illuminate their conscience and aid their spiritual growth. Early Quakers, with women given an equal role as missionaries and ministers, went out in pairs, Dyer among them, to proselytize through England and beyond, meeting persecution wherever they went. Even before Quakers arrived in Massachusetts, Puritan authorities knew their reputation as religious radicals and disturbers of government. On July 11, 1656, when Quakers Mary Fisher and Ann Austin sailed into Boston Harbor from Barbados, they were sent to prison without trial, kept five weeks, then sent back to Barbados. Eight other Quakers arrived, prompting the General Court to pass a law fining shipmasters if they brought Quakers, who would be arrested, whipped, and jailed.

When Dyer returned to America in 1657, she traveled the Boston area as a missionary and visited imprisoned Quakers until she was briefly jailed under the new laws, then released on bond to her husband. Back in Rhode Island, she served as the nucleus of a new Quaker group that felt called to return to the Massachusetts Bay Colony. Mary Clark went to Boston, where she was severely whipped and jailed 12 weeks. In October 1657, a stricter law was passed decreeing that banished Quakers who returned would have their ears cropped and tongues bored with a hot iron; three returning Quakers each lost an ear by August 1658.

Boston authorities passed a final decree that anyone convicted of being a Quaker should be banished on pain of death. Four Quakers were hanged, including Dyer, who returned to Boston in 1659 to minister to imprisoned Quakers, and then again in 1660. Twice arrested, she was condemned to death both times and, although reprieved in 1659, was hanged on Boston Common on June 1, 1660. When King Charles II and local public opinion forced authorities to abandon the death penalty, the Cart and Whip Act followed, under which any banished Quaker who returned would be tied to a cart and whipped through town, a fate endured by four Quaker women.

Although Hutchinson and Dyer are linked by their belief in the direct infusion of grace or light into the individual soul, the two controversies differ profoundly. Hutchinson's dispute with the ministers was a family quarrel over interpretation of Scripture, but she did not question the basic structures of the church. The Quakers, however, although rooted in Christianity and Scripture, departed from the entire church structure, professing no fixed set of theological tenets. Yet the links between Hutchinson and Dyer remain in Boston today. At the Massachusetts State House on Beacon Hill, a statue of Mary Dyer stands on the lawn opposite Boston Commons. Nearby stands a bronze memorial to Anne Hutchinson, portrayed as a young woman, eyes raised heavenward, one hand holding a Bible, the other a little girl. Dyer's inscription hails her witness for religious freedom, while

Hutchinson's plaque eulogizes her courageous advocacy of civil liberty and religious toleration.

References. Margaret H. Bacon, *The Quiet Rebels: The Story of the Quakers in America* (New York, 1969); David D. Hall (ed.), *The Antinomian Controversy, 1636–1638: A Documentary History* (Middletown, Conn., 1968); Amy Schrager Lang, *Prophetic Woman: Anne Hutchinson and the Problem of Dissent in the Literature of New England* (Berkeley, Calif., 1987); Selma R. Williams, *Divine Rebel: The Life of Anne Marbury Hutchinson* (New York, 1981).

                                                                    NINA TASSI

RENAISSANCE LITERATURE. English Lyric Poetry ranges from celebrating the creative generosity of the muse who inspires male authorship to postulating a realm of civilized discourse into which the language of woman intrudes as a barbaric or infantile disruption. With Sir Thomas Wyatt's introduction of the Petrarchan tradition into English lyric poetry in the mid-sixteenth century, Petrarch's representation of woman as the poet's Laura, his beloved, and his object to be scattered into verses becomes established in England. Yet poetry's attachment to the changing circumstances of England's court through the Renaissance also modifies the Petrarchan legacy. Wyatt's question "What vaileth truth?" echoes through the period and exposes the problematics of changing values in the court world. Whether the court was dominated by Henry VIII, Elizabeth I, or James I, court poets attached their uncertainties about their position to their representation of woman's mutability and woman's power. In the poetry of Sir Philip Sidney, John Donne, and Ben Jonson, male ambivalence about a woman's power renders the representation of woman all the more complex.

In Sir Philip Sidney's sonnet sequence *Astrophil and Stella*, that ambivalence is revealed in the two dramas of the sequence: the emergence of Stella, not simply a projection of the speaker's desires, and the speaker's reification of Stella. Although Sidney fails to dramatize a "real" beloved, involved in a relationship of mature mutuality, he does risk confronting an affective presence with a poised, articulate voice, in short, a woman with language. The sonnet sequence does, particularly in the Eighth Song, give space to Stella, a woman with her own story. This song inscribes Sidney's imaginative empathy with woman's culturally imposed muteness. Such empathy contrasts with Shakespeare's dominance over the Dark Lady's voice in his sonnets, a dominance that marks an effort of "will" to control or order his mutable world.

While John Donne's love lyrics celebrate the woman who inspires his love, his desire to return home in "A Valediction: Forbidding Mourning," and his longing to create a universe of two in "The Sun Rising," that woman remains tied to her limited world as he leaves to explore court advancement. While the wit of his metaphysical language compliments his beloved's intellect, the vituperative speaker of "Elegy VII" condemns his beloved as "Nature's Lay Idiot," whose entry into the world of love means no more than complicity in the deceits of love language.

As Queen Elizabeth aged without a dynastic successor and died in 1603, leaving James I, son of Mary, Queen of Scots, on the throne, the poets of the court circle adjusted the rhetoric of their love lyric to a new hierarchy of values. No longer were the final arbiter of worth and the ultimate source of identity a woman. When Ben Jonson demonstrates his worth as heir to his classical models, he does so at the expense of his "lady friends." Such poems as "Inviting a Friend to Supper" and the "Cary and Morison Ode" posit an exclusively male world, troubled at the fringes by sexual and political instability. Female generation itself is undermined in the troubling portrait of the "brave infant of Saguntum" as the "Cary and Morison Ode" opens.

While Jonson praises the poetry of Lady Mary Wroth, we must examine her lyric poetry, particularly the sonnet sequence presenting love from the woman's perspective, *Pamphilia to Amphilanthus*, to see a woman reflect on the representation of woman in the English Renaissance lyric. As Sir Philip Sidney's niece, Wroth stood in a critical relationship to the sonnet tradition. Wroth uses her sonnets to articulate the difficulty of adapting love language and the sonnet form to a woman's experience. In contrast to a tradition of woman's faithlessness, in Wroth's work, the male beloved, Amphilanthus, is the lover of two women. Pamphilia's pain and conflict in love, then, derive, in part, from her suffering loyalty to a disloyal man. In addition, however, Wroth's songs and sonnets begin to create the new discourse necessary for the new voice she is presenting. That discourse begins with a woman alienated "from knowledge of my self" but finds the forms, myths, and language to end in repose: "My muse now happy, lay thy self to rest." Wroth's achievement offers readers the opportunity to reevaluate the lyric tradition.

References. Josephine Roberts (ed.), *The Poems of Lady Mary Wroth* (Baton Rouge, La., 1983); Nancy Vickers, "Diana Described: Scattered Woman and Scattered Rhyme," *Critical Inquiry* 8 (1980–1981): 265–281.

NONA FIENBERG

RENAISSANCE LITERATURE. Italian Writers are divided into two groups: humanists and poets. In the fifteenth century many women, especially those of the upper classes, were given the same humanist education available to men. Educated in Latin, Greek, philosophy, and literature as young girls, they were regarded as prodigies by their established male counterparts, with whom they corresponded. However, upon reaching adulthood they either married or entered the convent, abandoning their writing. Such was the fate of Ginevra Nogarola (1417–1465) of Verona, Battista da Montefeltro Malatesta (1383–1450?) of Urbino, her granddaughter Costanza Varano (1426–1447), and Laura Cereta (1469–1499) of Brescia. Two exceptions were Isotta Nogarola (1418–1466), the sister of Ginevra, who chose to live in her family home and dedicate her life to scholarship; and Cassandra Fedele (1465–1558) of Venice, who as a young girl gave orations before the University of Padua, the Venetian people, and the doge. Seventeen years after marrying, Cassandra took up the pen once again.

In Florence, Alessandra Scala (1475–1506) wrote a Greek epigram in response to one written by her teacher, Poliziano. Using the vernacular, Alessandra Macigni Strozzi wrote 72 letters to her exiled sons. Lucrezia Tornabuoni d'Medici (1425–1482), the wife of Piero and mother of Lorenzo the Magnificent, wrote five short poems on biblical and evangelical themes and several lauds and hymns based on the life of Christ. Antonia Giannotti Pulci (1452?–?), the wife of writer Bernardo Pulci, wrote four *sacre rappresentazioni* (miracle plays).

In the sixteenth century many women rose to prominence as poets, imitating the style of Francis Petrarch, as did their male counterparts. Veronica Gambara (1485–1550) from Pratalboino (Brescia) wrote love poetry in her youth and passed to religious themes in maturity. Her sonnets, madrigals, and *stanze*, together with her correspondence, were published for the first time in 1759.

Vittoria Colonna (1490–1547) from Marino, Colli Albani (Rome), is known for her long-standing friendship with Michelangelo Buonarrotti and Galeazzo di Tàrsia. Her poetry was published on several occasions during her lifetime. In the 1544 edition of her *Rime* the poetry is divided into two sections: poems dealing with the death of her husband and poems on religious themes.

Gaspara Stampa (1523?–1554) from Padua moved to Venice in 1531, where her home became a musical and literary center frequented by Varchi, Vernier, Alamanni, and Domenichi. She was a member of the Accademia dei Dubbiosi. Her poetry (Venice, 1554), dedicated to her lover, Collaltino Collalto, consists of 311 poems divided into two parts: love rhymes and various rhymes.

Isabella di Morra (1520–1548) from Favale, Basilicata, wrote 13 poems, first published in 1559. She corresponded secretly with Diego Sandoval de Castro, who sent her poetry and letters. Upon discovering their correspondence, Isabella's brothers killed first her, then Sandoval.

Laura Bacio Terracina (1519–1577?) from Naples was a member of the Accademia degli Incogniti. She published seven collections of poetry, of which the first (1548) was reprinted five times in the sixteenth century, twice in the seventeenth. Her themes ranged from love expressed in Petrarchan terms to religious mysticism. In her *Discorso sopra tutti i primi canti di Orlando Furioso* (Venice, 1549; Discourse on All of the First Cantos of Orlando Furioso), the final line of each stanza was drawn from the first stanza of the corresponding canto of Ariosto's epic poem. A sequel followed in 1567. She also wrote *Sovra tutte le donne vedove di questa nostra città di Napoli titolate et non titolate* (Concerning All of the Widowed Ladies of Our City of Naples, Titled and Not Titled), an elegiac poem published in 1561.

Chiara Matraini (1514–1597?) of Lucca was a poet and scholar of philosophy and history. She wrote poetry in the Petrarchan style along with religious literature. *Rime e prose* (Lucca, 1555) was followed by *Rime e lettere* (Lucca, 1595) and *Lettere con la prima e la seconda parte delle rime* (Venice, 1597). Among her religious works are *Meditazione spirituali* (Lucca, 1581), *Considerazioni sopra i sette salmi penitenziali* (Lucca, 1586, Considerations on the Seven Penitential Psalms), *Breve discorso sopra la vita della Beata Vergine* (Lucca, 1590; Brief Discourse concerning the Life of the Blessed Virgin), and *Dialoghi spirituali* (Venice, 1602).

Olimpia Morato (1526–1555) from Ferrara moved to Germany following her marriage to Andreas Grunthler. Deep Lutheran convictions permeate her letters, important documents in the history of the Reformation. The humanist training of her youth led her to write several other works: three Latin *proemi* (introductions) to a commentary of the *Paradoxa* by Cicero; a translation into Latin of the first two tales of the *Decameron*; two dialogues in Latin; and eight *Carmi* (odes), three in Latin and five in Greek. Her complete works were published in 1558, 1562, and 1570.

Laura Battiferri Ammannati (1532–1589) from Urbino moved to Florence following her marriage to Bartolomeo Ammannati. She was a member of the Accademia degli Assorditi of Urbino and of the Accademia degli Intronati of Siena. Her poetry, acclaimed during her lifetime, was first published as *Primo libro delle opere toscane* (Florence, 1560, First Book of Tuscan Works). In 1564 she published a translation into the vernacular of the seven penitential psalms of the prophet David. Her correspondence with Benedetto Varchi was published in 1879.

Renaissance society had a special place for the so-called honest courtesans, women renowned for their beauty and culture who moved in the highest circles and presided over salons. Two of these courtesans were writers. Tullia d'Aragona (1508?–1556), born in Rome, was the lover of the writers Girolamo Muzio and Bernardo Tasso and was friendly with Benedetto Varchi and Piero Mannelli, to whom she dedicated many of her sonnets. Because of her poetry (Venice, 1547), she was excused by Cosimo I, duke of Tuscany, from wearing the yellow veil required of all courtesans. She also wrote *Il Meschino altramente detto il Guerrino* (Venice, 1560; Meschino, Also Called Guerrino), a romance in 36 cantos; and *Dialogo dell'infinità di amore* (1552, Dialogue on the Infinity of Love), a disputation on platonic love.

Veronica Franco (1546–1591) from Venice was admired and beloved by the princes and intellectuals of her time. Her portrait was painted by Tintoretto, and she was mentioned by Montaigne in his *Jornal de voyage*. She helped to found the Hospice of S. Maria del Soccorso in Venice for abandoned young girls and reformed courtesans. Her literary works consist of *Le terze rime* or *Capitoli* (1575), 18 rhymed letters written by Veronica and 7 written to her; and *Lettere familiari a diversi* (1580), 50 letters dedicated to the cardinal Luigi d'Este. Unlike Tullia d'Aragona, Veronica never attempted to hide her "profession" from the public.

References. Natalia Costa-Zalessow, *Scrittrici italiane dal XIII al XX secolo: testi e critica* (Ravenna, 1982); Margaret L. King and Albert Rabil, Jr. (eds.), *Her Immaculate Hand: Selected Works by and about the Women Humanists of Quattrocento Italy* (Binghamton, N.Y., 1983).

JOAN H. LEVIN

RENAISSANCE LITERATURE. Transalpine Writers. Perhaps the most seminally important contribution of Renaissance humanism to the burgeoning of female literary activity was the availability, on a large scale, of a diversified education to laywomen fortunate enough to have had access to books and teachers. Indeed, the education of women was one of the most persuasively argued topics in the famous Renaissance debate on women's worth, the *querelle des femmes*.* The availability of education created a large class of men and women who mastered the rudiments of humanist learning: proficiency in Latin, competency in Greek, knowledge of ancient and patristic literature, history, and moral philosophy, as well as the conventions of Petrarchism and Ficinian Neoplatonism. In particular, ladies of the upper classes and women relatives of the humanists profited from the humanist curriculum.

Marguerite of Navarre attracted leading poets and scholars; Marguerite of Navarre, educated with her brother Francis, the future king of France, was herself polyglot and wrote in many genres; the Dames des Roches consciously dedicated their lives to the pursuit of learning; and the Lyonnese school boasted such learned women as Louise Labé and Pernette Du Guillet. In England, Queen Elizabeth's philological training and knowledge of the classics dazzled the ambassadors at her court, and the erudition of Lady Jane Grey, Mary Sidney, and Margaret More Roper, to mention only a few, was eulogized by their contemporaries. Margaret of Austria and Louise of Savoy, both avid readers of the classics, ruled their realms with political and administrative acumen and their literary salons with erudition and wit. In Germany, Caritas Pirckheimer corresponded with the leading humanists of her day, and Margaret Peutinger was a noted biblical scholar. As during the Middle Ages, so in the Renaissance, a large portion of the works by women were of devotional or religiopolitical nature, but the ratio of religious versus secular texts became a great deal more balanced as time progressed.

Renaissance women writers could conveniently be categorized in six groups: the *grande dame*, the woman scholar, the nun, the religious or political activist, the *cortigiana onesta*, and the patrician. By and large, *grande dames* wrote secular and even public works, with lyric poetry, letters, translations, orations, and novelistic texts predominating, though some, notably Marguerite of Navarre and Vittoria Colonna, did compose devotional poems, and Elizabeth I penned several homilies. By and large, they wrote in the vernacular, and almost invariably they were held in high literary esteem by their contemporaries. Second, the woman scholar, occupying perhaps the most Renaissance of the six categories, was almost invariably related to a literary man and was frequently of well-to-do but not necessarily aristocratic descent. Renaissance women scholars devoted themselves to philological pursuits: translations, essays, letters, dialogues, and even invectives, both in Latin and the vernacular. This group, together with the writers of the urban patriciate (i.e., women for whom humanist education was not a matter of self-evident necessity), seems most concerned with educational opportunities for women and with the obligations women have to take advantage of these new opportunities. Women scholars were occasionally attacked and ridiculed, and they were the most vociferous advocates that women should learn for learning's sake. Third, the nun, the major representative of medieval women writers, no longer occupied that preeminent position in Renaissance letters. Writing in Latin and the vernacular, she came from all social classes, and her compositions include not only visions, revelations, and *vitae*, as in the Middle Ages, but also translations, biographies, and autobiographies. Fourth, the *cortigiana onesta*, the Italian Renaissance brand of the Greek hetaera, exemplifies the single woman's other alternative. Cultured, though rarely, if ever, of aristocratic descent, she most often wrote vernacular lyric poetry. Fifth, the religious political activist, militant descendant of the medieval Margery Kempe, often belonged to the urban poor, invariably wrote in the vernacular and was seldom rewarded for her activism and pamphleteering. Finally, the gentlewoman writer was usually a member of the provincial urban patriciate and was a Renaissance novelty. She was ordinarily learned as well as cultivated, she could be either single or married, she was rarely related to a literary man, and she composed almost always in the vernacular and in a variety of devotional or fictional forms. Conspicuously absent from this catalog of Renaissance women's writings are the learned commentary or treatise and the original epic or secular drama.

References. R. Kelso, *Doctrine for the Lady of the Renaissance* (Urbana, Ill., 1956); P. H. Labalme (ed.), *Beyond Their Sex: Learned Women of the European Past* (New York, 1980); M. E. Weisner, *Women in the Sixteenth Century: A Bibliography* (St. Louis, 1983); K. M. Wilson, *Women Writers of the Renaissance and Reformation* (Athens, Ga., 1987).

KATHARINA M. WILSON

REPRODUCTION, ETHICAL ISSUES IN. Perhaps no other area of human endeavor engenders more passionate debate and polarization than issues involving sexual activity, reproductive rights, abortion, and behaviors that challenge some of the traditional dogmas of American society. Over the course of the past decades, evolutions in technology have radically altered the role of women in society and, in many respects, shifted the power base for decisions regarding women's reproductive rights to their own bodies. This entry is intended as an overview of some of these issues, each of which could fill several books.

Sterilization of the Handicapped. In the early part of the twentieth century, public policy, at least in the United States, very much encouraged sterilization of those who were perceived as "mentally defective." Based upon eugenic principles and "societal interests" extrapolated from the ideas of Charles Darwin, state laws and judicial decisions were almost uniformly in favor of such actions. In the mid-1940s widespread revulsion against Nazi genocide swayed public opinion against the way sterilization of the handicapped was carried out, resulting in an abrupt decline in such procedures. In 1942 the U.S. Supreme Court declared human reproduction to be a fundamental human right. In response, many states reversed their position, thus making sterilization of the handicapped essentially impossible. The trend against sterilization of the handicapped culminated in the 1970s, when federal regulations officially prohibited the use of federal funds for sterilization of such persons.

More recently, dichotomized positions have softened in an attempt to move toward a more realistic middle ground. The general thrust of the ethical debate today is aimed at creating an environment in which decisions to consider sterilization of handicapped individuals are driven by a very serious attempt to balance the patient's best interests, her ability to care for herself, ability to understand consent for sexual activity, and a real—not a presumed—risk of pregnancy. Whereas 50 years ago it was common to sterilize handicapped children even before they went through puberty, today the evaluation is far more complex. Evaluation must consider at a minimum four categories of concern: (1) the appropriate decision maker; (2) reasonable alternatives to sterilization; (3) the best interests of the mentally handicapped individual; and (4) application of existing laws.

In most cases, parents or immediate family members and legal guardians are given the power to provide proxy consent for people who have been adjudicated and capacitated to provide such consent. The appropriateness and applicability of alternatives to sterilization, such as socialization training, abuse avoidance training, menstrual hygiene, or long-term contraception such as depo-provera, must be considered, and the best interests of the patient determined. Sterilization can be considered if there is a reasonable likelihood of fertility or sexual activity. The burdens of childbearing to both the individual and the family must be balanced against fundamental individual rights in specific cases.

AIDS and Pregnancy. Numerous volumes have been written about the impact of the human immunodeficiency virus (HIV) and acquired immunodeficiency syndrome (AIDS). It is abundantly clear that an expanding proportion of HIV cases is coming from the "vertical" transmission in which pregnant women transmit the HIV virus to their fetuses.

Initially, it was believed that there was no justification for prenatal HIV testing, since finding the virus would only stigmatize the patient and not lead to substantive alterations in obstetric management. However, with the development of antiviral compounds such as Acyclovir and newer-generation medicines to decrease the transmission rate of the virus, it can now be argued that knowledge and treatment of HIV in pregnancy have direct benefit to the fetus. However, it is vital that such arguments be made without shifting the balance against voluntary, and toward mandatory, testing for patients at high risk.

Another HIV/AIDS argument that has emerged concerns counseling of AIDS or HIV positive patients who are pregnant. Some have argued that such patients should be encouraged to abort rather than bring a diseased child into the world. While we certainly believe that abortion should be an option for such patients who so desire, HIV does not, and cannot, constitute an exception to the principles of noncoercion and neutrality that are fundamental to prenatal genetic counseling. It would be deemed completely unethical to tell a patient at risk for an autosomal dominant disorder such as Huntington's disease or an autosomal recessive disorder such as Tay-Sachs disease, both of which have fatal prognoses, that they must abort based upon odds that are similar or, in fact, even higher than that of transmitting the HIV virus. There needs to be a separation between the hysteria caused by HIV and an appreciation of its full societal impact.

It is now well-established public policy that physicians cannot avoid treatment of HIV patients based on irrational fears. Unfortunately, the history of physician behaviors in plague situations is not as altruistic as one might have hoped, dating back to the bubonic plague in Europe in the 1400s, when physicians fled the cities along with everybody else who was able. Nevertheless, the Hippocratic oath clearly proscribes sacrificing the welfare of patients for personal gain or safety, and physicians must balance reasonable risks versus obligations to patients.

Abortion. There is perhaps no more politically divisive issue in our society today than abortion,* nor is it likely that a consensus on the subject will be achieved. If one believes, on the basis of religion or theology, that the single-cell embryo is entitled to as much respect as the child, then, de facto, abortion must be considered murder, and steps taken to prevent such crimes. Conversely, if one believes personhood is realized at birth or relatively late in pregnancy, attempts to regulate female fertility, female sexual practices, or other controls over pregnancy must be considered inappropriately demeaning to women. Controls would be inconsistent with equality for women in society in general and in the bedroom specifically. The majority opinion of the American public appears to favor preservation of abortion rights, particularly during the early part of pregnancy and later under mitigating circumstances, such as significant fetal anomalies or in cases of rape or incest. Attempts to limit the availability of abortions have included the removal of Medicaid funding, imposition of mandatory waiting periods, proscription against specific procedures, and the introduction of numerous hurdles into the process. While some of these individual strategies are apparently reasonable, when taken as a whole they represent elements of a coordinated long-term strategy aimed at denying women access to abortion.

Prenatal Diagnosis. At roughly the same time that abortion rights were becoming recognized in the United States, first in a selected number of states such as New York, and finally with the *Roe v. Wade* decision in 1973, came concomitant advances in technology, allowing, in certain cases, prenatal diagnosis of fetuses with significant birth defects. The development of amniocentesis* and appropriate laboratory methods to handle the biologic products made possible the identification of conditions such as Down's syndrome and other serious chromosomal abnormalities, as well as biochemical abnormalities such as Tay-Sachs disease. The development of ultrasound made possible the detection of serious structural abnormalities such as neural tube defects and, later, heart and limb abnormalities. When such technologies were originally developed, and the demand for such services far exceeded capacity, it was commonplace to require parents to agree that should an abnormality be found, they would abort the pregnancy. It was felt that if parents would not "do anything" about the situation, the use of scarce services would be wasted on them. However, as the availability of such services has expanded, it has become a fundamental principle of genetics that there should be no linkage between information given to parents and what they choose to do with that information. It is well appreciated that reasonable and intelligent people will reach diametrically opposing conclusions under similar circumstances. Prenatal counseling should be no different. While there is considerable variability around the country and the world, in our experience, when couples are presented with a diagnosis of a fetal abnormality, and they are within their legal right to choose to terminate the pregnancy, approximately 50 percent choose to do so. Not surprisingly, the more severe the anomaly, the more likely it is that couples will choose to terminate. Clearly, if 100 percent of couples choose to terminate or choose not to terminate under given circumstances, the objectivity of such counseling is brought sharply into question.

Fetal Therapy. Since the late 1970s, it has become possible to not only diagnose selected fetal abnormalities but, in a limited number of circumstances, to actually treat them before birth. A major difference between treatment of the fetus and treatment of a child is the bodily integrity of the mother. In order to treat the fetus, one must operate on the mother or at least use her as a vehicle to reach the fetus. In our experience, most pregnant women are willing to do almost anything to preserve the health of their wanted fetus, and, in fact, one must often temper the enthusiasm of prospective parents to the realities of the situation in which they find themselves. Furthermore, while some of the in utero fetal surgical approaches have moved from being purely experimental to the status of high-tech, but routine therapy, many approaches are still clearly investigational. Under well-established ethical principles experimental therapies do not have to be offered to patients. Nor is there an obligation of patients to undergo such therapy.

Maternal–Fetal Conflict. Until our understanding of fetal developmental physiology and diagnostic capabilities such as ultrasound were developed, pregnancy was fundamentally a black box, at the end of which hopefully popped out a healthy baby. With the capabilities of diagnosing fetal status, potential conflicts arise between what is good for the mother but not necessarily best for the baby, and vice versa. The first known legal conflict between mother and baby came in 1981 in Georgia, when a woman diagnosed as having placental previa refused to have a cesarean section to save the baby. The physicians went to court to obtain an order compelling the woman to undergo the cesarean section. Ironically, while the order was being obtained, the women successfully and safely delivered vaginally, as the diagnosis had been mistaken. Since 1981 there have been numerous other examples of court-ordered cesarean sections. Analysis of these cases has revealed that in many instances the patients were either women of color or non-U.S. citizens, suggesting that attempts to compel women to undergo procedures may be partially driven by, or influenced by, cultural issues and perceived power differences, rather than a true appreciation for so-called fetal rights. Similarly, women who are drug abusers have occasionally been incarcerated during pregnancy to "protect the fetus." Such actions carry the potential for initiating a fall down a very "slippery slope." For example, while at first glance preventing women from taking illegal drugs that could harm the fetus seems rational and appealing, it is important to point out that the single most common teratogen today is alcohol, and alcohol consumption is perfectly legal. Similarly, tobacco, smog, and other airborne agents may have deleterious effects on pregnancy. The central question is, At what point do the rights of the individual pregnant woman supersede those of the fetus? We believe that, as laudable as it seems to protect the fetus from deleterious actions by the mother, coercing such behavior crosses the line of maternal autonomy. While inducements and enticements may be considered appropriate and reasonable, the incarceration of pregnant women is certainly not. There is ample precedent for preserving the physical integrity of individuals. For example, no private in the army has ever been forced to donate a kidney to save the life of a general or any other person. No person can be required to give blood to save another individual or even to offer help at the scene of an accident. Why, therefore, should a mother be compelled to undergo a major surgery to save the fetus?

Summary. Ethical issues involving reproduction provoke heated debate, perhaps because reproduction is such a fundamental issue and because its association with sexual behavior tends to render the debate more personal and less abstract. This overview is intended to highlight some of the fundamental issues at the forefront of ethical debate of reproduction in the late 1990s and to spark interest for further reading.

References. "Sterilization of the Handicapped," Committee Opinion #63, American College of Obstetricians and Gynecologists (September 1988); Mark I. Evans, J. C. Fletcher, A. O. Dixler, and J. D. Schulman (eds.), *Fetal Diagnosis and Therapy: Science, Ethics, and the Law* (Philadelphia, 1989); J. C. Fletcher and M. I. Evans, "Ethics of Genetic Diagnosis and Treatment," in F. A. Chervenak (ed.), *Ethics in OB/GYN (Clinical OB/GYN)* 35, 4 (1992): 763–782; J. C. Fletcher and M. I. Evans, "Ethics in Reproductive Genetics, in J. F. Monagle and D. C. Thomasma (eds.), *Health Care Ethics: Critical Issues* (Gaithersburg, Md., 1994), 24–42; M. R. Harrison, M. S. Golbus, and R. A. Filly, *The Unborn Patient: Prenatal Diagnosis and Treatment* (Philadelphia, 1990); P. G. Pryde, A. Drugan, M. P. Johnson, N. B. Isada, and M. I. Evans, "Prenatal Diagnosis: Choices Women Make about Pursuing Testing and Acting on Abnormal Results," in R. M. Pitkin and J. B. Scott (eds.), *The New Reproductive Genetics: Implications for Women and Their Physicians (Clinical OB/GYN)* 36, 3 (1993): 496–509.

MARK I. EVANS, WENDY J. EVANS, and MARK P. JOHNSON

REPRODUCTION OF LABOR POWER is the maintenance of the workers and the producing and raising of future workers who supply labor power for production. Although Marx does not include the reproduction of labor power within the sphere of surplus value production, feminist theorists, by assigning value to the reproduction of labor power, apply Marx's theory of value to the position of women under patriarchal social relations and the capitalist mode of production and to the relationships and contradictions between patriarchy and capitalism.

REPRODUCTIVE SYSTEM is those organs that are adapted to produce and unite sex cells in order to produce offspring. In human reproduction the organs, called *genitalia*, include (1) *gonads*, ovaries and testes, which produce ova and sperm cells, respectively; (2) *ducts*, which transport, receive, and store gametes (sex cells); and (3) *accessory glands*, which produce materials that support gametes. In addition, organs of the female system are adapted to support a developing offspring and to transport it outside the female's body.

Despite a common embryological origin and structure, the anatomy and physiology of the reproductive organs are the major differences between male and female. The reproductive system becomes functional when it is acted upon by hormones produced in the pituitary glands during puberty.

The male reproductive system is specialized to produce sperm and to deposit the sperm within the female reproductive tract. The system consists of the paired testes, contained in the external *scrotum*. Within the testes sperm are produced in *seminiferous tubules*. Between the seminiferous tubules are *interstitial cells (Cells of Leydig)*, which produce and secrete male sex hormones, predominantly testosterone. The duct system, which stores and transports sperm, includes the *epididymis, ductus deferens (vas deferens), ejaculatory ducts*, and *urethra*. Accessory glands include seminal vesicles, prostate gland, and bulbourethral glands. The *penis*, which surrounds the urethra, contains masses of erectile tissue and serves as the copulatory organ.

The female reproductive system is specialized for internal fertilization, implantation, fetal development, and parturition (labor and delivery). Although not actually a part of the reproductive system, the *mammary glands*, located in the *breasts*, are functionally associated since they secrete milk for the nourishment of the young.

The female reproductive system includes:

1. *Ovaries* are the female gonads, a pair of glands resembling an unshelled almond, 3.5 cm long, 2 cm wide, and 1 cm thick, located in the upper pelvic cavity, one on each side of the uterus. The ovaries produce ova and secrete the sex hormones estrogen and progesterone under the control of hormones LH (luteinizing hormone) and FSH (follicle stimulating hormone) produced and secreted by the pituitary gland.

Oogenesis is the process of cell division (meiosis) by which ova are formed. Prior to birth several million *primary follicles* develop in each ovary. These consist of a single large cell, the *primary oocyte*, and surrounding *follicular cells*. Many of the oocytes degenerate through a process called atresia and at birth about 2 million are present. Continuing atresia reduces this number to about 400,000 at puberty. Beginning at puberty, in response to pituitary hormones LH and FSH, some of the primary follicles are stimulated to grow and develop into *secondary follicles* each month. Only one normally completes the process and releases its ovum. The oocyte completes the first meiotic division into a large *secondary oocyte*, a future egg, and a small *polar body* that will eventually fragment and disappear. The surrounding follicular cells also divide. Some of these cells secrete increasing amounts of *estrogen* as the follicle grows.

Ovulation, stimulated by pituitary hormones, is the release from the ovary of the secondary oocyte and its surrounding cells. The secondary oocyte will complete the second meiotic division, to form an ovum and second polar body, only following fertilization by a sperm.

The *corpus luteum* is a structure formed as a result of structural and biochemical changes in the empty follicle left in the ovary following ovulation. The corpus luteum secretes both estrogen and progesterone. If fertilization of the ovum does not occur, the corpus luteum regresses about 12 to 14 days after ovulation.

Estrogen is a class of steroid hormones secreted primarily by the adult ovary. It is also secreted in small amounts by the adrenal cortex and in increasing amounts by the placenta during pregnancy. The functions of estrogen include development and maintenance of the female reproductive structures and the development and maintenance of the female secondary sex characteristics.

Progesterone, a steroid hormone, is secreted primarily from the corpus luteum of the adult ovary. It is also secreted in increasing amounts by the placenta during pregnancy. Progesterone promotes the changes that occur in the uterus to prepare it for implantation. It also affects the mammary glands and causes the mucus at the cervix of the uterus to become very thick and sticky.

The *ovarian cycle* is the cycle of events: maturation of a follicle, ovulation, formation of a corpus luteum, regression of the corpus luteum, with its accompanying cycle of estrogen, then estrogen and progesterone, release.

2. *Uterine (Fallopian) Tubes, also called Oviducts*, extend laterally from the uterus and open into the abdominal cavity near the ovaries. Each muscular tube is about 10 cm long and 0.7 cm in diameter and is positioned between the folds of the broad ligament of the uterus. The open funnel-shaped end, called the infundibulum, lies close to the ovary, and a number of fingerlike projections, the *fimbriae*, surround the ovary. Following ovulation the ovum is swept into the tube by ciliary action of the cells lining the infundibulum. Fertilization normally occurs within the uterine tubes.

3. *Uterus*. A hollow, thick-walled muscular organ, shaped like an inverted pear (7.5 cm long, 5 cm wide, 2.5 cm thick) which is the site of menstruation, implantation of the fertilized ovum, development of the fetus during pregnancy and labor. It is located in the pelvic cavity between the urinary bladder and the rectum. Anatomical subdivisions include the *fundus*, a dome-shaped portion above the entrance of the uterine tubes; the *body*, the major tapering portion surrounding the uterine cavity; and the *cervix*, a tubular, narrow portion that opens into the vagina. Normally, the body of the uterus is bent forward over the urinary bladder, and the cervix enters the anterior wall of the vagina at nearly a right angle.

Support of the uterus is both by muscles and by a series of ligaments including *broad ligaments*, a pair of folds of the membrane that lines the abdomino-pelvic cavity (peritoneum) and attaches the uterus to the sides of the pelvic cavity; *uterosacral ligaments*, which attach the uterus to bone at the base of the vertebral column (sacrum); *cardinal ligaments*, which extend laterally from cervix and vagina to the wall of the pelvis to maintain the position of the uterus and keep it from dropping down into the vagina; and the *round ligaments*, which extend from upperlateral wall to pelvic wall.

The *wall of the uterus* consists of three layers of tissue; the *serosa*, outer layer, is continuous with the broad ligament; *myometrium*, the middle layer, consists of three layers of smooth muscle fibers; and *endometrium*, the mucous membrane lining that consists of a layer closer to the uterine cavity (stratum functionalis) that is shed as menses during menstruation and a permanent layer (stratum basalis) that produces a new functionalis following menstruation.

4. *Vagina*. A muscular tubular organ, about 9 cm long, extending from cervix to vestibule. It serves as the receptacle for the sperm released from the urethra of an erect penis during coitus, the passageway for menses, and the birth canal. The wall of the vagina is very distensible due to the presence of a series of transverse folds, the *rugae*, and layers of smooth muscles that can stretch considerably. The lining, or mucosal tissue, consists of several layers that are maintained by estrogen. They form a tough protective lining. The normally acidic environment (ph 3.5 to 5.5) protects against microbial growth.

The *hymen* is a thin fold of mucous membrane that may form a border around the lower end of the vaginal opening (vaginal orifice), partially closing it. The hymen is the subject of folklore, misconception, and nonsense. It is a highly variable structure. It may be very thick or thin; vascular or avascular; cover all or only a very small portion of the vaginal orifice; may be very pliable or may rupture easily during physical exercise, sports, play, or coitus. An intact hymen is not proof of virginity; a ruptured hymen is not evidence that sexual intercourse has occurred. An *imperforate hymen* (very rare) covers the vaginal orifice completely and impedes menstrual flow and coitus. This condition is corrected by a small surgical incision.

5. *Vulva (Pudendum)*. The external genitalia of the female. It includes the following components:

Mons pubis (veneris): an elevation of adipose (fat) tissue that covers the anterior pelvic bones (symphysis pubis). At puberty it becomes covered with coarse pubic hair usually in a triangular pattern with a horizontal upper border.

Labia majora, two thick longitudinal folds of skin, fat, and muscle that extend from the mons pubis. They are covered with hair and contain sebaceous (oil) and sweat glands. The labia majora are the female homologue of the scrotum and function to enclose and protect other organs of the vulva. Toward the posterior end the labia are tapered and merge into the perineum near the anus.

Labia minora, flattened longitudinal folds of tissue located between the labia majora. They are hairless, do not contain fat, but do contain sebaceous glands. At the anterior end, the two labia minora unite and form a covering (prepuce) over the clitoris.

Clitoris, a small cylindrical mass of erectile tissue and nerves (2 cm long and 0.5 cm in diameter), is the female homologue of the glans penis of the male. The exposed portion of the clitoris is the *glans*. The unexposed portion is composed of erectile tissue that engorges during sexual excitement. The clitoris is richly supplied with the sensory nerve fibers that initiate the female sexual response cycle.

Vestibule, the cleft between the labia minora. Within the vestibule are the hymen, opening of the vagina, opening of the urethra (tube that transports urine from urinary bladder to outside), and openings of several ducts from:

(a) Paraurethral (Skene's) glands that are embedded in the wall of the urethra and secrete mucus. These are homologous to the male prostate gland.

(b) Greater vestibular (Bartholin's) glands that open by ducts into the vestibule near the lateral margin of the vaginal orifice. These correspond to the bulbourethral glands of the male and produce a mucoid secretion that supplements lubrication during sexual intercourse.

6. *Perineum (clinical perineum)* is the area between the vagina and anus. A small incision, episiotomy, is sometimes made in the perineal skin and underlying tissues just prior to delivery of an infant to prevent its tearing.

FRANCES GARB

REPUBLICAN MOTHERHOOD was an ideology that gave women a political function, that of raising children to be moral, virtuous citizens of the new republic, without their engaging in political activity outside the domestic realm.

During the American Revolution many women of all classes became politically active and participated in various ways for the cause. Women took part in boycotts and riots, served as "Daughters of Liberty," raised money, and spun and wove cloth in their own homes. Camp followers performed necessary services for their husbands, fathers, and other relatives in the army, and some women acted as spies and couriers; a few fought, disguised as men, in the army.

After the Revolution, although regarded as citizens of the new republic, women were not given a larger place in political life or allowed the franchise (except, briefly, in New Jersey). In the late eighteenth century, public and private spheres of activity were more sharply defined than ever before, and women's role was defined as wholly within the private sphere, even though such a separation would be possible only for the minority of women who were above the lower middle class. (See CULT OF TRUE WOMANHOOD).

Since the male thinkers who worked out the new relationship between individuals and the republican state paid very little attention to the role of women, it was left to the women themselves to discover their function and place in the great new experiment. Denied a part in political life, they invested their domestic sphere with political importance. The Great Awakening (the religious revival that swept the Atlantic Coast in the 1730s and 1740s) and the literary sentimentalism of the late eighteenth century gave woman the role of upholder and reformer of society's manners and morals. As a morally superior being she nurtured virtue within the home through her influence on her husband and as teacher of her children. Therefore, even if women did not take part in public life, through their role in the home they could raise their sons to become the upholders of the virtues needed by freemen in a free society. The role of Republican Motherhood, then, recognized the reality of restrictions on women but also gave them a vital role—ensuring the success of the republic by instilling in its future generations the moral and political values necessary for good citizenship.

Although the ideology restricted women to a narrow political role and may have delayed the legal recognition of married women as persons at law, it had a positive effect on women's education. Advocates of female education such as Benjamin Rush were able to argue that girls must be educated in order for them to properly perform their domestic function of instructing their sons in the duties and virtues they would need to maintain the liberty and self-government won for them by their fathers.

Reference. Linda K. Kerber, "The Republican Mother," in Linda K. Kerber and Jane DeHart-Mathews (eds.), *Women's America: Refocusing the Past*, 2nd ed. (New York, 1987), 83–91.

RESERVE ARMY OF LABOR. Women have been called a reserve army of labor, a pool of surplus workers who are drawn into the labor force in times of economic expansion or scarcity of male labor and are drawn back out of the paid labor force when male labor is plentiful. Although there is considerable evidence for the entry of women into the labor market in times of expansion (e.g., the world wars), as Ruth Milkman points out, the "reserve army" theory is too mechanistic to satisfactorily explain the situation of women in a highly sex-segregated labor market in times of recession.

Reference. Ruth Milkman, "Women's Work and the Economic Crisis," in N. F. Cott and E. H. Pleck (eds.), *A Heritage of Her Own: Toward a New Social History of American Women* (New York, 1979), 507–541.

REST CURE. See WEIR MITCHELL REST CURE

RETIREMENT may be defined as a stepping down from previous levels of labor market activity. The decrease in work effort may be abrupt, involving a onetime transition from full-time employment to complete retirement, or it may be a gradual move from full-time employment to part-time work ("partial retirement") and eventually to full retirement. This latter pattern of retirement has become more widespread among women and men, as pressures for early retirement from career jobs have continued at the same time that medical advances have prolonged the working life. In a sample from the 1969–1979 *Retirement History Survey* of the Social Security Administration, more unmarried women, for example, spent time in the intermediate stage of partial retirement than retired in the "classic" one-step move from full-time employment to full retirement.

The labor force participation rate of older women in the United States is already quite high and is expected to rise in coming decades. In 1992, 47 percent of women aged 55–64 were either working or looking for work. This proportion is projected to rise to 54 percent by 2005, according to the U.S. Department of Labor. Among unmarried women, 68 percent of those aged 45–64 were in the labor force in 1992. Their retirement decisions appear to be similar to those of men, the primary differences arising from the relative unimportance of self-employment among women and their greater reliance on income from Social Security rather than from employer pensions. The most important factors determining the timing and pattern of retirement in a sample of unmarried women in the *Retirement History Survey*, the most complete source of information on retirement behavior to date, were found to be age, health, earnings, labor force experience, and Social Security benefits. Women in poor health tended to retire earlier, as did those with larger Social Security benefits or other non-work income. Higher levels of education and longer experience in the labor force were found to be associated with delayed retirement. Unlike men in the *Retirement History Survey*, employer pensions did not appear to be an important influence on the retirement decisions of unmarried women, possibly because fewer women were covered by work-related pensions during these years (only 38 percent of women in the survey, compared to 66 percent of men).

Among married women in the *Retirement History Survey*, retirement behavior was strongly conditioned on the retirement decisions of husbands. Roughly two-thirds of wives retired prior to, or simultaneously with, their husbands. Wives' own economic opportunities, in the form of potential earnings or pension and Social Security income from additional work, appeared to be relatively unimportant. Interestingly, wives were more likely to continue working if their husbands were in poor health. They were also more likely to work if their husbands' income was relatively high, indicating marital selection in tastes for work. In 1992, 59 percent of married women aged 45–64 were in the labor force.

Upcoming changes in Social Security are likely to affect the retirement behavior of both married and unmarried women in the next decade. The 1983 Amendments to the Social Security Act provided for gradual increases in the age of eligibility for full retirement benefits from 65 to 67, beginning in 2000. This change effectively reduces benefits for those retiring before age 67. The potential decrease in Social Security benefits is especially critical for women, who, despite increases in coverage under employer pensions in recent years, still have relatively little income from sources other than Social Security.

A new data source has been developed by the Institute for Social Research of the University of Michigan to increase understanding of the retirement decisions of both women and men. Funded by the National Institute on Aging, the Health and Retirement Survey began in 1992 to follow a cohort of men and women aged 51 to 61. The first wave of data contains 12,564 respondents from 7,703 households, who will be reinterviewed every two years for several years. Survey content is focused on four basic areas related to the economics and demography of aging: labor force participation and pensions; health conditions and health status; family structure and transfers; and economic status. The retirement plans of women included in the first wave of these data indicate that the retirement behavior of married women may have changed in the 20 years since the *Retirement History Survey*. Married workingwomen now appear to take into account factors related to their own, as well as their husbands', retirement income, such as their expected pension benefits and whether their lower-cost employer health insurance will be available after retirement. Whether these factors eventually influence their retirement decisions will become evident with additional waves of this important new survey.

References. G. Hanoch and M. Honig, "Retirement, Wages, and Labor Supply of the Elderly," *Journal of Public Economics* 1 (1983): 131–151; M. Honig, "Partial Retirement among Women," *Journal of Human Resources* 20 (1985): 613–621; M. Honig, "Retirement Expectations: Differences by Race, Ethnicity, and Gender," *The Gerontologist* 36 (1996); T. Juster and R. Suzman, "An Overview of the Health and Retirement Study," *Journal of Human Resources* 30 (1995): S7–S56; S. Pozzebon and O. S. Mitchell, "Married Women's Retirement Behavior," *Journal of Population Economics* 2 (1989): 39–53; C. Reimers and M. Honig, "Responses to Social Security by Men and Women: Myopic and Farsighted Behavior," *Journal of Human Resources* 33 (1996): 359–382.

MARJORIE HONIG

ROMANCE, MEDIEVAL, is a literary genre that flourished from the twelfth to the fifteenth centuries in the literature of France, England, and Germany; examples of romance are also found in Provençal, Spanish, Portuguese, Italian, Hebrew, Greek, Dutch, and Norse. The English word "romance" is taken from the Old French term *romanz*, which evolved from the Latin adverb *romanice*, used as early as the ninth century to mean "in the vernacular." Since much of the material written *en romanz* in the twelfth century consisted of fictitious narratives with particular themes and formats, the English word "romance" has come to refer to those compositions and to the tradition they generated, as distinct from the epic tradition exemplified by the chansons de geste.

A form of narrative featuring love, adventure, or chivalry as a theme, medieval romance first appeared in verse and later evolved into prose. The subject matter of the romance was described at the end of the twelfth century by Jean Bodel, who divided vernacular literature into three groups: the *matière de Rome*, the *matière de Bretagne*, and the *matière de Charlemagne*. This latter group, also known as the *matière de France*, forms the basis for the chansons de geste, while the other two groups provide the basis for much of the romance material. The *matière de Rome* refers to legends and stories of antiquity on which were based the *romans d'antiquité*. The *matière de Bretagne*, or Breton material, includes the legends of both Arthur and Tristan. To the two romance *matières* included in Jean Bodel's classification should be added first the body of Graeco-Byzantine material, which serves as the subject matter for many *romans d'aventure*, and finally the "matter of England," a category added by modern critics to refer to romances set in England or concerned with English heroes.

The Old French *romans d'antiquité* have their predecessors in the classical romances, such as the early Greek romance of Alexander the Great. Following in this tradition is the first vernacular romance, the *Roman d'Alexandre* (c. 1100), a Franco-Provençal fragment that later appeared as a composite work in 12-syllable lines, which consequently came to be called *alexandrins*. An adaptation of Statius' *Thebaïs*, the *Roman de Thèbes* (c. 1150) was composed by an anonymous Norman author. Another Norman adaptation of a Latin work is the *Roman d'Enéas* (c. 1160), an imitation of Virgil's *Aeneid*. The *Roman de Troie* (1154–1173), a long compilation by Benoît de Sainte-Maure, is based on chronicles of the Trojan War.

The legends of King Arthur and his knights of the Round Table make up the body of material most often brought to mind by the term "romance." Early portraits of Arthur by William of Malmesbury (*Gesta regum Anglorum*, 1125) and Geoffrey of Monmouth (*Historia regum Britanniae*, c. 1136) underwent considerable elaboration by the Norman poet Wace in his *Roman de Brut* (c. 1155), later translated into Middle English by the twelfth-century Saxon poet Layamon. Some of the earliest and best-known Arthurian romances were written by Chrétien de Troyes, who composed his *Lancelot* or *Le Chevalier de la charrette* after 1164 for Marie, countess of Champagne. While Chrétien's romances, which also include *Erec et Enide*, *Cligès*, *Yvain* or *Le Chevalier au lion*, and *Perceval* or *Le Conte du Graal*, show both classical and Byzantine influences, his treatment of the Breton material in a new form of narrative had the greatest impact on the development of the romance genre, inspiring many imitations. The symbolism of the Grail theme, first introduced into European literature by

Chrétien, is continued in Robert de Boron's *Joseph d'Arimathie* (late twelfth or early thirteenth century) and in the series of prose Lancelot romances dating from the early thirteenth century. Chrétien's romances provided the sources for the Middle High German works *Erek* (c. 1190) and *Iwein* (c. 1200) of Hartmann von Aue and the *Parzival* (c. 1200–1212) of Wolfram von Eschenbach.

Marie de France, a contemporary of Chrétien, is the first known woman author of narratives based on the *matière de Bretagne*. Her *lais*, composed in the second half of the twelfth century, may be described as short romances dealing with Celtic and Arthurian themes. Written in octosyllabic couplets, Marie's *lais* contain strong elements of the supernatural (as in *Guigemar* and *Bisclavret*) and treat both happy and unhappy love; the *Lai du Chèvrefeuil*, one of Marie's most popular poems, presents one episode of the legend of Tristan and Iseult. Influences from Marie's *lais* may be seen in Gautier d'Arras' romance *Ille et Galeron* (c. 1170), thought to be based on Marie's *Eliduc*, and in Hue de Roteland's *Ipomedon* (c. 1185), which has parallels to the *lai Milun*.

The tragic love story of Tristan and Iseult first appears in the latter part of the twelfth century in the *romans* of Béroul and Thomas, as well as in a lost version by Chrétien de Troyes. The Norman poet Béroul's fragmentary work, written before 1191, most closely follows the lost Old French original (c. 1150–1160); a parallel version exists in German by Eilhart von Oberge (c. 1170). The *Tristan* of the Anglo-Norman Thomas (c. 1155–1178), also a fragment, presents the more courtly version of the legend, later continued by the German author Gottfried von Strassburg (c. 1210), by Brother Robert in the Norwegian *Tristrams saga* (1226), and by the anonymous author of the Middle English *Sir Tristrem* (c. 1300).

Romances with Graeco-Byzantine themes include the *Eracle*, written after 1164 by Gautier d'Arras, and *Floire et Blancheflor* (c. 1170), later translated into Middle High German, Middle Dutch, Norse, and Middle English; the early thirteenth-century *chantefable Aucassin et Nicolette* shows influences from *Floire et Blancheflor*. Other *romans d'aventure*, such as the twelfth-century works *Partonopeus de Blois* and *Robert le Diable*, are likely based on folk motifs.

The English romances developed in the thirteenth century with the early works *King Horn* and *Havelock the Dane*, followed by dozens of romances in the fourteenth century, including *Sir Orfeo* (c. 1320), a Celticized version of the myth of Orpheus and Eurydice, and the *Alliterative Morte Arthure* (c. 1360). *Sir Gawain and the Green Knight*, written by an anonymous Midland poet around 1375, and Chaucer's *Troilus and Criseyde* (c. 1385) are considered by some to be the greatest of the English verse romances. Although the romance genre declined in England in the fifteenth century, Sir Thomas Malory's prose *Le Morte Darthur* (1469) presented a synthesis of various Arthurian tales that later served as the basis for Tennyson's nineteenth-century reworking.

The Spanish *libros de caballería* appeared in the fourteenth century with the Castilian Zifar (c. 1300), taken from Oriental sources, and *Amadís de Gaula*, a neo-Arthurian work whose central plot parallels that of *Lancelot* and that later inspired Cervantes' *Don Quixote* (1605). In Italy the *matière de Charlemagne* is treated as romance in heroic epics such as Matteo Boiardo's *Orlando innamorato* (1483) and Ludovico Ariosto's *Orlando furioso* (1516).

Representing a vast collection of women's literature, the romance frequently features powerful female characters whose importance is seen not only in their interaction with other characters but also in their influence on the development of the plot. Their power, however, usually comes from an external source, such as the world of magic or the fateful love malady inflicted on male and female protagonists alike. The transfer of power from such strong female characters to the male hero is an enabling process that sustains narrative tension by provoking action and contributing to the resolution of the hero's quest for self-realization.

In Marie's *lai Lanval*, the fairy mistress possesses such power and exerts a controlling force on the plot. She seeks out Lanval and supports him both financially and emotionally. Similarly, in Chrétien's *Yvain*, Lunete transfers power to Yvain through her magic and moves him toward the accomplishment of his goals. In the *Chevalier de la charrette*, the lovesick Lancelot's obsession with Guenevere gives her such control over him that she is able to dictate his behavior. In the Provençal romance *Jaufré* (c. 1225), the hero's search for adventure and self-definition become inextricably bound up in his pursuit of the beautiful Brunissen, whose power comes from her ownership of some 100 châteaus. Christine de Pisan's courtly romance *Le Livre du duc des vrais amants* (1405) features an influential female character who brings about the end of the love affair between the married princess and the anonymous duke.

One of the best-known female characters of romance is Iseult, who often precedes Tristan in initiating action and moving episodes toward resolution. Wonderfully adept at creating ambiguous oaths, she saves both herself and Tristan from punishment by the court. Iseult's magic healing ability, a link to Celtic tradition, gives her real and symbolic power over Tristan's life and death, a power that is dramatically illustrated in the tragic ending of the romance.

References. R. S. Loomis (ed.), *Arthurian Literature in the Middle Ages: A Collaborative History* (London, 1959); Eugene Vinaver, *The Rise of Romance* (London, 1971); Katharina Wilson (ed.), *Medieval Women Writers* (Athens, Ga., 1984).

MARYLOU MARTIN

ROMANIAN REPUBLIC. The fall of the Ceauşescu regime liberated Romania's citizens from the tyranny of state control over their public and private lives. For women, the "revolution" also liberated their bodies from the repressive antiabortion law that had been in effect since 1966. Decree

770 had been at the center of a series of legislative and policy acts that linked politics with demography. In theory, socialist transformation involved all domains of social existence and required mobilization of the entire populace. This requirement gave critical importance to demographic factors, whose relationship to state policy bore directly on issues of gender. The instrumentalization of women's bodies for the alleged purpose of reproducing the labor force had particular consequences for women's lives.

In post-Ceauşescu Romania, as elsewhere in the former Eastern bloc, the institutionalization of democratic practices and market economies has produced complex, often negative results for women. In what follows, I briefly summarize the productive and reproductive roles of women during the Ceauşescu regime (as discussed in Kligman and Verdery) and then examine the effects of the transition on women in Romania.

Women in Ceauşescu's Romania. In the former Socialist Republic of Romania, as elsewhere in then Eastern Europe, gender equality was an ideological tenet as well as a policy objective. While achieved in legislation, gender equality remained problematic in practice. Women's participation in the labor force was largely a function of development strategies that emphasized raising industrial production. Although women's occupational opportunities expanded over time, women tended to work in spheres of the economy having lower political priority and status. For example, agriculture was feminized. The timing and implementation of policy decisions distributed men and women differently into the labor force.

Industrialization plans also entailed concern for creating the country's workforce. The Romanian state, like other socialist states, promoted population growth by providing positive incentives to stimulate childbearing, among which were maternal benefits, maternity leaves, "tax" incentives, and financial compensation for large families. The Ceauşescu regime also elevated reproduction to a national responsibility for every citizen. To this end, the positive incentives, themselves largely symbolic, were augmented by coercive measures. All modern forms of contraception were unavailable, making abortion the primary means of fertility control. Yet abortion was illegal under almost all circumstances. Increasingly stringent attempts to suppress the rise in illegal abortions resulted in the state's excessive intrusion into its citizens' intimate lives. Nonetheless, by 1989, Romania's maternal mortality rate was the highest registered in Europe, by and large the result of complications arising from illegal abortions.

Women in Post-Ceauşescu Romania. On December 26, 1989, one day after the execution of the Ceauşescus, Romania's provisional leadership liberalized abortion. Abortion remained the primary method of fertility control in 1996. Modern contraceptive knowledge is poor, and, for many, contraceptive alternatives are unaffordable and inaccessible. In reaction to the difficult socioeconomic conditions associated with political and economic restructuring, the birthrate has declined steadily (i.e., from 16 per

1,000 population in 1989 to 11.4 per 1,000 in 1992, to 10.4 per 1,000 by 1995). Women and men have been differently affected by "the transition," with women's opportunities in general being more limited.

Women's occupational options have both expanded with the opening of the private sector and been curtailed by downsizing, the recasting of occupational sectors, and the burgeoning of part-time labor. Women and men are still differently distributed in the changing labor market. Women's employment is not typically commensurate with levels of educational attainment. Women are generally absent from managerial ranks. The feminization of occupational sectors such as private agriculture and the service sector contributes to their market devaluation. The slow pace of privatization in Romania has made the service sector less dynamic than elsewhere in the region. Wage discrimination, although less pronounced than in the West, is characteristic (with an approximate gap of 11 percent). Women experience higher unemployment among all age groups, forming 55–60 percent of the total unemployed population. Young women under 25 seem to be most vulnerable, according to the National Commission for Statistics (AMIGO 1994, 1995). However, statistics vary from source to source. According to 1994 Ministry of Labor and Social Protection data, unemployment was highest among women between the ages of 25 and 29. Although women may not be the first to lose jobs due to economic restructuring, they remain unemployed for longer periods than men and have fewer new prospects. Women constitute the majority of part-time employees (a virtually nonexistent category before 1989). As elsewhere in the region, poverty is being feminized among all age groups, especially among homemakers, the unemployed, single mothers, divorcées, widows, and female pensioners.

Unequal economic access is mirrored in the unequal distribution of power in politics. Women's participation in national politics has decreased dramatically from 34.4 percent in 1989 to approximately 4 percent in 1992 and increased to 5.5 percent in the 1996 elections. Women are more engaged in local-level politics as well as in nongovernmental organizations (NGOs), although gender hierarchies persist in these realms. For example, women make up 6.11 percent of 39,831 local council members but only 2.74 percent of 2,954 mayors. NGOs have grown in numbers, with approximately 55 women's organizations involved in activities ranging from social to political initiatives. Their effectiveness has been relatively limited. Of these women's organizations, few claim to be feminist.

The transition has not been overly kind to women. State paternalism and "masculine democracies" differently relegate women and women's issues to secondary status. Women remain overburdened by domestic obligations. Moreover, child care is less available as social welfare measures are cut. Women are also victims of domestic violence, a critical and widespread factor in the increasing number of divorce cases (see Minnesota Advocates for Human Rights; Raboaca and Popescu). Public recognition of, and education about, violence are necessary. Government and nongovernmental organizations must also promote sexual and contraceptive education and usage. Shared parenting and household responsibilities form part of the democratization of gender relations, without which women cannot fully exercise their newly transformed citizenship rights and responsibilities or share equally in emerging economic opportunities.

References. M. E. Fischer, "Women in Romanian Politics: Elena Ceauşescu, Pronatalism, and the Promotion of Women," in S. Wolchik and A. Meyer, eds., *Women, State and Party in Eastern Europe* (Durham, N.C., 1985), 121–137; M. Fong, *Romania: Gender in the Transition* (Bucharest, 1996); G. Kligman, "The Politics of Reproduction in Ceauşescu's Romania: A Case Study in Political Culture," *East European Politics and Societies* 6, 3 (1992): 364–418; G. Kligman, *The Politics of Duplicity: Controlling Reproduction in Ceauşescu's Romania* (Los Angeles, 1998); G. Kligman and K. Verdery, "Romanian Socialist Republic," in H. Tierney (ed.), *Women's Studies Encyclopedia*, vol. 3 (Westport, Conn., 1991); 384–386; Minnesota Advocates for Human Rights, *Lifting the Last Curtain: A Report on Domestic Violence in Romania* (Minneapolis, 1995); Raboaca and Popescu (eds.), *The Condition of Women in Romania (1980–1995): National Report* (Bucharest, 1995); National Commission for Statistics, AMIGO, 1994, 1995.

GAIL KLIGMAN

ROME, ANCIENT. Legal Status of Women. Early Roman law accorded almost unfettered power to the oldest, male, lineal ascendant in each household, the *paterfamilias*. Apart from a handful of Vestal Virgins recruited mostly from upper-class families and consecrated at an early age to the service of Vesta, goddess of the hearth, women were freed from their paterfamilias' authority only if he emancipated them formally, if he died, or if they married in such a way that they passed into their husband's control, or *manus*.

Roman marriage was mostly a matter of intention: the desire to live together as husband and wife, not ceremony or contract, bound a couple together and alone served to distinguish marriage from concubinage (cohabitation). Marriage was of two types. The older type, marriage with *manus*, placed the wife in a legal position akin to that of a daughter. Property that she brought to the marriage belonged to her husband. In the later type, marriage without *manus*, which had become prevalent by the first century B.C., the wife remained under the control of her *paterfamilias*. Marriage without *manus* afforded some women more independence.

Most girls married in their teens. The minimum marriageable age was 12. Whether or not puberty had been reached was immaterial. It was probably not until the first century A.D. or later that the law required the consent of a girl who was under the control of her *paterfamilias*, and even then she could withhold it only if she could prove that her fiancé was morally unfit.

Like men, women were expected, and from the time of Augustus (ruled

27 B.C.–A.D. 14) were required, to marry and raise families. His marriage laws of 18 B.C. and A.D. 9 penalized unmarried and childless women between the ages of 20 and 50, including divorcées and widows who did not remarry within 18 months after their divorce or two years after their partner's death. They also barred senators and their descendants from marrying ex-slaves, actresses, and other women of disreputable profession. Slaves could never lawfully marry. Some formed quasi marriages, which had no status in law.

It was customary for a bride or her *paterfamilias* to furnish a dowry, usually of cash or goods. The law provided for its return in the event of the dissolution of the marriage. In the case of divorce, where no arrangements had been made for its return, the dowry was normally restored intact, less costs that the husband had incurred in maintaining its value (e.g., repairs to a house), a fraction for children, and another fraction if it could be shown that the wife's conduct had caused the divorce.

In early Rome, a man who divorced his wife for reasons other than adultery, poisoning a child, or tampering with the household keys was required to give her half his property. From at least the first century B.C., either partner could unilaterally divorce the other, without ceremony or formality, in person or by letter (from the reign of Augustus, a fully valid divorce seems to have required the presence of seven witnesses). Children of the marriage remained with the husband. A *paterfamilias* could dissolve his child's marriage, but it is unlikely that many did.

Adultery was a crime only for women. In the early law, an adulterous wife (or one who drank wine) could be killed by her husband or by her family acting with his consent. From the time of Augustus, adultery was a public offense, and a husband who caught his wife in the act was forced to divorce and prosecute her or himself risk prosecution for pandering. Convicted adulteresses lost half their dowries and were banished to a remote island. Women were not required to divorce adulterous husbands and were not allowed to bring them to trial. A double standard operated also in the law governing criminal fornication, or *stuprum*. Unmarried upper-class women, including widows, were forbidden to have sexual relations, but upper-class men were entitled to sex with prostitutes and other lower-class women. Rape was considered to be a crime against the victim's family and could be prosecuted by her, her *paterfamilias*, or her husband.

A woman who was released from her *paterfamilias'* authority when she was unmarried or married without *manus*, because she was judged to be incapable of managing her own affairs, was assigned a male guardian for life, usually a close relative. She required his approval of most legal and financial transactions, especially those that might result in loss to her, for example, selling land or freeing a slave. By the first century B.C., guardianship had been weakened by legal devices; for example, a woman could apply to the authorities to force her guardian to give his approval. From the reign of Augustus on, freeborn women with three children and ex-slaves with four were released from guardianship. It may be doubted whether many qualified.

Only women who were not under a *paterfamilias* or husband's control could own property in their own name. They could make wills, but until the second century A.D. this could be done only by a very complicated procedure and only with their guardian's authorization. The early law of succession treated women and men alike; for example, daughters and sons shared equally in the estate of a *paterfamilias* who died intestate. Equity was overthrown by the Voconian law of 169 B.C., which forbade anyone of the wealthiest class to appoint a woman his heir or to leave her a legacy of greater value than the property bequeathed to his heir or joint heirs. However, the law was easily and frequently evaded.

Reference. B. Rawson (ed.), *The Family in Ancient Rome: New Perspectives* (Ithaca, N.Y., 1987), 243–272, esp. 249–250, 255–257.

DAVID A. CHERRY

ROME, ANCIENT. Political Women of the Republican Period are well documented in the primary sources and are usually presented as powerful, energetic, and amoral. Women of elite families are alleged to serve as intermediaries in major political negotiations, to control access to male associates, to play a behind-the-scenes role in legal proceedings, and even to involve themselves in conspiracies (Sallust, Catiline, 24.3–25.5). Not uncommonly, they are also accused of sexual promiscuity and murder. Thus, Cicero in his forensic defense of Caelius blackens the name of Clodia, the widow of Metellus Celer, who had testified on behalf of the prosecution, by claiming that she engineered the whole trial out of thwarted lust for his client and exhorting the jury to curb this wanton abuse of female power. Uncritical acceptance of such denunciations prompted earlier scholars to create the familiar stereotype of the "emancipated," pleasure- and power-hungry Roman matron of the late republic. Recognition of the intensely rhetorical bent of Roman oratory, however, now leads skeptics to dismiss all accounts of women's political activity as tendentious exaggeration—while still frequently maintaining belief in lurid accounts of their sexual transgressions.

In contrast, feminist scholarship points to elite Roman women's structural place within the family and to the nature of political proceedings in Roman society to create a model in which all women, not simply an exceptional few, played a key role in power transactions in both the private and public spheres. As Suzanne Dixon observes, the Romans themselves perceived no absolute distinction between the political and social areas of life: formal power, limited to men, was an overt manifestation of informal power exercised through a patronage network, into which kindred ties were inextricably interwoven. Their place in that network as vital connecting links between families necessarily involved elite matrons in the day-to-day dealings of male kin. Judith Hallett constructs a theory of *filiafocality*: the daughter of a Roman *paterfamilias* (the male head of household) was valued emotionally for her own sake and strategically as a pledge of affiliation with a son-in-law, normally a close paternal associate. Consciousness of their filial importance would have given Roman daughters the confidence to deal assertively with brothers and sons and also placed them in an excellent position to act as brokers in complex negotiations between families.

Ancient sources provide a coherent picture of women regularly serving as mediators, patronesses, and family representatives, often with a marked degree of autonomy. Cicero's letters contain many instances of matrons performing as go-betweens for spouses or other relatives. Sestius' wife, Cornelia, informs Cicero's wife, Terentia, of Sestius' personal wishes, enabling Cicero to take them up with the Senate (*Letters to Friends*, 5.6.1); embroiled in a quarrel with the prominent Metelli family, Cicero himself appeals to Metellus Celer's half sister Mucia and wife, Clodia, to urge his case (*Letters to Friends*, 5.2.6); during the civil war between Caesar and Pompey, Terentia aids her absent husband, even applying on his behalf to Mark Antony's mistress, the actress Volumnia Cytheris (*Letters to Friends*, 14.16); in a family council, Servilia, mother of Brutus, promises to get a decree of the Senate reversed—an undertaking reported, significantly, without apparent astonishment and certainly without comment (*Letters to Atticus*, 15.11.2). Epigraphic material affords additional examples. The inscription known as the *Laudatio "Turiae" (Corpus Inscriptionum Latinarum*, 6.1527, 31670) shows its subject taking decisive steps to safeguard her inheritance, defend her home, support her proscribed husband in exile, and intercede for him with his enemies; her forcefulness and initiative are treated as praiseworthy. Ancient historians depict Fulvia, the formidable wife of Antony, assuming command of an army in his absence (Velleius Paterculus, 2.74.2–3; Plutarch, *Life of Antony*, 28.1, 30.1; Dio, 48.10.3–4, 13.1); her military visibility is confirmed by sling bullets inscribed with her name (*CIL*, 11.6721.3–5, 14).

Occasionally, we find women uniting in protest against oppressive government policies. In 195 B.C., female members of the propertied classes demonstrated in the streets to urge the repeal of the Oppian Law, a sumptuary decree curtailing the ownership and display of personal adornment (Livy, 34.1–8.3). Similarly, in 42 B.C., wealthy women whose male relatives had been proscribed protested against punitive taxes imposed upon them by massing in the Forum, where Hortensia, daughter of the orator Hortensius, appealed successfully to public sentiment in a speech admired by posterity (Appian, *Civil Wars* 4.32–34; cf. Quintilian, 1.1.6).

Oratorical denunciations of backstairs intrigue thus appear to reflect women's ordinary role within the Roman political system, albeit in a polemic fashion. Tales of female debauchery and violence are largely the products of patriarchal fantasy, warning male audiences that their womenfolk cannot be trusted with the informal power they exercise. Through a distorted lens, such accounts show us elite Roman women efficiently using kinship networks as their recognized vehicle of personal and political authority.

References. Richard A. Bauman, *Women and Politics in Ancient Rome* (London, 1992), 13–98; Suzanne Dixon, "A Family Business; Women's Role in Patronage and Politics at Rome 80–44 B.C., *Classica et Mediaevalia* 34 (1983): 91–112; Elaine Fantham et al., *Women in the Classical World* (New York and Oxford, 1994), 216–242, 260–329, 345–392; Judith P. Hallett, *Fathers and Daughters in Roman Society: Women and the Elite Family* (Princeton, 1984); Sarah B. Pomeroy, *Goddesses, Whores, Wives and Slaves: Women in Classical Antiquity* (New York, 1975), 176–189.

MARILYN B. SKINNER

ROME, ANCIENT. Private Lives of Women were characterized by a traditionally important role accorded to the citizen wife (*mater familias*). Despite legal checks on their freedom of action within and outside the house, Roman citizen women nonetheless frequently exercised considerable autonomy in their roles as daughters, wives, and mothers.

Perhaps because Rome developed for so many centuries as a predominantly agrarian and tribal society (eighth to second centuries B.C.), women's contributions to family and economic life retained value in male eyes. Despite their legal inferiority, wives and mothers were expected to act in the best interests of the family, and this expectation of female action allowed women considerable freedom of expression, especially within the household. Unlike the women of classical Greece, Roman women regularly attended social events and dined with the men in their family, thus hearing and participating in daily discussions of the family's and the community's problems and prospects.

Roman legend remembered not only women who bore strong sons, faithfully tended the family hearth, and made clothing but also women who, like the Sabines or the wife and mother of Coriolanus, actively interceded with husbands, fathers, and sons to restore peace and harmony to the general community. Thus, while women's lives focused mainly on domestic duties, they were not cut off from the events of the world outside their homes.

With the growth of the Roman empire and the increasing size of the city of Rome itself, the aristocracy became increasingly urban and wealthy. But conquest and riches did not work to drive Roman women into seclusion, as in classical Athens. In 195 B.C., women successfully pressed for the repeal of a law that forbade their display of wealth; their public demonstration reflects a sense of female solidarity and a network of friendships and associations among Roman citizen women that must have been developed in the context of their everyday activities.

When Rome later conquered the Hellenistic East (second through first centuries B.C.), the traditional values that accorded women a strong role within the home and some voice in public affairs absorbed features of Hellenistic noblewomen's lives, giving aristocratic Roman women an even wider sphere of activity. Still responsible for childbearing, household management, superintendence of the family's hearth and gods, and production of the family's clothing, the Roman matron could also conduct literary salons on the model of Eastern royal women and engage in politics through her influence on brothers, husbands, and sons. The ideal of Roman matronhood was Cornelia, daughter of a famous general and mother of prominent politicians (second century B.C.). A *univira* (married to only one man), mother of 12, and hostess to an important circle of philosophers and other learned people, she was renowned for her chastity, devotion to children and household, intellect, and simplicity of dress and style.

In the late republic and early empire (first century B.C. through second century A.D.), the great wealth of the aristocracy enabled its women to turn over the bulk of housework to legions of domestic slaves. Not all women followed Cornelia's noble model; many devoted their time to beautifying themselves and their homes, to education and music, to entertaining, to games and pets, and, increasingly, to amorous adventures. The tenets of Stoicism, however, which celebrated marital partnership and domestic life, tended to redirect many women's energies back to home and family, especially in the first two centuries A.D.

While some upper-class couples enjoyed long-lasting unions based on mutual respect and real affection, serial marriages were increasingly used by ambitious male politicians to further their careers, making it difficult for women to feel personal loyalty to their husbands. Moreover, Cornelia's large family was decidedly unusual; Roman upper classes did not replenish themselves. Despite high child mortality rates, couples generally chose to have only two or three children. The family's desire not to dissipate its estate among too many heirs combined with women's desire to avoid lifelong immersion in domesticity, dangers of childbirth, and potential separation from their children after divorce kept upper-class families small. Within these families, the affective bonds between father and daughter seem to have been stronger than between other dyads, strengthening Roman women's sense of worth and autonomy.

Compared with the instability of many upper-class families, especially during the late republic and early empire, greater emotional security may have been available to middle- and lower-class families of free and freed people. Funerary inscriptions attest to long marriages as well as strong affective ties between wives and husbands and between mothers and children.

Middle-class women living on farms or in the towns that dotted the Roman empire probably maintained the daily pattern of life modeled by

Cornelia, but without the luxuries and cultural advantages of her wealthy family. Graffiti from Pompeii show that town women made their political preferences for various local candidates known, participating as best they could in public life.

Familial solidarity probably gave the lower classes their greatest bulwark against the perils of poverty. Lower-class women regularly worked for pay outside the home; elderly female relatives or neighbors provided child care when possible. Urban families lived in crowded, wretched tenements and probably purchased ready-cooked food and bread for family meals. Rural women undoubtedly lived a precarious existence of endless work not only in their rude homes but also in the fields.

The middle and lower classes' emphasis on family life apparently extended into the swollen ranks of the slave community, especially in the cities. While slaves could not legally marry, *contubernium* (an informal, but socially recognized, union) united many a slave couple. Grave inscriptions show that either partner might buy first one of the couple then the other out of slavery, and then the couple's children. Many masters recognized and respected slave "marriages" and allowed couples to live together; for some slave women, daily life was much like that of lower-class women of free or freed status. However, other masters paid scant attention to their slaves' personal relationships and sold one of the partners or the slaves' children.

During the later Roman empire (third through fourth centuries A.D.), political and economic crises caused grave dislocations for the middle and lower classes, forcing many families—including women—to eke out a meager existence; poverty was so desperate that children were frequently sold into slavery. Upper-class women continued to exercise considerable authority within their homes, but they increasingly turned their attention and energy to religious activities, particularly to the goddess Isis, before whom men and women were equal. With the eventual conversion of the Roman world to Christianity and the establishment of a strong, institutionalized church, the archaic traditions that subordinated women to men, emphasized virginity and chastity, and stressed women's domestic duties returned to the fore; women were reconfined to the periphery of male life.

References. Judith P. Hallett, *Fathers and Daughters in Roman Society: Women and the Elite Family* (Princeton, 1984); Sarah B. Pomeroy, *Goddesses, Whores, Wives, and Slaves: Women in Classical Antiquity* (New York, 1975); Beryl Rawson (ed.), *The Family in Ancient Rome* (Ithaca, N.Y., 1986).

VALERIE FRENCH

ROME, ANCIENT. Women in Roman Poetry is of necessity the study of the role of women in the works of male Latin poets, since only one woman poet, Sulpicia, has survived, and her meager poetic remains are of minor merit and interest.

Drama. In the comedies of Plautus and Terence, women play a large part, but, despite some sharply drawn characters, the numerous female figures can be reduced to a handful of stock types: the wily maidservant, the predatory prostitute, the prostitute with the heart of gold, the nagging wife, and (kept mostly offstage) the virtuous young girl. A special case is the heroine of Plautus' *Amphitryon.* A faithful wife, she is seduced by Jupiter in the guise of her husband and becomes an almost tragic character amid the comedy.

Lucretius. Lucretius, the epic poet of Epicurean philosophy, deals extensively with women in his treatment of love and sex. Love is an unhealthy distraction from Epicurean detachment and serenity of mind in which the lover torments himself and blindly transforms the vices of a woman into virtues. Sexual desire and its satisfaction without emotional attachment or complications, on the other hand, are natural and permissible.

Catullus. The lyric poet Catullus, with a truly revolutionary attitude toward women, idealizes his mistress and the love of a man for a woman to a degree unparalleled by previous ancient authors. In an important group of poems he expresses and analyzes his overwhelming love for an aristocratic Roman matron named Clodia (given the pseudonym Lesbia). He pays tribute not only to her beauty but to her intelligence, learning, and wit.

Catullus' love for Clodia has an intensity heretofore found in ancient poetry only in homosexual attachments. Flouting the traditional notion that passionate love of a woman was acceptable only as a passing stage in adolescence but folly and madness for an adult male, he makes the woman the center of his life. Since Romans could not be expected to comprehend this novel conception of love (and Catullus seems to have some difficulty in understanding it himself), he struggles to describe something that was not a part of accepted Roman values by expressing it in terms that the Romans did understand and respect: religion, friendship, law, international relations, and business.

Unfortunately, Clodia, a very independent woman, seems not to have been interested in such a confining relationship. Catullus took this attitude as betrayal and responded with some brilliant, but often violently obscene, poems attacking her. Another attack on her came in a speech by Cicero, Rome's greatest orator, made in his defense of a man in whose prosecution Clodia was instrumental; Cicero defended his client in exactly the same manner as a modern defense lawyer in a rape case, by destroying the woman's reputation. It is regrettable that most of what we know about this remarkable woman comes to us in the writings of a disappointed lover and a designing lawyer.

Horace. In the odes and satires of Horace women are frequent, but they are quite unsubstantial figures. An exception is his ode on the death of

Cleopatra, which begins with the queen as the familiar monster of Augustan propaganda but ends by investing her with the nobility of those Roman statesmen who, like her, chose suicide over submission.

Love Elegy. Love elegy was a literary genre invented by the Romans, with no Greek prototype, and in it woman was of central concern. The leading elegists were Propertius, Tibullus, and Ovid. Propertius wrote many poems detailing his love for a woman whom he calls Cynthia, whose real name was probably Hostia. He spoke of her as a slave would speak of his mistress and idealized her by identifying her with the renowned heroines of the Greek legendary past. Although she is, to a great extent, a peg on which to hang his probings of his own emotions, a plausible portrait of a woman emerges. She was not only beautiful and temperamental, but also very well educated (she had to be to understand his constant allusions to Greek mythology) and accomplished in the arts. She was strong-willed and unwilling to be tied down. Like Clodia, she inspired a love that she refused to be bound by.

Virgil. Virgil, in the Roman national epic the *Aeneid*, creates a powerful woman in Dido. She is, in every respect, the equal of the hero of the poem, Aeneas, but when he leaves her to resume his mission to found the Roman people, the poet makes her react in a stereotypically female fashion, and women are seen to be obstacles to the serious enterprises of men. In addition, human and divine females are identified in the poem with the irrational and with the chaotic forces of nature.

Ovid. Ovid, of all ancient poets with the possible exception of the Greek tragedian Euripides, tries hardest to understand women and their psychology and to express what he has learned in his poetry, although at the beginning the knowledge he has gained through his close observation of women is used to portray them in a rather cynical fashion. In his *Art of Love* he instructs men in the manipulation of women, although the final third of the work is devoted to advice for women. By means of the "art" Ovid professes to teach—the Latin word meant both art and science—man must cultivate woman in the same sense that man cultivates nature in the art/science called agriculture. Like land, woman in a state of nature is rough, crude, and useless. A woman's "no" really means "yes" and the force a man may sometimes find it necessary to use is secretly welcome to her. On the positive side, the lover is exhorted to make himself worthy of love and to attend to his mistress' sexual satisfaction (even to the extent of ensuring mutual orgasm).

The *Heroides* (Heroines), a collection of letters in verse that Ovid imagines were composed by famous women at major crises in their lives, shows a good deal of psychological insight.

By the time of the *Metamorphoses* (Transformations), Ovid sees women in a new light. Of this lengthy collection of stories drawn largely from Greek mythology, many deal with encounters of men and male divinities with women. Ovid strips the stories of their glamour and romance and presents them as rape seen from the point of view of the victim. In contrast to the *Art of Love*, he now knows that women do not like to be raped. In addition, the poem, in its comprehensive analysis of the varieties of love and of the shifting instability of personal identity, constantly delves into the psychology of women.

Juvenal. Juvenal devotes a poem of over 600 lines to shrill, unrelieved misogyny. Although the encyclopedic listing of women's vices suggests a striving for exhaustiveness that may be rhetorical in inspiration, it is difficult to deny the presence of genuine hatred of women.

LEO C. CURRAN

ROME, ANCIENT. Women's Public Roles in the Roman Empire were determined by their social position, family connections, wealth, and residence: rural, urban, small town, or capital city. The evidence, most of it from inscriptions, testifies primarily about the well-off urban class.

At the top of the social hierarchy was the wife of the emperor, who shared her husband's public position. Augustus ruled (27 B.C.–A.D. 14), the first emperor, defined a position for his wife, Livia (58 B.C.–A.D. 29), that became a model for successive emperors to follow. She was the first woman in Rome to receive honorific public statues voted by the Senate and sacrosanctity, which protected her from verbal or physical abuse. Her husband also granted her, on the model of the Vestal Virgins, freedom from guardianship, so that she could administer her property independently. All three privileges, granted early in his career, established a public position for Livia. By his will Augustus bestowed his own honorific name on his widow so that she added *Augusta* to her name, a singular event, since no case existed in the Republic of a woman's inheriting a male relative's honorific name. She was also designated as the priestess of her newly deified husband, an anomaly in a society where even most female deities were served by male priests. While her new name and role as priestess conferred social prestige on Livia, none of her accumulated honors added up to a constitutional position in the state.

Inherent in Livia's position, as for most empresses, was a tension between a figurehead role—the chaste and devoted mother—and her actual ability to use her social prestige, vast wealth, and patronal connections to influence political life. In this regard she was, like the aristocratic women of the Republic, able to intercede, conciliate, and forge ties between her husband and other eminent Roman men.

Gradually, with successive emperors the honors for Imperial women escalated. The faces of empresses now appeared on state coins; they received ever more inflated honorific titles, such as Julia Domna's (d. A.D. 217) "mother of the (military) camps"; they were regularly deified and added to the Roman pantheon. Buildings were dedicated to them, or the empresses themselves practiced largesse on a grand scale. Agrippina the Younger (A.D. 15–59) started a temple for her deified husband, Claudius (ruled A.D. 41– 54); Julia Domna restored the temple of Vesta in Rome. The increase in public attention focused, beginning in the Tiberian period (A.D. 14–37), on *a domus Augusta*, "the house of Augustus," in which the wife and mother had a traditional and recognized role. The representation of emperor and empress as a divine couple from whom all benefits flow appeared as early as coins of Nero (ruled A.D. 54–68). Some empresses attempted to exercise political power openly, setting off vituperative attacks from the male authors who wrote histories of their husbands' reigns. The manipulative, power-hungry, domineering empress, a man-woman, is a staple of Roman literature. Yet a contradictory tension of playing the traditional and approved role of the modest, unassuming wife caused some empresses to stay in the background.

During the Empire well-off women, from the aristocratic elite to wealthy freedwomen, became benefactors of their communities, exercising a kind of public patronage unrecorded in the Republic, although our evidence (primarily inscriptional) shows that women were always in a very distinct minority. In the West perhaps 10 percent of the donors to local funerary societies or business groups were women. Forbis has shown how women in the West were honored by their towns as benefactresses in language similar to that for male benefactors, but the collected inscriptions list 32 women to 236 men in the first three centuries of the Empire. In the Greek East coins show 17 women to 214 men holding offices normally awarded to benefactors.

Why did women become more publicly visible during the imperial period? Van Bremen has tied the increased number of civic grants sponsored by women to increasing wealth and a common desire by the local rich, male or female, to become benefactors. It is hard to know if the example of the empress exercised any impression on local elite women and set a new model for public life.

Only a few women in the Republic served religious functions. Men controlled both the state cult and the domestic cult, and Scheid has observed that women were deliberately excluded from the sacral core of religion, the sacrifice. Apart from the Vestal Virgins, priestesses served Ceres, but they, although they had to be citizens, came from outside Rome. The rise and spread of the Imperial cult, especially of the deified empresses, opened opportunities for public religious service to women. Inscriptions for the cult of the deified empresses seem to reveal that priestesses were primarily freeborn, probably members of the local municipal elite. Scholars debate whether the title of priestess actually meant anymore than "wife of the priest," although some inscriptions do describe women without priest husbands and suggest an actual cultic role.

From the empress down to ex-slaves, inscriptional evidence attests to women in business. Numerous brick stamps and lead pipes show that women owned and invested in brickyards and foundries. The emperor Claudius offered rewards to women who would help finance shipbuilding; this offer presupposes a considerable number of women with capital to invest.

On the lowest social rung were slaves and ex-slaves. Female slaves did domestic work; in the households of the rich they had specialties centered on the women of the house. They were hairdressers, nursemaids, midwives, seamstresses, and personal maids. Some took their work with them into freedom, if they achieved it, or ran shops. A gender division existed in the kinds of work appropriate for women; the evidence of their tombstones reveals no female forays into men's work. Still, a sense of professional pride must have existed for the women or their family members to inscribe their work on tombstones. For these women, slave or ex-slave, a job title may have compensated for their inferior social position in Roman society. Within their own social circles a modest shop might signal success even if work outside the home was never an ideal of Roman society and, from the point of view of the free and wealthy woman, socially demeaning.

The change from a republic to an empire limited political rights for men and did not change the position of women, who were unable to vote or hold office or participate in political life. Yet signs for political candidates from Pompeii, painted on the walls, record the favorites of local women. These posters date from 80 B.C. to A.D. 79, but women appear only in the last 17 years of the city's history. Sauven has shown that 52 of the 2,500 posters included a woman's name; slaves and freedmen probably predominated. Some of the women may have been family members or clients of a patron running for elective office. The existence of the electoral notices assumes the women's belief in their ability to influence local political outcomes.

In the Empire as in the Republic women's public influence originated in, and supported, family status. An inscription from the city of Apollonia in Asia Minor records that the town and its Roman merchants honored a local woman with seven statues in public places, including a prestigious gilded image. The reason was the "excellence" of her parents and husband. High social status and wealth did not give women complete freedom to operate independently; their highest priority was to reinforce the public position of their families.

References. M. B. Flory, "Livia and the History of Public Honorific Statues for Women in Rome," *Transactions and Proceedings of the American Philological Association* 123 (1993): 287–308; E. F. Forbis, "Women's Public Image in Italian Inscriptions," *American Journal of Philology* 111 (1990): 493–512; R. MacMullen, "Women in Public in the Roman Empire," *Historia* 29 (1980): 208–218; L. Sauven, "Women and Elections in Pompeii," in R. Hawley and B. Levick (eds.), *Women in Antiquity: New Assessments* (London, 1995), 194–206; J. Scheid, "The Religious

Roles of Roman Women," in G. Duby and M. Perrot (eds.), *A History of Women in the West*, vol. 1 (Cambridge, Mass., 1992); 377–408; R. Van Bremen, "Women and Wealth," in A. Cameron and A. Kuhrt (eds.), *Images of Women in Antiquity* (Detroit, 1983), 223–242.

MARLEEN B. FLORY

ROYAL ACADEMY OF ARTS is the most prestigious British art organization, offering education, exhibition opportunities, and exclusive membership to aspiring painters, sculptors, and architects. Founded in 1768, the Royal Academy hoped to raise the level of British art by encouraging, according to its constitution, "men of fair moral characters, of high reputation in their several professions." Two prominent women painters were founding members of the academy: Angelica Kauffman (1741–1807) and Mary Moser (1744–1819). Unfortunately, from the beginning, women were excluded from holding any office within the organization and from assuming lectureships or attending life classes. Johann Zoffany's painting *The Academicians of the Royal Academy* (1772) aptly portrays Kauffman's and Moser's roles in the early academy. Zoffany depicts most of the Royal Academy members (RAs) arranging a nude model and drapery; Kauffman and Moser are represented only by portraits on the right-hand wall. After Kauffman and Moser died, the Royal Academy discouraged women from studying art in its school and failed to invite another woman painter to join until 1922, when Annie Louisa Swynnerton (1844–1933) achieved associate Royal Academy membership.

Excluding women from studying art and from full membership doomed women painters to second rank in England. Although painting was part of all educated women's regimen, women acquired primarily decorative skills. A typical middle-class woman learned to draw tolerably, paint landscapes, and copy artworks. Women painters excelled in watercolors, not oils, and focused on flower paintings, genre scenes, and touching love scenes suggested by literature. Although these paintings might gain a modest income for the artist, they could not successfully compete in Royal Academy exhibitions or gain support for membership. The Royal Academy valued large oil paintings, particularly historical or classical scenes, that displayed a painter's technical virtuosity and knowledge of human physique. Successful artists had to study anatomy and practice drawing nude models; women were not allowed this education.

Many art schools trained women to be lower-level artists; some of the most effective were the Female School of Design (founded in 1843)—which became the Royal Female School of Art in 1862—Henry Sass' School of Art (1842), Dickinson's Academy (1848), and the Slade School at the University of London (1871). The Royal Academy remained the school for serious painters, particularly for men intent on winning fame and titles. Although women were not expressly forbidden to enroll in Royal Academy classes, none tried until 1860. Sir Charles Eastlake suggested that Laura Herford, a prominent woman painter, apply for acceptance as a student. She submitted the requisite drawings under the name "L. Herford." She was accepted, as were 13 other women over the next few years, but women were restricted to studying from casts, reproductions, and clothed figures, never from living nudes. In 1863, the Council of the Royal Academy decided that its constitution did not allow women students. After protest from professional women painters, the Royal Academy allowed 13 women students to enroll.

Although many Victorian women became prominent painters, the Royal Academy remained adamant about not accepting women into full membership. Women were grudgingly allowed to study in separate classes, but not to teach or govern the institution. Artists of the caliber of Louisa Starr, Kate Greenway, and Elizabeth Thompson Butler were systematically ignored. Some intrepid RA members nominated prominent women for membership, but women lost every vote until 1922. Women were deemed less able to fulfill the necessary RA duties. Royal Academy membership entailed teaching and administrative responsibilities and guaranteed a painter's financial success. Victorians believed it improper for women to compete with, or supervise, men.

In 1903, the Royal Academy allowed mixed classes for most of its curriculum, and women were allowed to study nude figures in separate classes. Annie Laura Swynnerton and Laura Knight won associate membership in the 1920s. When, in 1936, Laura Knight achieved full status, the Royal Academy had, after 170 years, finally granted full rights and responsibilities of membership to women.

References. Ellen Clayton, *English Female Artists* (London, 1876); Sidney Hutchinson, *The History of the Royal Academy 1768–1968* (London, 1968); Charlotte Yeldham, *Women Artists in Nineteenth-Century France and England*, 2 vols. (New York, 1984).

JULIA M. GERGITS

RUSSIA. New Issues for Women Since 1991. The disintegration of the USSR in 1991 became the starting point of a deep socioeconomic transformation. Developments during this transformation have had a contradictory influence on women's status in the Russian Republic. This entry is confined to a consideration of women's economic standing (namely, employment, labor, unemployment, business), family conditions, health, and public activity.

Women in the Economy. High labor activity of women was a characteristic feature of the Soviet economy. Women made up 51 percent of the employed population, and the employment rate among the women of working age was 90 percent.

Restructuring of the national economy is being accompanied by a deep crisis in the production of goods and services, a decline in the total number of employed, and the growth of unemployment. Transition of men into employment sectors that in the USSR were considered "feminine," including banking, finance, retail trade, and so on, is a factor causing women to be actively excluded from the labor market. As a result of the economic conditions, women's share of employment has fallen significantly. In 1996 women constituted just 47 percent of the economically active population, and the employment level for women of working age fell to 76 percent. According to the Federal Employment Service, in 1996 women's share of the unemployed totaled 70 percent.

We must underline a distinctive "national" feature of Russian women's unemployment: about 70 percent of the unemployed women have had higher education; they are mostly engineers, economists, and researchers by profession. Under the structural economic transformations of the 1990s a woman has almost no opportunity to find a new job that accords with her level of education and experience, especially if she is over 30. Doles are trifling and quite insufficient to provide subsistence-level maintenance. Government authorities have retired completely from dealing with unemployment problems, and there are practically no programs to create new jobs or promote small business.

All economically active women can be divided into three groups: (1) those occupied in the public sector, (2) those in the private sector, and (3) women employed in the informal labor market.

Women in the public sector are occupied either in the so-called feminine industries, such as textiles, garments, and food, or in sociocultural industries financed from national and local authority budgets ("budgetary" industries). These include education, health care, science (the humanities, first of all), and social security. The drastic slump of output in public sector industries leads to falling earnings and to deteriorating conditions of work for women, who have to agree to any opportunity to earn.

According to official data, women now make up one-third of all those working in industry (both public and private sector industry) under harmful and dangerous conditions. For that reason, the number of occupational disease cases is growing, especially in mining, the aircraft, textile, garment, and metallurgical industries, and agriculture. Besides this, the greater portion of machinery and equipment used in "feminine" industries was long ago worn out and obsolete, and women operating these machines and equipment often sustain industrial injuries.

The standing of women occupied in "budgetary" industries, where they make up around 80 percent of the employed, may be characterized as much by extremely low salaries and irregular payments as by the existence of "hidden unemployment." This means that at a certain establishment or institution, when delays in receiving budgetary funds occur, the administration compulsorily gives a part of its employees so-called administrative leaves. In such cases people stay on the staff, but, in fact, for months they do not actually exercise their usual professional activities, and, of course, they do not receive their salaries.

There are many women within the actively growing private sector, but they are not present among owners and top managers in large businesses, and their share among owners in small and medium businesses does not exceed 36 percent.

On the other hand, women's employment in the private sector is essential; in 1995 it totaled 62 percent. However, employers' attitudes toward women in this new labor market are openly sexist and discriminatory. Now employers, even when advertising their vacancies, stipulate not only qualification but also sex, age, and, often, nationality of the possible applicants. As a rule, women, irrespective of their education, training, and experience, are offered low-skilled and low-paid jobs, such as cleaner, shop girl, nurse, secretary. Moreover, employment in the private sector is frequently linked for women with infringement of their labor rights, in particular with extended working hours, poor labor protection and safety measures, violation of laws on working mothers' rights, and so on. Cases of sexual harassment at the workplace within the private sector are becoming more and more numerous.

One can tell little about the standing of women forced to work in the informal sector, for the issue is practically unstudied. In the informal sector women earn their living and provide for their families by temporary, casual, or self-employment activities. These activities vary widely, from private teaching to baby-sitting, housecleaning, or peddling, to sex and drug trafficking. An interesting group of participants in informal self-employment are the "shuttles," people, men and women, who move as shuttles, to and fro, regularly traveling to Turkey, China, and the like in order to buy cheap garments and footgear there and later retail them in Russia at markets, small and often officially unregistered shops, or cafés.

As a rule, in this sector labor and economic relations between employers and their workers are not officially legitimated, being determined exclusively at the employer's will and having little to do with existing laws. In such circumstances the notion of labor rights itself is fictitious. Besides this, employers in this sector "because of economic considerations" make no obligatory payments to public funds for medical, social, and pension insurance, so that their women workers are not able to avail themselves of medical aid, any minimal paid leave, or pensions.

Thus, in Russia transition to a market-oriented type of economy is accompanied by the deterioration of women's standing in the labor market, changes in the structure and level of women's employment, feminization of poverty, infringement of women's labor rights, and aggravation of problems concerning workingwomen's health care.

According to the analysis made by the Federal Employment Service of

Russia in 1996, there will be no improvements in women's standing in the labor market within the next two years.

The Family and Women's Health Conditions. The economic crisis and political instability peculiar to the transformation period could not leave unaffected material and spiritual conditions of the family. In Russia more than one-third of all households now have incomes lower than the poverty level. Families consisting of a mother and one or more children (the condition of over 6 million families) have found themselves in most severe circumstances. The deterioration of their family's material conditions has caused a harder housekeeping burden for women, for such families often cannot afford to avail themselves of services provided by laundries, dry cleaners, hairdressers' shops, and so on. It is always a problem for workingwomen to care for their babies because many kindergartens have closed, and those that remain have raised their fees. Care for their ill or aged relatives presents similar problems. As a matter of fact, except for the so-called new Russians, who make up no more than 5 percent of the population, practically all families find it impossible to survive with a single breadwinner. For that reason, women are still forced to have permanent jobs or seek additional sources of income. It is difficult to estimate the physical and psychological overload borne by women.

Since the mid-1980s vital health indicators of Russian women and children have been sharply worsening. Statistics on morbidity have shown growth for almost all illness groups. The picture in regard to conditions for pregnant women is especially bad. The number of pregnant women suffering from anemia in 1995 increased threefold over the 1990 figure. The increase has been caused primarily by poor or bad nutrition. Maternal and infant mortality rates are rising. In 1995 the share of normal deliveries was as low as 36 percent. The number of officially registered abortions has fallen, but this is primarily a result of expanding the private health service system, where abortions are not usually registered. According to professional opinions, abortions still are the main means for natality control in Russia.

Life duration of the Russian population has also declined. In 1995 women's average life expectancy was 71 years, compared with 75 years in 1987.

Outbreaks of violence in intrafamily relations are now a particular problem. Wife beating by the husband has never been considered a crime in Russia. There is a well-known proverb saying, "If he beats, it means he loves." For that reason such cases have practically never been registered by the police or doctors. Recently, under the influence of international legal practice, registration of cases of women beaten or tortured by their husbands has begun, but only those with dangerous aftereffects. Based on registrations, it turns out that annually in Russia more than 15,000 women die and about 60,000 sustain severe injuries. However, official registration of such cases and necessary medical aid are all that the authorities are now able to give to victims of intrafamily violence. Asylums and "telephones of confidence" that can provide advice and moral support are now created, as a rule, at the initiative of various women's organizations.

The Women's Movement and Women's Organizations in Russia. In 1991 there was a single official women's organization in Russia, the Committee of Soviet Women, which incorporated numerous women's councils (*zhensovet*) acting at the factories under supervision of the local Communist Party committees.

In 1996 the Ministry of Justice officially registered over 300 women's organizations, clubs, and associations. Some of them are oriented to professional, regional, ethnic, or religious concerns. Some others were created for specific purposes, for example, to defend the environment, sons in service with the army (Soldiers' Mothers), or pensioners. However, a number of women's organizations are especially oriented to declare, present, and defend woman's rights. The impetus for this development was the Independent Women's Forum. The First Independent Women's Forum was held in Dubna in 1991, the second in 1992, by the Moscow Centre for Gender Studies, together with two feminist groups, the SAFO (Free Association of Feminist Organizations; now FALTA, Feminist ALTernAtive) of Moscow, and a group under the leadership of Olga Lipovskaya of Sankt-Peterburg. These forums with their gathering together of several hundred women from numerous Russian towns served as meeting places to introduce feminist theory to Russia for the first time and were the realization of the need to present and defend specific women's interests. Organizations established by women's initiative after the forums often call themselves the independent women's movement, to distinguish themselves from the former women's councils. By paying primary attention to enlightenment, education, and information on human and woman's rights, these organizations do actually help to wake up women's self-consciousness and to consolidate Russian women's efforts aimed at protection of their rights.

OLGA VORONINA

RUSSIA. Tsarist Russia was for centuries a feudal society characterized by strict social and gender stratification and hierarchy. Society was divided into social groups subject to the personal and total sway of the tsar.

The status of women differed by social group and region. Women of the propertied strata had the right to possess and manage private property, independently conduct business, and appear in court. The application of civil laws, however, did not extend to peasants, who were under the customary law (women in the eastern part of Russia, where remnants of the clan way of life persisted, were more deprived of rights than those in the western regions).

The same class differences can be traced in education. Although the vast majority of women remained illiterate up to the beginning of the twentieth century, some women of the upper classes did receive excellent educations. Among them were Princess Olga (?–969), the ruler of Old Russia, who laid the foundations of its state system (she introduced taxes, conducted a census, fixed the frontiers); Empress Catherine the Great (1729–1796), who founded the Russian Academy of Sciences and corresponded with Voltaire; her contemporary and friend Princess Catherine Dashkova (1744–1810), first president of the Russian Academy of Sciences, who debated with Voltaire, Diderot, and Adam Smith; and professor of mathematics and corresponding member of the Petersburg Academy of Sciences Sofia Kovalevskaya (1850–1891), whose memoirs record her struggle for the right to higher education and further scientific activity.

The 1860s were marked by social and economic reforms, the chief of which was the abolition of serfdom (1861). Civil law began to be developed more actively, although, as before, it was class-based. The principles of preserving the social and gender hierarchy of the society also governed policy on women. Legislation that determined the social and economic position of women was grounded on traditional patriarchal ideas. The Russian Orthodox Church was, and now remains, the principal social institution supporting the ideology of woman's destiny and inferiority.

Under the absolutist monarchy there was no question of suffrage for citizens. There were no citizens, only the emperor's subjects. With the formation of the State Duma, a legislative-consultative body, in 1906, some classes received the suffrage, but women (with students and soldiers) were placed in the category of disqualified citizens, with neither passive nor active suffrage (they could neither elect or be elected to government).

From the mid-1880s, with the development of capitalism the use of women in the industrial labor force began to grow. In the 1890s women averaged 25 percent of the workforce; in the 1910s, 40 percent (in the textile industry, about 70 percent). Women's working day lasted 12 hours, and their wages averaged 30 percent to 60 percent of those of men. The conditions of country women also remained very hard. After the abolition of serfdom men were endowed with land, but women still possessed no rights, and their working day on the family fields lasted 18 hours.

The range of professions for educated women was small: they could work as midwives, drugstore assistants, teachers in girls' schools, and, with special permission, doctors in women's hospitals. Chances of finding a state job were extremely limited: by imperial injunction (1871) clerical jobs in any state institution were closed to women.

In Russia up to the 1920s the absence of any sort of maternity and child protection law reflected badly on women industrial workers and peasants. Pregnant women got virtually no help from the state medical system, while the services of private doctors were far from available for everybody. In rural Russia, where the women's death rate was twice as high as men's, the life of women was especially hard. In villages girls were given in marriage at 16 or 17 years of age, and by 25 they usually had had five or six childbirths, excluding miscarriages, which ran from 25 percent to 70 percent. Abortions were prohibited and punished, according to the law, by loss of class rights and deportation to Siberia to become a convict settler.

In prerevolutionary Russia only religious marriage was legitimate and valid. As a rule the girl's parents chose her husband and provided a dowry. Divorce was not allowed. The family was a juridical alliance, with the wife obliged to obey her husband and submit to him in everything.

After the abolition of serfdom educational reform was among the principal reforms carried out. It formally gave girls access to education; however, education remained limited for them both because it was considered unnecessary for women and because access was based on class and property qualifications. At the beginning of the twentieth century girls made up 20 percent of primary school students, even less in higher forms. Also, standards were lower in girls' programs than in boys'.

Until the beginning of the 1870s Russian women of any class were forbidden to study at Russian and foreign universities. That is why the formation of the Higher Women's Bestuhzhev Courses in St. Petersburg in 1878 was such an important event. World-renowned scientists and scholars delivered lectures; however, the courses did not meet the requirements for further professional activity but satisfied only the want of higher education. The first institution of higher education for women was the Women's Medical University, established in 1895. By 1899 it had 386 students.

As a higher educational system for women was developing, the social structure was changing. In 1880, among the listeners of the Higher Women's Bestuhzhev Courses, 40 percent were representatives of the high strata, 7 percent were peasant women, and 23 percent were women workers. In 1914 women university students from the high strata averaged 20 percent, while peasant women increased to 25 percent, and women workers to 35 percent.

By the beginning of the twentieth century a twofold system of women's higher education had taken shape in Russia. There were various public higher women's courses (commercial, pharmaceutical, obstetrical, pedagogical, agricultural) attached to women's organizations, and there were a few state higher education establishments for women. But higher education remained sex-segregated. Until 1905 women could not study at the universities except as listeners at the Bestuhzhev Courses or as students at a "female" high school (e.g., the Women's Medical University), and even after 1905 they did so only as "lecturegoers," without the formal status of student. Therefore, women who wanted a full university education studied abroad. In 1889 two-thirds of the 152 women students at the Sorbonne were Russians; before World War I there were about 6,000 Russian women studying at Swiss universities.

From the middle of the nineteenth century the problem of women's emancipation began to be actively discussed. The novels and personality of George Sand (Aurore Dupin) and the ideas of Condorce, Saint-Simon, and John Stuart Mill were extremely popular. Male politicians, writers, natural scientists, and philosophers with positions across the spectrum took an active part in the public discussion.

From the mid-1860s there appeared in Russian society a new type of woman who by her behavior and outward appearance challenged the traditional norms and stereotypes of femininity, the so-called woman nihilist. Springing mainly from the middle and upper classes, these "new women" were, as a rule, well-educated professional women who sought work and economic independence, wore simple and rational clothes instead of the fluffy skirts usual at that time, cut their hair short, used no makeup, and advocated the simple way of life. Without rejecting values of love, they protested women's lack of rights in the traditional marriage and family. Negative reaction didn't stop them. Socially useful activity for the good of ordinary people became their principal life orientation. The need to work very often was not economic but part of their world outlook and way of life. It found its expression in the mass phenomenon of "going to the people." Young women became teachers, medical attendants, and midwives and went voluntarily to the countryside, where they devoted themselves to the medical care and education of the poorest people. The "new women's" contribution to the development of the Russian people's self-consciousness was not, and is not, appreciated at its true value by Russian historians.

The participation of these women in the revolutionary movement at the end of the century was a peculiar expression of the increase in their social activity and changes in their self-consciousness. Although their participation in revolutionary organizations was not a mass one, the very fact of their political activity had significant public repercussions. Among the best-known women revolutionaries was Sofia Perovskaya (1854–1881), a member of the revolutionary terrorist organization People's Will. In 1880 she took part in the assassination of Alexander II (the tsar who abolished serfdom and tried to carry out other social reforms). In 1881 Sofia Perovskaya was hanged, and these two events—the murder of the tsar and execution of a woman revolutionary—were long the subject of discussion.

As a whole, Russian society, trying at the end of the nineteenth century to free itself from its feudal chains, was undergoing deep socioeconomic and political crises that ended with the collapse of tsarism and the Russian empire. But before that happened, women had to bear the full brunt of hardships connected with the unsuccessful bourgeois, democratic revolution of 1905 and with World War I. During the war years many women volunteered at the front as nurses and in the rear worked actively in industry and in agriculture (by the end of the war women were 40 percent of the workers in heavy industry and 60 percent in textiles). Nevertheless, they still possessed no rights in society or the family.

OLGA VORONINA

RUSSIA. Tsarist Russia Women's Movement began in the late 1850s, when discussion of the emancipation of the serfs led to a consideration of women's position in Russian society. Influenced by feminist ideas of such thinkers as the French socialist Pierre Proudhon and the British liberals John Stuart Mill and Harriett Taylor, Russian writers argued for improving the education of women. Argument soon gave way to petitioning the government for higher education for women. Prominent among petitioners were upper-class, educated women such as Nadezhda Stasova (1822–1896), who also worked to organize aid societies for single women seeking work in cities.

The goals of the Russian feminist movement as it developed over the 1860s were similar to those of feminist groups elsewhere, as were the feminists themselves. For the most part from the nobility and the very small middle class, they sought educational and employment opportunities for women, crusaded for the outlawing of prostitution, set up programs to help women find work, and did charity among the poor. Under Alexander II (r. 1855–1881) they obtained admission not to the universities but to special lecture programs taught by university professors and roughly equivalent to the regular curriculum. Women also could train to be physicians. These advances were wiped out under Alexander III (r. 1881–1894), who did not approve of higher education for women, but Nicholas II (r. 1894–1917) reinstated the courses, and by the late 1890s, hundreds of young women were earning a college education in Moscow and St. Petersburg. Secondary and primary education for women grew as well during the late nineteenth century.

Feminists were less successful in their efforts to improve the marriage law, which was under the control of the Russian Orthodox Church. Divorce remained virtually unobtainable until the revolution of 1917. Nor could the feminists' charity projects do much to alleviate the enormous poverty of Russia. The autocratic government prevented campaigns for the vote before 1905. In 1905, however, a rebellion convulsed the country, and as men demanded self-government, feminists saw an opportunity to press for woman suffrage. Several organizations were formed, the most activist of which was the League for Equal Rights. They held rallies, marches, and petition drives but did not win enough support from male-dominated political parties to gain the vote.

Disappointed, the feminists fell into disarray after 1905. They busied themselves with charity projects until 1914; during World War I (1914–1918), they did volunteer work to aid the war effort. But they were not powerful politically, and during the revolution in 1917 they were swept away by the radical tide that brought the Bolsheviks to power. The main accomplishments of the feminist movement in tsarist Russia were gaining access to higher education and, by publicizing the arguments for woman's rights, winning widespread acceptance of the proposition that women's situation should be improved.

A second group advocated reforms for women in tsarist Russia—the socialists. From the early days of the debate on woman's rights, some said that improvements for women in Russia must be linked with a general reform of the entire society. Without revolution, argued such writers as Mikhail Chernyshevskii (1828–1889), women would remain enslaved, as were most men, by a fundamentally unjust social system that permitted the small nobility and burgeoning capitalists to control all power and most of the wealth. Women would be freed, as would men, by the destruction of the tsarist system and its replacement with public ownership of industry and agriculture. This argument, made first in the late 1860s and then reinforced in the 1880s and 1890s by the introduction of Marxist thought, had widespread appeal among young intellectuals, female as well as male. Some of these young people became revolutionaries, joining illegal underground parties. One such party, the People's Will, is estimated to have had several hundred female members, the most famous of whom, Sofia Perovskaia (1854–1881), organized and then participated in the assassination of Alexander II in 1881.

Subsequent revolutionary parties also espoused rights for women and included women in their ranks. The Social Democrats (SDs), a Marxist party formed in the late 1890s, advocated equal pay for equal work, protective labor legislation, maternity leave, publicly financed day care, and suffrage. After the Bolshevik faction of the SDs seized power in 1917, Alexandra Kollontai, Inessa Armand, and other female SDs laid the foundations for major reforms for women.

Thus, the success of the woman's movement in tsarist Russia was limited by the resistance of the conservative monarchy. Only after that monarchy had been destroyed by a massive revolution were genuine reforms in the lives of women from all social classes undertaken by a new, socialist government.

Reference. Richard Stites, *The Women's Liberation Movement in Russia* (Princeton, 1978).

                                                          BARBARA EVANS CLEMENTS

RUSSIAN WRITERS. Women appear relatively late in Russian letters. Up to the eighteenth century the cultural conditions in Russia, overwhelmingly molded by an Orthodox Christian worldview, restricted women's activities to domestic cares in unconditional obedience to the master of the household. Peter the Great (1682–1725) drew women from seclusion into participation in social life. Catherine the Great (1762–1796) followed up by founding educational institutions for girls. Despite these measures, however, a basic patriarchal attitude dominated the Russian way of life well into the twentieth century in spite of social and political upheavals. This attitude explains, in part, the modest literary value of early women's writing.

The first known work by a woman, *The Memoir of Princess Natalia Borisovna Dolgorukaia* (1767), was soon followed by several autobiographies of formidable Russian women: Empress Catherine II; talented, erudite Princess Ekaterina Dashkova (1743–1810), one of the first women to hold public office in Russia (president of the Academy of Science, 1783); and the "Cavalry Maiden," Nadezhda Durova (1783–1866) who, disguised as a man, served in the tsarist army during the Napoleonic Wars. Durova later wrote hyperromantic novels and tales.

During Catherine's reign some 70 women tried their talents at writing, yet professional women writers appeared only in the first half of the nineteenth century. Many adopted male pseudonyms to avoid conflicts with publisher and reader prejudice. They represented the trend known as George Sandism, advocating the right to a meaningful education and free choice of husband but, at the same time, reflecting the sad reality of women's position. Elena Gan (1814–1842, pseud. Zinaida R-va) in *The Useless Gift* (1842), Maria Zhukova (1804–1855) in Society's Judgment (1840), and Julia Zhadovskaia (1824–1883) in lyric poetry and prose lament the plight of intelligent women forced into loveless wedlock and constrained to a life of banality.

Karolina Pavlova (1807–1893), respected by literary contemporaries, including Pushkin and Mickiewicz, died forgotten and in poverty only to be fully appraised as a significant writer by the symbolists at the turn of the century. Her elegaic poetry is marked by bold, innovative rhymes, rhythms, and intellectual brilliance. Pavlova's novel *A Double Life* (Barbara Heldt [trans.] [Ann Arbor, 1978]) shows a sensitive girl's struggle to rise above the emptiness of society's lifestyle. Pavlova contrasts her daily routine, described in prose, with her ideal nightly dreamworld, rendered in verse. The shallow, hypocritical behavior of the upper classes is also castigated and ridiculed by the successful and prolific Countess Evdokia Rostopchina (1811–1858; e.g., "Rank and Money," in Helena Goscilo [trans. and ed.], *Russian and Polish Women's Fiction* [Knoxville, Tenn., 1985], 50–84) and Lidia Veselitskaia (1857–1936; pseud. Mikulich) in her *Mimochka* (1883–1893) stories.

Writers like Evgenia Tur (1815–1892; pseud. of Elizaveta Salias de Tournemir); Avdotia Panaeva (1820–1893; pseud. N. Stanitsky), remembered for her novels *The Talnikov Family* (1848), *A Woman's Lot* (1862), and *Memoirs* (1890); Marco Vovchok (1834–1907); Vera Figner (1852–1942); and Sofia Kovalevskaia (1850–1891), first Russian woman professor of mathematics, protest vigorously against discrimination and social oppression of women. In contrast, the gifted Slavophil Nadezhda Sokhanskaia (1823–1884) glorifies traditional patriarchal values. She draws bright pictures of the landed gentry's harmonious life in a spirited, colorful Russian.

After the turbulent 1860s and 1870s, with their stress on utilitarian literature, Russian modernism searched for new spiritual values and different artistic expression. Women participated effectively in all modernist trends: with the symbolists, Zinaida Hippius (1869–1945; emigrated to Paris 1919), Poliksena Solovieva (1867–1924; pseud. Allegro), and Mirra Lokhvitskaia (1869–1905) explored the "other Reality," the Absolute, the duality of human existence; Elena Guro's poetry was connected with cubo futurism; Anna Akhmatova (1889–1966; pseud. of Anna Gorenko) in her early stage the foremost representative of acmeism, favored precision of form and the aesthetics of reality. With Marina Tsvetaeva (1892–1941), whose idiosyncratic, lyrical voice defies any categorization, Akhmatova belongs among the greatest twentieth-century poets. Akhmatova's and Tsvetaeva's verse, memorializing the dramatic events of their times, appears in most anthologies of women's poetry. As modernism crested, Anastasia Verbitskaia's (1861–1928) voluminous novels popularized the themes of women's emancipation and free love with considerable success, despite their second-rate quality. These themes were picked up by Aleksandra Kollontai (1872–1952), a true feminist, who undertook to make women aware of their rights officially sanctioned by the 1917 Bolshevik revolution. Kollontai's heroines are totally devoted to party ideology and consider love affairs unimportant as "drinking a glass of water."

The typical heroine in the following decades of socialist realism, the dominant literary dogma since 1934, shares equal rights and equal duties with her male partner: she is industrious and successful in building socialism and, as an efficient homemaker, lives up to the high standards of the new Soviet family. The heroines of Galina Nikolaeva (1911–1963), of Vera Panova (1905–1973), and of the later fiction of Marietta Shaginian (1888–1982) approximate this ideal.

Many outstanding women writers fled Russia after the 1917 revolution and during World War II, joining émigré literary centers in the West. Lidia Chervinskaia (b. 1907), Anna Prismanova (1898–1960), Galina Kuznetsova (1900–1976), Nina Berberova (b. 1901), Lidia Alekseeva (b. 1909), and Olga Anstei (1912–1986) are among a score of remarkable women who have contributed brilliantly to the treasury of Russian literature in exile (see Pachmuss).

The Soviet totalitarian system has stifled literary initiative because the slightest nonconformity would meet with disapproval of dire consequence. Even after Stalin's death, when restrictions were somewhat slackened, no interesting experimentation took place in official literature. Yet many women writers have dealt with the horrors of Stalin's purges in shattering poems and memoirs: thus, Akhmatova's "Requiem"; Lidia Chukovskaia's (b. 1910) *The Deserted House* and *Going Under*; Nadezhda Mandelshtam's (1899–1980) *Hope Against Hope* and *Hope Abandoned*; and Evgenia Ginzburg's (1896–1980) *Journey into the Whirlwind* and *Within the Whirlwind* have been translated into most world languages but have not as yet been published in the Soviet Union.

World War II has inspired much of women's writings. Akhmatova, Olga Berggolts (1910–1975), and Vera Inber (1890–1972) wrote patriotic war poetry, particularly about the 900-day siege of Leningrad. The single, self-supporting, usually professional war widow, bravely coping with all odds of life, discrimination included, hoping for a reliable, strong man for moral support, appears frequently in the postwar fiction of I. Grekova (b. 1907, pseud. of Elena Ventsel), Margarita Aliger (b. 1915), and Olga Forsh (1873–1961). In contrast, Maia Ganina (b. 1927) and Victoria Tokareva (b. 1937) picture liberated, independent women who proudly reject any encroachment on their freedom. Natalia Baranskaia's (b. 1908) novelette *A Week Like Any Other* (1969) addresses candidly the emancipated woman's dilemma: how to pursue a career and simultaneously run a family.

Some innovative experimentation in prose can be detected in the latest works of writers born in the 1950s: Liudmila Petrushevskaia, Nadezhda Kozhevnikova, and Tatiana Tolstaia, the most original and exciting master of form. Poetry, a more suitable medium to obviate party restrictions, has shown revival in form, language, and motifs since the 1960s. The newest avant-garde includes first-rate talent: Bella Akhmadulina (b. 1937) and Novella Matveeva (b. 1934), as well as the dissident, now émigré poets Natalia Gorbanevskaia (b. 1936) and Irina Ratushinskaia (b. 1954), both victims of Soviet hard-labor camps and renowned for their unforgettable, poetic prison diaries. The avant-garde's most prominent member, though, is the exceptional Elizaveta Mnacakanova (b. 1922; emigrated 1975), who combines musical structures with transrational language to create a singular, evocative view of the world in her poetry, none of which was published in the Soviet Union.

Finally, frank discussions of unsolved feminist issues, muffled and discreet in official women's literature, are widely taken up by Tatiana Mamonova, Tatiana Goricheva, Julia Voznesenskaia, and other feminists who emigrated in 1980 (*Women and Russia*).

References. Barbara Heldt, *Terrible Perfection: Women and Russian Literature* (Bloomington, Ind., 1987); Tatiana Mamonova et al., in Tatiana Mamonova (ed.), *Women and Russia. Feminist Writers from the Soviet Union* (Boston, 1984); Temira Pachmuss, "Emigré Literature," in Victor Terras (ed.), *Handbook of Russian Literature* (New Haven, Conn., 1985); Temira Pachmuss (ed.), *Women Writers in Russian Modernism* (Urbana, Ill., 1978); *Russian Literary Triquarterly: Women in Russian Literature*, no. 9 (Spring 1974).

MARINA ASTMAN

S

SAINTS (MEDIEVAL) were an elite corps of "women worthies" venerated for their heroic pursuit of the *Vita perfecta* in the service of God. As cultural types or social constructs, they exemplified the highest ideals and spiritual needs of their age.

A collective study of women saints provides an indirect index of attitudes toward women as well as their actual status in the medieval church and society. On one level, celestial membership had a terrestrial base: those recruited to sainthood embodied the values and contemporary hierarchical order of their earthly society. With changes in the structure, values, and needs of society and the church, shifts occurred in the opportunities available to women—shifts that provided them with the visibility required for elevation to sainthood as well as with styles of sanctity.

Women saints were to serve as models of piety, or *exempla*—they were to inspire and mold imitative behavior. As sources of edification, their lives were used by the Church as instruments of socialization and control. Sometimes aimed at satisfying the psychological needs of churchmen, these lives also provided a variety of remarkable roles and experiences for the female imagination to act upon: they served as models of empowerment for women and inspired them with possibilities for their own lives of spiritual perfection.

As invisible interceders holding citizenship in two worlds, saints were believed to possess special divine, wonder-working powers. Many female saints were recognized as "specialists": their miracles were frequently gender-specific and favored women. They were especially called on by members of their own sex for their expertise in remedying problems of fertility, pregnancy and childbirth, bleeding, breast cancer, goiters, and childhood diseases.

The majority of saints recognized in the Middle Ages were products of popular sanctity. They were designated by the vox populi in a rather spontaneous, informal fashion, with their cults promoted by local pressure groups such as communities of nuns or monks, parishioners, or a bishop and his diocese. Therefore, most of the saints of this early period were venerated with something short of official, papal confirmation. Beginning with the Carolingian reforms, there was an attempt to regularize the veneration of saints and the establishment of their cults through extended episcopal and synodal control over the procedure. With the first papal canonization in 993, there appeared a growing intervention by the papacy in determining the legal status of new candidates for sainthood. During the thirteenth century the papacy attempted to establish complete control over canonization and its proceedings. In general, these procedural changes worked against the making of women saints, while formal canonization remained a male prerogative.

Although in theory the Church professed a policy of spiritual egalitarianism, a definite gender-based asymmetry (sometimes more exaggerated than at other times) existed among the membership of the holy dead. Invariably, it was much more difficult for women than for men to transcend their sex and enter the ranks of the celestial hierarchy. For the period from c. 500 to 1500 only approximately one out of six saints was female. This rather wide discrepancy among the elect can be explained, in part, by the exclusion of women from leadership roles in the secular church hierarchy. However, certain periods as well as geographic regions seemed to be more favorable than others in the making of women saints. During initial stages of various movements of the Church, women seemed to be provided with greater opportunities to achieve a visibility that could lead to a recognition of sanctity.

During the years 650 to 750, with the spread of Christianity in the north of Europe, a golden age of female sanctity emerged: approximately one out of every four saints was female, and in Britain, two out of five were female. Women with power and wealth were actively recruited by churchmen to aid in missionary work; establish churches, monasteries, and centers of education; and assume leadership positions. For their essential contributions to the Church, primarily as founding abbesses, these aristocratic women were frequently rewarded with recognition of sanctity. Some of the most prominent saints promoted during this golden age of female sanctity include Gertrude of Nivelles, Salaberga of Laon, Hilda and Elfleda of Whitby, and Etheldreda of Ely.

Beginning with the development of the Carolingian empire and various church reform movements and further exacerbated by the devastation and disruption caused by the Viking, Saracen, and Hungarian invasions, along with the development of feudal states, these earlier arrangements that had encouraged the exercise of power by women were transformed. Church and society became more regularized, structured, and right-minded, and the premature enthusiasm for women's active participation in religion waned. A strong preference for male leadership was asserted. The reformers' emphasis on celibacy fostered an exaggerated fear of women that frequently led to a strong misogynism. In some regions women's economic and formal political power (which had been based on the irregular powers of the aristocratic family) deteriorated. An increasingly rigid separation of public and domestic spheres and of male and female activities emerged. New feminine ideals of sanctity were promoted: the "privatized" domestic saint became especially popular. Through these basic changes, women's opportunities for leadership roles were circumscribed. These shifts are indirectly reflected in the growing asymmetry of the selection of male and female saints. For the period 1000 to 1150 only 1 out of every 12 saints was female: the nadir in female sanctity occurred in eleventh-century France, when male saints outnumbered female saints approximately 25 to 1.

In the late Middle Ages the locus of female sanctity shifted essentially to the cities of Flanders, the Rhineland, and especially northern Italy. From the mid-thirteenth through fifteenth centuries, another golden age of women saints emerged (a "feminization" of sainthood, according to Andre Vauchez), which encouraged and rewarded new styles of female piety. While the total number of saints declined during this period, the percentage of female saints increased so that approximately one out of every four saints was a woman. At this time there occurred a significant broadening of the social base from which saints were recruited. Many of the late medieval female saints came from middle or lower classes of urban society. Some acceded to sanctity through their ties with the new mendicant orders, while a significant number were drawn from the laity. For many, empowerment came through their prominent roles as contemplatives, mystics, and prophets. These special "gifts" allowed them to transcend the alleged liabilities of their sex and assume informal roles as critical authorities in the Church and society. Catherine of Siena, Bridget of Sweden, Clare of Assisi, Julian(a) of Norwich, and Joan of Arc are a few of these late medieval saints.

While women remained in a definite minority among the blessed, the very different worlds of the early and late Middle Ages provided environments favorable to the promotion of female saints. The central Middle Ages, in contrast, encouraged an exaggerated, asymmetrical pattern of sanctity.

References. David Herlihy, "Did Women Have a Renaissance? A Reconsideration," *Medievalia et Humanistica: Studies in Medieval and Renaissance Culture*, new series 13 (1985): 1–22; Jane Tibbetts Schulenburg, "Sexism and the Celestial Gynaeceum—From 500 to 1200," *Journal of Medieval History* 4 (1978): 117–133; Andre Vauchez, *La Sainteté en Occident aux derniers siècles du Moyen Age dapres les procès de canonisation et les documents hagiographiques* (Rome, 1981); Donald

Weinstein and Rudolph M. Bell, *Saints and Society: The Two Worlds of Western Christendom, 1000–1700* (Chicago, 1982).

JANE TIBBETTS SCHULENBURG

SAINTS AND MARTYRS (WOMEN) IN EARLY CHRISTIANITY were accorded the praise and fame usually given only to men and were held up as models of female holiness for other women to follow. During the outbreaks of persecution that occurred intermittently in the Roman empire until the legalization of Christianity under Constantine in 313, martyrdom was considered the best way for a Christian to imitate Christ and to be assured of a life after death, when there would be "neither male nor female." Thus, the first women revered as saints by Christians were martyrs. Even patristic writers, usually more disposed to blame women than to praise them, extolled the deeds of women martyrs as proof that every Christian, despite his or her sex or status in society, could share equally in the fellowship of Christ.

Many tales of courageous female martyrs circulated among Christians in late antiquity and the Middle Ages and provided inspiration for generations of Christian women. Most martyrdom stories are largely legendary, and even accounts of historical martyrs became overlaid with more and more fictional elements in the process of transmission. However, a few authentic accounts, written during the persecutions of the first three centuries, have survived, and they demonstrate conclusively the true importance of women martyrs in the early Church. The *Ecclesiastical History* of Eusebius, written in the early fourth century, records a number of such heroic women, including Blandina, the slave girl martyred at Lyons in 177, and the third-century Alexandrian martyrs Potimiaena and Apollonia. Other martyrs were commemorated by their local churches, as Crispina was in Numidia (North Africa); the three sisters Agape, Irene, and Chione at Thessalonica in Greece; Eulalia at Merida in Spain; and Agnes at Rome—though in the case of both Eulalia and Agnes, many legendary elements were soon added.

Of these historical accounts, perhaps the most highly acclaimed is the *Passion of Perpetua and Felicitas*. It is especially valuable because, in addition to a third-person narrative of the arrest and execution of the two women, it includes the prison diary of Perpetua herself, one of only a handful of works by women authors to survive from antiquity. The *Passion* is thus a unique, firsthand account of the personal experiences and thoughts of a Christian woman and provides precious insight into the motivations that led women to sacrifice their lives and their families for the new religion.

Perpetua was a 22-year-old convert from near Carthage, of good family and respectably married, when she and her slave Felicitas were arrested along with other Christians in A.D. 203. She was still nursing a young baby, whom she kept in prison with her until she was forced to let her family take care of him, and her diary reveals deep concern for the child and his

needs. Felicitas was pregnant and gave birth only days before her martyrdom (her baby was adopted by a Christian family). In the *Passion* of Perpetua, more than any other martyrdom account, the personal, domestic
side of the Christian–pagan conflict is apparent. Even more than her baby,
Perpetua's pagan father, who begs her over and over to deny her faith,
represents a family bond and a responsibility that she is forced to deny.
Through her own words we see a woman torn between two conflicting
identities: her socially ordained role as daughter and mother and her new,
deliberately chosen role as a Christian. The heroic martyrdom of Perpetua
and Felicitas in the Roman arena showed other women that they, too, could
achieve Christianity's highest distinction, but only if they relinquished their
traditional roles and responsibilities. After their death, their cult spread
quickly, and they are still venerated by the Catholic Church (on March 7).
Augustine honored them in several of his sermons.

Another female saint and martyr whose cult was extremely popular in
antiquity was Thecla. Among Christians of late antiquity and the Middle
Ages, Thecla was widely celebrated as a virgin, a disciple of the apostle
Paul, and the first woman martyr. Historians today have found no evidence
that she ever existed, but the early Christians certainly believed in her and
she can be said to have been the first role model for Christian women. Her
story is first found in the late second-century apocryphal *Acts of Paul and
Thecla*, a work written in a popular novelistic style that has been called a
"Christian romance." According to the *Acts*, Thecla gave up her home and
her fiancé in order to follow Paul and, after surviving several attempts on
her virginity and two martyrdom trials, continued his work by preaching
the new faith on her own. She was the first of a long line of virgin martyr
saints and was particularly popular in the fourth century after the end of
the persecutions, when virginity in a sense replaced martyrdom as the
means by which a Christian woman could reach the pinnacle of holiness.
In historical accounts of late antique holy women, Thecla is cited as an
exemplum, and a cult grew up around the site in ancient Seleucia (now in
southern Turkey), where she was believed to have ended her life. In the
Middle Ages she was also known as the patron saint of Milan and of
Tarragona in Spain.

These women, Perpetua the married woman and historical martyr and
Thecla the virgin and fictional heroine, as well as many other women
known for their purity and their bravery under persecution, provided models for Christian women in antiquity. At a time when women were being
pushed out of all positions of authority in the Church, they showed that it
was possible for women to achieve fame, holiness, and spiritual fellowship
with God.

References. Elizabeth Clark, *Women in the Early Church* (Wilmington, Del.,
1983); Stevan L. Davies, *The Revolt of the Widows: The Social World of the Apocryphal Acts* (Carbondale, Ill., 1980); H. Musurillo, *Acts of the Christian Martyrs*

(New York, 1972); Mary Ann Rossi, "The Passion of Perpetua, Everywoman of Late Antiquity," in R. C. Smith and J. Lounibos (eds.), *Pagan and Christian Anxiety: A Response to E. R. Dodds* (Lanham, Md., 1984).

JUDITH EVANS GRUBBS

SALONIÈRE is a woman in French society who organized and presided over intellectual conversations in her home and thus helped mold elite secular culture. The salons began in the seventeenth century as an alternative to court society. Women used the salons as a tool for "civilizing" language, literature, and social relationships between men and women. They provided the setting for authors to read their works and for nobility and upper bourgeoisie to refine their language and social customs and facilitated marriages between wealthy "robe noblewomen" and higher-status "sword noblemen." Thus, these salons served as an entrée into elite society. The *salonière* of the seventeenth century was ridiculed in Jean-Baptiste Molière's comedies for her pedantry, prudery, and preoccupation with love.

The *salonière* came into her own in the eighteenth century, when the salons became the center of the growing Enlightenment "Republic of Letters." Regular gatherings at the homes of women such as Mme. Geoffrin, Julie de Lespinasse, and Suzanne Necker served to encourage and organize the intellectual activity of those who began to call themselves the *philosophes*. The frequenters of these salons sought inclusion in the collective project of Enlightenment.

The *salonière* presided over her salon, a role demanding she orchestrate the conversation with wit and brilliance. Education was a prerequisite, but the salon provided continuing intellectual growth for the women, whose education in the convent or by tutors was often little more than social or moral instruction. Women like Mme. de Genlis devoured any books available for self-education.

The role of *salonière* was a career open to talent but did require significant financial resources. The *salonière* received no compensation, yet she was expected to maintain a suitable residential setting for the salon and to entertain her guests on a weekly basis. Eighteenth-century *salonières* served an apprenticeship in another woman's salon before launching their own. Mme. Geoffrin attended Mme. de Tencin's salon for 20 years before opening her own. In turn, Mme. Necker and Julie de Lespinasse frequented Mme. Geoffrin's salon. Julie de Lespinasse was also companion to Mme. du Deffand for 12 years. Thus, women acted as mentors for the future *salonières*.

The salons served as clearinghouses of information, news, and ideas; as meeting places for those involved in the business of the Enlightenment; and as models for an egalitarian, educated society of the future. The work of the Enlightenment and the discourse of the salon were centered on letters, as evidenced in the epistolary novel and the literary correspondence that were its trademark. This correspondence was frequently a joint project of the salon, making the *salonière*'s contribution invisible but invaluable. Salons sent out newsletters and established literary networks, and manuscripts were often read and critiqued there. In all of this, the *salonière* provided both the space and the occasion for this literary and political work termed the Enlightenment.

A similar phenomenon developed in England but lasted only from 1750 to about 1790. These salon women called themselves "bluestockings,"* a term that soon took on the negative connotation of pedantic women. As middle-class women, they tended to criticize the French salons as frivolous compared to their own diligence and intensity. They did not consider themselves ladies of leisure like their French counterparts. They worked, published, traveled, and championed women's education. Hannah Moore taught school, wrote plays and ballads, and published tracts. Other famous "Blues" included Elizabeth Robinson Montagu, Fanny Burney, Elizabeth Vesey, Elizabeth Carter, Mary Granville Delany, and Hester Mulso Chapone. In contrast to the French *salonières*, these women were held together by friendship and saw themselves as a group, independent of male approval.

Another salon society developed around Jewish women in Berlin between 1780 and 1806. Termed the *Rahelzeit*, this rich intellectual period is named after Rahel Varnhagen, née Levin, a young Jewish woman who chose a path of social independence and mastery of secular languages and skills, resulting in a salon that included foreign diplomats, déclassé noblewomen, and court figures. Varnhagen, Dorothea Mendelssohn, and Henriette Herz became famous figures in Berlin society for their high culture and assimilation into prominent Gentile circles. These *salonières* managed to bridge the gulf between German Gentiles and Jews, between classes in a rigid social structure, and between men and women, making them unique in German history.

The turmoil and social upheaval of the French revolutionary years brought an end to the salons in France, England, and Berlin. French noblewomen adopted a more domestic ideal. The bluestockings disbanded, but their crusade for female education would be revived by reformers in the second half of the nineteenth century. The Berlin salons were disrupted by anti-French and anti-Semitic reactions. The *salonières* demonstrated that women could play a significant role in intellectual life, a role that was lost once women returned to private lives.

References. Evelyn Gordon Bedek, "Salonières and Bluestockings: Educated Obsolescence and Germinating Feminism," *Feminist Studies* 3 (Spring/Summer 1976): 185–199; Dena Goodman, *The Republic of Letters: A Cultural History of the French Enlightenment* (Ithaca, N.Y., 1984); Deborah Hertz, *Jewish High Society in Old Regime Berlin* (New Haven, Conn., 1988); Carolyn Lougee, *Le Paradis des*

Femmes: Women, Salons, and Social Stratification in Seventeenth-Century France (Princeton, 1976).

ELAINE KRUSE

SANITARY COMMISSION. See U.S. SANITARY COMMISSION

SATI (SUTTEE) is a Hindu widow who was burned alive on her husband's funeral pyre or, in rare cases in southern India, buried alive with her spouse. The English word "suttee" has two meanings: (1) the widow who is burned and (2) the practice of widow burning. Today it is used only in its second meaning.

In Sanskrit "sati" means "a good woman" or "a true wife." The connection with widow burning stems from a Hindu myth recorded in the Puranas: Sati, an incarnation of the Goddess, took vengeance on her father for slighting her god-husband Shiva by burning herself. In ancient India the rite was known but rarely practiced. The classical texts of the Vedic period sanctioned widow remarriage, and the early Hindu lawgivers, such as Manu, simply recommended a chaste life for widows. In the medieval period suttee became established as a social practice, particularly in the Hindu states of Vijayanagar (south India) and Rajasthan (northwest India), where widows of the Kshattriya (warrior) caste became satis to glorify the princely rulers and their caste. During the eighteenth century widow burning was more prevalent among Brahmins and other twice-born castes in Bengal and Bihar, the early stronghold of the British. Because of extensive polygamy in these areas, at times 100 or more women became satis on the occasion of a Hindu prince's or Kulin Brahmin's death. At the beginning of the nineteenth century the practice was increasingly criticized, foremost by the Bengali Hindu reformer Rammohun Roy. Suttee was prohibited by Regulation XVII of 1829. Thereafter, widow burning was rare, but even today single cases are occasionally reported.

The practice of widow killing along with other human sacrifices existed in other societies outside India, for instance, among the Scythians, Thracians, Egyptians, Tongans, Fijians, and Maoris. Suttee, however, was exceptional with regard to two closely linked aspects: its survival until the beginning of the nineteenth century and its allegedly voluntary character. Only if a sati committed "suicide" would she gain the spiritual rewards for her late husband, his family, and herself. The attitudes of traditional Hindu society toward widowhood and suttee in particular were closely linked with the concepts of lineage, marriage, and female sexuality. Marriage was essential to secure the continuation of the lineage with pure male offspring to celebrate the death rites of their parents and ancestors. The chastity of the bride was essential for the purity of her sons and thus the future of her husband's lineage. Apart from this, a woman had no ritual identity independent of her father or husband. Because of the intimacy of the marital connection, her husband's death was seen as proof of her sins during an earlier life. Women were regarded as aggressive, malevolent, destructive, and even wanting to poison their husbands, if their *sakti* (power) was not under male control. However, if male spirit reigned over a woman's power, then femaleness could imply fertility and benevolence. Accordingly, permanent male control of women, their sexuality in particular, was necessary. Seen in this light, a young widow free of immediate male control was a constant threat to the purity of her husband's lineage. A sati symbolized the apotheosis of male control—even beyond his death.

Once a woman had internalized this ideal of purity and the danger of her own power, it was possible for her to become a sati "voluntarily," but only if we ignore the force that made her internalize the misogynist ideology in the first place. Moreover, the rituals involved in becoming a sati may have worked as an additional motivation. A sati took off her jewelry, had a ceremonial bath, and was then dressed in a simple sari. On her way to the cremation ground she was greeted by a crowd who had come for the spectacle and her blessing. Before mounting the pyre she circled the heap of wood murmuring holy mantras. In the absence of the husband's body, the widow was set on fire with one of his garments, for instance, his shoes or his turban.

If the widow was menstruating or a mother of small children, she was barred from becoming a sati. The impurity attached to blood and birth would hamper the purifying and redeeming act. In other cases, however, there was little choice. If a widow had doubts about the wisdom of self-immolation, the prospects of the deprived future that awaited many widows "helped" her decide. An element of immediate force was also involved. During the eighteenth century, for instance, when suttee was increasingly criticized, women were sometimes drugged and bound with cords to their husbands' corpses, or the funeral pyre was placed in a pit from which there was no chance of escape.

At times suttee reached epidemic proportions. During periods of extreme economic scarcity and famine, in eighteenth-century Bengal, for instance, the practice worked to curb population growth and helped circumvent rigid rules for the inheritance of real property. Moreover, suttee functioned as a social defense mechanism in a male-dominated society under threat. For Rajput warriors in northwest India and Vijayanagar princes in the south, the pain of defeat was sweetened by the knowledge that their women would not become the prey of their victorious enemies. In such cases, Rajput women committed mass suicide, *jauhar*, by throwing themselves into a fire or from a wall. In less martial societies, as in Bengal under Muslim and early British rule, men countered cultural alienation by reversion to traditional misogynist practices. Kulin brahmins, who were sometimes married to more than 100 women, coped with their economic and political impotence by enforcing their power over their wives.

Suttee was the most extreme expression of male sexual control within the Indian gender system; it glorified the power of women in order to justify their rigid subordination.

References. Lata Mani, "Contentious Traditions: The Debate on Sati in Colonial India," in Kumkum Sangari and Sudesh Vaid (eds.), *Recasting Women: Essays in Colonial History* (Delhi, 1989); Ashis Nandy, "Sati: A Nineteenth-Century Tale of Women, Violence and Protest," in A. Nandy (ed.), *At the Edge of Psychology* (Delhi, 1980), 1–31.

DAGMAR A. E. ENGELS

SAUDI ARABIA (population 12.3 million) is not only the birthplace of Islam but also a theocracy. All policies concerning the status of women are based on the interpretation of the ulemas or religious authorities.

Seclusion. Women in Saudi Arabia experience a gender segregation stronger and more extensive than the racial segregation that ignited the U.S. civil rights movement in the 1960s. Most Saudi women, however, do not question their segregation. They believe they should keep men at a distance, both physically and emotionally. This seclusion stems from Wahabism, a puritanical form of Islam that has not relaxed its grip on the kingdom since it took hold early this century. In the last two decades Muslim fundamentalists have further encouraged the rejection of Western culture. Fearful of their growing strength, the government has attempted to draw them into the system by placating them with expanding the power of the religious police.

Saudi society is based on male dominance, and women are under the authority of their fathers, brothers, and husbands. Sons are pampered and raised to believe they are entitled to respect and obedience, but they are also taught to protect their sisters.

The Prophet Muhammed, who was born in Arabia, is reported to have said, "The rights of women are sacred. See that women are maintained in the rights assigned to them." Most Saudi women accept that men, not they themselves, should safeguard their rights. Men lead. Always the husband, never the wife, leads the family in prayer. Whenever she leaves her home, a Saudi woman dons a loose, ankle-length black cloak (*abaya*). She also veils her face; women eager to demonstrate piety shroud themselves under two and three layers of silk and gauze. By veiling, a woman signifies that she is off-limits to men, and this deters them from making unwelcome advances. Since the honor of a family depends on the sexual conduct of its women (who are thought to be both highly sexed and lacking in control), both men and women look to the veil as a protective device. Although the Koran does not require women to veil, it is an ingrained custom, and the virtue of those who don't is held in question. They must counter well-meaning remarks of concerned relations who fret, "We will never meet in Paradise if you don't veil."

Although Saudis desire Western education and technology, most men and women reject Western cultural attitudes to women. Influenced perhaps by American soap operas popular in the kingdom, some Saudi women charge that Western freedom leads only to divorce, promiscuity, alcoholism, drug use, and a weakened family structure where the young do not respect their parents, and the aged are relegated to nursing homes. Gender segregation, they argue, promotes morality.

This segregation informs every aspect of life. Saudi Arabia is now an urban society, but women whose grandmothers and great-grandmothers used to ride camels are not allowed to drive. They can ride in gender-segregated city buses, although few do so. Wealthy families hire chauffeurs, but most women are dependent on the kindness of husbands, brothers, and sons to drive them around. To fly or take the train alone, a woman must obtain a letter of permission from her husband, father, or brother.

All public facilities are segregated. A few restaurants have family rooms where women are served, but most cater to men only. Despite the restrictions, however, women do get around, and there are "women's hours" at art exhibits, museums, and the zoo.

Education, Work, Control of Income. The veil arguably offers advantages to those who seek independence. It enables a woman to go about without harassment, writes Moroccan sociologist Fatima Mernissi. By lending a woman symbolic invisibility, the veil allows her to enter traditionally male spaces. She's not really there if she's covered up, so no one has to pay attention to her or tell her to go away. Veiling also demonstrates national pride, for it has been the national costume for centuries. Like an enormous pair of sunglasses, her veil allows a woman to see others, but they cannot see her as she shops for groceries or rides to the university.

Most of the ulema now support women's education. The Ministry of Education is divided in two sections, male and female; the female section is supervised not by the Ministry of Education but by the Department of Religious Affairs. When the first public schools for girls were established in 1959–1960, men rioted in the streets in protest. Today education for women is available in every village, town, and city. Through education, the conservative argument goes, a woman will learn to fulfill her role in life as a successful housewife, ideal wife, and good mother. The women's curriculum includes homemaking skills and has less science and more religion than the male curriculum. Women have been admitted to university since 1962, and currently 45 percent of university students are women. Most take degrees in teaching, nursing, and medicine.

Yet few graduates enter the workplace, even though at larger work sites women are entitled to maternity leave and child care. A company can legally hire a woman only so long as her job involves no contact with men. Critics charge workingwomen with nursing, teaching, and serving others rather than caring for the needs of their own families. In the segregated workplace, women can reach high positions, but they often lack the training in management skills to succeed. A woman's income (gained through dowry, inheritance, investment, and less often through work) is under her control and for her use only. Mai Yamani (research fellow at the School of Oriental and African Studies in London and daughter of former oil minister Zaki Yamani) indicates that 40 percent of Saudi Arabia's private wealth is in women's hands. More than 2,000 women are registered with the Riyadh Chamber of Commerce.

Marriage. Only women have the information necessary to arrange marriages, according to Saudi sociologist Soraya Altorki. A man's sisters will often suggest suitable marriage candidates for him among her friends, even showing him photographs of them. Marriages between first cousins, arranged by the parents of both parties, are common. Although a woman cannot be wed against her will, tremendous pressure can be brought on her to accept the family choice. Most trust their parents to choose wisely. When asked whether it was difficult to be betrothed to a stranger, a teenager replied that her parents would choose someone like her brother. "None of us chooses our brothers, but we get along with them. Marriage is the same," she said.

Men must pay a "bride-price" or dowry to the bride, often in the region of $30,000. Its purpose is to ensure a woman's financial security in case of divorce. In practice, however, the dowry sometimes goes to the father to pay for the wedding, to outfit the bride, or to help a brother with his dowry.

The conventional wisdom is that love follows marriage. Indeed, family life appears warm and welcoming. Polygamy is permitted but not widespread. It is easy for a man to divorce a woman. He can do so without the intervention of the courts, but a wife must petition the courts to obtain a divorce on her own account. Brides are expected to be virgins, and wives are expected to be faithful, and women do whatever they can to protect themselves from being the subject of gossip. If a wife is barren, the husband's family will often persuade him to divorce her or take a second wife. Few women question the justice of this. Both men and women generally prize sons more than daughters; the failure to produce sons is seen as the woman's fault.

Marriage exists primarily for procreation and for sexual gratification for both men and women. With little entertainment outside the home, the population growth is one of the world's highest. For companionship a woman looks to her female relatives and neighbors. Virtually all public and private gatherings are segregated.

In earlier times, when she married, a woman traditionally moved to the household of her spouse. With the rise of the cities, most Saudi newlyweds now live as a nuclear family in apartments separate from their parents. Yet at least symbolically, her mother-in-law is an authority figure for a bride.

Older women are honored, and a man and his wife are responsible for his mother's well-being throughout her life.

Most Saudi women spend their time in prayer, visiting, and watching television and videos. (There are no movie houses in the kingdom.) Among the kingdom's relatively few poor, some women work as sidewalk merchants or as cleaners and baby-sitters in schools, universities, women's banks, and airports. Women of the ever-diminishing Bedouin tribes spin and weave.

Middle-class families frequently recruit Third World nannies to clean house and take care of the children. In some cases, the nannies are treated as concubines by the men of the family. These women find themselves in a most unenviable position. Kept secluded, they find it difficult to prosecute the offenders or to protect themselves against abuse.

Feminism and Post–Gulf War Reform. After the Gulf War, a Constitution was established that allowed men more political participation. Women, however, were not consulted about the reforms, nor did they benefit. In fact, the Gulf War was followed by a backlash against women.

Many Saudis assumed that the American female soldiers were brought in as prostitutes for the comfort of the male troops. The very presence of these women inflamed conservatives. The fact they were allowed to drive, something no Saudi woman was permitted to do, only made it worse.

In 1991, 47 Saudi women drove through Riyadh to protest the ban on women's driving. Reprisals were swift. Religious leaders in mosques across the kingdom called them "prostitutes" and encouraged their harassment. Some of them were fired from their university teaching jobs. Their families received threatening phone calls. Even the liberals blamed the victims, calling their timing wrong. Since the drive-in, there has been little apparent action on the part of feminists. There are no organized Saudi feminist groups. The views of prominent women are well known by word of mouth among their peers. The government did not give visas to those who wished to attend the 1995 International Women's Conference in Beijing, China.

Future. After almost two decades of economic growth, the fall in world oil prices in the mid-1980s has led to economic stagnation. If the UN embargo against Iraq is lifted, a further fall might exacerbate internal problems in the kingdom. The government that used the women of the Riyadh drive-in as scapegoats to placate fundamentalist critics might be tempted to again blame women seeking basic human freedoms to divert attention from its inadequacy.

Both King Fahd and his successor-designate Prince Adbulla are aged, and it is difficult to predict what changes will occur after their passing. Despite media censorship, satellite television and the Internet are increasingly enabling Saudi accessibility to unsanctioned views. Wealthy, well-traveled Saudi women who have already seen the alternatives, for the most part, have preferred traditional ways. Yet the example of the courageous women of the Riyadh drive-in indicates that exposure to other lifestyles can lead not only to the will for change but also to action to enact it.

References. Soraya Altorki, *Women in Saudi Arabia: Ideology and Behaviour among the Elite* (New York, 1986); Leila Badawl, "Islam," in Jean Holm (ed.), *Women in Religion* (New York, 1994); Geraldine Brooks, *The Nine Parts of Desire: The Hidden World of Islamic Women* (New York, 1995); Fatima Mernissi, *Beyond the Veil: Male–Female Dynamics in Modern Muslim Society* (Bloomington, Ind., 1987); Mai Yamani, *The Economist* (1995). "Saudi Arabia: Silent Revolution."

JEAN GRANT

SCHOLARS AND INTELLECTUALS (ENGLISH RENAISSANCE). Writing in 1928, Virginia Woolf imagined a dreadful fate for Shakespeare's "sister" and explained cultural conditions as reasons women did not write in the English Renaissance. In fact, Woolf was wrong in thinking there were no women writers of the Renaissance, but scholars have only recently discovered and appreciated much of their work and significance. Many of the women scholars and intellectuals were women of immense courage as well as talent, such as Margaret More Roper, Catherine Parr, Lady Jane Grey, Elizabeth I, the Cooke sisters, and Elizabeth Cary, Lady Falkland. A woman who could read and write in the Renaissance was, however, unusual. It is difficult to know the literacy rates for women in this period, particularly since many people who could read could not write, and thus inability to sign names, one way of measuring lack of literacy, does not really work for this period. For both men and women, particularly in the countryside, literacy was probably low throughout the Renaissance. The work of English Renaissance women scholars and intellectuals was accomplished within a context where most of the population, but especially women, were illiterate. We should not believe, simply because there were a number of learned women in the English Renaissance, that the culture believed in the concept of education for upper-class women.

Of the women scholars and intellectuals, most are of the aristocratic or gentry class; in fact, a number of women of these classes were highly educated. Yet the lives of aristocratic women, although less confined than those of women of the lower classes, were still restricted by the emphasis placed on their being chaste, silent, and obedient. We should not consider that education necessarily came from a belief in women's capabilities and their potential role in public life. Humanist education (which included a study of the classics and foreign languages) served a very different function for women than for men. In the early sixteenth century, English scholars and humanists debated the question of women's education and their public role. Some humanists believed education would make women better wives: the Renaissance ideal was for women to be in a private rather than a public role. When writers such as Juan Luis Vives argued for women's education, they still perceived that education would fit a woman for her *private* function. Few believed that education would make women ready to play a public role.

The first really to advocate classical training for women was Thomas More, who provided such an education for his daughters and his female wards. In the 1530s and 1540s, Henry VIII appointed classical humanists as tutors not only for his son, Edward, but for his daughter, Elizabeth. This royal example caused several ambitious noble families to provide similar instruction to their daughters with the expectation this might lead to their making advantageous marriages. In the 1530s this argument over women's capabilities and their public position was mainly a theoretical issue; by the 1550s it had an immediate application, and John Knox called it a "monstrous" perversion for a woman to rule over men. Mary I's death in 1558, however, did not end this question, for her half sister Elizabeth would rule for the rest of the century.

Yet even in the second half of the sixteenth century, when a highly educated woman who was the author of some prayers and poems was herself ruling, people did not use the example of Elizabeth to give other women more of a role in public life. Instead, other rationales were used for female education. For example, the education of women also came from a desire to allow them to participate more fully in a religious life. Protestants especially believed that everyone, female as well as male, should be able to read God's word. One result of this belief was that most of women's writings in the English Renaissance were restricted to religious subjects, either in original works or translations.

Religion, both Catholicism and Protestantism, did give some women such a strong sense of purpose as to justify their writings and their actions. Margaret Roper, daughter of Thomas More, not only corresponded with her father while he was in prison but did translations and wrote poetry and theological commentary. Thomas More was very proud of her, but he also warned her that she should restrict her learning to her home circle. Unfortunately, much of Roper's own work has been lost, and one wonders what else she might have accomplished but for the restrictions placed on educated women.

Later in the reign of Henry VIII, his last wife, Catherine Parr, encouraged his daughters Mary and Elizabeth to read and translate Christian works. Parr herself was the author of *The Lamentation of a Sinner*. She may also have encouraged their cousin, Lady Jane Grey, who was also briefly a member of her household and an intellectual prodigy. Lady Jane Grey, a passionately convinced Protestant, died on the executioner's block at the age of 16, a victim to an abortive coup in 1553 that would have made her queen in place of her Catholic cousin Mary. Though she died so young, she left behind a number of letters and prayers.

Anthony Cooke, a devout Protestant, like More provided his daughters (he had five) with a thorough classical training. His daughters showed a remarkable zeal for study: Mildred Cooke Cecil, for example, did Greek translations. Her marriage to Elizabeth's principal minister, William Cecil, was a mutually devoted and intellectual partnership. Yet, because Elizabeth had no children, the emphasis on education from the royal household that had been so strong earlier in the century diminished. Educational treatises of the latter sixteenth century continued to tell women to be silent, chaste, and obedient. Despite this attitude, the end of the sixteenth and the early seventeenth centuries saw a number of brave, dedicated women, often inspired by religion, who used their scholarship creatively. For example, Elizabeth Cary, Lady Falkland, a converted Catholic, was the author of the play *The Tragedy of Mariam.* Cary's conversion led to her repudiation by her husband and great personal travail.

In Renaissance England a number of highly talented women were scholars and intellectuals. Yet their accomplishments were attained within a context that was extremely restrictive for women. The educated elite were often the more fortunate ones. Women of other social classes were economically marginalized and sometimes accused of witchcraft. Virginia Woolf was not so far off the mark after all. Shakespeare's sisters existed; they did not, however, have an easy time of it.

References. Margaret P. Hannay (ed.), *Silent but for the Word: Tudor Women as Patrons, Translators, and Writers of Religious Works* (Kent, Ohio, 1985); Retha Warnicke, *Women of the English Renaissance and Reformation* (Westport, Conn., 1983).

CAROLE LEVIN

SCHOLARS AND INTELLECTUALS (MEDIEVAL) are women whose careers reflect the opportunities available to women for intellectual and creative pursuits, c. 500–1400. More educated women are known by reputation than by surviving works: records show women who were teachers, students, patronesses, librarians, doctors, and lawyers. In the earlier Middle Ages, the abbeys provided most of the education for women in Latin and traditional school subjects, while noblewomen were taught at court, as were the daughters of Charlemagne. Latin education for women became increasingly rare toward the end of the period, although the convent of Helfta, which produced several important mystics in the thirteenth century, combined teaching of university subjects and devotional practice. Women known principally as scholars and intellectuals are the following:

Leoba. Leoba (Leobgy; 700–779) was an Anglo-Saxon nun in the monastery of Barking and a missionary with St. Boniface in Germany. The nuns of Barking were well educated; on the evidence of Aldhelm's *De Virginitate,* which was addressed to them, they studied Scripture, law, history and chronicles, grammar, and poetry. Only one letter written by Leoba exists, but it shows the influence of Aldhelm's complicated Latin and her pleasure in composing poetry. She was praised in her "Life" for her learning and love of scholarship. Boniface established her as abbess at Bischofsheim, where she proved a wise administrator.

Dhuoda. Dhuoda (b. c. 803) was a Frankish noblewoman who wrote a *Manual*, a handbook of instruction for her son. Out of the harsh circumstances of Dhuoda's life and her concern for the upbringing of her son, from whom she had been forcibly separated, comes her treatise, that reflects a particularly medieval way of looking at the world. Dhuoda draws on sapiential lore accumulated from church teaching, patristic exegesis, folk wisdom, quotations culled from the classical texts of the Middle Ages, and Scripture. Her *Manual* offers a unique view of a laywoman using her knowledge out of her fervent desire to prepare the life and the soul of her son in a difficult time.

Hrotsvit. Hrotsvit (Hrotsvitha or Hrotswitha) of Gandersheim (b. c. 935, d. after 973) was a Saxon canoness, one of the most prolific medieval women writers, who wrote Christian legends, plays modeled after the Roman dramatist Terence, and epic poetry. This activity has seemed to some incongruous or phenomenal, but Hrotsvit was a well-educated woman in an abbey that allowed an unusual degree of personal freedom and access to the outside world. Gandersheim, founded for noblewomen who ruled it autonomously, maintained an excellent school and library and had close connections with the Ottonian court. The details of Hrotsvit's life come only from her prefaces and comments in her works, but it is possible that she was educated at court and participated in the intellectual life there as well as at Gandersheim. Her work shows that she was well versed in both the ancient and Christian authors; characters in her plays speak scholarly disquisitions on subjects drawn from medieval learning. Disproving her use of the commonplaces of feminine frailty and inadequacy, Hrotsvit accomplished an ambitious plan of works.

Her legends and plays together make up a double cycle of stories in a scheme with thematic parallels and symmetries. Hrotsvit uses tales of fall and conversion, martyrdom, and triumphant virginity to illustrate the Christian ascetic ideal. Her particular genius in the plays is her wit and imagination in combining the serious and the comic. She shows the sincere heroism of the believers, most often women, while tempering the fates of the villains with comedy, thus revealing their absurdity in the light of the ideal of Christian life.

Anna Comnena. Anna (1083 to 1153–1155?) was a Byzantine princess who chronicled the reign of her father, Alexios I. Her work is one of the primary sources for the history of the Crusades. Inspired by epics and classical histories, in the *Alexiad* she combined good historical method, using official papers and oral sources, with her knowledge of Greek classical poetry. Anna was educated in the palace rather than in schools, and records that she studied the traditional course of subjects: rhetoric, philosophy, grammar, mathematics, church teaching, literature, and history. Her contemporaries held her in high esteem for her learning and her medical knowledge.

Héloise. Héloise (c. 1100 to 1163) was renowned for her learning at a young age; she had been educated by nuns and by her uncle, a canon in Paris, who hired Peter Abelard to be her tutor. In a scandalous episode that has put them into the ranks of legendary lovers, Héloise and Abelard married secretly, then separated and entered monastic life. Her story is known to us through her correspondence and Abelard's *Historia calamitatum*. Three of her four surviving letters are addressed to him, as is her series of scriptural questions called the *Problemata*, written from her position as abbess of the monastery at the Paraclete. Through these letters, Héloise displays the literary knowledge for which she was famous, and her skillful use of the rhetorical art of letter writing emphasizes the emotion from which the letters spring. They move from personal topics to theological and philosophical problems, which she argues ably. In addition, she is concerned with devising an appropriate monastic rule for women. Foremost in these letters is the sense of a woman in pursuit of truth through her philosophical inquiries in personal, practical, and spiritual matters.

Hildegard of Bingen. Hildegard (1098 to 1179) was a German abbess whose visionary works place her in the first rank of medieval intellectuals. At age 8 she entered the Benedictine monastery of Disibodenberg, where, 30 years later, she was elected abbess. Frequently ill all her life, she had kept her visions hidden until she was 40, when her physical suffering pressed her to make known what she had seen. A part of her first visionary work, the *Scivias*, was read by Pope Eugene and approved as prophecy at the Synod of Trier in 1147. This recognition of Hildegard as a prophet accorded her a freedom and an authority that other women in the Middle Ages were rarely able to achieve. She credited her vision with having given her understanding and knowledge of theological and philosophical works as well as her knowledge of Latin and music. But while she claimed little education, her writing reflects broad knowledge of the intellectual works important to her time; she was capable of writing complex and fluent Latin; and above all, she brought astonishing powers of intellect to every endeavor. From the time she began to record her visions to the end of her life, she engaged in prodigious activity, corresponding with religious leaders and heads of state, undertaking extensive preaching journeys, and engaging in an investigation of all aspects of humanity and divinity and the relationships among them. She wrote two more visionary works, hymns and sequences, and a play, now regarded as the first liturgical drama. Hildegard wrote on natural science and medicine, including discussions of women's physiologies and sexuality that appear to be completely original. A secret language and its alphabet complete the whole body of her works. All of

Hildegard's achievements are remarkable, but her visions are her principal work and are striking in their beautiful imagery and her interpretations of them, transforming the mystical experience into poetic experience and spiritual understanding. Hildegard's visions are encyclopedic, making up the whole of human history in relation to the divine, incorporating the spiritual and physical worlds, everything necessary for the understanding of the soul's ultimate end in God.

References. Karen Cherawatuk and Ulrike Withaus (eds.), *Dear Sister: Medieval Women and the Epistolary Genre* (Philadelphia, 1993); Peter Dronke, *Women Writers of the Middle Ages* (Cambridge, England, 1984); Joan Ferrante, "The Education of Women in the Middle Ages," in Patricia H. Labalme (ed.), *Beyond Their Sex: Learned Women of the European Past* (New York, 1980), 9–43; Marie Anne Mayeski, *Dhuoda: Ninth-Century Mother and Theologian* (Scranton, Pa., 1995); Barbara Newman, *Sister of Wisdom: St. Hildegard's Theology of the Feminine* (Berkeley, Calif., 1987); Glennis Stephenson and Shirley Newman (eds.), *Reimagining Women: Representations of Women in Culture* (Toronto, 1993); Mary Ellen Waithe (ed.), *A History of Women Philosophers: Medieval, Renaissance and Enlightenment Women Philosophers, A.D. 500–1600* (Boston, 1989); Katharina M. Wilson (ed.), *Hrotsvit of Gandersheim: Rara Avis in Saxonia?* (Ann Arbor, Mich., 1987); Katharina M. Wilson (ed.), *Medieval Women Writers* (Athens, Ga., 1984).

CLIA M. GOODWIN

SCIENCE AND WOMEN. Women have been more systematically excluded from doing serious work in science than from doing any other social activity except, perhaps, military combat. Given the many discriminatory barriers women have faced and the fact that women have frequently been ignored, robbed of credit, or forgotten when they have made important contributions to the sciences, it is not surprising that few women have been able to achieve eminence as scientists. The factors that account for the past suppression of women's voices in science are multifaceted, but because of the cognitive authority granted to science, none have been more pernicious or self-reinforcing than the theories scientists have produced (in the absence of women) about women's supposed intellectual inferiority.

The first systematic, scientific explanation of woman's intellectual inferiority can be traced back to Aristotle, whose theory that a defect in generative heat impairs female brain development influenced scientific thinking well into the eighteenth century. In the late 1700s, scientific views of sex and gender differences began to shift from a hierarchical model, in which woman was conceptualized as a defective man, to a model of complementary differences, which depicted woman as man's opposite and as perfect in her own way.

For women, unfortunately, this advance in thinking was more apparent than real. Because of the centuries-old tradition within Western intellectual thought of defining difference in terms of privation, the very characteristics presumed to make up woman's difference were perceived as having a lower degree of perfection than those of man. For example, emotion—one of woman's ascribed "perfections"—was characterized as resulting from the lack of rational control of the passions. Because of this defect in rational control, women's emotionality was also taken to be a mark of her inferiority and a reason to continue excluding members of her kind from science.

The alleged defect in women's minds that supposedly prevents women from excelling in science has changed over time—for example, from inadequate heat to inferior skull size, hormone deficiencies, and brain lateralization peculiarities. Because women have been defined out of science since ancient times, the question of women's real place in science is often approached by scholars as a matter of documenting the accomplishments of women scientists. Much of this work employs the "great man" approach to history, with the focus on women instead of men.

This approach has its difficulties: distinguished male scientists outnumber distinguished female scientists by a wide margin, and emphasizing "great women" does little to reveal the more usual patterns of women working in science. Even more problematically, perhaps, the focus on exceptional women scientists retains the norms and modalities traditionally associated with masculinity as the standard of excellence. This mode of doing history measures women's contributions to science against what men of European descent have valued and defined as science; and it tends to hide the racialized identities of women scientists, what the work of women scientists has meant to different populations of women and men, and how this work has underwritten and shaped elite men's very definition of science.

If the focus is shifted from recounting the stories of exceptional women scientists to examining the interplay between the social barriers to women's advancement in science and the strategies women have employed to secure a place in science, a more adequate picture of women's participation in science emerges. The vast majority of American women scientists in the modern era have been marginalized and underutilized, not for the lack of talent, hard work, or ability to seize enhanced opportunities, but because of what Margaret Rossiter has called hierarchical and territorial forms of occupational sex segregation.

Hierarchical discrimination has shaped women's participation in science by channeling them into auxiliary, low-status, low-paying positions, for example, as assistants in museums, "invisible" partners in husband–wife teams, technicians in industrial laboratories, educators in high schools, instructors in colleges, and scientific editors. The experiences of American women in astronomy in the late 1800s and early 1900s provide a vivid example of this type of occupational segregation.

Around the turn of the century in the United States, astronomy was experiencing rapid growth as larger observatories and bigger telescopes were being built, and new problematics, theories, methodologies, and techniques were being developed. For socially privileged women, these changes meant increased opportunities for employment. At the older observatories, women were offered some of the work once performed by male assistants, who now had new, exciting possibilities elsewhere. New technology such as spectrophotography created an increased need for cheap, intelligent labor. The type of work engendered by this technology—classifying, cataloging, and computing that required painstaking attention to detail—was easily categorized as "women's work."

Sex typing, however, was a mixed blessing, and it was a dynamic that operated primarily for socially advantaged women, since women belonging to racial and ethnic minorities were largely excluded from even the bottom rungs of the profession. While providing a place in the field for socially privileged women, the feminization of specific jobs within astronomy meant that the "lucky" few were confined to spheres of activity that afforded few opportunities for advancement, salary increases, or personal challenge. Because they worked essentially as "organic computers" under the control of observatory directors, the work they were assigned was not regarded as requiring much original or theoretical thinking. While women who secured positions in observatories were invariably indebted to the progressive attitudes of individual male directors, their participation in astronomy was nevertheless mediated by men, who were still subject to prevailing gender stereotypes and who, as project directors, received most of the credit for published work.

The alternative employment setting for women astronomers in the United States—the newly created women's colleges in the North—afforded some women more opportunities to undertake independent research. But because of heavy teaching loads and administrative responsibilities, poor funding for basic equipment, and external and internal pressure to pursue feminized research topics, women professors were not able to escape sex typing and sex segregation. This is not to say that women professors were unsuccessful at research. As with their counterparts in the observatories, despite considerable gender-specific barriers, they helped to advance their field, especially by contributing to the steady accumulation of small-scale discoveries, but also by making conceptual innovations.

The need for cheap labor was probably the engine driving the practice of sex segregation in astronomy; gender ideology simply provided the rationalization for this practice. Whereas certain types of work or roles within astronomy became feminized because they were low-paying and low-status, in other scientific arenas whole fields (e.g., home economics, nutrition, nursing) and entire specialties within fields were sex-typed as being inherently feminine and, therefore, the most suitable locations for aspiring women scientists. Psychology's evolution into the sex-segregated areas of theoretical science (male) and applied professional activities (female) illustrates this latter phenomenon of territorial discrimination.

In the early twentieth century, problems resulting from industrialization (e.g., poverty, overcrowding, child labor) created a somewhat expanded area of professional practice for women, especially for socially privileged women, but gradually also for women belonging to racial and ethnic minorities. Training institutes and psychological clinics were work settings that neither violated society's assumptions about "women's natural place" nor challenged the cultural assumption that women are too mired in the immediate and practical to apprehend the abstract and universal. Applied psychology quickly became identified and devalued as "women's work," and despite tremendous contributions by women psychologists to the growing fields of child development and education (as well as other related fields), by World War I a kind of territorial ghetto for women psychologists was firmly established.

During World War II, the military's need for psychological expertise in recruitment, training, psychometrics, and human factors research greatly stimulated the growth of traditionally male-dominated subfields. While women psychologists were often expected to volunteer their services to tend the "home fires" in the civilian population, men's "war work" achieved a status that was prestigious, highly paid, and decidedly "masculine" in the sense of being regarded as rigorous, objective, impersonal, tough, competitive, and unemotional. Masculinized subfields such as industrial psychology, psychometrics, and comparative and experimental psychology continued to flourish after World War II as increased educational opportunities and a restored confidence in science drove a greater wedge between "true" scientific psychology and its "distant" feminine relatives. To this day, the masculinized subfields of psychology enjoy a greater degree of scientific respectability than do the feminized ones—a fact that would seem to reflect the ways in which the dialectic between ideologies of gender and science has shaped the social construction of gender and science.*

What the examples of astronomy and psychology show is that while gender stereotypes enabled women to acquire a niche in science, they also locked women into a pattern of sex-segregated employment and underrecognition. This helped perpetuate the ideology of gender difference, and because of the racist and ethnocentric dimensions of the sexual division of labor, women belonging to racial and ethnic minorities were left stranded on the most distant perimeters of science.

In the late 1990s, significantly greater numbers and populations of women are undertaking graduate studies in every field of science and are working at every level in all scientific disciplines and employment sectors. As promising as these developments may seem, women still experience salary inequities at all levels, lower rates of tenure and promotion in academe, restricted opportunities for career advancement in nonacademic employment sectors, higher rates of schooling and employment in feminized fields, and greater levels of involuntary unemployment, part-time employment, employment out-of-field, and underemployment. At the same time, there continue to be subtle, but troubling, replays of the age-old notion that innate differences between the thinking of women and men preclude women from excelling in science.

Women's historical confinement to the periphery of science does raise important questions about gender and science. Is the past suppression of women's voices in science simply a matter of mistaken or irrational social differentiation? Have gender-based patterns of exclusion distorted the content, methods, norms, or practices of science? What are the limits, if any, of fighting sexist science with science in its present form? Full gender equity has proved elusive in science. For many feminists, the question about what should be done to improve the situation of women in science is also a question about how to expand the meaning of science.

References. G. Kass-Simon and Patricia Farnes (eds.), *Women of Science: Righting the Record* (Bloomington, Ind., 1990); Margaret W. Rossiter, *Women Scientists in America: Struggles and Strategies to 1940* (Baltimore, 1982); Margaret W. Rossiter, *Women Scientists in America: Before Affirmative Action 1940–1972* (Baltimore, 1995); N. Russo and A. N. O'Connell, "Models from Our Past: Psychology's Foremothers," *Psychology of Women Quarterly* 5 (1980): 11–54; Londa Schiebinger, *The Mind Has No Sex?: Women in the Origins of Modern Science* (Cambridge, 1989); Nancy Tuana, *The Less Noble Sex: Scientific, Religious, and Philosophical Conceptions of Woman's Nature* (Bloomington, Ind., 1993).

LYNNE S. ARNAULT and MARIA DITULLIO

SCIENCE FICTION. The relationship between women and science fiction (SF) encompasses women as characters in, and as authors and readers of, science fiction narratives and the critical attention that feminist science fiction has received. Each of these facets and the overall relationship differ in different countries. This entry is confined largely to English-language science fiction. For a discussion of French-language SF the Canadian journal *Solaris* is recommended. Information on science fiction of all countries is available in *Science Fiction Studies, Extrapolation,* and *Fantasy Review.*

Until very recently, SF was perceived as a predominantly male genre, written by and for males. Therefore, little attention was paid to possible differences that advanced technology might make in women's position and status. Women appeared as stereotypical excuses for males to stage rescue missions, as helpmates, lovers, mothers, and sisters to the world-conquering male heroes or as matriarchal monsters, aliens, or treacherous enemies who must be subdued or annihilated. (These images are still predominant.) Yet while Robert Heinlein, Andre Norton (Alice Mary Norton), and other writers of their generation gave stereotypical social roles to their women and girls, these same characters had adventures in space, performed their own rescues, and were often brilliant, energetic, exciting persons. To the generation of women now writing, reading, teaching, and criticizing SF, these stories, read during their childhood, gave hope in the imaginative space for which SF as a concept stood and represented possible alternative futures to those limited ones offered by day-to-day life. Depiction of women remained in this state until the publication of LeGuin's *The Left Hand of Darkness* in 1969, followed by many much more daring extrapolations and literary experiments in the early to mid-1970s. These extrapolations and experiments coincided with the influx of a significant number of women writers into science fiction.

There have been women writers of SF as long as science fiction has existed, its roots being traced back to E. A. Poe and Mary Shelley, H. G. Wells, Jules Verne, Francis Stevens, and Charlotte Perkins Gilman. But through the first half of this century, there was only a handful of women SF writers, such as C. L. Moore, Judith Merrill, Andre Norton, and in the early 1960s, Anne McCaffrey, Marion Zimmer Bradley, and Zenna Henderson.

In the late 1960s, however, the situation changed. More women entered the scene and began to achieve recognition for the first time. From 1968 to 1984 women received more than ten Hugo (fan-presented) and Nebula (colleague-presented) awards.

During the 1970s and 1980s SF realized a potential that was always there: to explore either the implications of allowing the patriarchy to continue on its present course or the possibilities for a future where gender equality is a quotidian fact. Writers such as LeGuin, Russ, James Tiptree, Jr. (Racoona Sheldon), and Kate Wilhelm were among the earliest to explore this potential (as were a few male writers such as S. R. Delany).

By the mid-1970s excitement began to mount: four major anthologies (Pamela Sargent's *Women of Wonder* [New York, 1975], *More Women of Wonder* [New York, 1976], and *The New Women of Wonder* [New York, 1978]; and Susan Anderson's *Aurora beyond Equality* [New York, 1976]) included stories by feminist novelists who were to become prominent in the latter part of the decade. The first panel on Women and Science Fiction was held at the 1976 World Science Fiction Convention in Kansas City. An amateur magazine, *Khatru*, had been printing letter interchanges on the issue of women in SF. A Canadian journal, *Witch and the Chameleon*, focused on that subject, and devotees in Madison, Wisconsin, who had just started an SF group and amateur magazine, founded an annual conference where a large percentage of the programming was specifically about women, feminist issues, and SF literature and where sexist programming would be discouraged. This conference continues despite early predictions of doom. Attention to women writers has also been drawn by the two journals *Aurora* (fan-oriented) and *New Moon* (critically oriented), both outgrowths of *Janus*, a fan magazine begun in 1975.

In the late 1970s major talents such as Octavia Butler, Suzy McKee Charnas, C. J. Cherryh, H. M. Hoover, Elizabeth Lynn, Vonda McIntyre, Kit Reed, Pamela Sargent, Joan Vinge, Chelsea Quinn Yarbro, Pamela Zoline,

Elizabeth Vonarburg, Katia Alexandre, Joelle Wintrebert, and Monique Wittig (French) joined the earlier writers, but women were still responsible for less than 15 percent of the SF published in any one year.

In the mid-1980s some critics and writers were attempting to dismiss the importance of women writers and feminist issues in contemporary SF, saying that women writers are disappearing or that their work is uninteresting. Nevertheless, established writers from other genres, such as Lessing, Atwood, and Piercy, as well as many new, excellent writers (e.g., Lois Bujold, Catherine Cooke, Zoe Fairbairns, Cynthia Felice, Mary Gentle, Megan Lindholm, R. A. McAvoy, Meredith Ann Pierce, Joan Slonczewski, Linda Steele, Sherri Tepper, Connie Willis, Cherry Wilder, Patricia Wrede) added their works to the existing corpus. The anthology *Despatches from the Frontiers of the Female Mind* (Green and LeFanu [eds.] [New York, 1985]) provides an introduction to some of them. With these new writers portrayals of both male and female characters have become more innovative as the powers of the imagination are stretched to encompass myriad possibilities such as alternative divisions of labor for the birth and nurturing of children, the provision of day-to-day needs, and the governance of societies or cautionary scenarios in which societies become more patriarchal, militaristic, or in other ways oppressive.

Critical studies began to appear with more regularity during the late 1970s and early 1980s, with groundbreaking articles in academic journals such as *Extrapolation* and *Science Fiction Studies*. Bibliographies, essay collections, single-author studies, dissertation-cum-critical texts, all of which are phenomena of the late 1970s, continue. Notable among these is Roger Schlobin's *Urania's Daughters: A Checklist of Women Science Fiction Writers, 1692–1982* (Mercer Island, Wash., 1983); Betty King's *Women of the Future: Female Main Characters in Science Fiction* (Metuchen, N.J., 1984); Nathalie Rosinsky's *Feminist Futures: Contemporary Women's Speculative Fiction* (Ann Arbor, Mich., 1984); and a collection of essays from a 1985 conference on women and SF held in Texas: *Women Worldwalkers: New Dimensions for SF and Fantasy* (Jane Weedman [ed.] [Lubbock, Tex., 1985]). The activity woven around and through women writing science fiction is a fact of the present as well as the future.

JANICE M. BOGSTAD

SCULPTORS. There are literary references to distinguished women sculptors in the ancient world, and medieval guild records list several women sculptors active in Paris during the thirteenth and fourteenth centuries. But only with the Renaissance and its elevation of the status of artists does significant information about women sculptors begin to become available. Even so, compared to women painters, from the sixteenth through the eighteenth centuries there are relatively few well-known female sculptors, because sculpture—viewed as a complex, expensive process, requiring great physical strength, a familiarity with human anatomy, and collaboration with numerous technical assistants—was not considered a suitable occupation for women.

Despite this prevailing attitude, Properzia de' Rossi (c. 1450–1530) won an important competition to produce marble sculptures for the western facade of San Petronio, a church in her native Bologna; the Spaniard Luisa Roldán (1656–1704) trained at her family's workshop in Seville and became court sculptor to Charles II; and Anne Seymour Damer (1748–1828), an English artist, made portraits of such distinguished sitters as Napoleon and King George III.

The nineteenth century marked the emergence of more internationally successful women sculptors than ever before. As the vogue for neoclassicism reached its peak, a group of American expatriate sculptors, all women, came to the fore in Rome. Nicknamed "the white, marmorean flock" (after their preferred medium, marble), they included Harriet Hosmer (1830–1908), known for both ornamental works and historical subjects; Anne Whitney (1821–1915), who sculpted likenesses of important liberal politicians; Emma Stebbins (1815–1882), responsible for a number of major fountain figures; and the remarkable Edmonia Lewis (1845–after 1911). The orphaned child of a Chippewa Indian and a black man, Lewis attended Oberlin College, studied sculpture in Boston, and made her reputation with a 12-foot-tall *Death of Cleopatra*, which was acclaimed at the 1876 Philadelphia Centennial.

Other notable nineteenth-century women sculptors are Vinnie Ream Hoxie (1847–1914), the first woman to receive a U.S. government commission for sculpture (at 15), and three more Americans—Anna Hyatt Huntington (1876–1973), who specialized in animal sculptures; Gertrude Vanderbilt Whitney (1876–1942), a student of Rodin, who produced several important war memorials; and Malvina Hoffman (1887–1966), another Rodin pupil, who created intriguing portraits of dancers and a series of 105 figures for the Field Museum of Natural History of Chicago. The German sculptor Elisabet Ney (1883–1907) established a successful career as a portraitist, while Frenchwoman Camille Claudel (1864–1943), Rodin's longtime assistant and companion, made works that demonstrate her mastery of expressive gesture and surface textures.

The pace of change has quickened enormously in all fields—from science to the arts—during the present century. Twentieth-century women sculptors have figured prominently in all the radical new artistic developments—most notably, modernism (abstraction). In fact, two of the most important pioneers of modernist sculpture were women: Louise Nevelson (1899–1988) and Barbara Hepworth (1903–1975). Nevelson was born in Russia and moved as a young child to the United States, where, by the mid-1950s, she had developed her signature approach—assembling discarded bits of wood into elegant and elaborate wall sculptures, painted all black, white, or gold. Hepworth was raised in Yorkshire, England, whose hilly terrain had a strong influence on her art—eloquent, curving shapes that suggest a human figure or a landscape. Most of Hepworth's sculpture was carved of wood or stone—sometimes embellished with wire, string, or paint.

Two French sculptors, Germaine Richier (1904–1959) and Louise Bourgeois (b. 1911), were also early modernist pioneers—Richier with her spectral, corroded-looking, cast bronze forms suggesting humans or other animals and Bourgeois with open-space, rectilinear wooden works and, later, rounded, organic shapes of stone, plaster, and rubber. The principal spokesperson for the surrealists, André Breton, was impressed with the fur-covered teacup exhibited by Swiss artist Méret Oppenheim (1913–1986) at the Museum of Modern Art in 1937. Ohio-born Dorothy Dehner (b. 1901) was trained as a painter but, beginning in the early 1950s, concentrated on three-dimensional art—simple, forceful works in metal or wood.

Pop sculpture is well represented by the work of Marisol (Escobar) (b. 1930), born in Paris of Venezuelan parents. Her blocklike, painted wooden figures reflect the artist's sense of sociopolitical satire. The "nanas" of French sculptor Niki de Saint-Phalle (b. 1930)—playful female figures with ungainly proportions, exuberant gestures, and bright colors—stand in stark contrast to the cerebral, minimalist rectangles sculpted by American Anne Truitt (b. 1921).

A wide variety of nontraditional materials and techniques has been explored recently in the works of such artists as Magdalena Abakanowicz (b. 1930), a Polish sculptor known for her haunting arrangements of repeated, humanoid forms made from burlap and rope; a whole host of Americans, including Lee Bontecou (b. 1931), who created an intriguing series of reliefs by stretching canvas fragments over welded steel frames; Greek-born Chryssa (b. 1931), who makes neon sculptures; and Americans Barbara Chase-Riboud (b. 1939), whose work is characterized by sensuous, textural contrasts of fibers and metal, Nancy Graves (b. 1940), who made her reputation by constructing a group of lifelike, life-sized, multimedia camels, Lynda Benglis (b. 1941), noted for her unusual combinations of materials (chicken wire covered with gesso and gold leaf), and Judy Chicago (b. 1939), who, in 1970, along with painter Miriam Schapiro, established the first American feminist art program at the California Institute of Arts and who is known for her massive, consciousness-raising* collaborative pieces, such as *The Dinner Party* (1979), a sculptural survey of women's history.

One of the most exciting late twentieth-century artistic developments is environmental sculpture—which, instead of being confined to a pedestal, projects into the viewer's space—like the eccentric abstractions of Eva Hesse (1936–1970), whose erotic, curved forms (made of rubber tubing or string dipped in fiberglass) were typically suspended from gallery walls and ceilings or laid across the floor. Judy Pfaff (b. 1946) creates playful, room-sized environments filled with brightly colored, "found" materials (twigs, electrician's wire), while Alice Aycock (b. 1946) invents large, complex machines with uncertain uses. Other examples are set outdoors, within the natural environment, either as permanent installations, like the startlingly original public parks developed by Nancy Holt (b. 1938), or temporary ones, like Beverly Pepper's (b. 1924) fabricated sand dunes on the northeastern Florida coast.

References. Charlotte Streifer Rubinstein, *American Women Artists from Early Indian Times to the Present* (Boston, 1982); Virginia Watson-Jones, *Contemporary American Women Sculptors* (Phoenix, 1986).

NANCY G. HELLER

SECOND SEX, THE is a pioneering and monumental study of woman by the French writer Simone de Beauvoir (1908–1986), published in 1949. *Le Deuxième Sexe* seeks to explore all aspects of woman's situation within the philosophical framework of existentialism. Starting from the Sartrean idea of original conflict between Self and Other, Beauvoir argues that man has always conceived of himself as the essential, the Self, and relegated woman to the status of Other, the second sex. In Beauvoir's analysis, two factors make the oppression of woman unique: first, unlike the oppression of race or class, the oppression of woman is not a contingent historical fact, an event in time that has sometimes been contested or reversed. Woman has always been subordinate to man. Second, women have internalized the alien point of view that man is the essential and woman the inessential.

The Second Sex is divided into two parts: "Facts and Myths" and "Woman's Life Today." Book 1 concerns woman as Other, woman as defined by biology, psychoanalysis, and historical materialism; the history of woman; and myths of woman. Book 2 concerns woman as Self, woman as she lives her situation through childhood, adolescence, adulthood, and old age; the experience of the lesbian, the married woman, the mother, and the prostitute; and woman's justifications in narcissism, love, and mysticism. Beauvoir concludes with an analysis of the independent woman, in which she argues the necessity of economic and emotional autonomy for women's liberation.

There is a consistent hostility in *The Second Sex* to woman's biology and especially to the maternal. One aspect of this hostility is Beauvoir's adoption of Sartrean existentialism and its rejection of the natural as antivalue. Another factor is the historical context in which Beauvoir was writing. In the late 1940s, France was still emerging from the trauma of Occupation and the Vichy regime. Although Frenchwomen had finally obtained the right to vote (1944), legislated, in part, in reaction to the misogynist policies of Vichy and in recognition of women's active participation in the Resistance, male rejection of Vichy propaganda did not go so far as to consider women's right to control their bodies. Not only did abortion continue to be outlawed, but even the sale of contraceptives remained illegal until 1967.

Beauvoir's personal history illuminates her philosophical assumptions and political priorities. Growing up as a dutiful daughter in the early part of the century, her childhood relation to her parents was in keeping with the traditional expectations and family structure of the time. Her mother took care of her moral welfare and day-to-day needs while her father was the authority figure who embodied the law and worldly knowledge. Françoise de Beauvoir, as evoked by her daughter, was a pious woman who accepted without question her prescribed duties as wife and mother, renouncing any self-expression outside those roles. She became for her daughter a warning, the image of what she wanted her own life not to be. Maternity always looked to Beauvoir like a trap in which women lose their autonomy and their happiness.

The most controversial statement of *The Second Sex* is Beauvoir's paradoxical formulation that "One is not born, but rather becomes, a woman." It expresses her view of woman's Otherness as fabricated, imposed by culture rather than biology. Rejecting any notion of nature or the feminine that defines woman's role in terms of sexual difference, Beauvoir sees the human body as a situation, a given that takes on meaning only in relation to individual and social contexts. "Woman" is thus a cultural sign for the male-created product she calls the second sex.

Beauvoir conceived of *The Second Sex* as a call to reflection rather than action, written to communicate her *prise de conscience* of what it means to be a woman. Not until 1972 did she publicly declare herself a feminist, which she defined in politically activist terms. Long before that time, however, she had been involved in the political struggles against women's oppression, from the campaign to legalize family planning in France in the late 1950s, to her efforts in the 1980s against the practice of genital mutilation in many Third World countries. In the 1970s she was at the forefront of the fight to legalize abortion.

In France, the ideology of equality that informs *The Second Sex* continues to be a major influence on contemporary feminists working for political and social change. During the 1970s and 1980s the book was often a counterpoint and focus of attack for feminist ideologies of sexual difference. In Beauvoir's analysis, the alternative to sexual difference is not becoming like men, as her adversaries insist, but an equality that would enable women "to be singular and universal at the same time." It is a claim to liberate the plurality and unexplored possibilities of individual difference, independent of gender definition.

References. Toril Moi, *Simone de Beauvoir: The Making of an Intellectual Woman* (New York, 1994); Hélène Vivienne Wenzel (ed.), *Simone de Beauvoir: Witness to a Century. Yale French Studies* 72 (1986).

DOROTHY KAUFMANN

SECONDARY SEX CHARACTERISTICS are anatomical differences between men and women, resulting from the action of testosterone and related androgen hormones (male characteristics) and estrogen and related estrogenic hormones (female characteristics) on nonreproductive tissues. These differences vary widely among individuals. It should be noted that these hormones are not gender-exclusive. The testes are a major source of androgen, predominantly testosterone, in males, and the ovaries are a major source of estrogen in females. In both sexes, the adrenal cortex also secretes small amounts of androgens and lesser amounts of estrogen.

Androgen hormones, by stimulating protein synthesis, effect muscle and bone growth. Hence, male secondary sex characteristics include muscular and skeletal development resulting in wide shoulders and narrow hips and a generally larger and more muscular body. The larynx (voice box) grows and enlarges in response to testosterone, resulting in a deep voice. Hair growth is stimulated on the face, along the midline of the abdomen, on the pubis, and on the chest and axillary region. In those individuals with a genetic predisposition to baldness, testosterone causes hair loss. Androgens promote activity in oil and sweat glands that may lead to acne, particularly around puberty. There is also evidence of behavioral effects of androgens. In both males and females androgens appear to be related to libido.

Estrogen causes cellular proliferation in many areas: glandular tissue in the breast grows, and fat is deposited in the breast; and increase in adipose tissue in the hips, buttocks, thighs, and subcutaneous areas results in rounded body contours; the pelvic bone structure grows and widens so the general body shape is narrow shoulders and broad hips. Although development of axial and pubic hair seems to be a response to adrenal androgens, the pattern of hair growth is estrogen-dependent. It cannot be overemphasized that within these general responses there is tremendous individual variation, and for all secondary sex characteristics there is more variation among same-sex individuals than there is difference in the average values between the sexes. (See also PUBERTAL PROCESSES.)

FRANCES GARB

SELF-DEFENSE. One area that has sparked considerable controversy is women's self-defense. For years the prevailing notion was that a woman should not fight a rapist because she would be hurt worse. Despite the absence of data to support this view, many police officers and even some rape crisis workers share the common assumption that if you fight, you get hurt more. The first major study to empirically dispute this notion was published by Pauline Bart and Patricia O'Brien, significant in that it was the first to challenge, with data, cultural myths about self-defense. Many recent studies have confirmed the importance of fighting back. Current research on self-defense concludes *unequivocally* that

1. Women who fight back and fight back immediately are less likely to be raped than women who do not.

2. Women who fight back are no more likely to be injured than women who do not fight back (in fact, it has been shown that victim resistance often occurred in *response* to physical attack).

3. Pleading, begging, and reasoning are ineffective in preventing rape or physical injury.

4. Women who fight back experience less postassault symptomatology due to avoidance of being raped.

5. Women who fight back have faster psychological recoveries whether or not they were raped.

6. Fighting back may strengthen the physical evidence should the survivor decide to prosecute for rape or attempted rape.

S. E. Ullman and R. A. Knight also dispute the idea that physical resistance provokes increased violence in particular types of rapists, such as sadists. Based on a sample of incarcerated stranger rapists, their study showed that, overall, the effectiveness of women's resistance strategies did not vary by rapist type. Women who fought in response to sadistic rapists were no more likely to experience physical injury than women who did not. These authors also admonish people from issuing warnings against the supposed dangers of physical resistance to sadistic rapists in the absence of any empirical data to support such claims. They also point out the futility of advising women to assess the "type" of rapist before determining whether or not to resist.

Victim resistance raises the "cost" of rape for the perpetrator (Kleck and Sayles). Resistance makes rape completion more difficult, increases the effort required by the rapist, and prolongs the attack, thereby increasing the risk of discovery and capture. It also increases the probability of injury to the rapist, possibly leaving marks that will contribute to later discovery.

Warning women not to fight back because they might get hurt is based in myth, not empirical evidence. Cooperation with the assailant does not guarantee safety, and resistance does not increase her risk (Koss and Mukai). Such myths serve only to assure more victims for would-be rapists, and they do an immense disservice to women by absurdly encouraging them to "bargain" with criminals. Only 3 percent of rapes involve some additional injury that is serious; usually the rape itself is the most serious injury suffered (Kleck and Sayles). Immediate and effective self-defense is the best way to prevent the hurt that comes from trying to recover from rape.

References. Pauline Bart and Patricia O'Brien, *Stopping Rape: Effective Avoidance Strategies* (New York, 1985); G. Kleck and S. Sayles, "Rape and Resistance," *Social Problems* 37, 2 (1990): 149– 162; M. P. Koss and T. Mukai, "Recovering Ourselves: Frequency, Effects, and Resolution of Rape, in F. L. Denmark and M. A. Paludi (eds.), *Psychology of Women: A Handbook of Issues and Theories* (Westport, Conn., 1993); S. E. Ullman and R. A. Knight, "Women's Resistance Strategies to Different Rapist Types," *Criminal Justice and Behavior* 22 (1995): 263–283.

PATRICIA D. ROZEE

SELF-FULFILLING PROPHECY is a concept of the social and behavioral sciences referring to the idea that one person's expectations for the behavior of others can help to bring about the expected behavior.

Social scientists have discussed the phenomenon at least since 1885, and a landmark exposition of the concept appeared in 1948 (Merton). Experimental evidence for the operation of this phenomenon, however, did not begin to appear until more than a decade later.

The earliest such research was conducted in laboratory situations. Psychological experimenters were given arbitrary expectations about the future behavior of their research subjects, who then tended to behave as their experimenters expected them to behave. For example, in one series of studies, some experimenters were told that their research subjects would tend to see photographs of other people as being of relatively successful people, while other experimenters were told that their research subjects would tend to see photographs of other people as being of relatively unsuccessful people. Results of these studies showed that the degree of success attributed to photographs of others was significantly affected by the expectations arbitrarily given the psychological experimenters who had shown the photographs to the research subjects. Further research implicated the role of nonverbal cues in the mediation of these interpersonal self-fulfilling prophecies; experimenters tended to obtain the responses they expected to obtain even when their verbal communications to their research subjects were carefully constrained.

An important incidental finding from these studies was that male and female research subjects were treated quite differently by their experimenters. For example, experimenters were much more likely to smile at their female subjects than at their male subjects, and it seemed likely that this differential treatment of female and male subjects might have affected subjects' performance. This finding was quite troubling methodologically since it suggested the possibility that some of the sex differences* obtained in psychological research might be caused not by genetic, constitutional, or socializational differences between the sexes but simply by the fact that they were treated differently during the course of the data collection.

Subsequent experiments on the self-fulfilling prophecy showed that these effects could be obtained even if the subjects were animals. For example, in one series of experiments, half the experimenters were told that the rats assigned to them had been specially bred to be "maze-bright," while the remaining experimenters were told that the rats assigned to them had been specially bred to be "maze-dull." In fact, of course, all rats had been bred normally and were neither maze-bright nor maze-dull. Nevertheless, after only a few hours the rats that had been arbitrarily labeled maze-bright had become better maze-learners than had the rats arbitrarily labeled maze-dull.

If rats became brighter when expected to by their experimenter, it seemed possible that students might become brighter when expected to by their teacher. Accordingly, the Pygmalion experiment was conducted in which teachers were led to believe that certain children in their classroom would show unusual intellectual development. The names of these children (who did not really differ from their fellow students) were then given to their teachers. Subsequent intelligence testing revealed that those children from whom teachers had been led to expect greater intellectual gains, in fact, showed greater intellectual gains than did the children of the control group for whom no special expectations were created.

Subsequent research suggested that there were two major factors contributing to the mediation of teacher's expectation effects. (1) *Climate*. Teachers tended to create a warmer socioemotional climate for those students for whom they held more favorable expectations. (2) *Input*. Teachers tended to teach more material and more difficult material to those students for whom they held more favorable expectations.

More recent research suggested that teachers teaching verbal material to males and quantitative material to females (the so-called sex-inappropriate materials) showed greater hostility toward their students in nonverbal channels of communication (video cues alone) than did teachers teaching the so-called sex-appropriate materials to these same students. These bias effects were smaller for female than for male teachers, and they were smaller for more androgynous than for more sex-typed teachers.

Currently, research is under way that is designed to show the degree to which sex differences of many kinds are increased or decreased by the differential treatment of female and male members of our society. This differential treatment may sometimes be quite overt, even blatant; often, however, this differential treatment may be quite covert, subtle, and unintended. Indeed, such subtle differential treatment may be detected in less than a minute of social interaction.

References. Robert K. Merton, "The Self-Fulfilling Prophecy," *Antioch Review* 8 (1948): 193–210; R. Rosenthal, *Experimenter Effects in Behavioral Research* (New York, 1966, enlarged ed., 1976); R. Rosenthal, "Interpersonal Expectations: Some Antecedents and Some Consequences," in P. D. Blanck (ed.), *Interpersonal Expectations: Theory, Research, and Applications* (New York, 1993), 3–24; R. Rosenthal and L. Jacobson, *Pygmalion in the Classroom* (New York, 1968; expanded ed., 1992).

ROBERT ROSENTHAL

SEMIOTICS AND FEMINISM. *Semiological Theory.* Semiotics began with the early twentieth-century work of American philosopher Charles Sanders Peirce and Swiss linguist Ferdinand de Saussure. In Peirce's theory of reality, though we have direct experience of a world of things, we have only indirect knowledge of them through their representations in our thoughts.

Peirce called these mental representations *signifiers*, and the objects of the world of things he called the *signified*. He acknowledged that language is related to conceptual objects, more often than not, only by convention and that therefore reality might not be truly represented by the signs, but he also believed that the true relationship between the signified and the sign could, over time, be established by what the "community" or culture continues to reaffirm.

Saussure's *Course in General Linguistics* (1916) proposed a science called semiology (from a Greek word meaning "sign") that studies the life of signs within society. According to Saussure, semiology "would show what constitutes signs and what laws govern them" and would be a general science with importance to many fields of study, such as psychology and anthropology. Central to his thought, however, was the argument that language is the most important and the most characteristic or ideal of all the sign systems because it is the most arbitrary. Like Peirce, Saussure designated two parts of any sign: the "signifier" and the "signified." Unlike Peirce, he did not believe that a true relationship between the signifier and signified could be established in reality or in the community's continued reaffirmation, but only in the study of language as a system of signs that established differences among the signifiers.

Saussure focused on several distinctions within linguistics: (1) between paradigmatic relationships (the similarities of signs at the level of signifier and signified) and syntagmatic relationships (the connections between and among signs used in a particular speech act or utterance); (2) between *langue* (the language system) and *parole* (manipulation of the language system within a concrete utterance); and (3) between synchronic, relational, and diachronic (historical) linguistic analysis. Working toward establishing a rigorous science of linguistic analysis that would yield structural rules, Saussure's insistence that signs can be understood only within a system began the structural approach to the study of language and gave the methodological foundation to structural linguistics, which maintains that language structures the mind.

Building on Saussure's linguistics, Roman Jakobson demonstrated that the smallest units of meaningful language, phonemes, necessarily operate as systematically binary oppositions that produce structural patterns through the gradation and mediation of the phonemes, for example, voiced and voiceless consonants. The anthropologist Claude Lévi-Strauss, assuming that Jakobson's structural linguistics had established structural rules that governed all language and that all of human culture was an extension of language, used this linguistic theory to interpret his cultural data. Lévi-Strauss used the linguistic principles of polarity and homology to show what he thought were universal laws of signification. He was ambivalent about why he thought language rules would be universal.

Roland Barthes continued Saussure's and Lévi-Strauss' ambition to use the principles of linguistic structuralism to interpret culture itself. To Barthes, all cultural complexes, linguistic and otherwise, are systems of signs. The general conventions governing a cultural complex are considered to be the equivalent of Saussure's *langue*; the individual instance is *parole*. Moving beyond the work of Saussure, Barthes says that the signifier and the signified have indicative levels that begin a suggestive or associative process. To Barthes, the associative level was the same as myth, the surreptitious expression of the dominant values of the dominant class. Barthes shows that in all kinds of cultural products, such as advertisements, the signifiers are related to one another and express one or many myths. Such displays of myth control people without obvious coercion.

Jacques Lacan uses semiotics to develop his theories of psychological structuralism. Deeply indebted to Freud, Lacan studies the unconscious as a sign system. Saussure's belief in the primacy of language meant that reality was differentiated and structured by language. Freud had shown that the unconscious was highly structured and usually made known through language. Lacan theorizes that the unconscious is constructed as language develops in the child and that the child's mass of instinctual drives becomes differentiated by language. The desires do not go away but become the unconscious, which "speaks" through dreams and complexes in rhetorical ways. Among Lacan's suppositions is that the father figure becomes the "reality principle" that says a child must not be the same as its instinctual desires, that is, cannot have the mother. The father makes the child repress desire and identify with the father. The subject is radically split into its imaginary and symbolic selves.

Feminism and Semiological Theory. The political implications of language have made linguistic study imperative for feminists. Feminist language theory has sought to study possible sex differences in the language of men and women, sexism embedded in language, and the mechanism of women's oppression through language. The use of semiotic theory has been very important in these investigations through the use and examination of structural linguistics, psychological linguistics, and the cross-disciplinary nature of signs.

Feminists have used semiotics in the same two ways linguists in general have, that is, by stressing either methodology or theory. Structuralism, Saussure's tool for analyzing sign systems, has been a dominant method of linguistic study even by those feminists who were less accepting of Saussure's insistence that the signified and signifier are arbitrarily related. For the feminist who is more concerned with Saussurean theory, meanings are made possible by language and language structures, rather than by the expression of an individual's experience. Experience and the individual are products of the institutionalized system of signs, and both function accordingly.

Feminists have intensively researched the differences in the language used by men and women. Much time and effort have gone into the description of the differences in order to see if women have their own language and if the power of men is related to the language men use. This purpose often necessitates the use of Saussure's concepts of *langue* and *parole* and shows women's speech as *parole* or variation from the norm, *langue*, which white males speak. Critics, often feminists themselves, point out that researchers within the language are not value-free, and they perpetuate stereotypes as well as skew the evidence. To these critics, only painstaking empirical research to establish paradigmatic and syntagmatic differences based on what women actually say will reveal the truer structures of the language sign-system and possibly gender differences in use of the language.

Feminists have not only been involved in collecting and interpreting the descriptive data of difference between related language structures but also employed Saussure's use of contrast as a principle of linguistic structure. Many feminists have made use of binary oppositions in their linguistic analyses, assuming, as do most nonfeminist linguists, that binary opposition as an ordering device is universal and possibly innate. Other feminists have looked hard at this assumption. Some, like Dale Spender, say the feminine opposite often doesn't really exist. Other feminists, such as Luce Irigaray and Hélène Cixous, say that paradigmatic and syntagmatic analyses do not show that antonyms form a persistent logical structure in the language sign-system. The duality, they say, lies outside linguistics but is in no way shown to be innate. Feminist criticism of the linguistic structuralists' assumptions about the necessity for polarity wishes to show that sexual dichotomy is not necessary.

Feminists find that sexist language becomes very noticeable in linguistic structural analysis when some paradigms become unbalanced by too many or too few relational words for one sex. Furthermore, as feminists have pointed out, linguistic structures involving negative relationships are often heavy in words related to women. Mary Daly, Dale Spender, Kate Millett, and Kate Swift are a few of the better-known feminists who specialize in investigating sexist language. Although feminist linguists use the methods of Saussure, they usually reject Saussure and semiology's point of stress that the signified and signifier are arbitrary relationships that have meaning only within the sign-system, not in reality. They focus occasionally on changing reality and therefore language and changing the sign-system, which must be a very long and difficult task.

Feminists who stay close to semiotic theory as well as to semiotic methodology are almost all French as opposed to the British-American school of feminists, which has adopted much of Saussure's methodology and only some of his theory. In general, French feminists insist on the arbitrary nature of signs and have found that Lacan's psychological structuralism elucidates semiotics. Feminists point out that his theories demonstrate how male and female children enter into language differently. Although feminists have been concerned about the patriarchal basis of his theory, he does not claim that the formation of the unconscious is outside the sign-system of language, a sign-system that is based in arbitrary connections. On the other hand, Lacanian theory believes that there can be no language until the mother–child relationship is broken, and absence is felt. The phallus or penis represents the loss of the mother's body; therefore, symbol making is dominated by the penis.

As is true of most French feminist critics, Julia Kristeva both admires and criticizes Lacan's theories. Kristeva's work builds upon Lacan's by discussing its importance and implications for women, but she rejects his "anatomy is destiny" principle, which he inherited from Freud. Kristeva's contributions to feminist semiological criticism are very important. Luce Irigaray is probably Lacan's most adamant critic. She challenges his idea of the language sign-system as incorrect because women have a language of their own that is not acknowledged by patriarchy. Moreover, she challenges Saussure's idea that the signified and signifier have a one-to-one meaning instead of multiple ones. These are challenges to structuralism and Lacanian theory at their base.

Feminism has shown continuing interest in semiotic theory as it extends beyond the language sign-system to other sign-systems. Applying the concept of sign-system to cultural analysis, as Lévi-Strauss does, or to myth viewed and written about in cultural products, as Barthes does, has proved a fertile area for feminists. The exposure of the myths that those in power perpetrate so that their values become the values of all the people has brought every cultural ritual and product under the scrutiny of feminists. Barthes illustrates his ideas with visual cultural products. This helped direct feminist theory toward the whole area of cinema as a sign-system. Semiological theory can be applied to all areas of study, as Saussure envisioned it would be, and feminists have not hesitated to do so.

GLORIA STEPHENSON

SETTLEMENT HOUSE MOVEMENT was a way of working for reform while providing social services at the neighborhood level. Although Stanton Coit established the first settlement house in the United States in 1886, women established the next two. Jane Addams opened Hull-House in Chicago in 1889, and graduates from several elite eastern women's colleges began College Settlement in New York about the same time. By World War I, several hundred settlement houses, two-thirds of which were headed by women, were operating in the United States. Women outnumbered men even more on settlement staffs and as volunteers and supplied the movement with its most charismatic leadership. Jane Addams, author of the classic *Twenty Years at Hull-House* (1910), winner of the Nobel Peace Prize, feminist, and supporter of numerous reforms, is by far the most famous. Others include Lillian Wald, who began Henry Street Settlement and developed the visiting nurse concept; Mary Simkhovitch, founder of Greenwich House; and Mary McDowell, who established the University of Chicago Settlement.

The fact that women dominated it gave the early settlement house movement its character. The women were actively committed to reform. Furthermore, many of their reforms were of special interest to women. They promoted the adoption of public playgrounds and innovations in the public schools, such as kindergartens, home economics classes, and adult education in English and citizenship for immigrants. To improve slum housing, they campaigned for local housing codes. In advocating better working conditions, they were especially concerned about the plights of women and child workers. The settlement workers supported a variety of social welfare measures, including mothers' pensions, a local innovation that foreshadowed the federal program Aid to Families of Dependent Children. Finally, the women settlement workers were particularly prominent in the suffrage and peace movements. Advocacy of these reforms was combined with daily settlement programming and serving their disadvantaged neighborhoods by emphasizing work with children, clubs, classes, and day nurseries.

The settlement method in carrying out these activities also reflected the female influence. Many of the settlement workers literally "settled" in the poor neighborhoods they served by actually living in the settlement house. There they created an environment akin to the college dormitories they had recently left. For the women leaders, most of whom never married, the settlement house resident group provided a family substitute and a female support network. The resident group at Hull-House was most prominent. It included Alice Hamilton, a pioneer in industrial medicine; Julia Lathrop, the first head of the federal Children's Bureau; and Florence Kelley, the leader of the National Consumers League. All three maintained lifelong ties to the movement, which gave them an initial base for their reform operations and a system of allies on whom they could call. Many other women were involved with the movement only briefly, but the experience was of lasting significance. Frances Perkins, the first woman in the cabinet and instrumental in the passage of the Social Security Act, lived at Hull-House as a young woman for only six months. Other well-to-do women, such as debutante Eleanor Roosevelt, never lived in a settlement house but did acquire firsthand knowledge of poverty by volunteering their services. In the case of Roosevelt, her experience teaching calisthenics and dancing on New York's Lower East Side gave her a sympathy with the poor that she would later carry into the White House as our most politically active First Lady. Settlement workers believed in a "consensus" approach to reform, bridging class lines, "interpreting" the poor to the rest of society, and utilizing established channels to advance their causes. In accord with these more passive approaches, they eschewed confrontational tactics and militant rhetoric.

The number of female settlement heads began to decline after World War II. The decline was probably due to a variety of factors, such as the end of residence in the settlement house, the trend toward hiring male social work graduates as administrators, the need to influence male-dominated Community Chests, which came to fund most settlements, racial turmoil in changing neighborhoods, growing settlement work with male juvenile delinquents, and the demise of the earlier feminist movement. Nevertheless, settlements still produced some outstanding women leaders. Lea Taylor, head of Chicago Commons and president of the National Federation of Settlements, courageously campaigned for the integration of her Near West Side Chicago neighborhood in the face of repeated arson attacks. Her successor as president of the National Federation, Helen Hall, served on the advisory committee that shaped the Social Security Act and was influential in the initial planning of Mobilization for Youth, the prototype program for the War on Poverty—all while heading Henry Street Settlement.

By the early 1950s, women were a minority among settlement heads, but Margaret Berry still became executive director of the National Federation, probably because of her skill in getting people to work together. However, by the late 1960s, blacks and other minorities had moved into the majority of settlement neighborhoods and were demanding minority leadership, including the directorship of the National Federation of Settlements. At the end of 1971, Margaret Berry yielded her position to a black male. The emphasis in the black power movement on strengthening the position of black men further eroded the number of women settlement heads to 29 percent by 1973. However, the movement still has some outstanding women leaders, such as Patricia Sharpe, who was head of Hull-House from 1980 until her resignation in 1989 and at the same time was active with battered women's programs.

References. Mina Carson, *Settlement Folk: Social Thought and the American Settlement Movement, 1885–1930* (Chicago, 1990); Allen F. Davis, *Spearheads for Reform: The Social Settlements and the Progressive Movement, 1890–1914* (New York, 1967); Elisabeth Lasch-Quinn, *Black Neighbors: Race and the Limits of Reform in the American Settlement House Movement, 1890–1945* (Chapel Hill, N.C., 1993); Judith Ann Trolander, *Settlement Houses and the Great Depression* (Detroit, 1975); Judith Ann Trolander, *Professionalism and Social Change: From the Settlement House Movement to Neighborhood Centers, 1886 to the Present* (New York, 1987).

JUDITH ANN TROLANDER

SEX DIFFERENCES (gender differences, sex-, gender-related differences, sexual dimorphisms) refer to physical, behavioral, and personality characteristics that differ for females and males. The term "sex" is used for biologically-based categories, and "gender" is more appropriate when referring to psychological and behavioral differences.

A topic of concern of Western philosophers throughout the ages, the formal study of sex differences by behavioral scientists received its theoretical impetus from Darwinian theory and its greatest empirical boost from the psychological testing movement. The issue has been heavily politicized throughout its history, with "facts" and theory often being fashioned to alternatively support or challenge dominant social attitudes about acceptable gender roles.* Recent advances have made the biases in this work more explicit.

The two major points of controversy have been the existence (and magnitude) of sex differences and their cause(s). A related issue has been the relevance (or irrelevance) of this research to social policy and attitudes regarding the appropriate roles of women and men.

Research on the existence of sex differences has been marred by definitional problems associated with using broad, heterogeneous, and culturally biased categories of behavior and with numerous methodological problems, including flawed experimental designs, biased observational techniques, inadequate data analysis, and distortions in the reporting of results. A more subtle, but important, issue has been the way a sex difference is defined. Most research compares average scores for males and females to determine whether a statistically significant difference exists. Few such differences account for more than 1 to 5 percent of the total variance. There is always considerable overlap between the female and male distribution. Thus, "significant" differences may not reflect large differences between the sexes. Little attention has been given to testing interactive models in which gender differences could occur under some conditions but not others or in which the impact of environmental extremes are more variable for one sex than for the other.

Physically, Homo sapiens is moderately sexually dimorphic. Boys are approximately 4 percent heavier and 1 percent longer at birth. Other differences that emerge during development include greater male muscular strength, lung capacity, metabolic rate, and ratio of lean body mass to overall weight and greater female tactile and olfactory sensitivity. Many of these differences increase with sexual maturity, which is approached more rapidly by girls than by boys, are maximum in adulthood, and decline with old age. Although biologically based, the expression of many physical sex differences is environmentally dependent. For example, differences in body size are maximum in plentiful environments but are reduced in populations under chronic nutritional stress.

Females have lower morbidity and mortality rates throughout the mid- to late prenatal and early postnatal periods. With the exception of the higher incidence among females of some nervous system malformations and autoimmune disorders, males are more frequently afflicted with virtually every neurologic, psychiatric, and developmental disorder of early childhood. Some of these are mental retardation, autism, hyperactivity, dyslexia, epilepsy, cerebral palsy, learning and adjustment disorders, and schizophrenia. However, when females are affected, it is frequently with greater severity. The development of females also appears to be less adversely affected by environmental hazards. Nonmutually exclusive hypotheses that have been proposed to account for these differences include (1) X chromosome-linked disorders for which males are more susceptible, (2) hormone differences during gestation, (3) the female's greater physical maturity at critical developmental stages such as birth, and (4) immunological incompatibility between mother and male fetus that might lead to fetal damage. Some of these causal factors also have been proposed to explain other sex differences that appear in older children and in adults.

Lower female morbidity and mortality continue into adulthood. Some differences also reflect biological factors, such as the relative protection against coronary heart disease afforded women by ovarian hormones. But historical changes in differential life expectancy and even reversals to higher female mortality in some less industrialized societies point to important interactions with cultural factors. These include sanitation, nutrition, and the level and availability of health care, particularly as it applies to dangers associated with pregnancy and childbirth.* They also include the relative contribution to overall mortality made by high-risk behavior such as smoking, alcohol consumption, accidents, homicides, and suicides, for which males show a greater excess in some cultures than in others.

Psychological differences between women and men are less clear-cut and are strongly influenced by cultural and social factors. Regarding abilities, there is some evidence that girls develop verbal skills earlier and that women on the average score higher than men on tests of verbal abilities, although the differences are small. Male scores on certain tests of spatial ability are higher, as are scores on mathematical achievement. However, recent evidence suggests that these differences must be qualified by the type of test used and, particularly in the case of mathematical achievement, whether the comparison is made between those scoring at the extremes (highest and lowest achievement) or between overall average scores. Differences in interests and prior experience also affect these scores.

Analysis of gender differences in personality variables suggests an even greater role for cultural and social learning factors. Men are more aggressive, although this must be qualified by the type of aggression being considered, as well as by the nature of the target and the perceived consequences. The clearest difference is for physical aggression that produces pain or physical injury, which is more likely to occur between men than between women. While biological factors such as circulating hormone levels may contribute to sex differences in aggression, the complexity of these differences suggests that learned aspects of gender roles play a critical role in their development. Other personality differences are not as large. Generally, women are more influenced by group pressures for conformity and are more susceptible to social influence. Related to this is a continuing finding that women are more sensitive to the nonverbal behavior of others and are more able to interpret nonverbal displays of others' emotions. All of these differences have been more clearly associated with traditional gender role enactment than with biological factors. Other personality characteristics that are stereotypically associated with women such as sociability and nurturance have received mixed empirical support at best.

In adulthood, women show a higher incidence of disorders such as depression,* anxiety, and eating disorders (anorexia, bulimia, and obesity). Men exhibit a higher frequency of personality disorders and of psychosexual disorders such as paraphilias (e.g., fetishism), sexual dysfunction, and disorders related to gender identity (e.g., transsexualism). Men are also more likely to be alcoholic or take illegal drugs such as heroin, although women take more medically prescribed, mind-altering drugs such as tranquilizers. Men have much higher rates of criminal behavior, including assault, rape,* and property crimes. For both teenage and adult populations more males commit suicide.

Overall, data on physical and psychological characteristics of women and men demonstrate many similarities and some differences. Past attempts to explain the differences that do exist focused on either biological or cultural determinants, but most researchers now argue for an interaction of biological, environmental, and socialization factors.

References. K. Deaux, "Sex and Gender," *Annual Review of Psychology* 36 (1985): 49–81; A. H. Eagly and V. J. Steffen, "Gender and Aggressive Behavior: A Meta-analytic Review of the Social Psychological Literature," *Psychological Bulletin* 100 (1986): 309–330.

ANTHONY R. CAGGIULA and IRENE H. FRIEZE

SEX SEGREGATION. See OCCUPATIONAL SEGREGATION

SEXISM refers to the selectively unjustified negative behavior against women or men as members of a social category. It is particularly used to denote discrimination against girls and women. Research has suggested four levels of sexism—individual, social/structural, institutional, and cultural—that interact with each other. *Individual sexism* involves stereotypic attitudes and behaviors. Part of the definition of gender roles in Western culture involves assumptions about the types of occupations, lifestyles, and abilities that are held to be appropriate for women and men. Distinctions have been in agreement with traditional stereotypes about personality traits. For example, men typically have been described by a series of characteristics that reflect rationality, assertiveness, and competency (i.e., objectivity, self-confidence, independence). Occupations stereotyped by individuals as "male-appropriate" that are associated with these personality characteristics include attorney, police officer, physician, and corporate officer. Traits such as submissive, subjective, emotional, and gentle have been used to describe women. Traditional "female-appropriate" occupations include elementary school teacher, typist, librarian, and nurse. Both masculine personality characteristics and occupations are rated by women and men as more desirable, important, and prestigious.

Sexist attitudes may lead to sexist behavior or sex discrimination against girls and women. Both women and men have been found to value the professional work of men more highly than the identical performance of a woman. Women are likely to be evaluated as being as competent as men when their performance is (1) acknowledged by an authoritative individual, (2) judged on explicit criteria, or (3) successful in male-dominated occupations or activities. The possibility that equivalent performances by women and men are evaluated differently because they are ascribed to different causes has been well documented. A man's successful performance is attributed to skill, while a woman's identical performance is attributed to luck and/or effort. A man's failure is more likely to be explained by unfair allegation of cheating, while a woman's failure is attributed to lack of ability. This overall discrimination has been found to be greater in men, who maintain more stereotypic values than women.

Social/structural sexism involves the interaction between people in dyads or within groups. Examples of this type of sexism include nonverbal behaviors that connote status and power. For example, women tend to take less personal space around their bodies than men do. Women are also assigned to smaller spaces, such as smaller offices or shared offices. From this specific nonverbal message, individuals infer that men are more dominant and have a higher status than women; the person who controls more physical space is more powerful and more dominant and has a higher status than the person who controls less space.

Another example of social/structural sexism concerns research in adults' evaluations and expectations of infant development. Experimenters requiring adults to play with infants have generally found that parents and nonparents interact and treat infants differently on the basis of the perceived or actual sex of the infant. Girls, for example, received more distal stimulation (i.e., touch and holding). Parents describe their newborn daughters as soft, fragile, and petite, while they describe newborn boys as strong, firm, and muscular despite no differences in babies' birth length, weight, or neonatal assessment. Differences in adults' responses to infants are not attributable to the infants' behavior. Rather, the results are directly related to the adult responsivity as a function of the infant's sex.

Institutional sexism refers to the manipulation or toleration of institutional policies that restrict the opportunities for one sex as compared with the other sex. Examples of institutional sexism include the impact of sex ratios within occupations and academic institutions and the effects of occupational status on women and men. When women and men in the same occupation are compared, women make a lower wage than men, are less likely to be accepted into postgraduate programs, and are less likely to receive financial support for their education. In addition, there may be higher admission requirements for women than men applicants, sex quotas for admission, discrimination in the award of financial aid, and age restrictions on enrollment that constitute an interface between age and sex discrimination against women. Women in the labor force are employed primarily in traditional women's occupations. Thus, the segregation of job categories by sex represents an institutional pattern of discrimination against women.

Cultural sexism focuses on women's lower social status and power. For example, while girls and women make up almost 53 percent of the human race, they are systematically omitted in our daily speech. Since girls and women are the majority, it would be logical to use "womankind" to refer to humans. However, "mankind" is the generic term meaning human race. In addition, cultural sexism is practiced by mental health practitioners. These professionals typically have described a mature, healthy, and socially competent man or adult (sex unspecified) similarly and significantly different from a woman. A healthy woman is considered less independent, less adventurous, less aggressive, and less objective, while more easily influenced, more excitable in a minor crisis, and more conceited about her appearance than either a healthy man or a healthy adult. Women are thus in a double bind with respect to their mental health: they cannot be a healthy woman and a healthy adult at the same time. Their double-bind status causes women to incur some social penalty regardless of their behavior.

Being male and, by extension, "masculine" activities, occupations, and personality characteristics are perceived as normative; the female and the "feminine" are a deviation from the norm. Another example of this "male as normative" theme is the sex bias in the psychological research process. The hypotheses tested by a researcher are shaped by a theoretical model but also by gender-role stereotypes. Stereotypes about women have influenced the kinds of questions researchers have investigated scientifically. In addition, there appears to be good evidence that sexism exists in selecting participants for research. Boys and men are used more frequently as participants than girls and women are. In fact, some entire areas of research have been conducted using males only. In addition, results of research using boys and/or men are likely to be generalized and discussed as "individuals are . . . ," while research based on girls and/or women is likely to be generalized only to this sex.

Thus, sexism has typically existed in the field of psychology inasmuch as it has led to a psychology of male behavior, not human behavior. Furthermore, there may be a tendency for research conducted by women scholars to be considered less authoritative than reports by men. In recent years, a constructive alternative to sexist research methodology has been offered, namely, feminist methodologies. These suggestions for nonsexist research provide the beginnings for an alternative approach to the study of human behavior, a shift in viewing the world as revolving around men to viewing it as revolving around men and women jointly.

References. J. Doyle and M. Paludi, *Sex and Gender: The Human Experience* (New York, 1997); R. Unger and Saundra Unger, "Sexism: An Integrated Perspective," in F. Denmark and M. Paludi (eds.), *Psychology of Women: A Handbook of Issues and Theories* (Westport, Conn., 1993).

MICHELE A. PALUDI

SEX-ROLE SOCIALIZATION refers to the process whereby an individual's behavior, attitudes, and perceptions come to resemble those prescribed by society for persons of his or her gender. Several different theories have been proposed to explain this process.

The first theorist to write extensively and influentially on this topic was Sigmund Freud. Freud believed that children discover the anatomical differences between boys and girls at around 4 to 6 years of age and that this event has profound implications for their differential development. Girls are supposed to envy boys for having a penis (penis envy) and turn toward the hope of having a child as a substitute. Boys are supposed to feel both proud of possessing a penis and fearful of losing it (castration anxiety). They also perceive a rivalry with their father for the love of their mother and fear him because he has the power to castrate them. Boys must, in the resolution of this conflict, shift their primary identification from mother to father. Freud's theory of socialization is not widely accepted by most contemporary psychologists. Because of the unconscious nature of the processes he described, it is extremely difficult to test any of the basic propositions.

Social learning theorists propose that general principles of learning can explain the process of sex-role socialization. If boys and girls receive different rewards and punishments for various behaviors based on their gender, then they would be expected to come to behave differently. Such differential rewards and punishments would include those administered by parents, teachers, and other adults, as well as by other children. Empirical research confirms that in a number of ways parents consciously and unconsciously respond differently to the behavior of boys and girls.

According to social learning theory, observational learning also plays a major role in sex-role socialization. By observing the behaviors of others, in real life and in the media, children learn that some behaviors are rewarded in males but not in females and that some behaviors are considered more appropriate for one sex than the other. It is assumed that girls learn it is more advantageous for them to imitate their mothers and other females, whereas boys learn to imitate their fathers and other males.

A third perspective on sex-role socialization derives from the cognitive-developmental theory of Lawrence Kohlberg. Kohlberg proposes that a key ingredient in the process of sex-role socialization is that children acquire the concept of gender constancy, the idea that gender is an aspect of a person that does not change with time or situation. Prior to age 5 children do not consistently give correct answers or explanations to questions such as, "When a boy grows up, can he become a mommy?" or "If a girl plays football, is she a boy or a girl?" According to Kohlberg, when a child acquires an understanding of gender constancy, he or she then tries to model his or her behavior to the way society defines masculinity or femininity,* as shown in the behavior of others, on television, or in books. That is, the child is intrinsically motivated to become competent, and becoming competent is equated with conforming to society's sex-role expectations.

Support for Kohlberg's theory comes from research showing that children who have a thorough understanding of gender constancy are more sex-typed than those who do not. However, a major limitation of Kohlberg's theory is that differentiation of behaviors according to gender appears much earlier than age 5 or 6, when gender constancy is typically attained. Boys play more with cars and trucks and girls with dolls as early as age 2.

The most recent theory of sex-role socialization is that proposed by Sandra L. Bem. It is also the only theory that evolves from a feminist perspective on sex roles and on development. According to Bem, the process by which children become socialized to society's sex-role expectations involves gender-schematic processing, which she defines as "a generalized readiness on the part of the child to encode and to organize information—including information about the self—according to the culture's definition of maleness and femaleness" (603). Gender-schematic processing is a direct result of society's emphasis on the importance of distinctions based on gender, distinctions consistently enforced, but unrelated to the biological characteristics that define men and women. Thus, gender comes to be a primary way of reorganizing input from the world.

Some support for Bem's theory comes from studies showing that children remember pictures that are sex-consistent better than those that are sex-inconsistent. She has also developed her theory so that it includes a framework for planning and implementing approaches to raising children who are not limited by traditional sex-role stereotypes. For these reasons Bem's theory represents a major contribution to the field. Like Kohlberg's theory, it cannot explain sex differences in the behavior of very young children, who are unlikely to have developed gender schemas.

In conclusion, Freudian theory of sex-role socialization is not held in high regard by most academic and research psychologists, although it probably continues to have substantial influence outside these disciplines. Social learning theory is a very broad-based theory that has great explanatory power. The cognitive-developmental theory of Kohlberg remains somewhat influential because of its emphasis on the influence of cognitive factors and on the child as an actor on his or her environment, not merely a passive recipient of its influences of others. Bem's theory is important because of the introduction of concepts from contemporary cognitive psychology and especially because of the integration of theory about sex-role socialization with feminist contributions to psychological thinking. (See DIFFEREN-TIAL SOCIALIZATION.)

References. Sandra L. Bem, "Gender Schema Theory and Its Implications for Child Development: Raising Gender-Aschematic Children in a Gender-Schematic Society," *Signs* 8 (1983): 598–616; Lawrence Kohlberg, "A Cognitive-Developmental Analysis of Children's Sex-Role Concepts and Attitudes," in Eleanor E. Maccoby (ed.), *The Development of Sex Differences* (Stanford, Calif., 1966), 82–173; C. Travis and C. Wade, *The Longest War: Sex Differences in Perspective* (Orlando, Fla., 1984).

JANE M. CONNOR

SEX-ROLE STEREOTYPES. See GENDER STEREOTYPES

SEXUAL AMBIGUITY. Those rare cases in which babies are born whose sexual gender is ambiguous or indeterminate offer an instructive illustration of the power of socialization on gender identity. Sexually ambiguous infants, who may either appear to be female but be biologically male or appear to be male but be biologically female, are sometimes called pseudohermaphrodites. When this condition is recognized early, gender is usually assigned by parents or the physician on the basis of chromosomal sex. Hormonal treatments or surgical treatment may be performed in order to enhance the chromosomal gender. In extensive investigations, J. Money and A. Ehrhardt conclude that gender assigned and accepted can have greater impact on self-image and self-identity than does biological gender. In virtually all the cases they studied, sex of assignment and rearing proved dominant even if the individual remained biologically the other sex. Biological males raised as females on the basis of physical characteristics developed female attitudes and sex-role identifications. Apparently, gender identity can be acquired independently of genes and hormones. Further, when chromosomes and hormones are incongruent with the sex of assignment and rearing, the cultural and social influences will prevail.

Reference. J. Money and A. Ehrhardt, *Man and Woman, Boy and Girl* (Baltimore, 1972).

ALLEN SCARBORO

SEXUAL DIMORPHISM refers to differences in form between males and females of a species. The obvious and biologically significant difference in humans is in the development of the reproductive system. The male develops testes, epididymis, vas deferens, seminal vesicles, prostate gland, bulbourethral gland, urethra, and penis. The female develops ovaries, uterine tubes, uterus, vagina, and clitoris. The sex of an individual is ultimately determined by a single pair of chromosomes (1 of 23 pairs in humans), the "sex chromosomes," designated X (a large chromosome) and Y (a small chromosome). A mature ovum always contains an X chromosome. A sperm may contain an X also, in which case the fertilized ovum, that is, zygote, will be XX and develop female. A sperm may contain a Y chromosome, in which case the zygote will be XY and develop male. All other chromosomes are identical in males and females. The reproductive structures in both sexes arise from identical embryological tissue. If a zygote is XY, genes are present that lead to the production of testosterone by the embryo. In the presence of testosterone, male internal and external genitals develop. In the absence of testosterone, that is, in XX embryo, the female internal and external genitals form. The development, then, is in response to the hormone environment.

Additional anatomical differences between males and females develop at puberty. These secondary sex characteristics* are extragenital and include such traits as size, body shape, breast development, body hair, fat deposition, size of larynx, and pitch of voice. All of these characteristics are tissue responses to differing amounts of various sex hormones produced by the primary sex organs (testes and ovaries) and, in smaller amounts, by the adrenal cortex in both sexes. There is great individual variation in all these characteristics.

There is also an important physiological sexual dimorphism in the human brain. The hormones LH (luteinizing hormone) and FSH (follicle stimulating hormone), which regulate the reproductive systems in adults, are released from the anterior pituitary gland under the control of releasing hormones from an area of the brain called the hypothalamus. (This is a tremendous simplification: the regulation is a complex interaction between levels of various hormones and numerous physiological and psychological factors.) In the female this control is a cyclic phenomenon, underlying the ovarian and menstrual cycles. In the male this control is a steady-state phenomenon. Studies on nonhuman species indicate that the male or female pattern of release of hypothalamic hormones depends on the prenatal hormone environment.

Sexual dimorphism is widely reported or assumed to exist in a wide variety of behaviors (aggression, compliance, emotional response), skills (dexterity, tactile sensitivity), and abilities (verbal, mathematical, visual-spatial). Some of these reported differences simply do not exist at all. In other cases, there may be small differences in average score between males and females, differences that are much smaller and less significant than those between same-sex individuals. There are not sex-exclusive behaviors, skills, talents, or achievements. In these areas where differences do exist, the complex interaction of biology, early experience, socialization, and so on makes it impossible to conclude that there is an exclusively biological explanation.

FRANCES GARB

SEXUAL DIVISION OF LABOR is traditionally seen as a natural arrangement that forms the basis of all economic specialization and social structuralization leading to the formation of kinship groups and the family. Scholars have focused their attention essentially on the consequences, rather than the causes, of the division of labor. Actually, its origins and causes are not known, though various hypotheses have been developed using factual and assumed biological differences between the sexes as the basis for an explanation. Thus, greater physical strength of males, female involvement in biological and social reproduction—usually perceived of as a handicap rather than a contribution—and differences in moral and intellectual development have been understood to be causal factors with regard to the division of labor by sex. Based on these assumptions, the most prominent of all hypotheses is the male-the-hunter thesis, which identifies the male as the first and main provider in human history who became the center of all economic and social development. This position, however, fails to acknowledge the significance of women's contributions as gatherers in early human history and thus their role in economic and social development.

This traditional approach likewise fails to explain (1) the variations of gender-specific task assignments cross-culturally (e.g., spinning is a female task among the Guajiro from Colombia but a male task among the Kogi, also from Colombia); (2) the distribution of same-task assignments between women and men in the same culture (e.g., among the Jivaro from Ecuador women are the horticulturists, but maize planting and harvesting are an exclusively male task); and (3) the flexibility of gender-specific task assignments (e.g., among the Mazahua from Central Mexico, women and men have interchanged tasks traditionally defined as gender-specific for prolonged periods of time during national and cultural crises). Thus, the variations in the division of labor by sex and the flexibility exercised in certain situations indicate clearly that it is not biologically determined but strongly affected by the ideological concepts of a social system. This is important since it is not the performance of an activity but the evaluation of a task's significance that determines the cultural meaning of the sexual division of labor.

Certain areas of scholarship are especially important to help us gain a better understanding of this phenomenon. *Prehistory* provides data on the first work arrangements of humans, and, indeed, the gathering and hunting complex of our early ancestors represents one of the core issues in the discussion. *Mythology* gives data on people's rationalizations, justifications, and explanations of how and why they do what they do. Mythical materials contain rich documentation on the question of gender-specific task assignments that allows us to understand the "sex-role plans" of societies and thus their explanations of their system of a division of labor between women and men. *Cross-cultural studies of socialization* are crucial in helping us to understand the goals and ideas of a society since they provide data on how a people prepare the next generation for its roles. Socialization patterns clearly express the gender concepts of a society and the significance attributed to them.

As a result of the interest in consequences rather than causes, the focus on the present, and the strong male-oriented bias in research, traditional scholarship has produced a one-sided picture of the division of labor between the sexes. As a result, hunting has been overestimated in its significance as compared to gathering. Instead of interpreting the early patterns of labor division in their own historical context, scholars have applied contemporary Western patterns of gender conceptualization to the beginning of human history. Roles of females in the mythic traditions as creators, initiators, and agents have been downplayed, and cross-cultural socialization studies have focused, with few exceptions, on males only. Traditional research on the sexual division of labor has essentially ignored female activities related to pregnancy and childrearing as well as male involvement in this sphere. Because of this, terminology, methodology, and theories reflect a male-oriented understanding of labor and its role in the evaluation of people's contribution to society.

Because Western nations assume a universal meaning of gender-specific task assignment and assessment, which in reality ignores the wide variation cross-culturally, the existing hypotheses on the sexual division of labor have gained global significance affecting national policies and international programs.

References. G. P. Murdock and C. Provost, "Factors in the Division of Labor by Sex: A Cross-Cultural Analysis," *Ethnology* 12 (1973): 203–225; Helen I. Safa, *The Myth of the Male Breadwinner, Women and Industrialization in the Caribbean* (Boulder, Colo., 1995); Peggy Reeve Sanday, *Female Power and Male Dominance: On the Origins of Sexual Inequality* (London, 1981).

MARIA-BARBARA WATSON-FRANKE

SEXUAL HARASSMENT has been ruled by the federal courts as a form of sexual discrimination that is outlawed by Title VII* of the Civil Rights Act of 1964. The law was extended to the field of education by Title IX* of the Education Amendments of 1972. Unwelcome sexual advances, requests for sexual favors, and other verbal or physical conduct of a sexual nature constitute sexual harassment when (1) submission to such conduct is made either explicitly or implicitly a term or condition of an individual's employment or academic advancement, (2) submission to, or rejection of, such conduct by an individual is used as the basis for employment decisions or academic decisions affecting such individual, or (3) such conduct has the purpose or effect of unreasonably interfering with an individual's work or academic performance or creating an intimidating, hostile, or offensive working or academic environment (Policy statement, University of Minnesota).

Though sexual harassment is not a new phenomenon, not until the rise of the women's movement in the 1970s and 1980s did this issue become an important item on the public agenda. While codified in the 1964 act, in 1976, for the first time, a federal court ruled that job retaliation toward a female employee who turned down sexual advances constituted sexual discrimination (*Williams v. Saxbe*, 413 F. Supp. 654, 66 D [DDC 1976]).

In 1980 the federal Equal Employment Opportunity Commission (EEOC) published its definition of sexual harassment as an amendment to its *Guidelines on Discrimination Because of Sex*. This definition covered the aforementioned areas of sexual submission as an explicit or implicit condition of employment and specifically included mention of an intimidating or offensive working environment. Court rulings and EEOC guidelines have further held that an employer is liable when sexual harassment takes place, "regardless of whether the acts were authorized, and whether they are known or should have been known of by the employer."

Despite clear guidelines in federal rulings, issues of sexual harassment remain sensitive and difficult. Myths of the victim's "inviting the relationship" are so pervasive that women tend to expect a skeptical reaction to their complaints. This, when added to the fact that sexual harassment often occurs in a situation of an unequal power relationship, creates an environment in which many victims are reluctant to file charges. However, in the face of growing public sensitivity to these issues, this environment appears to be changing.

Sexual harassment is an issue that our society has long swept under the rug. As an increasing number of victims are refusing to remain quiet, and as an increasing number of men and women in our society are defining acts of harassment as an ethical as well as legal violation, procedures are being adopted to inform and protect potential or real victims. Professionals who work in this field, however, warn that the problems are more persistent and widespread than is generally acknowledged.

References. B. W. Dziech and L. Weiner, *The Lecherous Professor* (Boston, 1984); C. A. MacKinnon, *Sexual Harassment of Working Women* (New Haven, Conn., 1979).

BETTY A. NESVOLD

SEXUAL ORIENTATION in Western cultures refers to an enduring erotic, affectional, or romantic attraction to individuals of a particular gender. Sometimes *sexual preference* is used as a synonym, although this term can be misleading because it suggests a degree of conscious choice in sexuality that most people do not experience and implies that those with a stigmatized sexuality could choose (or be compelled) to change it.

Sexual orientation is usually characterized as either *homosexual* (a primary or exclusive attraction to individuals of one's own gender) or *heterosexual* (a primary or exclusive attraction to individuals not of one's own gender). The term *bisexual* is used to describe persons with attractions to both men and women.

Discussions of sexual orientation have been rife with controversy. Prior to the 1970s, most scholars and professionals presumed the inevitability and desirability of a heterosexual orientation and sought to explain the "etiology" of homosexuality, though never with great success. In 1973, the American Psychiatric Association (later endorsed by the American Psychological Association) declared that a homosexual orientation is not inherently associated with psychopathology. This recognition helped to broaden inquiry from the "problem" of homosexuality* to the question of how sexual orientation develops generally. More recently, the question has been raised whether the very notion of "sexual orientation" is culture-bound, historically recent in origin, and confined to specific societies.

Current discussions of sexual orientation are dominated by two opposing perspectives. Social constructionists view homosexuality and heterosexuality* as categories that have developed over time in particular cultures; the most radical proponents of this view argue that all sexuality is completely determined by social influences. Essentialists, in contrast, view homosexuality and heterosexuality as universal categories that describe a core part of human nature; some essentialists go so far as to explain sexuality entirely in biological terms, emphasizing genetic and prenatal hormonal factors. Choosing sides in the constructionist-essentialist dispute may be unnecessary, however, since the two camps generally focus on different components of sexuality.

Sexual orientation includes at least four components. First, *sexual behavior* refers to specific acts that are defined as sexual by the individual or society. As primates, humans are born with a highly plastic behavioral repertoire and are capable of a wide variety of sexual behaviors. Sexual behavior is not synonymous with sexual orientation. People with homosexual orientation can engage in heterosexual behavior and yet remain homosexual (e.g., lesbians* and gay men who marry heterosexually), and heterosexual persons can engage in homosexual acts without changing their sexual orientation (e.g., in a gender-segregated institution).

A second component of sexual orientation is *psychological attraction*. Whereas sexual behavior is what a person actually does, psychological attraction refers to what a person would like to do if the environment permitted. A homosexual person's attractions are to members of her or his own gender and may or may not be expressed behaviorally. The same is true for heterosexual persons with members of the other gender. Heterosexual attractions are more likely to be acted upon than are homosexual attractions because no societal sanctions prohibit the former (although cultural norms prescribe appropriate settings and practices). The Kinsey studies (*Sexual Behavior in the Human Male* [1948], *Sexual Behavior in the Human Female* [1953]) demonstrated that significant numbers of U.S. citizens have consciously experienced both homosexual and heterosexual attractions and behaviors during their adult lives.

The sexual essentialists have focused primarily upon sexual behavior and psychological attraction in their discussions of sexual orientation. This perspective permits them to generalize across cultures and historical periods (and even across species), since sexual behaviors (and, most likely, attractions) of all varieties are ubiquitous among humans.

Because constructionists assume that sexual behaviors and attractions are endowed with meaning by one's social group, they emphasize two additional components of sexual orientation: *social roles*, which attach cultural meanings and expectations to various behaviors and attractions, and *psychological identities*, or ways in which individuals define themselves in terms of their sexual behaviors and attractions and their associated social roles. Defined in terms of socioerotic identities and roles, sexual orientation clearly is not a universal phenomenon; it is a way of categorizing human sexuality that has developed in Western societies relatively recently.

A cross-cultural example is illustrative. In many societies of Papua New Guinea, male sexual behavior appears to be shaped largely by situational variables. Adolescent males are expected to engage exclusively in homosexual behavior for several years. Later, they are expected to marry a female and engage in heterosexual behavior with her. Sometimes married adult males participate in the homosexual initiation of adolescents. Although many individual males in these cultures appear to develop preferences for particular behaviors and attractions to particular types of partners, no social role or psychological identity exists comparable to Western notions of "the homosexual" or "the heterosexual." In the constructionist sense, therefore, sexual orientation is not a meaningful term for describing these societies. From the essentialist perspective, however, males in these cultures can be said to have a sexual orientation to the extent that they have an enduring preference for partners of one gender over the other (which can vary over their life span).

Failure to recognize the differing emphases of the essentialist and constructionist schools has clouded consideration of the individual origins of sexual orientation within Western cultures. From a constructionist perspective, individual sexual orientation clearly has a sociocultural basis, since the very concept is viewed as a cultural construction. Nevertheless, constructionists have not yet adequately explained how behaviors and attractions (from which individual identities are constructed) initially develop. The essentialists have focused on prenatal factors and early experiences that shape individual behaviors and attractions; they have paid less attention to sociocultural roles. Empirical research on the contributions made by these variables to adults' sexual orientation remains inconclusive, however. Despite recurring arguments for the primacy of genetic or hormonal determinants, neither has been shown to be sufficient or necessary for the emergence of a heterosexual or homosexual orientation in humans. Nor have retrospective accounts revealed clear differences in the life experiences of homosexual and heterosexual persons. Future research is needed to illuminate how patterns of behavior and attraction are shaped by prenatal and experiential variables and how they come to be manifested as socioerotic identities within a particular culture.

References. A. P. Bell, M. S. Weinberg, and S. K. Hammersmith, *Sexual Preference: Its Development in Men and Women* (Bloomington, Ind., 1981); J. Boswell, "Revolutions, Universals, and Sexual Categories," *Salmagundi* 58–59 (1983): 89–113; G. Herdt, *Guardians of the Flutes: Idioms of Masculinity* (New York, 1981); Alfred C. Kinsey, Wardell B. Pomeroy, and Clyde E. Martin, *Sexual Behavior in the Human Male* (Philadelphia, 1948); Alfred C. Kinsey et al., *Sexual Behavior in the Human Female* (Philadelphia, 1953); J. Money, "Sin, Sickness, or Status? Gender Identity and Psychoneuroendocrinology," *American Psychologist* 42 (1987): 384–399.

GREGORY M. HEREK

SEXUALITY (FEMALE) is a social construct mixing sensuality, reproductive life, eroticism, and gender-role performance, diffused throughout all social and personal life in activities, feelings, and attitudes. The social construct and thus the values, experiences, and behaviors differ widely over time and across cultures, and they deserve our closest analysis and attention once we understand that ideas of "proper" and "normal" sexuality have served everywhere to socialize and control women's behavior.

A major impact of contemporary feminism* has been to shatter old beliefs about what sexuality was, could be, or should be. New feminist research in history, psychology, anthropology, and political science has altered earlier, more biologically based ideas and definitions regarding female sexuality. Although it would be patently false to claim unanimity in women's studies on the subject of sexuality, much current thinking rejects transhistorical ideas and sees biological sexuality only as a precondition that is never unmediated by social and individual experience.

Women's sexual freedom and women's sexual victimization have been both more closely analyzed and more visible in recent years than ever before. At first, feminists wrote at length about the need for transformation. Women were to reclaim and redefine their sexual identity, rechoreograph their sexual acts, and develop a sense of themselves as agents of their own sexual expression and satisfaction. Feminists called for more and better sexuality education, focusing not just on the facts of reproduction and plumbing but on the politics of pleasure, the potential of relationships and of fantasy. For a while there was a thrilling sense of new possibilities. But in more recent years, the pendulum within feminist writings has swung away from an emphasis on the power of self-definition to an emphasis on how women are victimized by coercive sexual acts and dehumanizing sexual images. The central metaphor for female sexuality seems to have moved from masturbation and vibrators to rape.*

The female body has always been contested terrain in patriarchal society, and we should expect that controversies over female sexuality will rage among feminists as well as in the wider society. Controversy can enrich feminist theory* and practice if the debate is creative and not destructive. Several issues concerning sexuality can be identified as especially important in current feminist writings:

1. The relationship of women's sexual opportunities and experiences to their political and economic status. Sociological research within societies, anthropological studies of disparate societies, and even microanalyses of status relations within couple relationships show that sexual freedom and satisfaction for women are intimately connected to women's self-respect, self-knowledge, and the sense of having options in life, which are, in turn, directly related to women's socioeconomic opportunities.

2. Meanings of lesbianism and bisexuality. Women's love for, and bonding with, other women take a wide variety of forms in different historical eras, cultures, and subcultures. Herstorians are frustrated by the paucity of materials with which to illuminate the nature and extent of sexual expressions between women but have determined that the concept and category of "lesbian" was established within the past 150 years, during a time of great emphasis on sex-role identity and on the medical development of categories of sexual normalcy and abnormality. Bisexuality has recently become a visible issue for women, although its prevalence is uncertain. Its appearance indicates both the increasing sexualization of society and the continuing reliance on identity categories to describe sexual expression. It seems safe to predict that both lesbianism and bisexuality will remain contested categories into the next century.

3. Roles of medicine and psychology in shaping definitions of sexuality and, through the definitions, society's and women's sexual expectations and experiences. Much feminist writing has properly criticized the Freudian disparagement of clitoral pleasure, the sexologist's selection of certain acts as "foreplay" and others as "the real thing," the ready classification of women who are not "adjusted" to current norms as having various forms of pathology, and so on. Whereas feminists at first celebrated the scientific evidence recognizing physiological similarity between male and female bodily sexual response (including the equivalence of male and female orgasm), later writers underscored the danger of a biological hegemony that might result from valorizing allegedly "objective" research. Instead of promoting respect for diversity, such research seems to establish new norms and new abnormalities. Moreover, all medical research seems

inattentive to relationship issues and the social contexts of such relationships and pursues a definition of sexuality that is excessively privatized and apolitical.

4. Changing priorities within feminist discourse for different aspects of female sexuality such as imaginal fantasy, relational intimacy, and physical pleasure. Because sexuality has not typically been seen as a social construction with psychological, sociological, biological, linguistic, legal, and other meanings, writers have competed to identify *the prime aspect* of sexuality, as if such a thing existed in the material world just awaiting empirical discovery. This has led to some destructive name-calling, with feminists who might emphasize one aspect of sexuality or another being labeled "male-identified" or "separatist" by others.

5. The impact on personal and social experience of female sexuality in a world where women's control over their own bodies is limited by real and threatened violence. Feminist writings have tried to assess the impact of patriarchal society on women's sexuality. As a strategy of adjustment, for example, have women learned to eroticize subordination and objectification? What are the differences between societies that criminalize aspects of women's choice (e.g., regarding abortion,* prostitution,* homosexual activities) and those where woman's rights to freedom of choice and expression are better protected and longer established? Feminist awareness of the global diversity of women's sexual situations currently emphasizes the pervasiveness of exploitation, for example, trafficking, involuntary prostitution, rape as a weapon of war. Global economic pressures will increase economic inequality and continue to make women's sexuality a commodity to be sold or stolen.

6. The relationship of sexuality to reproductive function (e.g., interconnections of sexuality and menstrual cycling, the effects of pregnancy or having birthed or nursed children on psychological and physiological sexual experience, life span shifts in sexual meanings and needs). Some feminists have claimed that female menstrual rhythmicity has special consequences for women in terms of sexual desire and experience. Others argue that the embodied aspect of female sexuality is a social construct from stem to stern and that menstrual rhythmicity is on the same subliminal and trivial level as circadian rhythms in enzyme production. This type of pro-biological and antibiological standoff denies individual differences and seems less likely to be resolved than to continue vacillating in tune with political emphases within the movement at large.

7. The role of learning. Although we experience our sexuality as immediate (even instinctive!) and are usually unaware of acquiring and changing psychological meanings and valences, we know that learning must be involved from the evidence of cultural diversity and our own changes over the life span. How and when are bodily meanings and pleasures learned? Some contemporary feminists have turned toward psychoanalysis with its focus on unconscious meanings, preverbal learning, and the symbolism that adheres to actions and attractions. Others use the ideas of social learning and reinforcement theory to show how what society teaches women to value and rewards them for choosing is what gets internalized and practiced.

8. Male sexuality. Feminists are agreed that, in a patriarchy,* male sexuality sets

the frame and the norm for women and that female sexuality is constructed to serve men's interests. But other than casual, usually pejorative references to male sexuality as "genitally dominated" or "inherently aggressive," feminists have chosen to write very little on the subject. Men's preoccupation with correct sexual equipment and its performance at the expense of emotional communication or enjoyment of their sensual potential needs to be understood as a function of their desperate need to establish and maintain proof of their masculinity. Because of the power relations in patriarchy, such masculinity is actually more directed toward establishing men's status with other men than with women.

9. Child sexual abuse. Feminist therapists and activists have increased public awareness of the prevalence and serious consequences of child sexual abuse, influencing policy, research, and legislation regarding offenders. However, feminists are deeply split regarding allegations of abuse at day-care centers, claims of ritualistic or "satanic" sexual abuse, and the validity of repressed and recovered memories of childhood abuse. Unfortunately, the emphasis on children as sexual victims has eclipsed the image of children as sexual agents, and children's sexuality education is currently focused almost exclusively on issues of protection and danger.

These are issues of interest to one feminist, but their listing only serves to point to the complex and syncretic nature of the subject and to the idiosyncratic perspective of any analysis. Each of us has her own list, her own definitions, her own experience. Female sexuality is the totality, no less.

References. L. Duggan and N. Hunter, *Sex Wars: Sexual Dissent and Political Culture* (New York, 1995); L. Faderman, *Odd Girls and Twilight Lovers: A History of Lesbian Life in Twentieth Century America* (New York, 1991); S. Jackson and S. Scott (eds.), *Feminism and Sexuality: A Reader* (New York, 1996); N. McCormick, *Sexual Salvation: Affirming Women's Sexual Rights and Pleasures* (Westport, Conn., 1994); S. Thompson, *Going All the Way: Teenage Girls' Tales of Sex, Romance, and Pregnancy* (New York, 1995); M. Valverde, *Sex, Power and Pleasure* (Toronto, 1987); C. S. Vance (ed.), *Pleasure and Danger: Exploring Female Sexuality* (Boston, 1984).

LEONORE TIEFER

SEXUALLY TRANSMITTED DISEASE (STD) discriminates against women, because women are less likely than men to have early symptoms or may have no symptoms at all. Late diagnosis and absent or inadequate treatment increase the likelihood of complications such as a pelvic inflammatory disease (PID), which can be life-threatening or result in infertility. Fifty percent of infertility in women is attributed to STD (Morbidity and Mortality Weekly 8-6-93). Chlamydia* is the STD most commonly responsible for PID, with gonorrhea* being the second most likely responsible organism.

Because of women's potential reproductive role, the health implications of negative influences on pregnancy, birthing, and offspring health status are of grave concern to women and to society at large. Finally, certain STDs such as genital herpes and genital warts (human papilloma virus) increase the risk of cervical cancer. The presence of selected STDs such as genital herpes, genital warts, and syphilis appears to increase the likelihood of acquiring HIV (human immunodeficiency virus) disease if one comes in contact with the virus.

Public attention focused on HIV disease over the last two decades has dominated concern and overshadowed potential risks of other STDs. Fear and panic about HIV disease have brought into the foreground misconceptions people hold about women's role in the spread of STD. Women— especially women who work in the sex industry—are regarded as a reservoir of disease, when women are actually more likely to contract the virus from men than men are from women. Sex workers have been leaders in education about the practice of safer sex (*Off Our Backs*, 18). Increased risk of transmission of HIV disease in sex workers is more a function of workers' and customers' use of shared needles in intravenous drug use.

Men are rarely admonished to utilize recognition of early symptoms of STD as a means to protect their partners—women—against the risk of sexually shared infections. A number of articles in the popular media have continued to propose the view of women as the moral repository responsible for halting the spread of HIV disease by curtailing their sexuality, being monogamous, and insisting that men use condoms.

Prevention of STDs and Promotion of Vaginal Health. Even mutually exclusive sex partners may experience and transmit a STD. Organisms such as candida (yeast) or bacteria and perhaps the protozoan trichomonas can cause infection in one or both partners neither of whom has any outside sexual contact. This occurs because such organisms may be present in most or all women at subclinical levels (i.e., causing no known harm) and then flare up and reach an infectious level requiring treatment, sometimes of both partners. Also, a given level of an organism may cause no symptoms in one person, but a second person exposed to that level may develop an infection.

Even within a mutually exclusive sexual partnership it is wise to use a physical and/or chemical barrier to reduce risks of infection in the unaffected partner. A sexual relationship should not be considered mutually exclusive from a STD risk point of view until after three to six months and after a negative HIV test of the partner at greater risk.

The level of vigilance and preventive action should be greater in those who have not been in a sexually exclusive relationship for six months. The single most important measure for a woman to use with male partners is the latex condom. (Natural skin condoms have been found to be somewhat permeable, thus allowing the transmission of some organisms.) The female condom is a valid alternative since research and experience have indicated that it is as effective at preventing transmission of STDs as the male condom, but it is more difficult to use properly. It tends to slip from proper placement if not carefully inserted and checked, jeopardizing prevention of both pregnancy and STDS. Other barrier methods such as the diaphragm used with the spermicide nonoxyl-9 or other products containing this spermicide are also effective in preventing the spread of STDs.

Vigilance should also include establishing a rapport with a potential sexual partner that allows for exchange of information about a history of STD. This is critical. It is also important to look at sexual partners and avoid sexual contact with persons who have inflammation, discharge from the penis or vagina, or bumps or sores on the genitals.

Women who are sexual with women may mistakenly think they have no risk of STD. It is true that their risk is largely related to each woman's previous or current sexual activity with men, if any. Women who call themselves lesbian may be reluctant to disclose sexual activity with men, but as many as one-third of one group of lesbians surveyed reported sexual contact with men in the previous two years. Therefore, women who have sex with women need to talk about their risks and use barriers appropriately. Male and female condoms can be adapted for use between women, as well as a latex barrier, formerly called a dental dam from its original use.

To the extent possible, women must avoid experiences that traumatize the vagina and genital area. Products such as deodorant tampons, hard plastic tampons, which may damage tissue upon insertion, perfumed douches and soaps, restrictive clothing made of synthetic fibers, and a diaphragm left in place longer than eight hours without adequate lubrication jeopardize the health and natural resistance of the vagina. Sexual interactions that do not feel pleasurable should be interrupted in order to avoid possible injury that may predispose to infection. Often, allowing more time for sexual response or adding lubrication (water-soluble) is sufficient.

Promoting vaginal health should be an active process of maintaining nutritional balance, including cultured yogurt and adequate fluids in the diet, avoiding excessive refined sugar intake, and avoiding the use of antibiotics that are not absolutely necessary, since vaginitis is often a side effect of antibiotic therapy. Regular sexual response and exercising the muscles surrounding the vagina help to build resilience. Bathing before and after sexual interactions reduces the chances of getting and giving STDs.

Sexual interactions involving the anus and rectum are extremely high-risk for spread of infection both between persons and from the anal area to the urethra and vagina. Latex barriers and sufficient lubrication are critical to safe interaction. Additionally, the tissue of the rectal and anal area is delicate and easily damaged and may provide an entry point for bacteria and viruses. Being cognizant of vaginal, vulvar, and abdominal sensations helps women detect early signs of imbalance or early infection. If modification of diet and health behavior does not alleviate the problem, or if a woman becomes aware that she has been in intimate contact with a high-risk person or situation, she should consult a health professional.

Reference. *Off Our Backs*, 18 (1988).

ELAINE WHEELER

SHADOW PRICE is a measure for valuing services, such as household production, that are not sold on the market and that therefore do not receive a market price. This concept is used in economic analyses of women's labor force participation.

SUSAN B. CARTER

SHAKERS. Shaker religion began with the visions of Ann Lee, an illiterate Englishwoman born to working-class parents in Manchester, England, in 1736. Very little is known of her early life, but she was apparently greatly troubled by religious questions and by the nature of human sexuality. In 1758 Lee joined a small Quaker-inspired sect and found a degree of comfort in their ritualistic dances, or shaking, as this was called. In spite of her fears of sexuality she married a blacksmith and became pregnant eight times. Four of those pregnancies ended in miscarriage, and her four children died in infancy; her experiences with sex, pregnancy, and childbirth confirmed her antipathy to the sexual side of human nature. During her marriage Lee suffered great mental and physical anguish, which culminated in 1770 in a series of visions and the conviction that she was the female Christ and that sexual relations were at the heart of human depravity. After this point her sect of "Shaking Quakers" demanded celibacy; membership thus remained small.

In 1774 Lee and eight followers sailed to the American colonies. The exigencies of earning a living caused them to scatter temporarily, but in 1776 they reunited in Niskayuna, New York, and began building their order. Aided by the strong revival spirit sweeping the new American nation in the late eighteenth century, the Shaker sect began to grow. Missionary efforts led to the founding of 10 Shaker communities. After Ann Lee died in 1784, a follower, Joseph Meacham, took charge of the group (1786) and gathered it into an ordered union with a published set of principles. The Meacham system became the Shaker way. At their peak in the mid-nineteenth century, 6,000 Shakers resided in 18 communities in eight states, in New York, Massachusetts, New Hampshire, Connecticut, Maine, Kentucky, Ohio, and Indiana. Fewer than a dozen members remain today.

Shaker society was communal. Members gave up private property to the group when they entered the sect and, in turn, received material support from the group. The Shakers believed in manual labor for all and took pride in their productivity, their husbandry, and their craftsmanship. The group was organized into "families" of 25 to 150 persons (50 was the optimal number) that became the center of religious and economic life. A Shaker community might include several families. Men and women of the family occupied the same dwelling under the dual leadership of two elders and two elderesses. Although its members were strictly regulated because of the Shaker commitment to celibacy, the family worked together as an economic unit to provide subsistence for itself and surpluses for sale. Shakers divided the burden of labor quite traditionally; women performed domestic "female" tasks, while males did the heavier outdoor labor. The Shakers were not economic separatists. They gladly traded with the world and took pride in the high quality of the goods they manufactured or produced for sale.

Shaker theological beliefs and the practice of celibacy made the group quite controversial, and the controversy continues today as scholars try to determine whether Shaker beliefs and practices liberated or confined its women members. The Shakers believed that Ann Lee was the female Christ, and they incorporated the idea of the equality of women into their governmental structure. Women controlled their own sectors of the Shaker family, for example, and were equals in respect to visions and revelations. Shaker theology, however, emphasized the radical differences between men and women; men were active and positive in nature, while women were passive and negative. Shaker doctrine also defined women as more sexual and animalistic than men; women and their sexuality must be controlled if the Shakers were to achieve perfection. Because men and women were so different, a female Christ was necessary to act as intercessor for the female half of the human race. Ann Lee had come to save women. She was also necessary for the salvation of men, however, because until women reached a position of dignity and self-control, society would be unable to create a new order and attain perfection.

Scholars who argue the liberating aspects of Shakerism for women point to the female Christ figure; to the leadership roles that included elderesses as the equals of elders; and to the replacement of the patriarchal family, childbirth, and motherhood with celibate communalism. Those who see Shakerism as less than liberating for women stress the theology that emphasized biological differences and the economic division of labor, which was very traditional. These scholars do concede, however, that the opportunity for religious leadership among the Shakers was empowering for Shaker women.

One active Shaker community remains. Seven women maintain the colony at Sabbathday Lake, Maine, where they continue their faith's rich musical and cultural practices. Historic Shaker designs in architecture, furniture, fabrics, and furnishings as well as their unique musical heritage are widely celebrated as vital influences on the American artistic and folk traditions.

References. Ken Burns and Amy Stechler Burns, *The Shakers—Hands to Work, Heart to God* (Florentine Films, Direct Cinema, 1985); Marjorie Proctor-Smith, *Women in Shaker Community and Worship* (Lewiston, N.Y., 1985); Suzanne Skees, *God among the Shakers: A Search for Stillness and Faith at Sabbathday Lake* (New York, 1998).

PAULA M. NELSON

SHAKESPEARE, FEMINIST CRITICISM OF. The first book-length work of American feminist criticism of Shakespeare appeared in 1980—a decade after Kate Millett's pioneering *Sexual Politics* demonstrated the relevance of the women's movement for literary criticism. However, a substantial body of work was published during the period 1980 to 1985, thus establishing a distinctive field with its own internal debate. The Modern Language Association (MLA) Bibliography Online confirms this growth of interest; in a September 1979 article in *Database*, Eileen M. Mackesy reported 16 records for a computer search combining the terms "Shakespeare" and "women," while the same search covering material from 1981 through August 1997 retrieved 326 entries.

The study of women in Shakespeare has not been a self-contained, marginal enterprise. From the outset it has been clear that the reassessment of female characters has direct implications for the status of male characters and for the status of Shakespeare. The ultimate issue is succinctly formulated in the introduction to *The Woman's Part* (Lenz, Greene, and Neely): "The extent to which Shakespeare aligns himself with patriarchy, merely portrays it, or deliberately criticizes it remains a complex question, one that feminist criticism is aptly suited to address."

One way to preserve the complexity and openness of this question is to assume that Shakespeare cannot be usefully labeled either misogynist or feminist since he occupies an intermediate position between these extremes. The dominant mood of a particular play may tilt toward one direction or the other without ever reaching the simple stance of either pole. Shakespeare's drama offers a mixture of uncritical investment in patriarchal structures and critical exploration of them, but the degree of awareness fluctuates and must be decided on a case-by-case basis. No one formula will suffice for all the plays, so the question is never settled in advance.

In order to assess Shakespeare's relation to the sexual politics in his drama, it is important to refine and clarify the concept of patriarchy—to see that the plays contain two sets of patriarchal values, not just one. A distinction between ruthless and benevolent versions of patriarchy avoids the claim that Shakespeare magically transcended patriarchal attitudes. Shakespeare's frequent undermining of tyrannical patriarchy demonstrates the existence of his critical standards and insight. His frequent endorsement of benevolent patriarchy shows that he remains enmeshed in the assumption that social harmony depends on male control, sensitively applied.

For example, the evaluation of male bonds in *As You Like It* leads to a reappraisal of comedy and of the links between genre and gender. The standard view that, whatever suffering women undergo at the hands of deluded men in the tragedies, female characters are allowed to come into their own in the comedies is revised. Rosalind's power has been overestimated because the countervailing force of male alliance has not been sufficiently taken into account. We cannot celebrate the occasions of Shakespeare's achievement of mutuality between men and women without also sharply noting that this mutuality is not unqualified but is strictly limited by a division of labor and power according to gender. Such mutuality does not constitute equality or independence for women.

In its first stage, feminist criticism of Shakespeare has produced fresh insights on a wide range of issues, including family roles, courtship and marriage, male bonding, female bonds, gender and genre, androgyny, and the boy-actor convention. The very success of this effort has led at the end of 1985 to a retrospective pause focusing on the questions, Has feminist criticism of Shakespeare finished its work? and What should be the next step? While it is impossible to predict the future course of the study of women in Shakespeare, there is a strong prospect for greater emphasis on cultural history and, in particular, on increased interaction between feminist criticism and new historicism—a line of development exemplified by Carol Thomas Neely's seminar on "Images of Gender and Power in Shakespeare and Renaissance Culture" at the World Shakespeare Congress in April 1986. Three preliminary observations can be made here about the possible combination of feminist and new historicist approaches.

First, current work suggests that the study of Queen Elizabeth as an enormously powerful woman cannot be used to disprove the fundamentally patriarchal character of Elizabethan culture and of Shakespeare's work. Allison Heisch shows that Elizabeth exercised power by employing rather than resisting gender stereotypes, while Louis Adrian Montrose analyzes how Shakespeare's emphatic patriarchal design in *A Midsummer Night's Dream* undercuts the nominal praise of Elizabeth.

Second, research on women in the period is a major trend, raising the question of how this material will affect our image of Shakespeare (*Women in the Renaissance*; Henderson and McManus; Hannay; Rose). Though the eventual impact of this new work cannot be anticipated, the likelihood now is that the contrast between actual women and Shakespeare's fictional women will be decisive, a contrast that may highlight the filtering effect by which Shakespeare narrows the range of possibilities open to historical women to create his own restricted version of women.

Third, a general consideration of the proper use of historical context is needed. Nonfeminist critics may raise the historical issue to block feminist approaches to the study of gender in Shakespeare; these are ruled out of bounds because Shakespeare is presented as a product of his times for whom feminist criticism is anachronistic and invalid. To this charge, the feminist critic answers that gender was not invented in the twentieth century and that Shakespeare's powerful dramatization of conflict between men and women and the intensity of his language in this regard demonstrate his probing of gender conventions. This reply is necessary but not in itself sufficient, however. The ultimate level of analysis is located in the critic rather than in the character or author since the critic provides the final perspective on patriarchal values—for a full discussion, see Peter Erickson. The feminist critic must acknowledge that our twentieth-century vantage point helps to make this perspective possible and must therefore squarely face our historical difference from Shakespeare.

The crucial point is that there are two distinct ways to respond to the question of historical difference. One way is to suggest that coming to terms with difference means simply to accept Shakespeare's perspective. This "love-it-or-leave-it" logic implies that if one cannot be satisfied with the Shakespearean ethic and make the best of it, then it is illegitimate to keep working on Shakespeare, and one ought to shift one's interest to contemporary women writers whose values one can find more compatible. One sign that feminist Shakespearean critics are vulnerable to this pressure is the attempt to avoid this difficulty by striving to make Shakespeare more feminist or transcendent than he is, to reduce expectations, and to settle for what one can get. Particularly with the late romances, the temptation can be strong to redeem Shakespeare and to make things come out right in the end. The result is that some feminist criticism becomes virtually indistinguishable from the traditional account exemplified by D. W. Harding, who asserts that the dramatist had "worked through" earlier problems with women. But the happy ending to Shakespeare's career is produced by a one-sided, idealized view that ignores the continuing problematic aspects of male–female relations. This false optimism may seem preferable when the price to be paid for accuracy and the full integrity of feminist critique is made to appear negative—when feminist criticism is alleged to lead to a sense of loss and sadness because one is cut off from emotional participation in Shakespeare's work and condemned to barren repetition of feminist attack. But we are not limited to these two unpalatable choices.

Another way to approach the question of historical difference is to view the use of historical perspective as a two-part process that involves not only attending to Shakespeare's historical position but also recognizing our own. Feminist criticism of Shakespeare engages the split between his past and our present by experiencing historical difference as a source of strength rather than weakness. One must make the negative criticisms of the literary tradition in order to take the positive step of revising it. Shakespeare will continue to hold a preeminent place in the canon of Western literature, but not as an unalterable fixture; our understanding of him will be decisively changed. Feminist criticism reexamines the claim that Shakespeare is "not for an age but for all time" by differentiating between what is enduring and what is not. Feminist Shakespeareans gratefully acknowledge and savor the lasting power of his verbal and dramatic brilliance, but without acceding to the pretense that his truths are permanent, as though one could find in Shakespeare an ethic that would be adequate to the lives we are living now. Studies that pursue a double focus by placing Shakespeare in relation to modern writers include Marianne Novy, *Women's Re-visions of Shakespeare, Cross-Cultural Performances*, and *Engaging with Shakespeare* and Peter Erickson.

From the perspective of 1995, what stands out as the single most important development in feminist Shakespeare criticism is the addition of race as an analytic category (Loomba; Erickson, "Representation of Blacks"; Hendricks and Parker; Hall). If *The Woman's Part* in 1980 is the symbolic landmark for the beginning of feminist criticism of Shakespeare, then *Women, "Race," and Writing* nearly 15 years later marks the start of a collective move toward a more inclusive feminist interpretation that encompasses race as well as gender.

References. Janet Adelman, *Suffocating Mothers: Fantasies of Maternal Origin in Shakespeare's Plays, Hamlet to the Tempest* (New York, 1992); Linda Bamber, *Comic Women, Tragic Men: A Study of Gender and Genre in Shakespeare* (Stanford, Calif., 1982); Peter Erickson, *Patriarchal Structures in Shakespeare's Drama* (Berkeley, Calif., 1985); Peter Erickson, "On the Origins of American Feminist Shakespeare Criticism," *Women's Studies* 26, 1 (1997): 1–26; Peter Erickson, "Representation of Blacks and Blackness in the Renaissance," *Criticism* 35 (1993): 499–526; Peter Erickson, *Rewriting Shakespeare, Rewriting Ourselves* (Berkeley, Calif., 1991); Peter Erickson, "Shakespeare and the 'Author-Function,' " in Peter Erickson and Coppélia Kahn (eds.), *Shakespeare's "Rough Magic": Renaissance Essays in Honor of C. L. Barber* (Cranbury, N.J., 1985); Shirley Nelson Garner and Madelon Sprengnether (eds.), *Shakespearean Tragedy and Gender* (Bloomington, Ind., 1996); Gayle Greene and Carolyn Ruth Swift (eds.), *Feminist Criticism of Shakespeare, Women's Studies* 9, 1–2 (1981–1982); Kim F. Hall, *Things of Darkness: Economies of Race and Gender in Early Modern England* (Ithaca, N.Y., 1995); Margaret P. Hannay (ed.), *Silent But for the Word: Tudor Women as Patrons, Translators, and Writers of Religious Works* (Kent, Ohio, 1985); D. W. Harding, "Shakespeare's Final View of Women," *Times Literary Supplement* (November 30, 1979); Allison Heisch, "Queen Elizabeth I and the Persistence of Patriarchy," *Feminist Review* 4 (1980): 45–75; Katherine Usher Henderson and Barbara F. McManus (eds.), *Half Humankind: Contexts and Texts of the Controversy about Women in England, 1540–1640* (Urbana, Ill., 1985); Margo Hendricks and Patricia Parker (eds.), *Women, "Race," and Writing in the Early Modern Period* (London, 1994); Jean E. Howard, *The Stage and Social Struggle in Early Modern England* (London, 1994); Lisa Jardine, *Still Harping on Daughters: Women and Drama in the Age of Shakespeare* (Sussex, England, 1983); Coppélia Kahn, *Man's Estate: Masculine Identity in Shakespeare* (Berkeley, Calif., 1981); Carolyn Ruth Swift Lenz, Gayle

Greene, and Carol Thomas Neely (eds.), *The Woman's Part: Feminist Criticism of Shakespeare* (Urbana, Ill., 1980); Ania Loomba, *Gender, Race, Renaissance Drama* (Manchester, England, 1989); Louis Adrian Montrose, " 'Shaping Fantasies': Figurations of Gender and Power in Elizabethan Culture," *Representations* 2 (Spring 1983); Louis Adrian Montrose, *The Purpose of Playing: Shakespeare and the Cultural Politics of the Elizabethan Theatre* (Chicago, 1996), 61–94; Carol Thomas Neely, *Broken Nuptials in Shakespeare's Plays* (New Haven, Conn., 1985; Urbana, Ill., 1993, with new preface); Marianne Novy, *Love's Argument: Gender Relations in Shakespeare* (Chapel Hill, N.C., 1984); Marianne Novy (ed.), *Cross-Cultural Performances: Differences in Women's Re-visions of Shakespeare* (Urbana, Ill., 1993); Marianne Novy, *Engaging with Shakespeare: Responses of George Eliot and Other Women Novelists* (Athens, Ga., 1994); Marianne Novy (ed.), *Women's Re-visions of Shakespeare* (Urbana, Ill., 1990); Mary Beth Rose (ed.), *Women in the Middle Ages and the Renaissance: Literary and Historical Perspectives* (Syracuse, N.Y., 1985); *Women in the Renaissance*, special issue of *English Literary Renaissance* 14 (Autumn 1984); Valerie Traub, *Desire and Anxiety: Circulations of Sexuality in Shakespearean Drama* (London, 1992); Valerie Wayne (ed.), *The Matter of Difference: Materialist Feminist Criticism of Shakespeare* (Ithaca, N.Y., 1991).

PETER ERICKSON

SHEKHINAH is a feminine Hebrew noun designating the divine indwelling presence, perceived as God's immanent, nurturing aspect; sometimes personified as a divine mother or bride. *Shekhinah* is especially important in Jewish mysticism, where some traditions say the universe is in a state of disharmony, with the masculine, infinite element of God separated from the feminine, accessible *Shekhinah*. Humanity's goal is to restore harmony to the cosmos by reuniting the male and female aspects of the deity, a union often described with erotic imagery. This is a rare instance of the feminine having any part in Jewish mysticism or, indeed, in any Jewish thinking about the divine. For some contemporary Jewish feminist theologians *Shekhinah* is a preferred divine designation. (See JEWISH FEMINIST THEOLOGY.)

References. Arthur Green, "Bride, Spouse, Daughter: Images of the Feminine in Classical Jewish Sources," in Susannah Heschel (ed.), *On Being a Jewish Feminist: A Reader* (New York, 1983), 248–260; Moshe Idel, "Sexual Metaphors and Praxis in the Kabbalah," in David Kraemer (ed.), *The Jewish Family: Metaphor and Memory* (New York, 1989), 197–224.

JUDITH R. BASKIN

SISTER FORMATION CONFERENCE was a grassroots organization among American women that was religious, formed to meet the needs of changing times. Its specific goal was to upgrade and integrate the intellectual, professional, social, and spiritual education of women religious. From 1954 to 1964 the conference functioned within the National Catholic Educational Association. In 1964 it was suppressed by the Vatican as an independent entity. The conference anticipated many of the reforms of Vatican Council II and prepared sisters for carrying them out. Its archives are housed at Marquette University.

References. Ritamary Bradley (ed.), *Sister Formation Bulletin*, 1954–1964; Mary Schneider, *The Transformation of American Women Religious* (Notre Dame, Ind., 1986).

RITAMARY BRADLEY

SLAVES, AFRICAN AMERICAN. Their experience of slavery began when the first Africans arrived in the American colonies in 1619. At that time they were free persons indentured for a period of four to seven years. As indentured servants, African women labored beside African men and white settlers to develop the first communities in the Virginia colony. As labor force needs became difficult to solve, laws were created placing Africans in permanent servitude, and for the next 240 years, slavery was imposed on African people.

The African women torn from their homeland and forcibly brought to the Western Hemisphere came with a culture and a mind-set. They brought a sense of pride based on their various roles in Africa as landowners, farmers, leaders of state, entrepreneurs, and family members. Their ability to shape their own culture and values now served to facilitate their survival and their involvement in creative living.

As the institution of slavery was systematically and deliberately imposed on them, this quality of competence and this African frame of reference served as resources in confronting new experiences in an unfamiliar and unfriendly land. The artistic and creative qualities of African women were ignored as their skills, intellectual abilities, and physical strengths were exploited by whites. They were unpaid agricultural workers on large plantations and small farms and factory workers in cities. Normally the slave women worked 14 hours a day, but it was not uncommon for the workday to last 16 to 18 hours, seven days a week. The so-called aristocrats of bondage who worked in the "big house" were on 24-hour call under the constant watch of the white family. Whether in the field or home of the white family, black women were expected to produce a predetermined amount of work.

The slave women working in the "big house" maintained the home, serving as laundresses, housemaids, cooks, and nurses. They planned menus and developed recipes using a combination of ingredients, spices, and seasonings from Africa and the colonies. They were early fashion designers who spun, wove, and knitted clothing for the members of the white household. They created doilies and niceties for the homes of the mistresses and from the scraps made things to make their own cabins pleasant and attractive. The homes of the white masters were supposedly favored places to work. However, those who labored there were often one mistake or a punishment away from the tobacco, rice, indigo, or cotton fields, where the majority of slave women worked. Black women cleared the land, plowed, and drove single and double mule teams; they ginned, sorted, and separated foreign particles from the cotton; stacked and threshed the rice; and ginned sugarcane. On smaller farms the fieldwork was more varied; gender was not used in determining the type of work expected from African women. They chopped and hauled wood, cut trees, and rolled logs. At times they were seen repairing roads, pitching hay, and putting up fences. A few were skilled carpenters, tanners, blacksmiths, and copper workers.

Although most African American slave women were agricultural workers, a few labored in factories. It was not uncommon for factories to own their own labor force. The mines, cotton and woolen mills, saltworks, and foundries introduced slave women to a new work experience. They processed food and tobacco, refined sugar, milled rice, and tapped turpentine trees. They were forced to cord wood, load ore in furnaces, lay railroad tracks, dig ditches, and pull trams in the mines. They faced many hazards in and around the factories: wild animals, toxic materials, fires, and poisonous snakes, as well as bodily injury or loss of limbs suffered from equipment without safety devices.

While many worked the rigorous schedule in the factories, fields, or white homes, others were hired out to earn additional funds for the slave master. In such situations some black women were able to earn extra money and purchase their freedom. Independent efforts such as this exemplify the drive of slave women to exercise control and find creative ways to have some say over their lives.

The slave quarters afforded slave women the greater opportunity for self-direction. In the church, African American women exhibited leadership qualities as preachers and singers. In bush-harbors (informal churches) religious ceremonies held in secret allowed slave women the opportunity to sing and pray to a God they believed would free them. There they could address their cruel treatment by their masters.

A few slave women were conjurors and fortune-tellers and were feared by both whites and blacks because of their supposed power. Older female slaves were recognized for their knowledge of medicine and midwifery and as herbalists. These women prepared potions and remedies from roots, cedar gum, cotton seeds, camphor, and herbs. They also aided in the birth of black and white children. Their African background provided them with a knowledge of obstetrics and cesarean section. Often they treated childhood diseases and as nursemaids reared and cared for white and slave children alike. In the slave community and the "big house," slave women treated common ailments, minor cuts, and wounds.

The slave family cushioned its children against the shock and pain of slavery and offered them support in understanding their life situation. In spite of the long workday, women found time to socialize and spend time with their children and husbands. They shared folktales and had social dances and picnics. Women worked together to make quilts, cultivate gardens, and support the family with as many comforts and conveniences as possible. Although not permitted to marry in the Euro-American way or to maintain African family traditions, slave men and women were committed to each other and their children.

This commitment to the family, particularly the children, limited the control slave women could exercise over their home and work life. They responded to cruel treatment in ways that would not cause them to be sold away from loved ones or create conflict between their household and that of the master. Although they could not strike or quit, they exercised what control they could. Slaves organized work slowdowns, damaged or destroyed equipment and products, and refused to work, and a few ran away. Some black women responded to cruelties by striking the master or mistress or by giving them a verbal lashing. In fact, a slave woman could make the life of a mistress very miserable and uncomfortable. But such acts of resistance could meet with severe retaliation. Cuts with butcher knives, brandings, scaldings with boiling water, and beatings were just a few of the punishments that frequently resulted in permanent scarring, mutilations, and death.

Such punishments were inflicted on both men and women. Throughout slavery African women suffered the same barbarous treatment as men and were required to bring the same strength and productivity to the work situation. However, female slaves had an additional burden to bear: they were victims of sexual abuse and rape by their white masters and any other white males who had access to them. As breeders their value was measured in terms of their ability to produce many children.

This sexual coercion and forced role as instruments of fertility made childbearing a dilemma—motherhood was both a joy and a strain. The joy of giving birth was clouded by the knowledge that the child would become the chattel of the slave master and be subjected to various forms of cruel treatment.

During their entire pregnancy, slave women maintained the same work routine. Some were relieved of their work responsibilities a few weeks before giving birth, but after birth they were given only a few days off. They received little or no physical care, and infant mortality was high. Numerous pregnancies, hard work, poor working conditions, and the absence of physical care resulted in backaches, infected uteruses, fever, dysentery, and worms. These poor health conditions were not conducive to healthy births, so those babies who survived were fortunate.

The girl babies who survived the trauma of birth and reached the age of 5 were expected to pick burrs from the wool and seeds from the cotton and spin thread. Between the ages of 6 and 12 years, the young girls performed numerous tasks in the fields and "big house." In the home of the mistress they were instructed to make beds, wash and iron clothes, help prepare and serve snacks, and meet the personal needs of the white mistress and her family. Young slave girls served drinks, fanned flies, and made the fires in the chilly bedrooms. They were expected to gather the eggs, pluck the chickens for the evening meal, drive the cows, and act as scarecrows in the fields. They carried food and water to the field hands. These many simple tasks were preparation for their role as adult slave women.

The restraints placed on the childhood of slave girls were enormous. They prepared them for the limited control over their lives as adult slaves. However, in spite of all restrictions, slave women contributed to the vitality of black life and, at great sacrifice to their own race, contributed to the growth and development of this country.

References. Angela Y. Davis, *Women, Race and Class* (New York, 1981); Jacqueline Jones, *Labor of Love, Labor of Sorrow* (New York, 1985); Gerda Lerner, *Black Women in White America* (New York, 1972).

ELEANOR SMITH

SOCIAL FEMINISM is feminist activity directed toward reforms affecting the health and welfare of women, homes, and family rather than toward women's rights. William L. O'Neill coined the term to distinguish between what he called "hard-core" or "extreme" feminists and the larger, less radical group of "social" feminists who were more interested in social reform than in equal rights.

Since O'Neill's first use of it, the term has been associated especially with those women activists from the Progressive movement in the 1890s who worked through organizations such as the League of Women Voters, the Parent-Teacher Association, and the National Consumer's League for social justice causes. Their efforts to increase government intervention into health and social welfare issues led to protective legislation for women workers, child labor laws, and other social reform measures. In general, they held the traditional view of women's sphere, accepted the necessity of different treatment of women, and opposed the Equal Rights Amendment because it could wipe out the protective legislation they had worked to achieve. The disagreement between social feminists and the National Women's Party on this issue developed a serious rupture within the ranks of women activists.

By the second half of the 1920s, the social reform impulse declined, and social feminists had to take a defensive stance as clubs once devoted to reform became social and professional organizations without broad reform goals. Charges of communism rising out of the Red Scare and the "Spider Web Charts," attempts to link leading social feminists with international radicals in a Bolshevik conspiracy to take over America, caused social feminist organizations to become much more conservative in tone and in commitment.

As the depression refocused attention on the need for social welfare, social feminists trained in settlement house and volunteer agency work entered the New Deal and were crucial to the social legislation of the administration. (See NEW DEAL.) But as the women who entered the federal government during Roosevelt's first term left, they were not replaced, nor had they been particularly concerned to fight the discrimination they had encountered in the bureaucracy. Women's organizations worked against laws and government regulations prohibiting the employment of married women with husbands who had jobs, but their activism was limited largely to trying to influence legislation.

Through the 1940s and 1950s, major women's organizations continued to be conservative and limited in their aims. Still, they functioned as vehicles for expressing concern and mobilizing support for reforms that would improve the health and welfare of women, home, and family.

The final victory of woman suffrage owed much to the backing of social feminists, who joined the fight not because they were interested in equality but because they became convinced the vote was necessary to achieve reform. After attaining the vote they promoted many desirable reforms, but few of these reforms were concerned with improving woman's rights. They have been criticized for their refusal to recognize class as a barrier among women, for their promotion of protective legislation, and for the very limited success of their reform programs. Nonetheless, through the 1920s they continued, almost alone, to carry the banner of reform, and leading social feminists like Jane Addams and Eleanor Roosevelt proved the capability of women leaders on the national level.

References. Lois W. Banner, *Women in Modern America: A Brief History*, 2d ed. (New York, 1984); J. Stanley Lemons, *The Woman Citizen: Social Feminism in the 1920s* (Urbana, Ill., 1973); William L. O'Neill, "Feminism as a Radical Ideology," in Alfred F. Young (ed.), *Dissent: Explorations in the History of American Radicalism* (DeKalb, Ill., 1968), 273–300.

SOCIAL PURITY MOVEMENT was a movement to elevate morality and improve the sexual treatment of women, largely through the abolition of prostitution and the double standard.

From the last three decades of the nineteenth century to the end of World War I, an international crusade to purify sexual conduct focused on the need to reeducate society, particularly men, in the control of sexuality. Rooted in earlier women's temperance and moral reform traditions, the American Social Purity movement was influenced by the "rescue" work of British prostitution reformers like Josephine Butler and W. T. Stead and the revelations of international groups for the suppression of "white slavery."*

Composed of widely diverse groups divided on the issues of free love and women's political and economic rights, the American movement, like its British counterpart, was united in the need for a single moral standard, and the word "chastity" figured frequently in the literature. Because Social Purists believed in woman's need to resist sexual subjection by men, the movement had feminist participation. Suffragists were featured speakers at the first American Purity Congress in Baltimore in 1895, and Purists and feminists alike favored abolition, rather than regulation, of prostitution and moral equality in the relations between the sexes.

Prostitution was clearly the focus of much Social Purity agitation. Americans were particularly effective in combating systems of regulated tolerance. Women's voluntary religious and charitable organizations lobbied successfully to abolish legalized prostitution in St. Louis in the 1870s, and there were no further regulationist attempts in the United States thereafter. From the 1880s onward, Social Purists fought for a variety of abolitionist reforms, including prosecution of customers as well as prostitutes, improved prison conditions and rehabilitation for prostitutes, and centers and activities to safeguard the virtue of urban working girls. Movement advocates were also instrumental in establishing municipal vice commissions, raising the age of consent laws, and passing the 1910 Mann Act.

Since its inception Social Purity was criticized, not without reason, as morally repressive. Women like Deborah Leeds, whose husband, Josiah, was an ally of the nation's chief censor, Anthony Comstock, herself personified the movement's censorship wing with her Department of Pure Literature. However, recent research has demonstrated that the movement was also dedicated to the dissemination of sex hygiene information, suggested by its motto "Purity through knowledge, not innocence through ignorance."

As Linda Gordon has pointed out, the birth control ideas of Social Purists were feminist in that advocates urged voluntary motherhood and woman's control over her own body. Yet Social Purists were opposed to contraception and abortion. Furthermore, their eugenic arguments, which at first were aimed to increase woman's power, foundered in a "cult of motherhood" essentially opposed to woman's professional advancement.

At the core of the Social Purity movement was the conviction that sexuality had to be controlled. Many reformers believed that because incontinence was basically associated with man, it was woman's mission to reeducate him. To the extent that it accepted the idea of feminine moral superiority and, by implication, the traditional "separate sphere" for women, the movement was not fully feminist. Nonetheless, in urging women to resist sexual domination and exploitation, it aided the advancement of feminine autonomy.

References. Edward J. Bristow, *Vice and Vigilance: Purity Movements in Britain since 1700* (Totowa, N.J., 1977); Linda Gordon, *Woman's Body, Woman's Right: A Social History of Birth Control in America* (New York, 1976); David J. Pivar,

Purity Crusade: Sexual Morality and Social Control, 1868–1900 (Westport, Conn., 1973).

LAURA HAPKE

SOCIAL SECURITY. Old Age and Survivors Insurance (OASI), generally called Social Security, was established in the United States by the Social Security Act of 1934. Since the 1930s Social Security has expanded to include disability insurance (it is now OADSI) and the vast majority of Americans. In 1994 about 95 percent of all jobs in the United States were covered by Social Security.

Earnings subject to Social Security tax are credited to each person's separate account, but since the program was intended to provide a basic minimum income for retired workers, benefits are not proportional to the moneys paid into each account. As earnings rise, the proportional return of the benefits is reduced. Lower-paid workers, who are expected to have fewer savings, receive payments covering a larger portion of their pre-retirement income than more highly paid workers receive.

Since 1939 Social Security has paid extra benefits to married workers. At the time this change was instituted, more than 85 percent of wives did not work for pay outside the home. To give some support to housewives, benefits to married couples include a spousal benefit of 50 percent of the worker's benefit. Working wives are dually entitled. They receive either their own retirement benefits or the spousal benefit, whichever is greater. As the gap between men's and women's earnings narrows (in 1994 women's median earnings were 72 percent of men's, up from 60 percent in 1980), more women should earn retirement benefits greater than their spousal benefits would be; the reverse has been true since 1939.

If the husband predeceases the wife, which normally happens, the widow receives her husband's benefit if she is of retirement age (except in those rare instances in which her retirement benefits are greater than his). Until reforms were made in the 1970s, however, a widow who remarried lost her widow's benefits, and a divorced woman who was married for less than 20 years received no spousal benefits at all. In 1978 the time was cut to 10 years.

There are equity concerns with the present system. One is that a two-earner couple whose combined income equals that of a one-earner couple will receive lower combined benefits than will the one-earner couple. Feminists have been especially concerned with the way Social Security policy affects divorced women and housewives. One concern is to allow the divorced wife to collect benefits as soon as she reaches minimum retirement age, whether or not her ex-husband has retired. This is part of the broader issue of separate accounts for housewives, or "earnings sharing." Various methods have been proposed for crediting a housewife's account (e.g., having 50 percent of the husband's earnings credited to his wife's separate account). Some recommend more comprehensive changes, such as the "double-decker plan," giving all persons of retirement age an across-the-board sum as the principal part of their benefit, with a smaller sum, based on earnings, added. However, strains on the system caused by increased longevity have made any reforms that will increase the costs or administrative burden of the system virtually impossible.

SOCIALIST WOMEN. From its beginnings in early nineteenth-century Europe, the modern socialist movement has attracted numbers of women into its ranks. Pledged to overcoming both class and gender inequalities through social and economic reconstruction, socialist movements formulated the first political theories to encompass the rights of women. They also organized the first political parties that admitted women to membership and, to varying degrees, gave them opportunities for political action and leadership. Modern socialism originated in the era of the French Revolution and, influenced heavily by Henri Saint-Simon, Charles Fourier, and Robert Owen, took shape in the 1830s and 1840s. Labeled by Karl Marx and Friedrich Engels "utopian socialists" (a designation commonly used today), the early nineteenth-century socialists believed it possible to establish harmony among all human beings and to mitigate the worst effects of industrialization, by the rational reorganization of human society according to universal (natural) law. A new order consistent with industrial and technological development could be shaped to provide for useful work by all members of society, for satisfaction of individual needs—and for improvement of the condition of women.

Adding to the French critique of property the economic analysis of the Englishman David Ricardo and drawing on the work of German thinkers, especially Georg Hegel and Ludwig Feuerbach, at midcentury Marx and Engels constructed a new philosophical system that they termed "scientific socialism." They drew from Fourier the principle that the degree of progress of a given society could be measured by the status of its women. Also contributing to the appeal of socialism to women was the association of socialists with movements for the liberalization of autocratic, repressive regimes in countries such as Russia, where women took a leading role in, and constituted up to one-third of, revolutionary circles, including populist and terrorist groups active in the 1870s and 1880s. During the period of the Second International, socialist women, led by the German Clara Zetkin, formed an international organization and held international conferences in Stuttgart in 1907 and Copenhagen in 1910. At the latter, they called for demonstrations of socialist support for women's suffrage through celebration of an International Women's Day, which is now commemorated in many countries by women of all classes on March 8.

On the eve of World War I, some 175,000 women belonged to Europe's largest socialist party, German Social Democracy, while much smaller numbers participated in France (probably about 1,000), Italy, Russia, and elsewhere. Although often nominal members only, having joined the socialist party primarily to support their husbands' political goals, women in many cases gained distinction disproportionate to their numbers. Sometimes ambivalent about the relative urgency of the "woman question," socialist women, along with most socialist men, accepted the argument of Engels' *The Origin of the Family, Private Property and the State* (1884) that women's subordination in society resulted from the development of private property and the monogamous family, which was purportedly required to assure that men's wealth would be transmitted to "legitimate" heirs. Therefore, according to Engels and his followers, the emancipation of women would accompany socialist revolutions that abolished private property (capital) and "restored," at a higher level, an originally "classless," communal society characterized by equality of the sexes. (See ORIGIN OF THE FAMILY, PRIVATE PROPERTY, AND THE STATE.)

Outstanding women associated with utopian socialism were the Frenchwomen Claire Demar, Pauline Roland, Suzanne Voilquin, and Flora Tristan, whose study of the working classes in London preceded Engels' better-known work and whose call for an international union of workers prefigured Marx's famous call, "Workers of the World, Unite"; and the Englishwomen Anna Doyle Wheeler and Fanny Wright. The most notable Marxist women were Louise Saumoneau and Madeleine Pelletier in France, Rosa Luxemburg (called "the best mind after Marx") and Clara Zetkin in Germany, Eleanor Marx in England, Angelica Balabanoff and Anna Kuliscioff in Italy, Adelheid Popp in Austria, and Alexandra Kollontai in Russia. Leaders in revolutionary populist groups included Sofya Perovskaya, Maria Spiridonova, and Vera Zasulich in Russia.

In related anarchist movements, Louise Michel in France, Federica Montseny in Spain, and the Russian-born Emma Goldman, who earned fame in, and suffered expatriation from, the United States, stand out. Though not easily linked with specific socialist parties, Sylvia Pankhurst in England and Charlotte Perkins Gilman in the United States also deserve recognition. With the rebirth of feminism in the United States in the late 1960s, socialism again attracted adherents among women seeking female liberation, and the work of Marx and, especially, Engels, brought class and gender issues together for another generation. Socialist women today are more apt than their predecessors to understand revolutionary transformation to encompass social relationships along with political economy.

References. Marilyn J. Boxer and Jean H. Quataert (eds.), *Socialist Women: European Socialist Feminism in the Nineteenth and Early Twentieth Centuries* (New York, 1978); Mari Jo Buhle, *Women and American Socialism, 1870–1920* (Urbana, Ill., 1981); Jane Slaughter and Robert Kern (eds.), *European Women on the Left: Socialism, Feminism, and the Problems Faced by Political Women, 1880 to the*

Present (Westport, Conn., 1981); Barbara Taylor, *Eve and the New Jerusalem: Socialism and Feminism in the Nineteenth Century* (New York, 1983).

MARILYN J. BOXER

SOCIÉTÉ DES RÉPUBLICAINES RÉVOLUTIONNAIRES was a radical women's political organization chartered in Paris in 1793 and dissolved by the National Convention as a politically dangerous society less than six months later.

During the early years of the French Revolution (1789–1793), women participated in popular manifestations in favor of constitutionalism, the right to petition, property rights, and economic reform. Female leaders emerged who had strong working relations with the Cordeliers and the Jacobin Clubs; and since their agendas for revolutionary change appeared to be parallel, male leaders of the revolutionary societies solicited continued and active participation of women citizens during the early months of 1793.

Radical women in Paris, who accepted literally the rhetoric of egalitarianism, organized the Société des Républicaines révolutionnaires, which was registered with municipal authorities in May 1793. Two particularly energetic spokeswomen emerged to guide the organization: Pauline Léon, a chocolate manufacturer, and Claire Lacombe, a newly arrived actress. As spokeswomen for their society, they advocated the enforcement of laws dealing with public morality, occupational training for girls and women, expanded educational opportunities, and rigorous measures to guarantee economic subsistence, to suppress hoarding, and to push social revolution further.

By the fall of 1793, the Société des Républicaines révolutionnaires had allied itself with one of the most radical revolutionary groups in Paris, the Enragés. They actively campaigned for the rights of women to participate politically, to join the military, to direct revolutionary festivals, to play guiding roles in education and the family, and to wear nontraditional dress. To show allegiance to the French Revolution, they demanded that all women be required to wear the tricolor cockade. Both their ideas and their allegiance with the Enragés, however, were too radical; the Jacobins and conservative market women viewed them as subversive to good order in society. If they were so active in the halls of government and in the streets, their detractors questioned, then who was in the home rearing the children to be good republicans?

In September the problems between the Républicaines révolutionnaires and the Jacobins emerged openly in heated debate. Although the attacks by the Jacobins were, at first, accusations of political subversiveness, later the attacks became blatantly sexist. On 9 Brumaire II (October 30, 1793), Conventionnel André Amar demanded that exclusively female societies be disbanded. Citing "evidence" of their "bizarre, unnatural behavior," he noted that women did not have the knowledge, attention span, devotion, self-direction, or capacity to participate in the political process. That same day, the National Convention prohibited the existence of all women's organizations. Shortly thereafter, the government began legally to restrict all collective demonstrations, thereby eliminating one of the few channels for women's participation in social, economic, and political change.

References. Margaret George, "The 'World Historical Defeat' of the Républicaines-Révolutionnaires," *Science and Society* 40 (1976/1977): 410–437; Darline Levy, Harriet Applewhite, and Mary Johnson, *Women in Revolutionary Paris, 1789–1795* (Urbana, Ill., 1979).

SUSAN P. CONNER

SOCIOBIOLOGY, a subfield of biology, first appeared in 1975 with the publication of E. O. Wilson's book *Sociobiology: The New Synthesis*. It is defined by its practitioners as the systematic study of the biological basis of all social behavior, from social insects to humans. The importance of sociobiology derives from its role as a theory of human nature. Using the "new synthesis" or "modern synthesis," sociobiologists mean to transform the study of society. As Wilson says, "One of the functions of sociobiology, then, is to reformulate the foundations of the social sciences in a way that draws these subjects into the Modern Synthesis" (4).

Biologists and anthropologists adopted sociobiology very quickly, and books, articles, and journals proliferated. It is now widely accepted as a field, positions have been created for sociobiologists, and courses in the subject are taught at many universities. Sociobiological arguments have made their way into other fields such as economics and political science and are widespread enough that they appear in high school and even grade school material. Opposition to sociobiology has also been widespread, however. Critics have pointed to the flaws in assumptions and methodology that result in conclusions about human behavior that do nothing more than reflect the cultural biases of the sociobiologists. These critics have also drawn attention to the relationship of sociobiology to earlier, discredited theories of biological determinism (Lewontin, Rose, and Kamin; Hubbard and Lowe).

When applying the theory to humans, sociobiologists assert that human social behavior and social institutions are the result of the action of genes. They argue that these genes have been selected during evolution because they give rise to behaviors that increase the reproductive success of individuals. At times the sociobiologists do not claim complete genetic determination but speak of propensities or say that genes promoting flexibility in social behavior are strongly selected. However, these qualifying statements have little force, since the body of the theory is based on the assumption that the details both of the structure of human society and of the social behavior of individuals are genetically determined.

Sociobiologists have claimed biological control for a large part of human

social behavior, such as warfare and aggression, religion, rape,* xenopho-
bia, territoriality, conformity, competition, cooperation, altruism, entrepre-
neurial ability, a hierarchical structure of society, differing birthrates of the
rich and poor, women marrying rich men, and children not liking spinach.
In particular, a number of sex differences in behavior are claimed to exist
and to be genetically determined, for example, differences in aggression, in
nurturing and parenting, in representation in male-dominated professions
such as business, politics, and science, and in philandering.

When theorizing about an observed human behavior, sociobiologists do
not prove genetic control but instead assert that it exists, at best trying to
make the assertion plausible. The heart of sociobiological argument is the
attempt to show that given behaviors are adaptive, that is, that natural
selection results in that particular behavior. For example, in dealing with
the sexual division of labor in our society, sociobiologists have argued that
since females certainly share half of their genes with their children, while
males cannot be completely sure of their paternal contribution, it is adaptive for females "to invest heavily in the well-being of the children" but
not for males. This "suggests why women have almost universally found
themselves relegated to the nursery while men derive their greatest satisfaction from their jobs" (Barash). A genetic basis is assumed, not demonstrated, and then an evolutionary story is developed to explain what is
observed. Furthermore, since behavior is said to be shared so as to be
adaptive, the sociobiological explanation carries the suggestion that the end
result is the optimal one.

Sociobiological explanations require that behavior be under genetic control, at least to some extent. Since no one has yet identified any social
behavior in humans that is controlled by a specific gene or genes, sociobiologists resort to several arguments to try to demonstrate genetic determination of behavior. The first is the proposal that traits observed
universally in human cultures are genetically based. No one, however, has
demonstrated convincingly that any traits, including often-cited sex differences in behavior, are universal. There are fundamental problems with the
methods sociobiologists have used to try to demonstrate universality, given
the wide variation in behavior shown both within and across cultures. Furthermore, even if a trait were to be identified as universal, this in itself
would not be evidence of a genetic underpinning except in the most trivial
sense.

A second, related line of argument points to social behaviors that are
said to be similar in both humans and other primates, such as aggressive
dominance systems. However, there are the same basic problems in identifying such behaviors across species as within. A more fundamental objec-
tion is that even if similar behaviors could be identified, similarity alone
does not allow one to draw the conclusion that the traits share the same
evolutionary or genetic basis.

A final claim is that some traits, such as schizophrenia, IQ, and dominance, have been directly shown to be somewhat heritable and that this is indirect evidence that others may be as well. This argument is no stronger than the previous ones, however, since no reliable evidence exists to show that any human behavioral trait is heritable. Furthermore, the ground of the argument has shifted here, since heritability measures the degree to which differences in behavior are due to genetic factors.

Since there is thus no evidence that human social behavior is under genetic control, the evolutionary stories are pure speculation. Furthermore, if a given behavior is not known to be genetically determined, then one can, in general, just as well explain its appearance through cultural development or adaptation. There are no criteria for choosing either the biological or the cultural explanation or some particular combination of the two. The wide cross-cultural variations in behavior make it clear that environment plays at least some role in behavioral development. However, despite the claims of the biological determinists, one cannot say more than this about the origins of human social behavior.

Sociobiology is neither a new phenomenon nor an isolated one. In the nineteenth century, theories claiming to have scientifically demonstrated a relationship between biology and behavior were very prevalent and widely accepted (Fee; Hofstadter). These nineteenth-century theories of biological determinism, collectively known as social Darwinism, were eventually discredited, but they have now reappeared in modernized forms. The revival began in the late 1960s, and there has been an increasing interest in them since. Sociobiology is only one of a wide variety of theories purporting to show that biology determines human social behavior. Most of the other theories, however, are not evolutionary models but attempts to find direct biological underpinnings of behavior by looking at such things as brain function or hormones (Fausto-Sterling; Lewontin et al.). The current theories are often direct descendants of their nineteenth-century predecessors and rest on arguments and scientific underpinnings that are no firmer than those of the social Darwinists.

The wide acceptance of sociobiology and other theories of biological determinism may well be due to their political implications. Such theories offer support for the status quo, since our social organization is said to be due to nature. Sociobiology particularly suggests that we live in the best of all possible worlds, since behavior is held to have evolved adaptively. The sociobiologist Barash, for example, has said that "there should be a sweetness to life when it accords with the adaptive wisdom of evolution" (310). Sociobiological theories claim to give us the limits of possible change, or at least of desirable change. They are also, at bottom, theories not about the origins of human society but about the origins of inequalities in human society. They are works used to justify social inequities such as sexism* and racism. Starting from the very questionable assumption of meritocracy that is, that ability is the primary determinant of social position, they add that abilities are largely determined by biology. It then follows that if people are in positions of privilege, it is not because of unfairness but because their genes are better. The importance of differing and inequitable sex roles in our society is reflected in the fact that sex differences play a large part in all the theories of biological determinism. It is also not surprising that much media attention has been directed to theories of the origins of sex differences.

A disturbing trend is the appearance of a number of feminist versions of biodeterministic theories in response to sociobiology and other works. Alternative evolutionary and hormonal theories have been suggested by A. S. Rossi, E. Morgan, and S. B. Hrdy. In addition, results from works on brain lateralization have been widely adopted, with a left brain versus right brain dichotomy identified with male versus female thinking. These ideas attempt to counter the stories of mainstream biological determinists that accept the male stereotype as the norm and devalue women. They attempt instead to assert the legitimacy of the cultures and values that are typical of women's worlds. These theories, however, have no better basis than any of the others. The search for understanding human societies lies elsewhere than in studying our biology.

References. D. P. Barash, *Sociobiology and Behavior* (Amsterdam, 1977); R. Bleier, *Science and Gender* (New York, 1983); R. Dawkins, *The Selfish Gene* (Oxford, 1976); A. Fausto-Sterling, *Myths of Gender* (New York, 1985); E. Fee, "Science and the Woman Problem: Historical Perspectives," in M. S. Teitelbaum (ed.), *Sex Differences: Social and Biological Perspectives* (New York, 1976); R. Hofstadter, *Social Darwinism in American Thought* (New York, 1959); S. B. Hrdy, *The Woman that Never Evolved* (Cambridge, Mass., 1981); R. Hubbard and M. Lowe (eds.), *Genes and Gender II* (New York, 1979); R. C. Lewontin, S. Rose, and L. J. Kamin, *Not in Our Genes* (New York, 1984); E. Morgan, *The Descent of Women* (New York, 1972); S. Mosdale, "Science Corrupted: Victorian Biologists Consider the Woman Question," *Journal of the History of Biology* 11 (1978): 1–55; A. S. Rossi, "A Biological Perspective on Parenting," *Daedalus* 106 (1977); J. Sayers, *Biological Politics: Feminist and Anti-Feminist Perspectives* (London, 1982); E. O. Wilson, *Sociobiology: The New Synthesis* (Cambridge Mass., 1975).

MARIAN LOWE

SOUTHERN BLACK WOMEN'S NETWORK (1900–1930). Black women have a long history of making a public imprint on American society. Beginning in the nineteenth century, they organized and participated in benevolent and literary societies. By the beginning of the twentieth century, black women's clubs had emerged in response to policies of exclusion from white women's clubs, in opposition to lynching, and in protest against the continuing sexual abuse of African American women. Members of these clubs became leaders in organizations of educational, civic, social, recreational, and political groups around the country. They also became organizers of groups that supported and endorsed racial solidarity and economic independence. Branches of these civic and social action agencies were established throughout the country, even in the Deep South.

Southern black women organized and developed programs to improve the quality of life for African Americans in the South. This network of southern black women instituted day-care centers, kindergartens, medical clinics, mothers' meetings, settlement houses, reading rooms and libraries, playgrounds, academic and industrial art classes, literary clubs for young adults, and houses for delinquent boys and girls. They fought discrimination, prejudice, segregation, and racism in order to provide equal services and opportunities for African American black children and young adults—especially girls—in the South.

Though these women protested and petitioned the law of separate but equal, their immediate objective was to fight for the equality that the nation professed. They fought to have black school facilities equal to those of white schools, to have the standard of living conditions in the black communities equal to those in the white communities, and for the hiring of black personnel to serve and protect their communities. Where there was a void in services, these women established neighborhood clubs designed to meet the needs until local officials or charitable agencies assumed the responsibility, in full or in part. Such was the original intent of the Sunset Club of Orangeburg, South Carolina, founded by Marion Wilkerson; the Tuskegee Women's Club of Tuskegee, Alabama, founded by Margaret Murray Washington; and the Neighborhood Union of Atlanta, Georgia, founded by Lugenia Burns Hope. (See GRASSROOTS ORGANIZATION.)

The southern black female network consisted basically of educated, middle-class women with opportunity, obligation, and commitment to confront racism, segregation, and sexism as they promoted the study of blacks in the world. Their activism was designed to service the needs of both rural and urban areas. They saw themselves responsible to their less fortunate sisters. They became the black caucus that developed black Young Women's Christian Associations (YWCAs) in the South, worked with the interracial movement in the Commission on Interracial Cooperation (later the Southern Regional Council), were the core of the Southeastern Federation of Colored Women's Clubs, and were the primary founders of a Pan-Africanist group, the International Council of Women of the Darker Races. Emerging as regional and national leaders, they attacked the issues of the plight of domestic workers, child welfare, segregated railroad facilities, disfranchisement of blacks, and abolition of the convict-lease system, lynching, and double school sessions and low pay for black school teachers. These women, being products of Victorian America, accepted the morals and values of the era. They sought to introduce to the "better class of white America" the "better class of the black community" in order to improve race relations. They defined moral and racial appropriateness using their standards as guidelines in order to "morally" clean up their communities.

By the early twentieth century, activists in this network included Lugenia B. Hope (Ga.), M. L. Crostwait (Tenn.), Mary McLeod Bethune (Fla.), Lucy Laney (Ga.), Nettie L. Napier (Tenn.), Charlottee H. Brown (N.C.), Nannie Helen Burroughs (D.C.), Janie P. Barnett (Va.), Maggie Lena Walker (Va.), Florence Hunt (Ga.), Margaret Murray Washington (Ala.), Jenie Moton (Ala.), Mary J. McCrorey (N.C.), and Marion B. Wilkerson (S.C.)

References. Paula Giddings, *When and Where I Enter . . . The Impact of Black Women on Race and Sex in America* (New York, 1984); Cynthia Neverdon-Morton, "The Black Woman's Struggle for Equality in the South, 1895–1925," in Sharon Harley and Rosalyn Terborg-Penn (eds.), *The Afro-American Woman: Struggles and Images* (Port Washington, N.Y., 1978), 43–57; Cynthia Neverdon-Morton, *The Afro-American Woman of the South and the Advancement of the Race, 1895–1925* (Knoxville, Tenn., 1989); Jacqueline A Rouse, *Lugenia Burns Hope, Black Southern Reformer* (Atlanta, Ga., 1989).

                                                                    JACQUELINE A. ROUSE

SPAIN. Civil War (1936–1939) made women indispensable in positions till then held exclusively by men. Overnight many Republican women became soldiers since the army was drawn from trade unions and "proletarian" parties. Aurora Arnaiz organized the first column of the *Juventud Socialista* (Socialist Youth) for the defense of Madrid, in Barcelona women fought in the streets, and in Valencia they demanded arms in order to go to the front. Lina Odena, a seamstress prominent in the Communist Party, fought to the last bullet, which she fired against herself so as to escape falling into enemy hands, thus becoming a martyr and a symbol. Shortly thereafter, however, the army was regularized, and women were relegated almost exclusively to the rearguard. "Men to fight, women to work" was the slogan, and many women went to work in factories.

Dolores Ibarruri, "La Pasionaria," insisted that women should have access to administrative posts both in industry and in the Communist Party. A party organization, Women against War and Fascism, was created. It published the bimonthly journal *Mujeres*. Its activist branch, the Committee to Aid Women, organized women in industry, collected money, trained nurses, founded day nurseries and asylums for war orphans, replaced men in public transportation, regularized the mail services, distributed food and clothing, supervised hygiene, worked in factories, and cultivated the fields. A very important organization was the Catalonian Union of Anti-Fascist Women, which began publishing the journal *Trabajadora* in 1938. Madrid's Union of Young Girls was open to all ideologies but controlled by the Union of Young Socialists and Communists. Its journal *Muchachas* emphasized equality with male comrades.

In 1936 the Anarchist Lucia Sánchez founded *Mujeres libres*, a publication of the Free Women's Association whose members sought permanent liberation for women and considered the sexual revolution as another aspect of the fight for freedom. Federica Montseny, minister of health and welfare, legalized abortion in 1936. Courses on contraception were offered. A school for mothers and one for housewives were instituted to prepare future homemakers. Campaigns against venereal diseases were waged. Soldiers were urged to stay away from brothels and to be conscious of the dignity of women. Women who wished to give up prostitution were welcomed by asylums, which gave them medical, moral, and financial assistance as well as job training to make them financially independent.

All these women's liberation movements encountered resistance not only from many women who continued to believe that a man should provide his own well-being and that of his family but even more so from men who continued to consider woman as a fundamentally domestic being. Whatever progress had been made and whatever promise of future progress existed were cut short by the whirlwind of defeat in 1939.

The women in the Nationalist camp never went to war as soldiers, nor did they gain the prominence in industry that distinguished the women on the Republican side. In 1934 Pilar Primo de Rivera, sister of the founder of the Falange, the Spanish fascist party, created the Feminine Branch of the party. It began by assisting the families of dead or imprisoned fascists but soon became active in disseminating propaganda and fund-raising. It was a fundamental component of the regime of the Nationalist leader General Francisco Franco during and after the war. Through its Social Welfare Taskforce it expanded its activities to include other right-wing women's organizations.

According to Franco's ideologists, the primary function of women was to procreate for the glory of the motherland, as it was in Nazi Germany or fascist Italy. For those who were not contributing to the preservation of Spain via motherhood, a six-month period of social service was instituted in 1937. Although not compulsory for all, it was expected of those women wishing to work for the government or in any professional job. In contrast to the Republicans, who were plagued by internal dissension, the better-organized Fascist Feminine Branch made the social service a very effective instrument of war. It contributed to the victory of the Nationalist cause but not to the progress of feminism, to which it was ideologically opposed. After Franco's victory, the Fascist Feminine Branch became the official organ for the ideological and cultural instruction of Spanish women.

References. C. Alcalde, *La Mujer en la guerra civil española* (Madrid, 1976); Geraldine M. Scanlon, *La polémica feminista en la España Contemporánea: 1868–1974* (Madrid, 1974); Julio Iglesias de Ussel and R. M. Capel, *Mujer española y sociedad: Bibliografía 1940–1984* (Madrid, 1984).

ANTONIO H. MARTÍNEZ

SPAIN. Medieval. Women's lives were influenced by the various ethnic and religious groups that dominated the country over the centuries. From the fifth through the fifteenth centuries, Spain was governed first by the Visigoths, later by the Muslims, and finally by the Christians, who completed the Reconquest in 1492. The role of women, however, was not determined solely by the ruling society but also by class, for every element of their lives depended on their place in the social structure.

The women of nobility enjoyed a privileged existence of leisure and protection. Some were sent to convents to be educated, although not all learned to read and write Latin. A daughter's duty was to obey her father's wishes, especially concerning the choice of a husband. The primary importance of a young noblewoman was her marriageability: unions were arranged for political and economic advantages meant to ensure the future viability of a family or kingdom, and formal betrothals usually took place when the bride and groom were adolescents. Noblewomen who did not marry, were widowed, or were repudiated by their betrothed often opted for the convent. These nuns were not necessarily devoted to the monastic life, and stories of scandalous behavior abounded as they continued their luxurious existence and enjoyment of laic life inside the convent walls.

The lifestyle of townswomen was quite different from that of their wealthy counterparts, although it did vary according to their family's means and the size of the town in which they lived. The majority of women married, and although parental consent was generally required, it was often not imposed without consultation of the future bride. Once married, a woman looked to her husband for shelter and protection and was expected to be obedient to him; nevertheless, traditional Visigothic laws that remained in effect for centuries allowed her to retain many rights. She could inherit both real and movable property and pass it on to her children, although marriage without parental consent was cause for disinheritance. At betrothal the future bride and groom typically exchanged property as well as symbolic rings; the man was expected to furnish his wife with at least one-third of his possessions, and a widowed woman typically retained this endowment for her own support and the inheritance of her children.

The law provided for continued separation of property after marriage; only those possessions acquired after the wedding were considered common property. Regardless, the husband was considered the administrator of all properties, even those held separately by his wife, and by law could dispose of any of them at his will. Upon his death, however, she could challenge such actions, or her heirs could do so in the event that she preceded her husband in death. Widowed women could administer their own property in addition to their late husband's inheritance, although remarriage once again subjected them to their new spouse's supervision. Unmarried women also had certain rights even if they left the home of their parents before marriage.

Concubinage was not uncommon in medieval Spain and was therefore regulated by law; a *barragana* was a woman supported by a man she could not legally wed. This arrangement usually came about because the man in question was already married, a widower unwilling to wed again, or a priest. Although a *barragana* had no legal right to her partner's inheritance, her children retained rights as long as they were recognized by their father and were not born in adultery.

Because of their domestic and child-rearing responsibilities, most married women or concubines did not work outside the home; generally, they were supported by their husbands in addition to any income they might have had from separate property. It was not unheard of, however, for married or unmarried women to work as bakers, fishwives, barmaids, innkeepers, or shopkeepers. Those who were the inhabitants of rural environments were limited to domestic and agricultural chores and led a more difficult existence. Most lived with their families in the poverty of rustic huts, sustaining themselves on what they could raise on their property and trade.

Life was very different for women living under Islamic rule. Thousands of the Muslim soldiers who settled on the Iberian peninsula arrived without Islamic women but soon took Christians for wives, many of whom were taken by force as prisoners of war. Islamic law allowed a man four legal wives and as many slaves as he wished, and could afford, for his harem. (See ISLAMIC LAW.) Harem slaves were bought and sold at markets where the fair-skinned persons of the northwestern part of the peninsula brought the highest price. Some of these captives became the favorites of a rich master, who would bestow upon them luxurious gifts. Family life was dominated by the Muslim husband, who kept his wives and daughters veiled and secluded from other men. Women could be repudiated and thereby divorced from their husbands but could not initiate separation themselves. The daughters of wealthy families were generally educated only in the art of catering to men and were married without their consent or consultation to spouses they would typically not see until the wedding. Most Muslim men, however, could probably afford only one wife, who, with her daughters, was expected to care for the household. Throughout the Middle Ages these households might alternately find themselves in Christian or Muslim territory as the borders between the two powers shifted back and forth.

References. Claudio Sánchez Albornoz, *España y el Islam* (Buenos Aires, 1943); Heath Dillard, *Daughters of the Reconquest* (Cambridge, 1984).

NANCY F. MARINO

SPAIN. Since 1975. The 1978 Constitution legalized and stimulated the forces that work on behalf of women. Spanish women have now come of age: they have equal rights, educational possibilities similar to those of men, and wide-ranging employment opportunities. Married women have acquired legal identity and complete control over acts related to their persons.

The figure of the dominant and all-providing male has ceased to be supported by the law.

Modern home appliances, the availability of prepared or semiprepared foods, the contraction of the immediate family and its social activities, legalized abortion, and the decrease in infant mortality have given Spanish women a big reduction in the domestic workload and a new freedom. A longer life expectancy and individualized family planning now allow women to pursue jobs and professional careers.

All these changes have occurred in a few years, much more rapidly than elsewhere in Europe. In Spain, the reactionary forces that defeated the progressive elements in 1939 had to be overcome first, something that was possible only during the last phase of Francisco Franco's regime and the period immediately following his death in 1975.

The emigration of entire families seeking work in the more industrialized European countries during the 1950s and early 1960s put hundreds of thousands of Spaniards in contact with social realities that they wished to transplant to Spain upon their return in the late 1960s and early 1970s. The returning émigrés made good their demands as the country became democratized. Tourism also brought millions of Spaniards into contact with millions of foreigners who had more liberal and democratic mores. Television, which is much more difficult to manipulate than radio or the press, brought daily broadcasts and images of life from all over the globe. There was also the cinema, along with publishing houses and bookstores, which presented enviable standards and ways of life. Journalists filed reports from more democratic countries about their political processes. Graduate students went to study in Europe and the United States to return later with new ideas and different lifestyles. The decisive factor amid these changes was, however, the new industrial development of Spain in the 1960s, which required a large number of women to join the workforce. Financial independence also meant freedom of action. Prior to the 1960s, Spanish women were not allowed to wear slacks or bikinis in public. Now it is not uncommon to see even topless women, of varied age, on beaches and at swimming pools.

In the 1980s, women studied at all levels of higher education. In comparison to men, the differences are not quantitative but qualitative. More women major in the social sciences than in the natural sciences, and only 2 percent study engineering. The majority of women still go into supportive fields such as nursing, social work, and teaching. Women fill 94 percent of the teaching positions at the elementary level, a little less than 50 percent at the secondary level, and 25 percent at the level of higher education, where their rank is usually lower than that of men. Only 5 percent of university full professors are female. Illiteracy is still greater among women than among men, especially in rural areas and in working-class neighborhoods.

In 1986, 28 percent of women worked outside the home, and they constituted 30 percent of the labor force. Fifty percent of the women aged 18 to 24 worked as compared to 30 percent of those aged 24 to 35 years. There is a correlation between level of education and employment: more education makes it easier to enter and remain in the workforce. Thus, there are more unemployed women than men. Thirty-six percent of women lack stable employment as opposed to 16 percent of men.

From 1974 to 1986 the average age at marriage was 26 for men and 24 for women. Many women now wait as many as four years after marriage to have their first child. They plan their maternity around their professional situation. The birthrate was reduced by 6 percent from 1984 to 1986. The fertility rate dropped from 2.8 children in 1974 to 2.6 in 1978 and to 1.7 in 1984. The use of contraceptives, illegal until 1979, was, nevertheless, frequent prior to legalization and has since become very common. Thirty-eight percent of married women had an average of more than four children in the 1930s; that rate dropped to 17 percent in the 1980s. Most young couples now have a maximum of two children. Divorce, which was legalized in 1981, still occurs less frequently in Spain than in the rest of Europe, except Italy. Cohabitation has become accepted among people with middle to high levels of education; it has always been common among the lower classes.

The influence of women in politics is growing slowly. More men than women vote in elections. Women tend to avoid political extremism and vote for parties oriented toward the center. Their active participation is reflected in the fact that 13.5 percent of the candidates running for Congress were female in 1977, 18 percent in 1979, 19 percent in 1982, and 22 percent in 1986. As of 1986, female candidates for the Senate had reached a maximum of 15 percent. Of the candidates, 6.5 percent had been elected to Congress and 5.5 percent to the Senate. The percentage of women in government posts continues to increase, especially at the medium and lower levels of the administration. Only 6 percent of top-level positions are held by women. In 1986 there were some female ministers, several governors, a few university presidents, a substantial number of mayors, and a number of undersecretaries. The head of the National Television Network, a government agency, was a woman, Pilar Miro. The traditionally male-only Royal Academy of the Language, whose quarters used to be off-limits to women even when not in session, elected Carmen Conde its first woman member in 1978. Elena Quiroga was the second woman elected, in 1983. The army, the navy, and the air force, however, continue to refuse to enlist women, although there has been talk that they may recruit females for noncombat duties.

The situation of women in contemporary Spain has undergone radical changes since 1975, and it can be said that women have attained adulthood in their legal status. Yet many battles remain to be won. Even though the family is evolving toward freer, less rigid forms of life, when there is an economic crisis, such as the one witnessed in the late 1970s, women are still the most adversely affected. They are still expected to sacrifice their jobs and careers to the needs of their families.

In short, women are moving away from their former status of "queens of the home" without having fully acquired the status of "first-class" citizens. They are liberating themselves from paternalistic attitudes and structures, but they have not yet gained full equality with men.

References. Spain, Ministerio de Cultura, Instituto de la mujer, *Situación social de la mujer en España* (Madrid, 1987); Julio Iglesias de Ussel and Rosa María Capel, *Mujer española y sociedad: Bibliografía 1940–1984* (Madrid, 1984).

ADELAIDA LÓPEZ DE MARTÍNEZ

SPAIN. Women's Movements did not exist per se in the late nineteenth century, but there were individual feminists. Cecilia Böhl de Faber (1796–1877), using the pseudonym Fernán Caballero, accurately depicted the inner struggles and outward difficulties of the women of her times. Concepción Arenal (1820–1893), who caused a scandal by attending university dressed as a man, and Emilia Pardo Bazán (1852–1921) opposed in life and in writing the social customs and mores of their time.

Women's education was advanced by the Association for the Education of Women, founded in 1871, where all lecturers were men, and professional schools offering courses in teaching, business, languages, drawing, music, printing. New ideas were promoted by *Instrucción de la mujer* (Education of Women), founded in 1882. Concepción Jimeno, a member of the upperclass Women's Council on Ibero-American Union, advocated a conservative feminism aimed not at equality but at an intelligent collaboration with men.

El pensamiento femenino, with a female editorial board, began publication in 1913. It presented feminism as a humanitarian and charitable movement. In 1918 the National Association of Spanish Women (ANME), founded by Celsia Regis and María Espinosa de los Monteros, became the most important feminist organization in Spain. Its journal, *Mundo femenino* (1921), attacked the Right for supporting woman suffrage against their principles, in the belief that women were by nature conservative; it attacked the Left, which, contrary to its own principles, opposed woman suffrage for the same reason. The Club Lyceo, founded by María de Maeztu, although not professedly feminist, made a significant contribution to woman's rights and to the upgrading of their educational level.

At the turn of the century the Spanish feminist movements unfortunately tended to split into leftist and rightist movements with subsequent limitations and exclusions. The more perspicacious members of the Catholic hierarchy realized that they needed to defend woman's rights if they were to retain the loyalty of educated women and workingwomen. The Federation of Catholic Women Workers was founded in 1912, and the Young Catholic Women was founded in 1929. The workingwoman was to be saved from socialism by Catholic trade unions, and the middle classes by Catholic feminism.

Efforts to improve working conditions for women were linked to various socialist movements. In 1884 Teresa Claramunt created a Union of Textile Women Workers. New ideas regarding divorce, free love, and the right to vote were advanced more by strong-minded women than by feminist movements. Carmen Hildegarte wrote in favor of legal and sexual equality. Parliamentary Deputy Margarita Nelken, in *La mujer en las Cortes Constituyentes* (Women in the Spanish Parliament, 1931), urged the Republican government to introduce new labor hours, support the rights of illegitimate children, legalize divorce, and abolish prostitution. Clara Campoamor, another active deputy, fought tirelessly for the right to vote, which was achieved in 1931. Victoria Kent, also a deputy, dedicated her humanitarian efforts to reforming the prison system. On the right were the Women's Association for Social Services, supported by the church, and the Feminine Branch of the Falange (the Spanish fascist party). (See SPAIN, Civil War.)

At the end of the Civil War (1936–1939), the indoctrination and development of women were monopolized by the Feminine Branch of the Falange, which dealt with household tasks, choral music and dancing, and political development under the auspices and for the service of General Francisco Franco.

María Campo Alange, author of *La guerra secreta de los sexos* (The Secret War of the Sexes, 1948) and *La mujer en España. Cien años de su historia (1860–1960)* (Spanish Women: One Hundred Years of Their History, 1964), was instrumental in the creation of the Seminar on the Sociology of Women, which was involved in studies rather than direct action. Formed in 1965, the Women's Democratic Movement (MDM) was an active group with communist tendencies. In 1974 it added Women's Liberation Movement (MLM) to its name, thus becoming MDM-MLM. An offshoot of this movement was the Association of Castilian Homemakers, which published the influential journal *La mujer y la lucha.* The Association for the Promotion of Women's Education (APEC), founded in 1973, proposed a cultural revolution that would change ideas about women in order to bring about reforms.

The year 1975, Women's International Year, was decisive for the feminist movement in Spain. Franco's death that year brought about significant changes in the political system. The number of movements increased along with their membership and public recognition. A Feminist Seminar was created in anticipation of The Hague Tribunal to Judge Crimes against Women. Cristina Alberdi, a lawyer, organized Madrid's Feminist Group, whose purpose was to study the social oppressions of women. The Democratic Association of Women (ADM) in 1976 organized housewives of the lower socioeconomic class and began publishing the *Gaceta feminista*. Attorney Maria Telo, a leader of the Association of Spanish Women Lawyers (1971–1976), worked for the civil, penal, and labor rights of women. Although divorce was not legalized until 1981, the Association of Separated Women has been legalized since 1973. Several other radical feminist groups surfaced but were short-lived. In 1976 Jimena Alonso opened a bookstore for and about women. Since 1980 María Angeles Durán has directed, with great scientific rigor, the Women's Studies Seminar. Also in 1980 the Ministry of Culture established an undersecretary for women, which has carried out a rigorous campaign to legalize feminist groups. In 1983 the Center for the Dissemination of Women's News (CIM) was created to study the condition of women in the fields of law, education, health, and sociopolitical involvement.

Reference. Julio Iglesias de Ussel and R. M. Capel, *Mujer española y sociedad: Bibliografía 1940–1984* (Madrid, 1984).

ANTONIO H. MARTÍNEZ

SPAIN. Writers. Women writers, a rare phenomenon before the twentieth century, had to surmount numerous barriers in a conservative, male-oriented society. This achievement was feasible because the women often were aristocrats or had a foreign education. In the golden age, Renaissance idealism accompanied by religious fervor produced several great mystics, including Spain's first woman writer, Santa Teresa de Jesús (1515–1582), a Carmelite nun of exalted spirit. She adapted love poetry symbols into divine poetry: mystic experiences are sketched through images of worldly love. In addition to three autobiographical books, she wrote *Camino de perfección*, a spiritual guide for nuns, and *Las Moradas*, describing the mystic's path to God (*Way of Perfection* and *Interior Castles*, in *The Complete Works*, 1957). In a simple and sometimes humorous style, they are a major contribution to the mystical tradition.

In the baroque period María de Zayas (1590–1661), an upper-class feminist with, except in matters regarding women, aristocratic values, created some narrative masterpieces. Her collections, *Novelas amorosas y ejemplares* (Love and Exemplary Novels) and *Desengaños amorosos* (Love Disillusions), follow structurally the *Decameron* model, have a didactic purpose, and promote equality: they condemn male chauvinism and the intellectual oppression of women, who are urged to be independent.

The nineteenth-century Romantic movement brought a new subjective lyric expression, free from neo-classical norms. Gertrudis Gómez de Avellaneda (1814–1873) marked this transition with several elegies and nature poems of neo-classical pattern, followed by passionate love verses, nostalgic descriptions of Cuba's landscape, and religious exultations based on biblical themes. Carolina Coronado (1823–1911), also influenced by the Bible, wrote simple, spontaneous poems of love, nature, and religion. Her social awareness led to satirical and feminist compositions like "Libertad," or freedom everyone can enjoy—except women. Lyric poetry reached new heights with the neo-Romantic Rosalía de Castro (1837–1885). Her meta-fictional "strange story," *El caballero de las botas azules* (The Gentleman in the Blue Boots), scrutinizes writers, readers, and popular literary genres. But Rosalía is, above all, a poet. *Cantares gallegos* (Galician Songs) and *Follas novas* (New Leaves) offer an idyllic vision of her native Galicia, while echoing the voice of its oppressed farmers. Social concerns develop into existential thought and tender compassion in her symbolist masterpiece *En las orillas del Sar (Beside the River Sar, 1937)*, where she encompasses human suffering and loneliness with tears of desperation. Rosalía is a prominent precursor of contemporary poets.

Among novelists, Cecilia Bohl de Faber (1796–1877, Fernán Caballero), an ultraconservative, defended upper-class privileges. Popular customs and anecdotes provided raw materials for her narrative, heavily ballasted with strict moral principles. Idealized peasants stage colorful romantic scenes in *La gaviota* (The Sea-Gull), subtitled "original novel of Spanish customs," while *Cuadros de costumbres* is a collection of short stories portraying Andalusian folklore. Countess Emilia Pardo Bazán (1851–1921) was the first woman to hold a university professorship and a pioneer in the feminist movement. Complaints about double standards are a leitmotiv of her works, which include several volumes of literary essays and more than 500 short stories in a wide thematic range. A key essay, *La cuestión palpitante* (The Burning Question), molds literary naturalism to her religious beliefs. *Los pazos de Ulloa* (The Manor of Ulloa) and *La madre naturaleza* (Mother Nature), novels stemming from this version of Spanish naturalism, present a pessimistic view of life in a rural setting. *Una cristiana* (A Christian Woman) and *La prueba* (The Test), published together (1890), portray types: the frivolous little doll, the ideal Christian, the liberated "new woman." Russian narrative influenced her last novels.

A second golden age of rich lyric followed the avant-garde movement of the early twentieth century. But the Civil War (1936–1939) shattered the country, forcing into exile many writers such as Ernestina de Champourcín (b. 1905), who produced most of her poems in Mexico. *Presencia a oscuras* (Presence in the Dark), inspired by her rediscovery of God, has deep religious roots. In *Poemas del ser y del estar*, trying to reconcile poetry with the poet, similar religious feelings surface. Carmen Conde (b. 1907), prolific in several genres, is the first female member of the Royal Academy of Language. Her passionate verse celebrates love and life but also expresses grief for the broken dreams of postwar Spain. Tenderness defines her "Poemas a la madre."

Until the 1950s, social poetry appeared isolated and timid; thereafter it became a rebellious trend. To Angela Figuera (b. 1902) poetry is a tool for improving the world. The mild tone of maternal love in *Mujer de barro* (Woman of Clay) turns anguished and fierce in *El grito inútil* (The Useless Shout) and *Los días duros* (The Hard Days), fiery cries of compassion and impotence. Another strong social poet, Gloria Fuertes (b. 1918), evolves from self-pity in *Isla ignorada* (Ignored Island) to sarcastic criticism of the inane middle class in *Aconsejo beber hilo* (My Advice Is to Drink Thread). Her poems about daily life, naive at times, exude anguish and solitude. A new sensibility emerges from the voice of Ana María Moix (b. 1947), defending absolute freedom of forms while rehabilitating materials judged apoetic before, in *Baladas para el dulce Jim* (Ballads for Sweet Jim) and *No Time for Flowers*.

The narrative fiction of Concha Espina (1877–1955), bridging the centuries, combines traditional realist techniques with a new social awareness. Her best novels are *El metal de los muertos* (The Metal of the Dead), about labor problems the miners face, and *La esfinge maragata (Mariflor*, 1924) concerning women's marginal lives. Because of the civil war, however, the novel, isolated from current Western innovations, nearly suffocated in its own tradition of outdated realism. The recovery starts with Carmen Laforet (b. 1921). In her early novel *Nada (Andrea*, 1964), a best-seller and winner of the first Nadal Prize (1945), the heroine's dreams clash with a sordid environment and anomalous family members. Although conventional in structure and narrative techniques, it reveals an acute feminine sensibility combined with a wide existential scope: life's ups and downs lead to disenchantment, to "nothingness," because of the uncertain future and lack of communication. Elena Quiroga (b. 1921), member of the Royal Academy of Language, gained immediate fame with the rather conventional *Viento del Norte* (Northwind) (Nadal Prize, 1950). But her narrative prowess is evinced in *La sangre* (Blood), with its technical novelty of a centennial chestnut tree narrating its impressions of four generations of a family, and in her psychological novels, *Algo pasa en la calle* (Something's Happening in the Street) and *La careta* (The Mask), with multiple points of view and stream of consciousness. A champion of social narrative and recipient of prestigious literary prizes, Ana María Matute (b. 1926) defends the novel as a vehicle for revealing human problems and striking society's conscience. The civil war and its consequences give the historical background to her best novels, *En esta tierra* (In This Land) a political, nonconformist defense of the poor, and *Los hijos muertos (The Lost Children*, 1965), a message against hate. Like the previous novels, *Primera memoria (School of the Sun*, 1963) protests lack of justice, deceptive charity, and indifference to suffering. A fatalistic view leads her narrative to themes of envy, destruction, and loneliness. Carmen Martín-Gaite (b. 1925), one of today's foremost novelists, writes introspective novels where existential queries find an answer in the meaning of writing. All human conflicts are related to the need for communication, and *Retahílas* (Threads) deals with the lack of it. *Entre visillos* (Between the Blinds) (Nadal Prize, 1957) criticizes the provincial narrow-mindedness of middle-class young people without a clear purpose in life. Innovative and abreast of current trends, *El cuarto de atrás (The Back Room*, 1983) (National Literary Award, 1978) is a mystery novel that weaves fantastic elements with memoirs and metafictional thoughts.

References. J. M. Díez Borque (ed.), *Historia de la literatura española* (Madrid, 1980); Carmen Conde, *Poesía femenina española* (Barcelona, 1967, 1971); José Simón Díaz, *Manual de bibliografía de la literatura española* (Madrid, 1980); Janet Pérez, *Contemporary Women Writers of Spain* (Boston, 1988).

J. BERNARDO PÉREZ

SPANISH AMERICA. Colonial Convents in the New World. Convents gave the secluded and strictly supervised women of the New World several forms of liberation: they offered the devout an authentic religious life, provided support and safety to women who could not marry, constituted true financial centers often controlled by women, and, finally, promoted intellectual and literary activities.

The most important and logical function of the convent was to satisfy the spiritual hunger of truly religious women. Above all others stands Madre Francisca Josefa del Castillo in Colombia, whom Menéndez Pelayo compared to Saint Teresa. Other mystics were Sor Jacinta de San José, Sor María Anna Agueda de San Ignacio, Sor Sebastiana Josefa de la Santísma Trinidad, Madre Inés de la Cruz, and Doña Guerra de Jesús, who was canonized. The fervor of these nuns is evidence of their genuine religious spirit and gives the lie to allegations that women of that day usually entered a convent for other than religious reasons. The mysticism practiced by the nuns represented a form of escape from the rigorous sociomoral control to which women were subjected.

During the colonial period, if a woman was unable to marry because she lacked a suitor or an adequate dowry to bring to the marriage, a convent could serve as a refuge. Although entering a convent meant renouncing secular life, it did not necessarily represent pious seclusion, for nuns were surrounded by friends and relatives; moreover, they were allowed to take with them two slaves and two maids to serve them. This meant that many nuns did not even comply with the vows of obedience, chastity, and poverty, nor with the rule of leading a cloistered life.

As regards the vow of obedience, we have knowledge of rebellions staged by nuns, such as the one in 1660, when the nuns of the Franciscan order of New Spain opposed restrictions on the number of maidservants they could bring to the convent; in 1770 the protest was against the imposition of communal life.

The vow of chastity, which demanded a pure life dedicated entirely to God, was not always honored: during the seventeenth and eighteenth centuries nuns had very personal relationships with monks, clergymen, or lay-men; these relationships were known as "devotions" and constituted a curious form of courtship in the confessional, at the barred convent win-dows, or in an exchange of letters and gifts. In extreme cases, the relation-ship was carnal; however, recent sociological studies show that this occurred less frequently than was previously believed. Nonetheless, at the porter's lodge of the convents a worldly atmosphere prevailed.

In her study of the Convento do Destêrro in Brazil, the sociologist Susan Soeiro proved that the high dowries demanded by this convent, as by many others, forced parents to mortgage their properties. Some convents grew so rich that they also operated as lending institutions. It is also known that some nuns held property and received a considerable annual income, called a "reserve," for their personal expenses. Some cells were true palaces with every kind of luxury, like the one owned by Sor Juana de Maldonado y Paz in Guatemala. Many nuns became moneylenders; for example, Madre Catarina de Monte Sinai became so wealthy that when she died, her estate was worth the sum of 4,402,000 reals.

Generally, nuns knew how to read; some could write more or less, and a few knew enough Latin for their prayers. However, despite their limited learning, the nuns of the New World carried out some richly creative work. The most prominent, among many, were the Mexican Sor Juana Inés de la Cruz, Madre Castillo in Colombia, Sor Juana de Maldonado y Paz in Gua-temala, Sor Leonor de Ovando in Santo Domingo, and Sor Ursula Suárez and Sor Tadea García de la Huerta in Chile.

In summary, according to sociohistorical studies of the colonial era, con-vents often represented an opportunity for women to become independent of a repressive society and to fulfill themselves in areas prohibited outside the convent walls. In other words, many convents in the colonial period were true centers of feminine liberation.

Reference. Susan Soeiro, "The Social and Economic Role of the Convent," *Hispanic American Historical Review* 54, 2 (1974): 209–232.

RIMA DE VALLBONNA, translated by BERTIE ACKER

SPANISH AMERICA. Colonial Period. Colonial Spanish America pre-sented the phenomenon of widespread racial mixture; the most important feature being the birth and growth of a new hybrid race, the mestizo, re-sulting from the union of Spanish male and Indian female, either through casual intercourse, concubinage, or marriage. Spanish women first arrived in the New World on Columbus' third voyage (1498) and before 1600 were found in practically all settlements. Black females imported as slaves arrived in the early 1500s and also spread through Spanish America. Three centuries of miscegenation aided the process of acculturation as the women of each race responded to contact with males of other races in keeping with their own cultures. In the colonial society that developed, white women from Spain were at the apex followed by creoles (American-born Spanish women). Lower levels were made up of mestizo, Indian, mulatto, and black women. Although a woman's position was determined principally by the socioeconomic status of her family, upward mobility, achieved through either acquisition of wealth or marriage, prevailed throughout the colonial period and in all areas. Wealth and social status were not the sole prerogatives of white women, however, and among the poor as well, women of all racial groups were to be found.

Women married early, usually not for love but to forge or consolidate family alliances. If not married by age 25, they were considered unmarriageable and hence were relegated to spinsterhood or entry into a convent. A woman brought not only the social prestige of her family into marriage but also a dowry that could be in the form of land, livestock, mortgages, slaves, or similar assets. Marital fidelity was a female obligation. Married women of the elite were guarded from admiring eyes by jealous husbands and hence were not often seen in public. A colonial ecclesiastical court could terminate a marriage by annulment or by divorce (legal separation), which allowed the parties to live apart but forbade either to remarry during the lifetime of the other. While many upper-class women in urban areas lived in comfort and luxury, at the lower end of the social scale were black female slaves whose contributions to colonial economic development were made under dehumanizing conditions from which only a few escaped through manumission. Throughout the period women were regarded as morally and spiritually superior to men, with great capacity for sacrifice and hardship.

Women's education sought to impose cultural standards as well as to integrate girls into family life and the social or racial group to which they belonged. A few of the creole elite hired tutors to teach their daughters drawing, song, and music in the hopes that this would qualify them for marriage to a rich, socially acceptable man. Practical or vocational instruction offered in convents and day schools was supplemented by the teaching of Christian doctrine, respect for the clergy, and reverence for the symbols of the faith. Girls were urged to practice the virtues of purity, unselfishness, and charity. The teaching of reading, spelling, and arithmetic came about slowly. Girls and boys received instruction separately. Schools were few in number, and most women were illiterate. Higher education was exclusively for men.

By law women were subject to the authority of their fathers and then their husbands. A married woman could not act without her spouse's consent, but a single woman had practically all the rights of a man. In addition to being legally classified as single or married, women were also classified as either decent and virtuous (those who feared "shame" if they violated behavioral norms) or "shameless" (those who showed disrespect for such norms). The latter group was ostracized from the protection of the family and had no refuge, often living on the fringes of society as vagrants or prostitutes.

Many Spanish, creole, and mestizo women participated actively in family business ventures, most often as silent partners in management, while other mestizo women as well as Indians, black freedwomen, and mulattoes became owners or operators of bakeries, cafés, inns, taverns, and small farms. Concentrations of women that became economically important during the period included convents that acquired capital through endowments and dowries for the inmates. Once invested, this wealth stimulated economic development. Although intended for those choosing to lead a communal life of prayer, chastity, and obedience, many convents became places of sumptuous living, with some of the nuns being waited on by slaves, having meals served in their cells, and even adopting children. By the end of the colonial period, convents had come to be populated by unmarried women, widows, divorcées, and reformed prostitutes, in other words, those for whom there was no place in society. (See SPANISH AMERICA, Colonial Convents in the New World.)

A symbol of independence and revolt against the subordinate role of women in society was the *tapadas* (veiled women) of Peru, whose stylish dress and provocative use of the shawl enabled the wearers to flaunt publicly the code of acceptable female behavior and arouse men's erotic interest as well. At the other extreme were the *beatas* (pious laywomen), whose daily religious devotions, acts of charity, and nunlike habits reflected Christian virtues.

For 300 years women contributed significantly to the social, cultural, and economic evolution of Spanish America according to their status in society. With limited or no education and existing in an inferior relationship to men, they raised children, managed large households, directed economic activities, transmitted the social values and customs of their particular group to their children, and provided social stability. The fact that many women of lower social status propelled themselves upward to positions of influence within society attests to their personal initiative and strength of character.

References. Julie Greer Johnson, *Women in Colonial Spanish American Literature: Literary Images* (Westport, Conn., 1983); Ann M. Pescatello, *Power and Pawn: The Female in Iberian Families, Societies, and Cultures* (Westport, Conn., 1976); Steve J. Stern, *The Secret History of Gender: Women, Men, and Power in Late Colonial Mexico* (Chapel Hill, N.C., 1995).

                                                                    E. V. NIEMEYER, JR.

SPANISH AMERICAN POETS. Nineteenth Century. The social status of women in Latin America regressed during the nineteenth century, and women found themselves even more confined than before independence. They were especially handicapped in that very few women received any schooling beyond the elementary level unless they entered a convent or came from the aristocracy.

Given the fact that very few women benefited from the fruits of higher education, it is not surprising, then, that one finds so few of them among the intellectual luminaries of the nineteenth century in Latin America. In countries as large as Brazil and Argentina, a history written by males, does not record a single woman poet in the nineteenth century. In some Spanish American nations, however, a few women made a significant contribution to poetry: Gertrudis Gómez de Avellaneda of Cuba, Dolores Veintimilla de Galindo of Ecuador, Isabel Prieto de Landázuri of Mexico, María Bibiana Benítez of Puerto Rico, and Salomé Ureña de Henríquez of Santo Domingo. Minor poets were María Josefa Mujía (1813–1888) of Bolivia, Mercedes Marín del Solar (1804–1866) and Rosario Orrego Uribe (1834–1879) of Chile, Josefa Murillo (1860–1898) of Mexico, and Carmen Hernández de Araújo (1832–1877) and Úrsula Cardona de Quiñonez (1836–1875) of Puerto Rico.

Gertrudis Gómez de Avellaneda (1814–1873), poet, novelist, and playwright, was a person who lived intensely the 59 years of her life. Twice she married and twice became a widow. Her love affairs were full of turmoil, and she often found haven in her Catholic faith. In fact, she seriously considered entering the convent. From 1836 to 1859 she lived in Spain, where she earned accolades and was treated by the Spanish intellectuals as one of their own. In 1863 she returned home to play an influential role in Cuban letters as a lyric poet. Her Romanticism is full of emotional intensity and conveyed in neo-classical form, for she was a disciple of Quintana and Meléndez Valdés. Her *Devocionario poético* (1867) reveals a deep faith and a soul thirsty for God. "Al Partir," one of her best sonnets, expresses her love for her homeland. The best of her poetry can be found in *Obras* (4 vols., 1914–1918).

The Ecuadoran Dolores Veintimilla de Galindo (1821–1857) is perhaps the most fascinating and certainly the most tragic of the nineteenth-century women poets. She married the Colombian physician Sixto Galindo and accompanied him to Quito and Cuenca, where she became well known by distinguishing herself in literary contests. In Cuenca, however, she dared to oppose the death penalty imposed on a man convicted of killing his father. She wrote and dedicated a poem to this man, Tiburcio Lucero, whom she did not even know. She was violently attacked in the press and mercilessly slandered, and her life was threatened. Alone in her desperate sorrow, she committed suicide at the age of 36. Veintimilla's Romantic poetry is passionate and poignant, as was her life. Called the "Sappho of Ecuador," she left not only vibrant and moving verses but also the example of a woman who stood alone for the basic human right to life against a society that constantly denied it. Her poems were published in *Producciones literarias* in 1908.

Mexico's Isabel Prieto de Landázuri (1833–1876) was born in Spain and died in Germany but was wholly Mexican in literary training, expression, and temperament. She arrived in Mexico at the age of 5 and moved with her family to Guadalajara. She was especially adept in expressing maternal love in moving lyricism and Romantic emotionalism. Her poems were assembled, edited, and published in 1883 by the Mexican poet and humanist José María Vigil. Her contemporaries were so moved by her poetry that they called her the "Twin Sister of Sor Juana Inés de la Cruz."

Puerto Rico's two most important women poets of the nineteenth century were María Bibiana Benítez (1783–1873) and her daughter Alejandrina Benítez (1819–1879). María Bibiana lived to be 90, far outlasting most nineteenth-century women in Latin America. She began writing verses in her middle life and was the first woman to write poetry in Borinquen. She first came to public attention in 1832 with "La Ninfa de Puerto Rico," a poem dedicated to the installation of the Real Audiencia de Puerto Rico (Royal Court and Council). She modeled her neo-classical and Romantic poems after Calderón and Fray Luís de León without ever achieving much originality.

María Bibiana's daughter Alejandrina Benítez proved a better poet than her mother, singing the beauty of the Puerto Rican landscape and displaying her enthusiasm for modern inventions and the achievements of nineteenth-century science in beautiful verses. She also gave Puerto Rico its best Romantic poet in her son Gautier Benítez.

Another Latin American woman poet who expressed great hopes and optimism about the capabilities of science in creating a better world was the Dominican Salomé Ureña de Henríquez (1850–1897). Her education was extensive because of the privileged position of her family, for she was the wife of Francisco Henríquez, president of the Dominican Republic. Salomé began to show her poetic inclinations at the age of 15 while using the pseudonym "Herminia." Her *Poesías* were first published in 1880 and reveal a patriotic and Romantic soul. Her greatest contribution to her country, however, was the establishment of the first Normal School for Women, the equivalent of the first Dominican Teachers' College. Two of her sons, Max and Pedro Henríquez Ureña, became distinguished writers and novelists. Her best poems, "La gloria del progreso" and "La fé en el porvenir," can be found in *Poesías Completas*, published in 1950.

References. Isaac J. Barrera, *Historia de la literature ecuatoriana* (Quito, 1954); Enrique Anderson Imbert and Eugenio Florit, *Literatura Hispanoamericana* (New York, 1960); Carlos González Peña, *History of the Mexican Literature* (Dallas, 1969); Cesareo Rosa-Nieves, *La Poesía en Puerto Rico* (San Juan, 1958).

TARCISIO BEAL

SPANISH AMERICAN POETS. Twentieth Century. Latin American poetry offers a rich spectrum of themes and styles, yet it has not been easy for the woman writer to be recognized by the patriarchal establishment with its rigid, critical canons. Despite all adversities, the lyrical heritage left by the early women writers as well as by those who continue working today is vast and vital.

In the 1920s there emerged in Spanish America a group of four important poets who would have an impact on future generations. The year 1920 is in itself a key date, for in that year women begin to appear in the public and intellectual circles of their respective cities, emerging from the habitual, intimate, and cloistered privacy in which so many of their contemporaries had remained hidden and silent.

Alfonsina Storni (1892–1938), poet of Buenos Aires, is one of the pioneers who began to speak out without false euphemisms or modesty concerning the condition of women. One of her most famous poems, entitled "Tú me quieres blanca" (You Want Me White), emphasizes the fact that man demands perfection and especially chastity of the woman, while he himself is exempt from judgment. This critical stance toward the society in which she lived, in addition to her profound identification with the woman who transgresses, is demonstrated in another poem, "La loba" (The She-Wolf). Here Storni portrays a woman who chooses to lead her own life through the image of an animal that separates from the pack and chooses a life that is solitary but dignified. This image represents one of the principal tendencies in Storni's work: her poetry champions, above all, the creative woman's right to freedom and pleasure.

Storni's opus, including seven volumes of poetry, children's theater, and prose poems, makes her a prolific, yet little studied, creator. Her subtle irony and sharp critique of Buenos Aires society (also found in Mistral's poetry) and her deep concern for the marginal, the weak, and the oppressed open the way for the new voices of the future.

Gabriela Mistral (1889–1957), contemporary of Alfonsina Storni and the first Latin American woman to win the Nobel Prize in literature, is also a fundamental lyrical voice that blazes paths for future generations. Mistral is characterized by a primal attachment to the land that surrounded her. Her poetry is rooted in her native Elqui Valley in northern Chile. A profound regional attachment characterizes all her work, especially her important *Poema de Chile* (Poem of Chile) of 1954, dedicated to the topography of her country, and the famous long poem "Sol del trópico" (Tropical Sun), dedicated to all of Latin America.

A language studded with powerful images, sober verse form, and expressive sensuality characterizes this extraordinary woman, who wrote of maternity, frigidity, madness, and children. Because of this array of themes, she was always labeled as a traditional Romantic "woman poet." Yet the rich language and the original focus of these themes put her ahead of her time and caused her to be misunderstood.

Delmira Agostina (1887–1914) and Juana de Ibarbourou (1895–1977) draw a pattern different from that of Storni and Mistral; they also belong to a different poetic generation. The poetic of Agostini is characterized by an expansive eroticism and a concern centered on the discovery of her own freedom and autonomy. Through her intensely sensual poetry, unlike Agostina, Ibarbourou exults in conforming to the patriarchal standards of her time and in praising her own body, always in relation to a masculine object.

The Mexican Rosario Castellanos (1925–1974) is without doubt one of the most brilliant voices of the period. Born just as the preceding generation was beginning to publish, Castellanos took on the dynamism and the impetus of her predecessors and went on to produce one of the most profound and seminal bodies of work of contemporary Latin American literature. From *Travectoria del Polvo* (1948) through the poems collected after her premature death in 1974, the theme of Castellanos' poetry is, above all, the condition of the Spanish American woman, to whom "things" have been "taught mistakenly." With this phrase Castellanos draws the first coordinate of her poetry: the reevaluation of female passivity and the championing of a new search for fulfillment and freedom. Just as Storni scoffed at the "hombres pequenitos" (the little men), who shut women up in canary cages, Castellanos exposes the cult of confinement and domesticity, that is, the Latin American female destiny.

Castellanos denounces woman's immersion in petty detail, her subjugation to the prescriptions of motherhood, and the cult of eternal love. In so doing she casts doubt on almost all the values that have dominated Hispanic society. Her poetry, like that of Storni and Mistral, is rich in imagery conveyed by means of everyday language. The contribution of these women can be summed up as the exposition of new themes and the exposure of the female condition through the elaboration of a new language linked to feminist postulates.

The poetry of three very important and highly original poets, the Argentines Olga Orozco (b. 1931) and Alejandra Pizarnik (1936–1972) and the Puerto Rican Rosario Ferré (b. 1942), should also be mentioned. Orozco's poetic voice is unique in current Spanish American literature. It is occasionally obscure, though not in imagery but in the existential mystery of what is enunciated. Her copious and well-known poetic production possesses a coherence that reflects the recurrent ambiguity of the poetic word itself. She manifests a strong attraction to the unconscious and a desire to release and liberate its energy. Her first book, *Desde lijos* (From Afar), published in 1946, already conjures up that sense of an unknown and perilous game with an inverted world. Orozco's poetry is highly dreamlike, sculpted with perspectives where dream takes on the outlines of reality. The same could be said of her fellow Buenos Airean, Alejandra Pizarnik, who, like her, inhabits a world dominated by the surreal and the transfiguration of immediate reality.

There are many other important women poets in the Spanish American lyrical tradition, but it is primarily these women whose originality and daring mark an indelible path in poetry written by women of the twentieth century.

MARJORIE AGOSIN, translated by LORRAINE ROSES

SPANISH AMERICAN PROSE. Nineteenth Century. With independence and the formation of the new republics during the early decades of the nineteenth century came an invigorating commitment to women's education, which had a correspondingly invigorating effect on women's writing. The work of educators such as Juana Manso and Rosa Guerra in Argentina, Rita Lecumberry Robles in Ecuador, and Ana Roque de Duprey in Puerto Rico and the proliferation of schools for girls assured the literacy of a large number of women and their consequent increased participation in a variety of literary activities. Poetry, the novel, and the essay were cultivated, and periodicals by and for women proliferated, they being one of the most popular and accessible outlets for women to express themselves and communicate with one another. Among the periodicals were *El Album cubano de lo bueno y lo bello* (The Cuban Album of the Good and the Beautiful; Havana, Cuba, 1860), founded and directed by Gertrudis Gómez de Avellaneda; *El Album* (The Album; Lima, Peru, 1874), founded by Argentine exile Juana Manuela Gorriti; *La Mujer* (Woman; Bogotá, Colombia, 1878), founded by Soledad Acosta de Samper.

Letter writing, a common form of written expression during the colonial period, continued its importance as an outlet for women. Well-known correspondence is that of María de Sánchez (Mariquita) (1786–1868), who presided over an important salon in Buenos Aires in the early decades of the nineteenth century and corresponded with Esteban Echeverría, Domingo Sarmiento, and other political and literary figures, and that of Manuela Sáenz to Simón Bolívar. Many nineteenth-century writers maintained a lively correspondence with friends, family, and one another, but those that have perhaps most captivated readers are the love letters of two Cuban writers, Gertrudis Gómez de Avellaneda (1814–1873) and Juana Borrero (1877–1896). Much work remains to be done in collecting and publishing the letters of Spanish American women. As Sergio Verqara Quiroz demonstrates in his groundbreaking publication *Cartas de mujeres en Chile, 1630–1885* (Chilean Women's Letters), the correspondence of women who have not been remembered for singular acts of bravery, for their relationships with famous men, or for other literary accomplishments can have great literary as well as social and historical value.

A number of women combined a prolific and varied literary output with an active involvement in education, woman's rights, and social reform. Gertrudis Gómez de Avellaneda, who was born in Cuba but spent most of her productive literary life in Spain, wrote poetry, numerous plays and novels, travel narratives, letters, and essays. Besides her journalism, Soledad

Acosta de Samper (Colombia, 1883–1903) wrote biographies, history, travel narratives, and essays, among them "La mujer moderna" (The Modern Woman), a book-length text of scholarly research that is still useful today as a source of information on women's contribution to the arts and sciences. Juana Manuela Gorriti's (Argentina, 1819–1892) voluminous production includes history, biographies, novels, stories, legends, an autobiographical narrative, and even a cookbook. Clorinda Matto de Turner (Peru, 1852–1909) was active in journalism and wrote several novels. *Aves sin nido* (Birds without a Nest) is considered a forerunner of the Peruvian Indianist novel. Her forthright attacks on the clergy and on government officials caused her excommunication from the Catholic Church. Other women suffered similar punishments or ostracism for their bravery in criticizing the Establishment in their novels. Mercedes Cabello de Carbonera (Peru, 1845–1909) attacked the corruption of urban Lima society in her novel *Blanca Sol*. She spent the last 10 years of her life in an insane asylum. In Honduras, Lucila Gamero de Medina (1873–1964), credited with writing the first Honduran novel, was excommunicated for her criticism of the clergy in *Blanca Olmedo*.

Juana Manso (1819–1879), Rose Guerra (d. 1864), and Eduarda Mansilla (1838–1892) enriched the literature of Argentina with their novels, journalism, and travel narratives, while Lindaura Anzoátegui is considered a forerunner of the *costumbrista* (literature of manners) movement in Bolivia because of her text *Como se vive en mi pueblo* (Life in My Town). Ana Roque de Duprey (Puerto Rico, 1853–1933), besides her work in education, journalism, and women's rights, wrote 32 novels, including *Sara la obrera* (Sarah the Worker), an example of social realism. The Cuban Luisa Pérez de Zambrana (1835–1922), although best known for her poetry, wrote two novels and contributed to various periodicals.

Two writers who deserve special mention are María de la Merced Santa Cruz (la Condesa de Merlin) and Flora Tristan. La Condesa de Merlin was born in Cuba in 1789 but went with her father to live in France and thereafter made that country her home. She maintained an attachment, however, to her native land, and her works *Mes douze premieres annees* (My First Twelve Years) and *La Havane* (Havana) were translated into Spanish and are considered a valuable contribution to Cuban letters. Flora Tristan (1803–1844), born in Paris to a French mother and a Peruvian father, at the age of 23 traveled to Peru to claim what she considered to be her rightful inheritance. The account of her travels through Peru and her descriptions of people, places, and events are a unique and fascinating text.

References. Lynn Ellen Rice Cortina, *Spanish American Women Writers: A Bibliographical Research Checklist* (New York, 1983); Meri Knaster, *Women in Spanish America: An Annotated Bibliography from Pre-Conquest to Contemporary Times* (Boston, 1977); Diane E. Marting (ed.), *Women Writers of Spanish America:*

An Annotated BioBibliographical Guide (Westport, Conn., 1987); Sergio Verqara Quiroz, *Cartas de mujeres en Chile, 1630–1885* (Santiago, 1987).

JANET N. GOLD

SPANISH AMERICAN PROSE. Twentieth Century. In the period after World War I, when Latin American literature needed alternatives to highly rhetorical and ornamental modes, women writers helped develop a simpler prose. Gabriela Mistral of Chile (b. Lucila Godoy Alcayaga, 1889–1957; Nobel Prize in literature, 1945) in her essays recognized women as teachers, mothers, and counselors. Alfonsina Storni (Argentina, 1892–1938), also a poet, was a noted journalist and passionate feminist. Teresa de la Parra (Venezuela, 1889–1936) focused on upper-class, Europeanized ladies in her novels *Iphigenia* (1924; Eng., 1993) and *Mamá Blanca's Souvenirs* (1929; Eng., 1959). Early recognized as a stylist, she was rediscovered as a student of women's culture.

In the 1930s and 1940s Buenos Aires, known for sophisticated, fantastic fiction, featured Chilean novelist María Luisa Bombal (1910–1980) of *The House of Mist* (1934; Eng., 1947) and *The Shrouded Woman* (1938; Eng., 1948), Victoria Ocampo (1891–1979), an influential editor, and her writer-sister Silvina (b. 1903). Writers of realism at this time included Marta Brunet (Chile, 1901–1967), who showed rural women as more independent than traditional codes would suggest. Nellie Campobello (b. 1900) depicted the Mexican revolution through a small girl's eyes in *Cartucho* (1931; Eng., 1988) and the lives of revolutionary era women in *My Mother's Hands* (1937; Eng., 1988). Women folklorists studied and popularized crafts and lore. Lydia Cabrera (Cuba–United States, 1900–1991), adapted Afro-Caribbean tales. María Elena Walsh (Argentina, b. 1930), folksinger and writer, used folk narrative conventions to help children understand such issues as shifting sex roles and environmental dilemmas.

Currently being rediscovered are women who pursued both learning and social change during the 1930s and 1940s: the literary critic and feminist Concha Meléndez (Puerto Rico, 1895–1984); the Costa Rican short story writer, activist, and student of Central American society Carmen Lyra (María Isabel Carvajal, 1890–1949); and Yolanda Oreamuno (Costa Rica, 1916–1956), psychological novelist and legendary nurturer of intellectuals and activists.

By the 1950s and 1960s, many more women participated in literary life. Social novelists included Rosario Castellanos (Mexico, 1925–1974), whose *The Nine Guardians* (1957; Eng., 1961) gave an inside view of Tzotzil Indian and Hispanic cultures in rural Mexico. Castellanos was an important feminist voice. Marta Lynch (Argentina, 1925–1985) developed a political and yet highly personal novel; *La Señora Ordóñez* (1967) analyzes a woman's confused attempts at autonomy. Elena Garro (Mexico, b. 1920) veils social criticism in the enigmatic, lyrical novel *Recollections of Things to Come* (1963; Eng., 1969). Two best-selling Argentine writers, Silvina Bullrich (1915–1990) and Beatriz Guido (1925–1988), leaven social commentary with melodrama.

In Mexico, Elena Poniatowska (b. 1933), Margo Glantz (b. 1930), and María Luisa Mendoza (b. 1931) practice innovative journalism. Poniatowska obtains revealing oral histories from actors in Mexican history (*Massacre in Mexico*, 1971; Eng., 1974). Mendoza's journalism and novels transmit, in eccentrically cluttered style, social criticism and examine women's culture. Glantz is a supporter of cultural experimentation and a feminist.

Writers of the postboom era include the Argentine–U.S. Luisa Valenzuela (b. 1937); Chilean Isabel Allende (b. 1942), author of *The House of Spirits* (1982; Eng., 1985); Ana Lydia Vega (Puerto Rico, b. 1946); Angeles Mastretta (Mexico, b. 1949); Magali García Ramis (Puerto Rico, b. 1946); Laura Esquivel (Mexico, b. 1950); Rosario Ferré (Puerto Rico, 1942); and Albalucía Angel (Colombia, b. 1939). Enjoying renewed attention are the Argentines Griselda Gambaro (1928), Sara Gallardo (b. 1929), and Angélica Gorodischer (b. 1929), Inés Arrendondo (Mexico, b. 1928), Claribel Alegría (Nicaragua/El Salvador, b. 1924), and Armonía Somers (Uruguay, b. Armonía Etchepare de Henestrosa, 1917), as well as women essayists in anthropology, activism, and social thought. While today's writers are often feminists, women's studies should also reexamine earlier authors who, without open feminism, understood women's status and culture.

References. Debra A. Castillo, *Talking Back: Toward a Latin American Feminist Literary Criticism* (Ithaca, N.Y. 1992); Jean Franco, *Plotting Women: Gender and Representation in Mexico* (New York, 1989); Amy K. Kamisky, *Reading the Body Politic: Feminist Criticism and Latin American Writers* (Minneapolis, 1993); Naomi Lindstrom, *Women's Voice in Latin American Literature* (Washington, D.C., 1989); Adelaida López de Martínez (ed.), *Discurso femenino actual* (San Juan, P. R., 1995); Diane E. Marting (ed.), *Spanish American Women Writers: A Bio-Bibliographical Source Book* (Westport, Conn., 1990).

NAOMI LINDSTROM

SPANISH AMERICAN WRITERS (COLONIAL). The deficient education of women during the colonial period made New World literature predominantly the domain of men. Additionally, criticism tended to pay little attention to literature written by women and in some cases has even denied feminine authorship of works written under pseudonyms. Recent scholarship gives us a better perspective of the epoch, for it has revealed formerly unknown names and texts, most from religious centers.

Despite the lack of intellectual stimulation, women in religious orders produced creative works that deserve consideration. The most outstanding are, from Mexico, Sor Juana Inés de la Cruz (1648?–1695) and, from Colombia, the Venerable Mother Josefa del Castillo y Guevara (Mother Castillo; 1671–1742). Others whose names remain but whose works lack any great importance preceded and followed them. They and a few laywomen writers are listed in catalogs and collections of the time, lists copied by Carlos Sigüenza y Góngora, José Toribio Medina, Manuel Orozco y Berra, and Alfonso Méndez Plancarte.

The 4,000 or more volumes in the library of Sor Juana Inés de la Cruz and the instruments she possessed for the study of mathematics, physics, and music made her cell an intellectual sanctuary that attracted the most notable men of that epoch. In a reactionary period of extreme distrust toward all scientific or technical activities, Sor Juana distinguished herself as a solitary figure of genius dedicated to speculation and to experiments that prefigured the Cartesian spirit of the age of Enlightenment. She was a feminist and since the seventeenth century has been considered one of the greatest geniuses of baroque poetry. She was also outstanding in drama and in prose. Her complete works were collected in four thick volumes by Méndez Plancarte.

The works of Mother Castillo were not published until a century after they were written. Menéndez Pelayo called her the St. Teresa of America: not only did she dedicate herself to the mystic life, as did the saint of Avila, but she also recounted her own life at the urging of her confessors. Moreover, her mystic-literary works reveal the obvious influence of St. Teresa, and, although she was not canonized, she was beatified. Her literary production, collected and published in 1968 by Darío Achury Valenzuela, consists of *My Life*, an autobiographical book, and *Spiritual Affections*, a mystic treatise. There are also poems attributed to her, but Méndez Plancarte has shown that some are adaptations of poetry by Sor Juana Inés de la Cruz. Therefore, although she is assured a place among American prose writers, there remains a question of whether she should be included among the lyric poets of the colonial period.

Santo Domingo, then known as the Athens of the New World, was the home of the first woman poet whose work can be seriously considered part of American literature, Sor Leonor de Ovando (?–1610?). Of her work only five sonnets and a composition written in blank verse are known.

Thomas Gage (*A New Survey of the West Indies*, 1655) was the first to speak of the "Tenth Muse," Guatemalan Sor Juana de Maldonado y Paz (1595–1665?). From then on, her name was regularly included in histories of Guatemalan literature, even though until recently we did not have a single poem as evidence of a talent worthy of the place given her among her country's lyric poets. The research of Ernesto Chinchilla Aguilar and Mariano López Mayorical brought to light some documents that might confirm Gage's assertions. They tell of the small, but lavish, palace that Sor Juana possessed in her convent in Guatemala; the protests throughout the city when she was named abbess; Montúfar's painting of her in the pose of St. Lucía, condemned by the Inquisition; her cell as the meeting place for the most prestigious poets, artists, and intellectuals among her contemporaries. However, the poems attributed to her in Fray Antonio de Arochena's *Catalogue of the Writers in the Order of San Francisco of the Province of Guatemala* have never been located. The little that has so far been retrieved is not sufficient proof of an exceptional literary talent. Much research must still be done before a definite conclusion is reached.

There are many more nuns in the annals of mystic poetry, for example, Venezuelan Carmalite Sor María de los Angeles (María Josefa Paz del Castillo [1750–?]), Capuchin Sor Juana de Hazaña, and Sor Paula de Jesús of the Barefoot Merced order. Poems of the latter two were included in Rubén Vargas Ugarte's anthology *Peruvian Classics*.

A flood of the Mapocho River in 1783 led Sor Tadea de San Joaquín (Tadea García de la Huerta [?–1827]) to write a long ballad to her confessor, who was absent from the city. The ballad relates how the lives of the nuns were threatened when the water beat against the walls of the monastery. It was published in Lima in 1784 and is considered the first poem by a Chilean woman.

Autobiographies were also written in the convents, some of questionable literary value. They do, however, provide valuable sociohistorical information. In addition to the brief, but important, autobiography of Sor Juana Inés contained in the letter she addressed to Sor Filotea (pseudonym used by the Bishop of Puebla) and the autobiography of Mother Castillo, they include one written in 1757 by Sor Mariá Marcela (1719–?) of New Spain in 1757; by Sor Sebastiana Josefa de la Santísima Trinidad (?–1757), in the form of epistles addressed to her confessor; by Sor María Anna Agueda de San Ignacio (1695–1756), author of several devout works of poor literary quality and doubtful spiritual value; and, by Sor Ursula Suárez (1668–1749) of Chile, the *Story of the Singular Mercies the Lord Has Shown a Nun, His Bride*, which, according to Toribio Medina, is a product of her imagination. Mother Inés de la Cruz, founder of the convent of San José de Carmelitas Descalzas de Mexico, wrote an autobiography, as did Ecuadoran Sor Catalina de Jesús María Herrera (1717–1795, *Secrets between the Soul and God*).

Of special interest is *The Life and Adventures of the Nun-Ensign, Doña Catalina de Erauso* (1592–1648?), published in 1828. The novelesque character of the life this singular woman led induces the suspicion that it is an apocryphal text: from the age of 4 she was isolated from the world in a convent in San Sebastián de Guipúzcõa. At 15 she ran away and, dressed as a man, served several masters as a page for a couple of years, but, fearful of being discovered by her family, she sailed to Chile. There she fought against the Araucanian Indians as a valiant soldier and later in Peru became famous as a gambler and a swordsman. After 19 years of adventures she revealed her identity and was forced to return to her native country. Under the name Antonio de Erauso she immediately embarked for New Spain, where she worked as a mule driver transporting goods between Veracruz and Mexico City. Between 1648 and 1650 she disappeared mysteriously. The written account goes up only to 1626, the date of her return to her native land. In it there is a basis of truth that probably comes from the oral or written tale that Catalina de Erauso herself told; however, along with the passages verified by the Archives of the Indies appear many fictitious ones that seem to be interpolations by another author. A meticulous, in-depth study could prove that a process of fictionalization has occurred, characteristic of the colonial narrative, a process noted in studies by Enrique Pupo-Walker. For that reason it could be called fictionalized autobiography. Regardless of the identity of the interpolator, the important thing is that the manuscript that has been preserved was written between 1626 and May 24, 1784, the date Juan Bautista Muñoz deposited it in the Royal Academy of History in Madrid. This is a text that should be taken into account in future studies dealing with the narrative of that period.

Some women writers of great literary talent hid behind pseudonyms. Perhaps because their works stood out as superior, it was contended that those fictitious appellations really hid the identity of men. Amarilis and Clarinda in Peru are two cases worthy of mention.

Of Amarilis' work only one excellent lyric poem has been preserved. Entitled "Epistle to Belardo," it was addressed to Lope de Vega in 1621, begging him to write the biography of Saint Dorothea; it recounts that the author is the descendant of Peruvian conquistadors, explains that she is in a convent in Lima, and, above all, expresses her tendency to love boldly the most impossible things, among which she counts "the hopeless love" that he awoke in her with his "peerless works." In 1630 Lope de Vega included this poem in his *Apollo's Laurels*.

Clarinda, called the "Great Anonymous Writer," became known for her poem "In Praise of Poetry." Diego de Mejía included it in his *Antartic Parnassus*, explaining that the author was "an illustrious lady in the Kingdom of Peru, well versed in Tuscan and Portuguese," whose name Mejía withheld following her order and out of due respect. Some critics agree with the Colombian poet Rafael Pambo that "in Spanish seldom has anyone pronounced a more practical and elevated discourse on poetry."

Women outside the convent also made their mark. In the baroque literature of Mexico, Catalina de Eslava (1534–1601) and María de Estrada Medinilla are recognized. The former dedicated to her uncle, dramatist Fernán González de Eslava, a sonnet, "The Laurel Wreathes Our Brow," which was included in the preface to his book *Spiritual and Sacramental Orations*. Méndez Plancarte considers María de Estrada Medinilla the precursor of Sor Juana Inés de la Cruz. Two lengthy lyric poems of hers were published in 1640.

In conclusion, in colonial literature mystic poems and autobiographies by nuns predominate. In drama, Sor Juana Inés de la Cruz was the outstanding figure. Of all the writers mentioned, only the complete works of Sor Juana, Mother Castillo, and Sor María Anna Agueda of San Ignacio have been published. In general the works are ruled by the literary codes of Spain and Europe; by patriarchal conventions; and by norms imposed by phallocentrism and by scholastic philosophy. The restless clairvoyance of Sor Juana did not conform to the latter, and for that reason the church silenced her lyrical voice and her spiritual anxieties—an intellectual death that caused her demise within two years, but the Mexican nun still towers over the panorama of colonial literature. In general, the rescue of texts written by women remains today a challenging task for researchers.

References. Electa Arenal and Stacey Schlau, *Untold Sisters—Hispanic Nuns in Their Own Works* (Albuquerque, 1989), 5; Madre Francisca Josefa Castillo y Guevara, *Obras completas*, 2 vols., ed. Darío Valenzuela Achury (Bogotá, 1968); Catalina de Erauso, *Vida i sucesos de la Monja Alférez* (Tempe, Ariz., 1992); Thomas Gage, *Nueva relación que contiene los viajes de Thomas Gage en la Nueva España* (Paris, 1838); Tadea García de la Huerta, *Relación de la inundación que hiso [sic] el Río Mapocho de la ciudad de Santiago de Chile, en el Monasterio de las Carmelitas*, ed. José Toribio Medina (Santiago, Chile, 1899); Pilar Gonzalbo Aizpuru, *Las mujeres en la Nueva España—Educación y vida cotidiana* (Mexico City, 1987); Sor Juana Inés de la Cruz, *Obras completas*, 4 vols., ed. Alfonso Méndez Plancarte (Mexico City, 1951–1956); Julio Jiménez Rueda, *Sor Juana Inés de la Cruz en su época* (Mexico City, 1951); Julie Greer Johnson, *Women in Colonial Spanish Literature—Literary Images* (Westport, Conn., 1983); Guillermo Lohmann Villena, *Amarilis Indiana* (Lima, Peru, 1993); Alonso Méndez Plancarte, *Poetas novohispanos—Segundo siglo (1621–1721)*, vol. 2 (Mexico City, 1944); Marcelino Menéndez Pelayo, Historia de la poesía hispanoamericana, 2 vols. (Madrid, 1948); Octavio Paz, *Sor Juana Inés de las Cruz o Las trampas de la fe* (Barcelona, Spain, 1982); *Revista Iberoamericana—Literatura colonial* 2, 172–173 (July–December 1995): 605–649); Carlos Sigüenza y Góngora, *Vida de la V. M. Ynés de la Cruz, refiriendo con sus propias palabras . . . —Paraíso Occidental, plantado y cultivado en su magnífico Real Convento de Jesús María de México* (Mexico, 1684).

RIMA DE VALLBONNA, translated by BERTIE ACKER

SPORTS. Women's participation in public sporting events in Western society has been limited to Bronze Age Crete, Classical Sparta, and the twentieth century. Although women's participation is still much more limited than men's, within the last 50 years the track-and-field, winter, and aquatic events and the team sports in which women publicly engage have grown enormously.

In 1896, the modern Olympic Games began in Athens, Greece. In the early years of this competition, almost all of the events were considered "men-only affairs." Not until the 1900 games did women officially enter the Olympics and then only in two events, golf and tennis. Next to be added were archery and ice skating, with swimming following in 1912. Although women began applying for the inclusion of track-and-field events to the Olympics in 1919, not until the 1928 games was any women's track and field offered, and even then participants were allowed only five events in a provisional program.

Besides their late entrance into sports participation, women in the United States have faced additional restrictions in their athletic involvement. First, only white women were initially allowed to participate in sporting events, and only upper-class women could generally afford to do so. Second, individual sports were socially acceptable much earlier than team sports, which might involve physical contact. Third, women's involvement in sports was considered acceptable only if the women had "feminine" motivations, for example, weight control, sociability (in high schools and colleges "competition" was "unfeminine," but noncompetitive "play days" with other schools might be allowed). Finally, even today, many women with interest and ability in athletics lack the opportunity to participate. Scholarships, facilities, and adequate training and coaching needed to participate in athletics are not available to women on a level comparable to their availability to men.

Despite the fact that women were latecomers in sports participation and that they continued to face additional restrictions once in the sports arena, women have made dramatic improvements in their level of performance. In fact, when comparing women's with men's times in speed events over a 50-year period, the statistics show not only that women have improved their times but also that their improvement has proceeded more rapidly than men's. These female athletes' improvements have been so great that K. F. Dyer suggests that women will "catch up" with men in the near future (see this work also for more detailed comparisons of women's and men's times).

Of the many factors involved in this greater improvement in women's athletic accomplishments, one is the increase in medical knowledge of the female body. Social factors include greater societal acceptance of female participation, changes in female socialization toward sports, and the emergence of positive female role models for younger female and male athletes. There have also been political and legal factors, such as the women's liberation movement, the drive to ratify the Equal Rights Amendment (ERA),*and Title IX* of the Educational Amendments of 1972.

Women have made impressive advances in performance level over the last 50 years. But the future of women's sports in the United States was suddenly jeopardized in 1984 when the Supreme Court, in its *Grove City College v. Bell* decision, determined that Title IX applied only to those specific programs receiving federal funds. Since athletic programs in the nation's schools do not normally receive federal funding, it was feared that the *Grove City* decision might send women's athletic programs back to their pre–Title IX condition. However, after several failed attempts, in 1988 Congress passed a law undoing the *Grove City* decision and overrode President Reagan's veto. The future of women's sports in the United States again looks hopeful, but the lesson of the *Grove City* decision needs to be remembered. Constant pressure is still needed to see that all educational institutions offer girls and women athletic opportunities comparable to those they offer boys and men.

References. M. A. Boutilier and L. SanGiovanni, *The Sporting Woman* (Chicago, 1983); K. F. Dyer, *Challenging the Men* (New York, 1982); R. Howell, *Her Story in Sport: A Historical Anthology of Women in Sports* (New York, 1982); E. McGrath, "Let's Put Muscle Where It Really Counts," *Women's Sports and Fitness* 8 (December 1986): 59.

MELISSA LATIMER

SPORTS. Gender Equity In. Gender equity in sports has improved since 1972 but is far from being achieved. Before the passage of Title IX* of the Education Amendment of 1972, which prohibits gender discrimination in educational programs or activities receiving federal financial assistance, women constituted only 5 percent of the total number of athletics participants in high school and 15 percent of those in college. By 1993–1994 only 38 percent of high school participants and approximately 36 percent of athletes in college programs affiliated with the National Collegiate Athletic Association (NCAA) were female. During the 1970s, after the passage of Title IX, athletic opportunities for women increased dramatically at both the high school and college levels. By 1980, however, increase in participation began to level off, and it drastically decreased after the Supreme Court's *Grove City College v. Bell* (1984) decision narrowed Title IX's coverage from the entire institution to the specific program or activity that received federal financial assistance (Berry and Wong). In 1988, the Civil Rights Restoration Act counteracted the *Grove City* decision and restored strength to the administrative enforcement of Title IX as it related to athletics.

In 1979 the Office of Civil Rights (OCR) released initial guidelines that would need to be followed in order for a sports program to be in compliance with the federal mandate:

1. substantial proportionality of intercollegiate athletics opportunities to the respective enrollments of each gender (e.g., if full-time undergraduate enrollment is 50/50, athletics opportunities should be 50/50);

2. history and continuing practice of program expansion for the underrepresented gender: the institution must demonstrate a continuing practice (to date, very few institutions meet this criterion);

3. extent of equal and effective accommodation of the athletics interests of the underrepresented gender.

In October 1995, the OCR released a new interpretation of the three-prong approach that allows institutions to abide by one of the three prongs. The interpretation stated that Title IX compliance is not meant to deny opportunities for either gender. The OCR also focuses on athletics program components to determine compliance. These components are accommodation of interests and abilities (sports offered), athletics financial assistance, equipment and supplies, scheduling of games and practice times, travel and per diem allowances, tutoring, coaching, locker rooms/practice and competitive facilities, medical/athletics training facilities and services, housing/dining facilities and services, publicity, support services, and recruitment of student athletes. Comparisons are made on a total program basis (i.e., total men's to total women's opportunities and benefits, because Title IX protects opportunities and benefits on the basis of gender, not on the basis of basketball or volleyball). These same components are also used at the interscholastic level where applicable.

The OCR has developed a manual to assist institutions in complying with Title IX. This manual walks institutions step by step through a self-study to determine compliance or noncompliance.

The role played by the OCR in complaints of gender discrimination has increased dramatically. The OCR responds to any complaint of gender discrimination filed with its office and also selects institutions at random to investigate for compliance.

Participation numbers indicate that a large majority of institutions of higher learning are not in compliance if the "proportionality" prong is addressed. In 1993–1994, the undergraduate enrollment for men and women at NCAA Division I institutions was 49.2 percent men and 50.8 percent women, but the percentage of participants in intercollegiate athletics was 66.4 percent men and 33.6 percent women. Though the first half of the 1990s enrollment percentages have remained fairly stable, improvement in the percentage of women participating in athletics has been small. In 1990–1991, the proportion of men and women participants was 69.1 and 30.9 percent, respectively; in 1993–1994, 66.4 and 33.6 percent, and in 1994–1995, 63.1 percent and 36.9 percent.

The "Equity in Disclosure Act" of 1994 requires institutions to disclose gender equity information on a team-by-team basis: number of participants (on the day of first contest), total operating expenses attributable to each team, number of coaches/assistant coaches (including number of male and female coaches), total amount of money spent on athletics-related aid, total recruiting expenditures (separate for men and women), total revenue (men and women), and average annual salaries of all coaches (these are not done on a team-by-team basis).

The Civil Rights Restoration Act brought strength back to the Title IX federal mandate. Institutions not in compliance will continue to see lawsuits brought against them by coaches and student athletes who face gender discrimination. As long as the court system continues to mandate compliance with Title IX, and as long as the desire for equitable programming remains strong, athletics participation by women will increase. The federal mandate of equal opportunity is over 20 years due, but equity will be achieved only when girls and women are provided with full opportunities to actually participate in sports.

References. R. C. Berry and G. Wong, *Law and Business of the Sports Industries*, 2d ed. (Westport, Conn., 1993); D. Blum, "Slow Progress on Equity," *The Chronicle of Higher Education* 41 (October 26, 1994): A45–A51; NCAA, *Achieving Gender Equity: A Basic Guide to Title IX for Colleges and Universities* (Overland Park, Kans., 1994); *NCAA News* 31 (36) (1994): 3, 16; 32 (4) (1995): 1, 16; 32 (5) (1995).

JANE MEYER

SPORTS ISSUES. The history of girls and women in sports has seen tremendous change since the passage of Title IX* in 1972. Women have seen change on both ends of the athletics spectrum, participation in sports and access to leadership roles. Girls are being afforded increased opportunities to participate at all grade and high school levels, but job opportunities have actually declined so that access to leadership roles has yet to be realized. Numerous studies have been conducted to determine both participation opportunities for girls and women and the status of women in sports leadership positions. Also, the court system is becoming heavily involved with gender and equal pay discrimination lawsuits, especially at the intercollegiate level.

The major sports issues for women have been participation in sports; access to leadership roles, (and, once access has been achieved, equitable compensation levels in sports leadership roles); and increasing leadership opportunities for minority women.

One method of increasing athletics access to leadership positions for women is to provide appropriate role models for girls. This has been overwhelmingly documented by R. V. Acosta and L. J. Carpenter, who showed that the only way to increase female representation in sports leadership positions is to provide role models. Unfortunately, the number of role models has declined drastically. In 1972, 90 percent of coaches and administrators of women's college teams were women. In 1992 only 48 percent of coaches and 17 percent of administrators of women's teams were female, and women held just 30.8 percent of all administrative jobs in athletics programs. Among women's programs, 27.8 percent had no women at all involved in their administration. If this trend continues, there may be no women coaches at the college level in another 20 years.

A small piece of good news is that women have broken the barrier with regard to administering NCAA (National Collegiate Athletic Association) Division I athletics programs with I-A football. In the mid-1990s, then, a limited number of women were given the opportunity to administer major college athletics programs, which had not been the case five years earlier.

The NCAA conducted a study in 1988–1989 to gain a better understanding of the "perceived barriers of women in intercollegiate athletics careers." Female coaches and administrators who participated were primarily white, single with no children, and under 40 years of age. Eighty-five percent of the administrators surveyed said they would enter the athletics field again, even though they face some form of discrimination on the administrative side of athletics (i.e., there are many qualified women who apply for jobs but are not hired).

Ninety-five percent of the surveyed coaches "stated they would enter the profession of coaching again and 70% plan to stay in their current position for another year." Coaches must recognize the importance of mentoring young females and addressing with them the possibility of coaching as a viable profession for women.

Women officials revealed that 62 percent had previously been college coaches and officiated at a variety of levels (NCAA, National Junior College Athletic Association [NJCAA], National Association of Intercollegiate Athletics [NAIA], and high school). Officials also obtained their positions by marketing themselves and performing part-time duties of officiating for an average of eight years.

The top five reasons that there is a decline or lack of women in athletics leadership roles as perceived by both men and women in intercollegiate athletics administration were success of the "old boys club" network, lack of support systems for females, failure of the "old girls club" network, female "burnout" (women leave coaching and/or administration sooner than men), and failure of females to apply for job openings. Costa and Carpenter, *Perceived Causes.*

Women can serve as positive role models as administrators, coaches, teachers, and officials in sports. It is important for women to position themselves as leaders and to promote the importance of mentoring to young girls as these girls discover the positive influence sports can have on their lives. It must all begin by women's obtaining leadership positions and mentoring each other to obtain additional leadership opportunities for other women.

Active leadership positions obtained by women must be equitably compensated. The 1963 Equal Pay Act stipulated that an employer must pay equal salaries to men and women holding jobs that require comparable skill, effort, and responsibility and that are performed under similar working conditions. It is the individual's responsibility to establish that the job is substantially equal to one held by an employee of the opposite gender who is being paid more. The person filing the discrimination charge must also prove that gender is the sole reason for the pay inequity. When a salary discrepancy exists, and jobs are determined to be essentially equal, the court examines whether the wage differential is justifiable based on criteria other than gender. Institutions find that they need to be very careful in the wording of contracts for coaches because if the wording in job descriptions and qualifications is comparable, the pay for coaches should be the same or comparable. If discrepancies exist, they must be able to demonstrate why the discrepancy exists and that it is not based solely on gender (Wong and Barr).

Participation of women increased, but not dramatically, in the 1985–1995 decade. In 1994–1995, participation numbers, 63.1 percent for men, 36.9 percent for women, in intercollegiate athletics were only slightly improved from 1990–1991, when participation was 69.1 percent and 30.9 percent, respectively. Enrollment percentages of men and women were similar in both academic years. It is quite evident that women's percentages have increased, but not at the rate that male participation numbers rose in the same decade. Participation in sports for women is not proportional to the opportunities being provided at collegiate-level educational systems. In 1994–1995, only 110,524 females participated in sports at NCAA institutions compared to 189,084 males.

Female intercollegiate sports that are gaining popularity include basketball, which continues to be the most popular for women, based on number of institutions that offer the sport for women and the number who actually participate in the sport; volleyball; tennis; and cross-country. Sports gaining in popularity and increasing number of participants at the intercollegiate level are soccer, crew, softball, and outdoor track and field. This trend is very exciting since the squad sizes needed to field these teams provide access to increased numbers of females.

At the high school level in 1993–1994 over 2 million girls participated in sports, compared to only 817,073 in 1972–1973 (NCAA NEWS 32, 51). (Over 3.3 million boys participated in interscholastic athletics in 1993–1994 as compared to over 3.7 million in 1972–1973.) Girls' participation levels are nowhere near those of boys over this time frame, yet a definite increase in female participation has occurred at the interscholastic level. The most popular sport for girls at the high school level is basketball (in terms of the number of schools that offer that sport and number of participants), followed by outdoor track and field, volleyball, softball, soccer, tennis, and cross-country.

It is very important that female leaders not lose sight of increasing opportunities for minority women. Population projections indicate that by the year 2000, approximately one-third of the elementary and secondary students will be ethnic minorities, yet nearly all of their teachers (this includes a large majority of coaches and administrators) will be white. As our culture becomes more diverse, it becomes very important that opportunities for ethnic minorities increase to provide role models for students. According to Crase and Walker black physical educators are rapidly becoming "an endangered species." This is occurring because very few African Americans are entering the profession or enrolling in graduate school to further their education in this field. Once again, if role models do not exist, it is difficult to persuade individuals to enter a field that is "unknown" (Smith).

The number of minority women leaders in athletics has not increased since the 1970s, even though sports participation by minorities has. Discrimination in hiring practices has been documented, and this discrimination has limited the number of ethnic minority women in sports leadership roles. It has been shown that "black women have to deal with both racism and sexism particularly at predominantly white institutions" (Abney and Richey).

The Black Coaches Association was started to assist with the recruitment, retention, and support of black male and female coaches. This association has developed a common voice on the importance of providing role models for young ethnic minorities looking to pursue professional opportunities in administration, coaching, officiating, and other sports leadership positions.

In conclusion, women in athletics leadership positions in the 1990s were faced with tremendous pressure to continue the fight to provide additional participation opportunities for girls and women in sports. These opportunities are not only on the competitive field but also in coaching, officiating, teaching, and administration. Women must look to increase access to these opportunities. Once access is attained, then the issues of equitable treatment and equitable pay must also be addressed. These issues are all important. Each must be addressed by all leaders in sports, not just women, in order to provide participation and leadership opportunities for any person, regardless of gender or race, in the ever-changing world of athletics.

References. R. Abney and D. L. Richey, "Opportunities for Minority Women in Sport—The Impact of Title IX," *Journal of Physical Education, Recreation and Dance* 63 (1992): 56–59; R. V. Acosta and L. J. Carpenter, *Women in Intercollegiate Sport: A Longitudinal Study—Fifteen Year Update, 1977–1992* (Brooklyn, N.Y., 1992); R. V. Acosta and L. J. Carpenter, *Perceived Causes of the Declining Representation of Women Leaders in Intercollegiate Sports: 1988 Update* (Brooklyn, N.Y., 1988); R. C. Berry and G. Wong, *Law and Business of the Sports Industries*, 2d ed. (Westport, Conn., 1995); D. Crase and H. Walker, "The Black Physical Educator: An Endangered Species," *JOPERD* 59 (1988): 65–69; Y. R. Smith, "Recruitment and Retention of African American and Other Multi-Cultural Physical Educators," *Journal of Physical Education, Recreation and Dance* 64 (1993): 66–70; *NCAA News* 32 (5) (1995); 32 (7) (1995); G. M. Wong and C. A. Barr, "Pay Attention: Athletics Administrators [and Coaches] Need to Understand Equal Pay Issues," *Coaching Women's Basketball* 9, 1 (1955): 20–21.

JANE MEYER

STATISTICAL DISCRIMINATION. This theory was developed as a way to explain why employers whose goal is to maximize profits might nonetheless have a preference for one worker over another equally qualified worker. Given imperfect information about an individual's productivity but known differences among groups, say, women and men, a person's sex may be assumed to provide relevant information. Hence, men may be hired in preference to, or paid more than, women because they are, on the average, more productive or, for that matter, because their productivity varies less.

It has been argued that such behavior does not constitute economic discrimination if the employer's perception of the differences between the groups is correct (Aigner and Cain). In such a situation, however, a woman may be less likely to be hired and may be paid less than equally qualified men, because each is judged as a member of a group rather than on individual merit (Borjas and Goldberg).

There are two additional reasons statistical discrimination is a matter for concern. One is that information about groups may also be imperfect and that the employer's perception about them is not necessarily correct. This might happen because real differences existed in the past and are erroneously projected to the present and even into the future. A second and equally serious problem is that unequal treatment of equals is likely itself to result in unequal outcomes. Assume, say, that a man and a woman are both looking for a job, fully intending to remain in the labor force until they reach retirement age. The man is offered a better job, promoted more rapidly, and paid more. If the woman then decides to drop out of the labor force, this is likely to be a case of self-fulfilling prophecy.*

It is clear, therefore, that statistical discrimination, like other forms of discrimination, must be expected to lead to both unfair treatment of workers and inefficient allocation of resources.

References. D. J. Aigner and G. G. Cain, "Statistical Theories of Discrimination in Labor Markets," *Industrial and Labor Relations Review* 30 (1977): 175–187; K. Arrow, "Models of Job Discrimination," in A. H. Pacal (ed.), *Racial Discrimination in Economic Life* (Lexington, Mass., 1972), 83–102; K. Arrow, "The Theory of Discrimination," in O. Ashenfelter and A. Rees (eds.), *Discrimination in Labor Markets* (Princeton, 1973), 3–33; G. J. Borjas and M. S. Goldberg, "Biased Screening and Discrimination in the Labor Market," *American Economic Review* 65 (1978): 918–922; E. S. Phelps, "The Statistical Theory of Racism and Sexism," *American Economic Review* 62 (1972): 659–661.

MARIANNE A. FERBER

STATUS OFFENSES are legally proscribed acts for which only juveniles, with their "disabilities of minority" status, can be arrested, petitioned (or charged), adjudicated, and detained. Status offenses include curfew violations, incorrigibility (ungovernable by parents/guardians or other adults such as teachers in the capacity in loco parentis), running away, truancy, and underage liquor law violations (minor in possession of alcohol, underage drinking, etc.). Operating under a philosophical doctrine of *parens patriae*, where the state is the ultimate parent of every child, juvenile justice officials exercise broad discretionary power over the socialization of youth. This latitude allows the juvenile court to intervene in status offense cases that involve issues of morality (as opposed to criminality).

Since the inception of the juvenile court in 1899, the administration of juvenile justice has been particularly susceptible to cultural definitions of "appropriate," gender-specific behavior (Platt) and certainly since Paul Tappan's early focused investigation. This susceptibility has led the juvenile court to be protective of young women, especially when they are suspected of being sexually active. Calls for the reform of juvenile justice often include, therefore, the need to remedy the juvenile court's reinforcement of gender stereotypes and the sexual double standard.

The impetus for such concerns can be gleaned from the latest summary statistics provided by the Office of Juvenile Justice and Delinquency Prevention (OJJDP). While female adolescents account for only 23 percent of the 2.3 million juvenile arrests in 1992, they represent 42 percent of the 17,300 officially handled or petitioned status offense cases. For status offenses that predominantly involve young women, the statistics are even more disparate. For example, adolescent women accounted for 62 percent of all runaways in 1992, and, among all status offenses, runaways account for 32 percent of all detentions. In summary, young women are particularly susceptible to state intervention in cases of status offenses; and for offenses where their representation is disproportionally high, state intervention is most intrusive.

That female offenders are relatively rare has worked against young women. The misconduct of female adolescents is frequently attributed to deficient families, precocious sexuality, and emotional and developmental problems. Overall, since young men are much more likely to offend (72.4 cases per 1,000 youth at risk in 1992) than are young women (17.5 per 1,000), adolescent female offenders are more likely to be considered "abnormal" or at further risk (Campbell). Such attributions result in more obtrusive, "child-saving" court actions with girls than with boys.

Evidence of such a protective philosophy has led to charges of juvenile justice paternalism. A review of juvenile justice investigations into discrepant gender-specific standards in juvenile justice led William A. Reese and Russ L. Curtis to conclude that female status offenders are more likely to be arrested, detained, petitioned, adjudicated, institutionalized, and placed in reformatories for longer average confinements than is often true for young men, even delinquent boys. This punitive treatment of female status offenders has been attributed to the traditionally male-dominated juvenile court by commentators (Sarri).

The necessity and legitimacy of the juvenile court's jurisdiction over the socialization needs of youth have been questioned for reasons other than the introduction of gender inequity. These other issues include the sanctity of the family unit, parental rights, individual freedom, constitutional safeguards against unlawful detention, the stigmatizing effects of state intervention, dubiety about the "career escalation model" (predelinquent teens will become delinquents if state intervention does not sanction status offenses), and growing evidence that many troubled youth need greater integration into society, not removal from society. The breadth of these issues has galvanized opposition to continued juvenile court jurisdiction over status offenses across traditional ideological lines—from conservative law-and-order advocates to liberal civil libertarians. For example, "just desserts" advocates have argued that less concern with status offenses would allow the juvenile court to better serve as a more traditional criminal court with more focused attention to the deterrence potential of delinquent sanctions.

As a result of gender inequity and these other concerns, over the last 30 years the federal government has moved to curtail the juvenile court's intervention in cases of status offenses. This policy initiative began with a report by the Presidential Commission on Law Enforcement and Administration of Justice that included a recommendation that status offenses be decriminalized—youths who have committed no delinquent acts should be spared any state intervention or, if absolutely necessary, "diverted" (referred by the state) to private therapeutic agencies. Federal policy guidelines also include the Juvenile Justice Act of 1974, which called for the "deinstitutionalization of status offenses" or "DSO," which was intended to discourage the commitment of status offenders to secure facilities.

These federal efforts have resulted in unanticipated consequences for youth accused of committing status offenses. While residential admissions to public facilities declined by 18 percent from 1975 to 1984, admissions to private facilities increased by 78 percent (to 101,007 admissions in 1984) (U.S. Department of Justice). Efforts to decriminalize status offenses also resulted in a 20 percent increase from 1977 to 1984 in the number of private facilities that administer to the needs of troubled youth.

Parallel changes in the statistics for female status offenders were more dramatic. The admission of young women to public facilities declined by 37 percent from 1975 to 1984, but private admissions increased by 121 percent (to 41,079 admissions in 1984). In effect, while state commitments for status offenders have witnessed significant declines, much of the progress has been offset by commitments to private, often profit-seeking facilities where accessibility and public scrutiny are more difficult. This outcome has undermined the ability to monitor the treatment of female adolescents (Bergsmann).

In addition, juvenile courts have retained jurisdiction over many status offenders by reclassifying repeat status offenders as delinquent, by the revocation of probation and incarceration of status offenders who violate valid court orders (VCO), or by classifying youth as "children in need of supervision" or "CHINS." Meda Chesney-Lind has observed that this is a particular problem for young women who are suspected of being sexually active by juvenile justice officials. The number of young women in custody in public and private facilities for status offenses per se declined by 29 percent from 1977 to 1985, but the number of detained and committed female delinquents and CHINS increased by 18 percent and 39 percent, respectively. The net result was that in 1985, there were 7 percent more young women in public or private custody on a given day than was true in 1975.

The cases of most status offenders continue to be handled informally (e.g., for the United States in 1992, of 181,300 arrests for running away, only 17,300 cases [or 9.5 percent] were petitioned or handled officially), and the number of status offenders who are detained in public facilities continues to decline (a decrease of 8 percent from 1988 to 1992). Nevertheless, the overall number of petitioned status offenses in 1992 (97,300 cases) represents an 18 percent increase over 1988 statistics (OJJDP). Critics have noted that many of these children would have been informally warned and released before DSO or diversion—a phenomenon referred to as "net widening."

The recalcitrance of the juvenile court in the face of 30 years of reform efforts to decriminalize and to deinstitutionalize status offenders is testimony to the dilemma confronting juvenile justice administrators. Radical nonintervention leaves the court with no remedies to save the child and subjects many young women to the risks of street life. Institutionalization protects the girl from these dangers but disrupts the family, stigmatizes the young woman, and surrounds her with delinquent influences. This dilemma, perhaps as much as entrenched male dominance, explains why the paternalistic protection of young female status offenders has been institutionalized into juvenile justice and is, therefore, so resistant to change.

References. Ilene Bergsmann, "The Forgotten Few: Juvenile Female Offenders," *Federal Probation* 53 (1989): 73–78; Anne Campbell, *The Girls in the Gang: A Report from New York City* (New York, 1984); Meda Chesney-Lind, "Judicial Paternalism and the Female Status Offender: Training Women to Know Their Place," *Crime and Delinquency* 23 (1977): 121–130; OJJDP, *Offenders in Juvenile Court, 1992* (Washington, D.C., 1994); Anthony Platt, *The Child Savers: The Invention of Delinquency* (Chicago, 1977); Presidential Commission on Law Enforcement and Administration of Justice, *Task Force Report: Juvenile Delinquency and Youth Crime* (Washington, D.C., 1967); William A. Reese and Russ L. Curtis, "Paternalism and the Female Status Offender: Remanding the Juvenile Justice Double Standard for Desexualization," *The Social Science Journal* 28 (1991): 63–83; Rosemary Sarri, "Juvenile Law: How It Penalizes Females," in Laura Crites (ed.), *The Female Offender* (Lexington, Mass., 1976); Paul Tappan, *Delinquent Girls in Court* (New York, 1947); U.S. Department of Justice, *Children in Custody. 1975–85* (Washington, D.C., 1989).

WILLIAM A. REESE II

STEREOTYPICAL HEROINE IN VICTORIAN LITERATURE consists of the portrayal of women as the angel in the house, the old maid, or the fallen woman. The stereotype functions to idealize the passive, self-sacrificing mother for the benefit of a patriarchy. Often contrasted with the motherly angel, the old maid, in her unattractiveness, bitterness, or dislike of her role in the home, is seen as deserving of her lonely spinsterhood. The fallen woman, though usually portrayed as a martyr, is an example of the consequences awaiting women who unheedingly choose love before marriage.

The angel in the house is the perfect helpmate. She serves and obeys her husband, is moral adviser and guide to the children, and ensures peace and stability in her home. Beautiful, sweet, passive, and self-sacrificing, her identity is derived solely from her role as wife and mother. Charles Dickens' Agnes Wickfield (*David Copperfield*) and Esther Summerson (*Bleak House*), being loyal to family unity, embody Victorian domestic values. But in their passivity and tireless self-denial to men who are unworthy of them, such heroines as William Makepeace Thackeray's Amelia Sedley (*Vanity Fair*) and Anthony Trollope's Lily Dale (*The Small House at Allington*) become almost masochistic parodies of the feminine ideal. Even women novelists who portray female characters striving for a life of their own suggest an ambivalence about independence and domestic security. Charlotte Brontë's Jane Eyre (*Jane Eyre*), Elizabeth Gaskell's Margaret Hale (*North and South*), and George Eliot's Dorothea Brooke (*Middlemarch*), though achieving strength, individuation, and self-knowledge through deep and enduring psychological struggles, eventually marry and become primarily the stabilizing forces in their husbands' lives.

Wilkie Collins' Marian Halcombe (*The Woman in White*) and Dickens' Miss Havisham (*Great Expectations*) represent stereotypes of the old maid. Though self-sacrificing in her devotion to Laura Fairlie, Marian Halcombe is unattractive and masculinely active, intelligent, and willful, traits repugnant in a Victorian wife. In her cruel scheming to keep Pip and Estella apart, Miss Havisham embodies the bitter vindictiveness of the betrayed and solitary woman. Brontë's Lucy Snowe (*Villette*), however, is a portrayal of a heroic old maid. Lucy lives a drama based on lack and need because of her determined attempt to define herself in what is, to her, an alien world, but her discipline through despair as she achieves independence is equated with her reemergence into society on her own terms.

The fallen woman is allowed more sympathy than is expected from a society that insisted upon harmony in the home and chastity in single women. Though she is an example of the woman who has, if only for an instant, strayed from morality and therefore must deal with both her own guilt and society's ostracism, she is often a passive innocent. Gaskell's Ruth (*Ruth*) and Thomas Hardy's Tess (*Tess of the D'Urbervilles*) suggest the double standard of a society that at once teaches innocence as womanly duty and virtue and punishes those who are seduced. In these novels, the authors twist the moral lesson so that, rather than blaming the innocent heroine for her mistake, they present her as a victim of society's standards for women. In death, both Ruth and Tess become martyrs to a society that fails to see its own lack of morality in its victimization of women. Nancy, in Dickens' *Oliver Twist*, too, though an accomplice to underworld characters, is presented sympathetically. She is a victim of circumstances, the product of a society that provides no work for the uneducated woman. Thus, with no status or options, Nancy falls into prostitution. In her loyalty to Sikes, though, Nancy parallels the angel because her self-sacrificial death to save Sikes expiates her sins. George Eliot is the least sympathetic to the fallen woman. She not only condemns the vanity and ambitious sexuality that engender Hetty's seduction (*Adam Bede*) but compounds her selfishness with infanticide. Hetty, too, is ostracized and isolated from society and dies alone.

In the Victorian novel, women were stereotyped to ensure the dominance of the patriarchy. Presented as a role model and ideal for the family fireside readers, the sweet and beautiful angel is the arbiter of domesticity in the face of an uncaring world. In return for her loving devotion, she is rewarded by a marriage that provides her security and identity. In contrast, those women who are too willful or intelligent or who are embittered and unlovable are punished through spinsterhood. Preferring independence to obedience, the old maid is destined for loneliness and, probably, guilt. The precarious sexual position of young single women is depicted by the fallen woman, who is most often a victim of her own innocence. While presenting a warning to the adolescent female reader, however, the authors' sympathetic portrayals also suggest that society should be both more compassionate toward the innocent heroine and more wise in educating her.

Female authors tend to be more ambivalent about stereotyping their heroines as angels than do male authors because women authors' heroines often embody conflicts within the authors themselves. While passionately striving for independence, the heroines also desire love, but society's inability to accept and encourage autonomy in a woman blocks the heroines from resolving this conflict. The solution is to show the heroine's growth through struggle, from which she emerges as a stronger and more self-assured and assertive individual. But this strength, instead of allowing her social autonomy, enables her to be a more interesting, more worthy helpmate to her husband. The heroine is still idealized as the self-sacrificing angel, albeit a more admirable one.

References. Nina Auerbach, *Woman and the Demon: The Life of the Victorian Myth* (Cambridge, Mass., 1982); Richard Barickman, Susan MacDonald, and Myra Stark, *Corrupt Relations: Dickens, Thackeray, Trollope, Collins and the Victorian Sexual System* (New York, 1982); Francois Basch, *Relative Creatures: Victorian Women in Society and the Novel 1837–67*, Anthony Rudolph (trans.) (London, 1974); Katherine M. Rogers, *The Troublesome Helpmate: A History of Misogyny in Literature* (Seattle, 1966).

LAURIE BUCHANAN

SUBJECTION OF WOMEN, THE, by John Stuart Mill, an English social theorist and feminist activist, was written in 1861 and published in 1869, after he introduced a parliamentary petition for woman suffrage. The delay was due to Mill's sense of political timing. With the end of slavery in the United States and the growing women's movement in both the United States and England, Mill believed that his analysis of the need to abolish the last form of slavery—domestic slavery—could finally have a proper hearing.

To build support for the feminist cause, Mill presented different arguments intended to appeal to different audiences. Today we would label the arguments liberal feminist, radical feminist, and socialist feminist. First, he addressed progressive men who accepted the liberal ideas of formal equal rights, individual liberty, and equal opportunity but were unwilling to apply them to women. Second, he reinforced the radical feminists, who knew exactly what he was talking about when he dissected the tyranny of men as a sex-class. Third, he appealed to socialist feminists, who came out of the Owenite utopian socialist tradition, which had analyzed the connection between women's emancipation and the achievement of socialism but had not always recognized the importance of legal changes such as the suffrage. Mill's multidimensional treatment of marriage illustrates the three audiences and three levels of his argument for women's emancipation.

For the liberals, Mill dissected the legal inequalities of the late nineteenth-century marriage contract. According to the law, the husband could seize the wife's property, including her wages. He was the final authority on the care of the children; domestic violence was seen as his right. Legal separation was possible only for the very wealthy. Divorce was such a controversial issue that Mill decided not to treat it in *Subjection*. He was also probably hesitant to deal with the issue in his most public feminist essay because of his involvement with Harriet Taylor, a married woman. Until her husband died, which allowed them to marry, they traveled together and led their lives as soul mates.

For the radical feminists, Mill went further than issues of formal equality to uncover the unequal power relationship in the family. He assumed that this relationship of sex-class domination shaped and was shaped by the legal structure. He believed that "the generality of the male sex cannot yet tolerate the idea of living with an equal" and that the public inequalities were rooted in men's desire to keep women subordinated in domestic life. He described the power of husbands and fathers as despotic. By using the language of politics to describe a relationship that was seen as natural and voluntary by his contemporaries, Mill challenged the liberal public/private distinction by illustrating how, indeed, the personal was political.

As with our modern-day radical feminists, Mill's most persuasive examples of male domination involved sexuality and domestic violence. (Perhaps this was why Sigmund Freud was attracted to the essay and ended up translating it into German.) Wife battering was of particular concern to Mill and his partner, Harriet Taylor. They responded to numerous newspaper articles dealing with the subject. In *Subjection*, Mill analyzed the complex reasons that women did not rebel against this violence as much as one would expect. He also testified during public hearings on the issue of prostitutes and contagious diseases. He argued that legislation that held the women, and not their male clients, responsible for the spread of venereal diseases was unjust. In *Subjection* he recognized the existence of marital rape. Finally, in letters he defended birth control as a means for giving women more control over their lives. As with divorce, he was not willing to raise the issue of birth control in an essay intended to help women gain the suffrage.

Clearly, for Mill sexual relations could involve a large degree of coercion and domination. For a celibate man he showed remarkable sensitivity to the politics of sexuality. As for why most women were not as radical as he was, Mill explained, "It must be remembered, also, that no enslaved class ever asked for complete liberty at once." Thus, legal equality was only the first step in the eventual overturn of sex-class domination of women in the most private aspects of people's lives—the bedroom.

For the socialist feminists, Mill alluded to their analysis of the family as a supporter of competitive cutthroat capitalism and to their position that relations between men and women had to be transformed at a very fundamental level. In his *Autobiography*, Mill supported the socialist feminist aim of evolutionary development of worker-owned and -managed cooperative communities. In *Subjection* he presented two points for the socialist feminist. First, legal changes were a necessary first step in trying to transform sexual relations. Second, the family transformed into an arena of egalitarian participation could operate like the cooperative production unit: it could teach men and women the habits needed in a more emancipatory society. By placing Mill's idealized view of the family within the context of his evolutionary socialism, it becomes clear that he was not simply legitimating some bourgeois notion but rather that he saw the egalitarian family as a transitional emancipatory form.

In the end, Mill's analysis of women's emancipation rested on all three levels. He felt that legal changes were needed, especially the vote. Since legal changes in themselves could not transform the way men treated women in their most unpublic moments, he assumed that the political battle would also have to enter the bedroom. Finally, he placed both types of change within the context of his vision of a socialist society in which equal economic power would help to undo the historical subjection of women.

References. John Stuart Mill and Harriet Taylor, *Essays on Sex Equality*, ed. and intro. Alice S. Rossi (Chicago, 1970); Wendy Sarvasy, "A Reconsideration of the Development and Structure of John Stuart Mill's Socialism," *The Western Political Quarterly* 38, 2 (June 1985): 312–333.

WENDY SARVASY

SUBSTANCE ABUSE represents a point on a continuum between abstinence and addiction. The term refers to the misuse of illegal and legal drugs that continues despite negative consequences. Substance abuse and addiction are both characterized by a repeated misuse of drugs that causes negative consequences. However, addiction involves physiological effects such as tolerance and/or withdrawal symptoms, while substance abuse often includes a psychological reliance on a drug but not a physiological one. In addition, substance abusers tend to use lesser amounts of a drug and use less frequently. Women use and abuse both legal and illegal substances. Legal substances include alcohol and prescription medications such as sedatives or tranquilizers. Illegal substances include such drugs as marijuana, cocaine, opiates, and sedatives or tranquilizers that are used without a prescription. In general, gender affects the type and frequency of drugs used, the course of the abuse process, the types of consequences experienced, and the treatment of substance abuse. Further, age seems to be related to the drug of choice among women, with older women (over age 35) using alcohol and/or prescription medications, and younger women being polysubstance users.

Women are, by far, the highest consumers of prescription medications. Women have historically been disproportionately diagnosed with emotional problems and treated with prescription medication, a phenomenon that continues today. Abuse of prescriptions can occur in different ways. First, physicians may fail to adequately assess the other medications that are currently being taken and can prescribe additional drugs that have serious interaction consequences. This is particularly a problem among elderly women. A second avenue to abusing prescription medications is the overreliance on medications to address normal emotional distress. Women have long been prescribed tranquilizers, rather than being urged to consider therapeutic or supportive services, when seeking help for traumatic experiences such as physical abuse, rape, or incest. At its worst, this practice can lead to drug-seeking behavior where women will seek treatment from multiple physicians or emergency rooms with false claims of pain in order to receive additional medication.

Although women use far more prescription medications than men, women use and abuse less alcohol and illegal drugs than men. On a fairly consistent basis, national survey results find that only slightly more men than women report drinking sometime in the last year. The difference becomes more striking as the frequency of drinking increases, with far more men reporting symptoms of alcohol abuse and alcoholism than women. However, women do drink alcohol abusively, though typically less in both quantity and frequency than men. Women are more likely to drink by themselves and are less likely to binge-drink (drinking excessive amounts in a single period of time lasting hours, perhaps, days) when compared to men. Although women tend to begin drinking and developing abuse problems at later ages than men, they progress more quickly into the different stages of abuse. Women also process alcohol differently than men so that drinking the same amounts of alcohol can result in a higher blood alcohol content (BAC) for women when compared to men. When abusive drinking continues over the years, women often develop more severe cases of gastrointestinal, cardiovascular, and liver diseases relative to men, despite having comparable drinking patterns.

Much less is known about women's use of illegal substances. Women are most often introduced into drug use by their male partners and usually live in a relationship with someone who is also abusing drugs and/or alcohol. In general, the number of men who are current users of marijuana and cocaine (use sometime within the last month) outnumber women by a 2 to 1 ratio. Women report that using both marijuana and alcohol at the same time increases their level of energy and sociability. However, heavy smoking of marijuana is associated with fatigue, irritability, and low mood. Women cocaine abusers are apt to begin using the drug at earlier ages than men, which is thought to result from a woman's tendency to be in a relationship with an older male. Women often report using cocaine as a way to alleviate depression and feelings of guilt.

Despite the drug of choice, antecedents and consequences of drug use are fairly similar for women. There is an overriding social disapproval for the use of drugs and alcohol by women, thought to relate to women's roles as wives and mothers. This disapproval ranges from being relatively mild in the case of alcohol, to fairly severe in the case of cocaine, narcotics, or polysubstance abuse.

Women substance abusers are often more harshly judged because of their role as the primary caregiver of children. For example, some states have recently attempted to criminalize the use of illegal drugs during pregnancy. Women have been charged with such crimes as criminal neglect when their babies have been delivered with an illegal drug in their system and also for providing an illegal substance to a minor via the umbilical cord. Surveys of drug-abusing women have found that criminalizing illegal drug use during pregnancy would make them less likely to seek treatment services and prenatal care.

The deleterious effect that drug and alcohol abuse has on a developing fetus is a significant consequence that is unique to women. Research on women's substance abuse is most often done in the context of their roles as mothers, so much of what is known about the abuse of drugs and alcohol by women is because of the effect those substances have on a fetus. Drinking alcohol and the use of prescription and illegal drugs during pregnancy have been related to such problems as low birth weight and premature delivery, both of which are linked to infant mortality. Further, the abuse of substances can result in a child's having growth problems, neurological consequences, and mental retardation. In some cases, children can be born with fetal alcohol syndrome, or be addicted to a drug and experience withdrawal symptoms upon delivery. More recently, it has been suggested that a woman's use of drugs and alcohol during pregnancy is associated with the development of learning disabilities and attention deficit disorder in her children. Other problems associated with reproduction include amenorrhea, an inability to ovulate, and spontaneous abortions.

Women's abuse of drugs and alcohol is also more highly stigmatized because of concerns about their sexual virtue. Some research suggests that women under the influence of drugs or alcohol are seen as less moral. It is presumed that drug and alcohol abuse is a sexual disinhibiter, making women more likely to behave sexually in a way that is socially inappropriate. Substance abuse is also believed to contribute to prostitution and makes it more difficult to avoid and resist physical or sexual abuse. Women are often perceived as being more responsible for, or more deserving of, being battered or raped when they are under the influence of drugs or alcohol.

Significant in the psychosocial histories of substance-abusing women is harmful or painful experience with men. Women substance abusers are typically from alcoholic families where the father is the primary drinker. Further, many women have experienced physical and sexual abuse both in their families of origin and in their current relationships. Physical abuse and unwanted sexual experiences are more common among younger women, a phenomenon that is increasing in prevalence.

In their current families, women tend to experience psychosocial consequences such as divorce, separation, sexual and reproductive dysfunction, or estrangement from children as a result of their substance abuse. Women are also less likely than men to miss work or be arrested for drunk driving, and their substance abuse tends to be more private and with their substance-abusing partners. Women are therefore less likely to come to the attention of those professionals trained to assess substance abuse and referred for appropriate treatment services. The use of drugs and alcohol is increasingly being connected to criminal activity, as many of the women in prison are there because of drug-related crimes or were under the influence while committing their crime. Women substance abusers also experience a higher rate of suicide attempts than nonabusing women.

Contracting HIV, the virus that causes AIDS, is another significant potential consequence of drug use. Injection drug users (typically, heroin, cocaine, or a combination of both) are at highest risk for HIV infection because sharing needles contaminated with HIV-infected blood is the primary way women contract the virus. Also associated with cocaine use in particular is trading sex for drugs. Heterosexual transmission of the virus through unprotected sex is the second most common route of infection for women and the only category of transmission where women outnumber men. Women are at particularly high risk, as injection drug use is most often in the context of a primary sexual relationship with a drug-abusing male, where the sharing of needles has a strong sexual connotation.

Outreach for women substance abusers is difficult because of the reliance on men to obtain their drugs and the lack of public consequences of their drug use, such as employment or legal repercussions. It appears that regardless of the drug of choice, women seek treatment for their substance abuse problems sooner in the abuse process than men. However, while substance abuse is more stigmatized for women because of child care responsibilities, it is precisely those responsibilities that make it more difficult to obtain treatment services. Women consistently report that the lack of child care services is a major barrier to seeking and remaining in treatment. Women also report a fear that their children will be removed from their custody if they seek treatment and are unable to provide supervision for their children. Further, pregnant women have difficulties finding treatment that is able to meet their dual needs of substance abuse and pregnancy. Children, however, are a major motivator for women to seek services, and women are more likely to choose treatment programs that involve their children.

Gender is a significant factor in behavior related to substance abuse. In general, drinking or using behavior and the consequences of substance abuse are related to the role expectations of women and involve the more private sphere of women's' lives.

References. B. Lex, "Some Gender Differences in Alcohol and Polysubstance Users," *Health Psychology* 10 (1991): 121–132; S. C. Wilsnack and L. J. Beckman (eds.), *Alcohol Problems in Women* (New York, 1984).

DINA WILKE

SUFFRAGE DES FEMMES was the first active organization devoted to woman suffrage in France. It was a small society (50 to 100 members at its founding in 1876 and 25 to 50 members at its collapse in 1926), but it was the center of militant French suffragism in the period before World War I.

Hubertine Auclert (1848–1914) founded Suffrage des femmes (originally Droit des femmes) to organize radical feminists who opposed the moderation of the mainstream French feminist movement led by Maria Deraismes and Léon Richer. In Suffrage des femmes and her weekly suffragist newspaper, *La Citoyenne* (1881–1891), Auclert insisted on obtaining full political participation for women in the French Third Republic.

Auclert, perhaps the first activist anywhere to use the term "feminist" (*La Citoyenne*, 1882), urged the use of militant tactics. She and the members of Suffrage des femmes tried a tax boycott, a census boycott, court cases, demonstrations in the streets, and violence at a polling place (which led to Auclert's trial of 1908). This militancy attracted considerable publicity but alienated the majority of French feminists.

Suffrage des femmes frequently had a socialist tone, particularly after

Auclert participated in the socialist congress of Marseilles in 1879, but its foremost characteristic was republican feminism. After Auclert's death, the society became more moderate under her sister, Marie Chaumont.

References. Patrick Bidelman, *Pariahs Stand Up: The Founding of the Liberal Feminist Movement in France, 1858–1889* (Westport, Conn., 1982); Steven C. Hause, *Hubertine Auclert, the French Suffragette* (New Haven, Conn., 1987); Claire G. Moses, *French Feminism in the 19th Century* (Albany, N.Y., 1984); Charles Sowerwine, *Sisters or Citizens: Women and Socialism in France since 1876* (Cambridge, 1982).

STEVEN C. HAUSE

SUPERMARKET ROMANCES. Popular romance novels (supermarket romances) are fictional works written to transport readers from their everyday lives into a world of excitement and romantic fantasy. Typically, these romances follow a basic formula: a woman encounters and falls in love with a man who, at first, seems unattainable. Over the course of the novel the heroine and hero must overcome numerous obstacles in order to find true happiness, usually in marriage.

In general, novels in the 1990s feature a more liberated heroine seeking a sensitive man as an equal partner rather than the submissive, naive, younger heroine and dominant, macho heroes described by critics in the late 1970s and early 1980s (Modleski). As romance writer Judith Arnold explains in Jayne Krentz, contemporary romances require contemporary characters. The heroines have structured, challenging lives and are loved by men who welcome them as equals. The hero needs the heroine as much as she needs him, and the relationship they form is a "balanced" one, based on traditional values of marriage, home, and family. Within the past 10 years, two significant changes have appeared in contemporary romances. The first is a recognition of the need for safer sex practices; the use of condoms is common practice among the main characters in modern novels. A second change is the inclusion of gay and lesbian minor characters who are multidimensional, loyal friends, usually of the heroine. While the alternative lifestyles of these gay and lesbian characters are not explored in detail, their presence is a recognition that choices other than compulsory heterosexuality do exist.

A more traditional pattern occurs in historical novels. While the heroines of historical novels have become increasingly competent in their domains, they are limited by the social constructs of the historical time. In this way they are forced to be subservient and are often subjected to rape, dominance, and violent abuse. Helen Hazen argues that romances include rape fantasies because "rape fantasy is quite healthy" (17). Despite Hazen's justification, heroes of historical novels written in the 1990s are less likely to be the perpetrators of violence against the heroine, yet they remain stereotypical, dominant males. The juxtaposition of a multidimensional heroine with a somewhat one-dimensional hero is a characteristic of the romantic historical novels written today.

Most readers are introduced to romance novels through series romances made popular in the 1970s by Harlequin and Silhouette. These shorter romances of 200 pages or less are published monthly and rarely require advertising, as faithful readers know when to expect the next publication. Over time, readers often progress from a "steady diet" of series romances to longer, more detailed romances, with fully developed characters and variations in plot patterns. These novels typically contain specific erotic content and feature independent and sometimes older heroines. Carol Thurston traces the rise in popularity of the development of these "erotic romances" during the late 1970s and early 1980s.

Romantic fiction is immensely popular and profitable. An estimated 45 million people read them in North America alone, and *Publishers Weekly* estimated sales of these novels in excess of 1 billion in 1997. This figure does not take into account the numbers of books traded or sold at garage sales, auctions, and secondhand stores. According to Harlequin Enterprises research, readers range in age from 15 to 105, 68 percent are college-educated, approximately 55 percent work outside the home, and they have an average household income of $45,300. Although the numbers and demographics are impressive, they do not explain the popularity of this genre.

In the past 20 years, a number of feminist critics and researchers have analyzed the mass appeal of popular romances and argued over the significance of their effect on women readers. Janice Radway in her seminal study, explores the demographics, reading history, and leisure patterns of romance readers and their knowledge and evaluation of romances. Radway argues that women are empowered by the control they exert over their reading choices and their individual interpretations of the novels. In a recent study of a small reading group (Mitchell) one reader, who is terminally ill, describes her reading as a matter of survival. Powerless to change her situation, she uses her reading as a way to escape and to take control of her life through her reading. Romance novelist Susan Elizabeth Phillips (Krentz, 55) refers to this phenomenon as "a fantasy of female empowerment," in which romance reading offers the reader an opportunity to take control of the chaotic events in her day-to-day life by indulging in a fantasy over which she (the reader) has control. Seven of the nine women in Mitchell's study stated that their reading increases in times of crises, especially when the crises are beyond their control, such as during the Desert Storm conflict in Iraq, extended illnesses, or other periods of instability in their lives.

Supermarket romances, with their reliance on traditional values of heterosexual marriage, motherhood, and self-sacrifice, continue to win the hearts of devoted readers and provide fertile ground for aspiring writers. Several organizations (e.g., Romance Writers of America) offer seminars, tip sheets, and books advising novice writers how to write and sell their romances. *Romantic Times Magazine* columns offer similar material and feature articles from successful writers. Authors, publishers, and organizations have Web pages and on-line chat groups to discuss and promote current romances, thereby making it effortless for readers and hopeful writers to remain current on trends and changes in the marketing and selling of romances.

While it may appear on the surface that romance reading is a harmless escape that provides comfort to the reader, some critics call the romance a "quick fix" that offers few benefits to help women change the course of their lives. As Keya Ganguly explains in her critique of Radway's work, "reading romance novels doesn't appear to contribute to change; at best, it may give them (the readers) the energy to continue positions of subordination" (135). Ganguly's argument has serious social and political implications for women, particularly when the content of romance novels is examined closely. In addition to portraying heroines in traditional heterosexual relationships, romance novels also reflect specific erotic behaviors of the characters. Although a heroine may be sexually experienced, she is involved in monogamous relationships only, as is the hero once he has made love to the heroine. More troubling for feminists such as Ganguly is the theme of sexual dominance of men over women and the inclusion of sexual encounters that depict violence and rape. Although less overt violence and physical dominance occur in novels currently being published, patriarchal values still reign as the preferred choice of heroines, and, as the numbers of sales indicate, the preferred choice of readers as well.

References. Keya Ganguly, "Alientated Readers: Harlequin Romances and the Politics of Popular Culture," *Communication* 12 (1991): 129–150; Helen Hazen, *Endless Rapture: Rape, Romance and the Female Imagination* (New York, 1983); Jayne Krentz, *Dangerous Men and Adventurous Women: Romance Writers on the Appeal of Romance* (Philadelphia, 1992); Karen S. Mitchell, "Ever After: Reading the Women Who Read (and Re-Write) Romances," *Theatre Topics* 6 (1996): 51–67; Tamia Modleski, *Loving with a Vengeance: Mass-Produced Fantasies for Women* (London, 1982); Janice Radway, *Reading the Romance: Women, Patriarchy, and Popular Literature* (Chapel Hill, N.C., 1984); Carol Thurston, *The Romance Revolution: Erotic Novels for Women and the Quest for a New Sexual Identity* (Urbana, Ill., 1987); Romance Writers of America, *Romance Genre Statistics: Update* [Online], (1997) available e-mail: www.rwanational.com (April 23, 1998).

KAREN S. MITCHELL

SUPREME COURT (U.S.) AND WOMAN'S RIGHTS. Except for a few years between 1970 and 1980, there has never been a significant number of U.S. Supreme Court justices who have taken an active interest in the issue of equal legal rights for women. Before passage of the Fourteenth Amendment in 1868, almost no cases involving claims of discriminatory treatment of women were even heard by the Supreme Court. *Bradwell v.*

Illinois (83 U.S. 130 [1873]), was the first case brought by a woman under this post–Civil War amendment, which guarantees equal protection for all citizens. In other words, states are prohibited from enforcing discriminatory laws and engaging in discriminatory practices. Even before *Bradwell*, however, the Supreme Court had ruled that Congress intended the amendment to fight race discrimination and nothing else. In Myra Bradwell's case, the Supreme Court found that an Illinois law prohibiting women from becoming lawyers was constitutional. In a concurring opinion, Justice Joseph P. Bradley stated:

The civil law, as well as nature herself, has always recognized a wide difference in the respective spheres and destinies of man and woman. Man is, or should be, woman's protector and defender. The natural and proper timidity and delicacy which belongs to the female sex evidently unfits it for many of the occupations of civil life. . . . The paramount destiny and mission of woman are to fulfill the noble and benign offices of wife and mother. This is the law of the Creator.

This approach to the role of women set the stage for Supreme Court opinions for almost 100 years. The Court heard few cases challenging state law on the basis of sex; the ones that were heard tended to continue the "benign protection" view first enunciated in *Bradwell*. *Muller v. Oregon* (208 U.S. 412 [1908]), involved a challenge to an early protective labor statute. Even though the Court had invalidated a similar law applying to male workers a few years before on the grounds that it violated freedom of contract, in the *Muller* case the Court decided that such laws were valid if designed to protect women. A law limiting the workweek to 60 hours for female employees was designed, the Court said, to protect "the future well-being of the race." The justices pointed to the physical burdens of motherhood, the different "physical structure" of men and women, the superior strength of men, and the historical dependence of women on men as support for their argument.

The *Muller* case put liberals of the time in a difficult position: was it better to argue that women should be treated equally with men or to use this opportunity to provide at least some workers with protection from the rapacious employers of the time? In the famous "Brandeis brief" in the case, future justice Louis Brandeis, with the extensive assistance of Josephine Goldmark of the National Consumer's League and his sister-in-law, took the latter course and used statistics and medical and social research to argue that oppressive working conditions had a marked, adverse effect on women's health.

Other cases were decided on similar principles throughout the years that followed. Montana could make a special exemption from licensing for small laundries run by women (*Quong Wing v. Kirkendall*, 223 U.S. 59[1912]); Michigan could prohibit women bartenders to protect the morals of women (*Goesaert v. Cleary*, 335 U.S. 464 [1948]). Even as late as 1961, the Court found valid a Florida law exempting women from jury duty on the grounds that "woman is still regarded as the center of home and family life" (*Hoyt v. Florida* 368 U.S. 57).

In 1971, the Court began to see laws affecting women in a different light. In *Reed v. Reed* (404 U.S. 71), it found an Idaho law giving men a preference over women in administering estates of deceased relatives to be unconstitutional. While this signaled a major change in direction, the message the Court was sending was difficult to interpret. The case did not extend the full protection of the Fourteenth Amendment to women; it simply found that the law had no "rational basis"—the state had no reason at all for preferring one sex over the other in such cases. Unlike situations involving race discrimination where the presumption is that a discriminatory law is unconstitutional, the Court continued to presume state laws constitutional and require plaintiffs alleging discrimination on the basis of sex to meet a very heavy burden of proof in order to prevail.

The passage by Congress of the Equal Rights Amendment (ERA) in 1972 sent a signal to the Court that politically the time had come to take a closer look at government-mandated sex discrimination. Cases in the early 1970s struck down differential family allowances for male and female members of the armed forces, differences in Social Security benefits for widows and widowers, and other sex-based differences in legal treatment. At the same time, however, the Court was carving out areas where it would not find sex discrimination unconstitutional: real physical differences, such as the ability to get pregnant, could justify different treatment under the law (*Geduldig v. Aiello*, 417 U.S. 484 [1974]), as could laws designed to remedy past discrimination, such as navy regulations allowing women to stay in the service for a longer time without getting promoted (*Schlesinger v. Ballard*, 419 U.S. 498 [1975]).

The case that set the current standard for deciding sex discrimination claims was *Craig v. Boren* (429 U.S. 190 [1976]), which dealt with the singularly unimportant issue of the age at which people could consume 3.2 percent beer. Oklahoma set the age for women at 18 and for men at 21 and justified the difference by saying that men were more likely to cause traffic accidents as a result of drinking and driving. Instead of applying the difficult-to-prove "rational basis" test, whereby almost any reason the state could give would render a law constitutional, or the easier standard applied in race discrimination cases, in which virtually all discrimination was seen as unconstitutional, the Court applied an intermediate standard. States would be required to prove, first, that the statute serves an important government objective and, second, that the method they have chosen is substantially related to that objective. The Court found the state's traffic safety objective to be a valid one but could find no significant relationship between the objective and the differential drinking age. Therefore, the law was found unconstitutional.

The political events of the early 1980s had a dampening effect on the

Court's treatment of sex-based discrimination cases. As the passage of the ERA had spurred the Court to activism, its failure to ratify it brought activism to a stop. The election of conservative president Ronald Reagan had a similar political effect on the Court, but even more important, it led to the appointment of three justices to the Supreme Court (Sandra Day O'Connor, Anthony Kennedy, and Antonin Scalia) who held traditional views of sex roles almost reminiscent of the *Bradwell* Court.

The Supreme Court continued to mouth the words of the test developed in *Craig v. Boren*, but in terms of the results it reached, many legal scholars believe it really went back to the old "rational basis" standard. In a 1981 case testing the constitutionality of a California statute that made it a crime for men, but not women, to have consenting sexual intercourse with a person under the age of 18, the court found that the state's avowed purpose of preventing teen pregnancy was a valid one, and this law was a reasonable way of pursuing it, in spite of the fact that such statutes were shown to have no effect on teen pregnancy rates (*Michael M. v. Superior Ct. of Sonoma County*, 450 U.S. 464). In the same year, the Court found male-only draft registration requirements constitutional because women are not permitted in combat by the military services (*Rostker v. Goldberg*, 453 U.S. 57).

It would be an exaggeration to say that the Court has come full circle since *Bradwell*, but it is certain that its direction changed after the 1970s. Given the makeup of the Court, that trend is likely to continue.

While abortion rights are included in a different set of legal principles than those discussed here (the constitutional right of privacy), there are clear connections between the two. Traditional views of sex roles and morality in both areas will continue to affect the Supreme Court's views of woman's rights, as *Webster v. Reproductive Health Services* (488 U.S. 1003 [1989]), which in significant ways allowed states to limit the right to choose abortion, indicates. That case appears to set a direction for abortion issues that will undercut the principle of women's control over their own bodies enunciated in *Roe v. Wade* (410 U.S. 113 [1973]). *Roe v. Wade* held that the right of privacy prevented state and federal governments from interfering in a woman's right to choose abortion, at least in the early stages of pregnancy. Cases from the late 1980s involving the interpretation of federal employment discrimination laws, affirmative action, and protective labor practices also indicate that the trend in the majority of the U.S. Supreme Court is toward a much more traditional view of the role of women in American society. The conservative justices tend to be considerably younger than the more liberal justices, who were all nearing retirement age in the early 1990s.

Justice William Brennan's resignation in 1990 marked the end of an era in Supreme Court history. Brennan was the political force behind many important decisions furthering women's legal rights and wrote the majority opinions in many key cases, such as *Craig v. Boren*. Until 1980, appointments to the High Court tended to be based on ability rather than politics (the conservative Dwight Eisenhower appointed Brennan), but the process has become much more politicized since then. Given that the next several appointments to the Supreme Court are likely to be conservative, the future does not look bright for advocates of equal legal rights for women.

References. Barbara Babcock, Ann Freedman, Eleanor Norton, and Susan Ross, *Sex Discrimination and the Law* (Boston, 1975); Ann Freedman, "Sex Equality, Sex Differences, and the Supreme Court," *Yale Law Journal* 92 (1984): 913; Herma Hill Kay, *Sex-Based Discrimination*, 3d ed. (St. Paul, Minn., 1988); J. Ralph Lindgren and Nadine Taub, *Sex Discrimination* (St. Paul, Minn., 1988); Wendy Williams, "The Equality Crisis: Some Reflections on Culture, Courts, and Feminism," *Women's Rights Law Reporter* 7 (1982): 175.

KATHRYN WINZ

SWEDEN since the 1970s has promoted equality of men and women through reforms to strengthen women's position in the workplace and men's responsibility for the home and children. Women's organizations have been important in shaping the attitudes and opinions that have made these reforms possible. The first Act on Equality between Men and Women at Work was passed in 1980. In 1988 the government established a Five Year Plan of Action to achieve equality, with set goals in the economy, labor force, education, family, and "influence of women." As a part of the plan, a new Act on Equality went into effect in 1992. It strengthened the rules on equal pay, indirect discrimination, and sexual harassment. The review of the plan led in 1994 to another bill (Shared Power–Shared Responsibility), which further tightened the Equality Act.

Female employment in Sweden is roughly twice that of the European Union. In 1993, 50.6 percent of Sweden's 8.7 million people and 48.9 percent of its 4 million labor force were women. The labor force participation (LFP) rate of women (aged 16 to 64) had risen from 54.9 percent in 1967 to 79.1 percent; the LFP rate of women with children under age 7 had risen from 37.6 percent in 1967 to 81.3 percent.

Since women generally entered occupations that were extensions of women's traditional roles, the workforce was, and remains, highly sex-segregated. In 1988 only 4 occupational fields had an even sex distribution (40 percent to 60 percent). Reforms in the educational system and a series of actions and special programs were launched to encourage women to go into nontraditional fields. While the goal of an equal sex distribution in 10 occupational fields was not met by 1994, overall a somewhat better balance was achieved, and the efforts continue.

Although differentials are small compared to other countries, women earn less than men. Crowding in traditional women's occupations (women in white-collar jobs in industry earned 63 percent of men's salaries in 1973;

in 1993, 80 percent) and a smaller share of overtime and shift work bonuses contribute, but the major reason for the differential is women's greater share of part-time work. The percentage of employed women who worked part-time (less than 35 hours a week) declined from 44 percent in 1986 to 40 percent in 1994 (compared to 8.69 percent for men), and the average number of hours increased. Of workingwomen, 25.9 percent worked from 20 to 34 hours a week; 4 percent, for less than 20 hours. The figures for men were 4.9 percent and 1.7 percent, respectively.

Swedish children share a single, nationwide curriculum in the nine-year comprehensive schools. Both boys and girls study home economics and technology and learn typing, textile handicrafts, and wood- and metalworking.

Secondary schools offer a choice of programs, only a few of which have equal sex distribution. Although the percentage of girls in some traditional women's fields dropped slightly between 1971 and 1988 (e.g., nursing and care dropped from 98 percent to 91 percent), and the percentage in some traditionally men's fields rose (e.g., natural science from 41 percent to 51 percent, technology from 7 percent to 22 percent), traditional attitudes persisted. Efforts to achieve a more even sex distribution in certain secondary education programs were undertaken, and the number of girls and boys entering nontraditional programs in 1990 increased, but the dropout rate was very high (e.g., for boys in textiles, over 40 percent, for girls in building and construction, over 65 percent). Secondary school reforms in 1991 were designed, in part, to try to not only achieve but also retain a more even sex balance in certain programs. Summer courses in technology, engineering workshops, and temporary classes in natural sciences were offered to girls to try to broaden their choices of study tracks.

The proportion of women in higher education has increased steadily since the late 1970s. However, the large statistical increase in the 1980s was largely the result of a transfer of postsecondary programs that attracted mostly women to the higher educational system. A 1991 review showed that sex-role stereotyping actually increased in all educational sectors except engineering. The percentage of women in nursing and care rose from 83 percent in 1980 to 86 percent in 1990; those in teaching, from 75 percent to 83 percent. Women in technology, however, increased from 9 percent to 22 percent. In 1990 women made up 20 percent of engineering students, 43 percent of those in medicine.

The proportion of women declines on the postgraduate level (38 percent in 1990), and they receive the doctorate less often (28 percent). Although their proportion in all teaching categories in higher education increased during the 1980s, in 1990 women still made up only 28 percent of teaching faculty, 20 percent of lecturers with doctoral qualifications and held only 7 percent of full professorships.

Changes in law and policy since 1970 have been designed to give both men and women the opportunity to participate equally in work, family, and society. Advice on family planning and contraception is readily available free of charge in the health services, and in many places school medical services and youth centers also give advice. About 70 percent of sexually active couples use contraceptives.

The first exceptions to a total abortion ban were allowed in 1938. In the 1960s the law and its interpretation were liberalized, and in 1974 abortion became, generally, possible on demand up to the 18th week. Since 1974 abortions have averaged about 35,000 a year. In the 1970s they were most common among women around age 25; in the 1990s the age has risen to 30.

Although the divorce rate is high (45 percent), 80 percent of preschool children live with both parents. Parents are jointly responsible for children; when divorced, joint custody is automatic unless one parent opposes it. The parent who does not live with the children pays maintenance according to financial ability. In cases of failure to pay maintenance, the social security system advances the money to the caring parent.

The social security system in Sweden covers health and medical services (free for children and mothers), child allowances, old age pensions, parental and other benefits. Although economic problems in the 1990s necessitated the reduction of some benefits and the tightening up of conditions, the basic system remained intact, and reforms aimed at giving both parents the opportunity to combine work and family life continued.

Parental benefits allow parental leaves of absence with compensation to care for young children. For each child a total of 12 months of parental leave may be taken, up to the child's eighth birthday. Half of the leave is designated for each parent, but all except 30 days may be given over, in writing, to the other parent. The 30 days are exclusive to each parent and nontransferable.

Since, in 1987, only one father in five chose parental leave during his child's first year, steps were taken to increase the number of fathers taking parental leave. Projects to inform fathers-to-be and new fathers about childbirth and child care proved popular, and participating fathers have taken longer leave. Almost 40 percent of fathers of children born in 1991 used an average of 15 percent of the total benefits during the first year.

In addition to the parental benefit, fathers are entitled to a 10-day leave at the time of birth, and 72 percent take an average leave of 9 days. Either parent may take up to 60 days compensated leave a year to care for a sick child. In 1993, 33 percent of the sick days were taken by men. Another reform introduced in 1995 allows parents of children under 8 years of age to reduce their workday to six hours, but with loss of pay.

As more women return to work within a year of giving birth, child care services are essential. Public child care is the responsibility of the municipalities, and since 1995 municipal authorities have been required to provide day-care center and family day-care places for all children aged 1 to 6 and some form of leisure-time activity for 7- to 12-year-olds.

Public day care expanded rapidly from the 1970s. In the early years, strong central control guaranteed minimum standards, but as the system developed, it was characterized generally by the easing of state controls and greater decentralization. Virtually all child care was municipal until the 1990s, when economic constraints led municipalities to encourage, with some financial support, private facilities operated by cooperatives, foundations, limited companies, and so on. The proportion of private child care has grown steadily. In 1992 about 70 percent of children aged up to 6 and about 37 percent of children aged 7–12 years with both parents employed were enrolled in child care. Private facilities accounted for 7 percent, up to 18 percent in some municipalities, of that care.

In 1987, although 38 percent of the members of Parliament were women, women made up only 16 percent of the standing committees and commissions, where most of the important work is done. A goal of the Five Year Plan was to increase women's influence by increasing the representation of women in public bodies to 30 percent by 1992 and 40 percent by 1995. In state government this goal was exceeded.

The largest political party, the Social Democrats, helped increase the number of women candidates in the 1994 elections by alternating men and women on its candidate lists. In the new government women gained 41 percent of the seats in Parliament and held 43 percent of the seats on standing and other committees and government commissions. For the first time men and women held an equal number of cabinet seats, 11 each (in 1989 women had held 7 of 21 seats), and there were two women undersecretaries of state. In indirectly elected positions on national-level public boards the number of women rose from 16 percent in 1986 to 37 percent in 1993.

In local elections women won 41 percent of municipal council and 48 percent of county seats, but men continued to dominate nearly all policymaking bodies. They also dominate senior positions in employer and employee organizations and political parties and in management. In the private sector less than 10 percent of managers are women; in the public sector, the percentage is 30 percent.

The Five Year Plan of Action was most successful in the political sphere, but some progress was reported in every area, and, where goals were not met, efforts to reach them continue. Women's increased political representation puts pressure on them to push forward in the quest for equality.

SWEDISH WRITERS' literary history begins with religious writings in the Middle Ages, as exemplified by the revelations of Birgitta (1307–1373). Other signs of beginnings can be seen in Hedvig C. Nordenflycht (1718–1763), of aristocratic stock, who set pen to paper to support her family.

Well aware of women's precarious position in society, she defends her sex, demanding acknowledgment of woman's intellect and capacity for deep emotion. But personal loss and grief remain central to Nordenflycht's writing, evidenced in her collection of poems *Den sörgande Turtur-Dufwan* (1743; The Mourning Turtle-Dove), important for introducing the subjective into Swedish literature as well as for its lyrical and artistic style.

Anna M. Lenngren (1754–1817) continues the budding feminist tradition of Nordenflycht in her "Några ord till min k. Dotter, i fall jag hade någon" (1798; A Few Words to My D. Daughter, in Case I Had One). Lenngren in short satire, realistic idyll, comical portrait, song, and epigram records everyday life.

During the nineteenth century Swedish realistic prose is, in part, shaped by three women writers from widely different intellectual and social milieus (Sophie Knorring [1797–1848], Emilie Flygare-Carlén [1807–1892], and Marie S. Schwartz [1819–1894]). It is, however, Fredrika Bremer (1801–1865) whom Sweden claims as its first major woman novelist. She presents the reader with realistic portraits of everyday life of the middle class, examining relations between the sexes, between parents and children, and especially between father and daughter. During the 1830s Bremer shapes the Swedish family novel, strongly mirroring social reality in many works. Her early female portraits show women obedient to convention, humble, submissive, self-sacrificing, but by the time she finishes *Hemmet (The Home)* in 1839 this presentation has changed. Bremer here presents a provocative study of parents' and society's violations of a young woman's endeavor to develop herself. Her new woman is still firmly rooted in the family, but *En Dagbok* (1843; *A Diary*), influenced by Bremer's visit to Harriet Martineau, attacks the patriarchal family in a bleak description of women's conditions. A penetrating analysis of society, its realist technique is clearly influenced by Balzac. In 1856 Bremer again returns to the theme of the home brutalized by the patriarchal father in *Hertha*, her best-known work. It describes a young woman's fight against overwhelming odds to gain a sense of self. The heroine, a teacher struggling to instill in her students the urge to become free and self-sufficient, transgresses radically and dies young. Bremer's vision of a future for woman is the beginning of a literary theme pursued by Swedish women writers to our own times. It must be stressed, however, that her women figures best exert their "natural" and important influence within the home as wives and mothers.

Truth seekers as feminists (Sophie Adlersparre, Alfhild Agrell, Ellen Key, Anne C. Leffler) or as a reluctant feminist (Victoria Benedictsson) dominate the literary and critical scene of the 1880s. With strong foremothers such as Bremer, Mathilde Fibiger (Denmark), and Camilla Collett (Norway) and encouraged by the intellectual ferment of the Modern Breakthrough, these women set out to rewrite marriage, the relations between the sexes, womanhood, and sexuality. Among the best known are Leffler and Benedictsson. Although Leffler (1849–1892) daringly analyzes the nature of female sexuality under patriarchy, the life and work of Victoria Benedictsson (1850–1888) have attracted feminist scholars. She is recognized by many as second only to Strindberg as an innovator of Swedish realistic prose. Her diary *Stora Boken* (1884–1888; The Big Book) must be seen as a great contribution to Swedish memoir literature. Hers was a tragic life; her writing was her way out of intensely oppressive living conditions. *Från Skåne* (1884; From Skåne), a short story collection, presents life among the peasants and lower classes in the provinces. It has an unmistakably feminist perspective of the sex-war problematic and the oppression of women trapped within the marriage institution. Benedictsson's first novel, *Pengar* (1885; Money), launches the author as the new, fresh voice in Swedish literature. In step with the Modern Breakthrough she delivers a scathing attack on the sexual, social, and psychological conditions of women. *Pengar* is exciting as a novel about self-development and self-destruction. Benedictsson's unmistakable ambivalence, in spite of the often outright statements to the contrary in the diary, about man's inherent superiority over woman, remains at the core of her subsequent writing. *Fru Marianne* (1887; Mrs. Marianne), in a complete turn from *Pengar*, presents a harmonious, ideal family. The novel describes the education of a spoiled city belle who, in the end, shines as the worthy wife, lover, companion of the Great Man and worthy mother of his son.

The greatest Swedish woman writer of the nineteenth century is Selma Lagerlöf (1858–1940). Her tales, legends, gothic thrillers, historical novels, and realistic short stories have won her enormous popularity as well as critical acclaim. *Gösta Berlings Saga* (1891) single-handedly rejuvenates a flagging narrative art. The novel's poetic, imaginative language with its archaic expressions, its borrowings from tale and legend language, and its very lively and emotional emphatic characteristics all made *Gösta Berlings Saga* appear as something entirely new in literature. A trip to Italy resulted in *Antikrists mirakler* (1897; The Miracles of Antichrist), the author's attempt to bring about a union of socialism and Christianity. In *Herrgårdssägen* (1899; The Saga of the Manor) she returns to the world of *Gösta Berlings Saga*, but in spite of its fantastic elements the story is a manifestation of Lagerlöf's interest in psychology, especially theories of the split personality. Her favorite themes of madness and guilt and retribution return with a vengeance in the magnificent *Herr Arnes pengar* (1903; Lord Arne's Hord). The year before that she published *Jerusalem* (2 vols.), a penetrating and at times brilliant study of religious fanaticism and social disintegration in a northern province in Sweden. In her later work Lagerlöf ponders the nature of the occult and evil, the various destructive forces that wreak havoc with the individual and with society. To the end of her life, however, Lagerlöf believes in the possibility of a good, decent world order beyond the ugliness and chaos of World War I.

In the early part of the twentieth century Agnes von Krusenstjerna (1894–1940) is especially noteworthy for her effort to break down literary taboos by writing openly about female sexuality, as in her antifamily novel series *Fröknarne von Pahlen* (1930–1935, 7 vols.; The Misses von Pahlen), which created a bitter feud among critics and social commentators. Krusenstjerna's work, with its emphasis on peace and matriarchal ideals and on motherhood and giving birth and its stance against patriarchy, fascism, and oppression of women, challenged many of the women writers who followed, among them Karin Boye and Ellen Wägner. The latter (1882–1949) uses realistic prose to describe concrete political and social issues, particularly those dealing with women's emancipation. Influenced by the writings of the feminist theoretician Ellen Key, Wägner becomes a pacifist, arguing that it is a specific female role to work for peace and freedom. One of her best novels is *Åsa-Hanna* (1918), the story of a woman torn among choosing self, choosing the family, or working for world peace. *Väckerklocka* (1941; The Alarm Clock) reveals Wägner's belief in, and search for, an ancient matriarchy, and in *Fred med jorden* (1940; Peace Be with the Earth) she takes a strong environmental stance. Swedish feminist and environmental movements of the 1970s and 1980s are indebted to her work.

Although women are predominantly prose writers, there is one central female poet, modernist Karin Boye (1900–1941). As a member of the Clarté group she is an activist and a pacifist. Her poem collections are central to Swedish literature. She renews poetry with her absolute ethical loyalties, with her intrepid exploring of the unconscious. The collection *För trädets skuld* (1935; For the Sake of the Trees), containing the well-known "Prayer to the Sun," exemplifies her technical boldness, her intensity in insisting that nature is the source of life and energy, the Originator. To come to grips with her lesbianism, she underwent psychoanalysis, described in the novel *Kris* (1934; Crisis). Published posthumously were the important collection *De sju dödssynderna* (1941; The Seven Deadly Sins) and her antiutopian science fiction novel *Kallocain* (1941).

The feminine mystique that characterizes much of the writing during the 1930s and 1940s is met head-on by the one major female proletarian writer, Moa Martinson (1890–1964). She gives a strong, clear, new voice to women's experience by allowing the maternal body to speak, specifically about sexual experience, giving birth, sagging breasts, scar-ridden stomachs, abortions, sterility, and aging. Best known is her *Kvinnor och äppelträd* (1933; Women and Apple Trees), with its two heroines, both in their 50s. It is the story of how life and brutal conditions have literally formed these two bodies, but it is also the story of how these unlikely leading ladies fight to make life meaningful, after all. Importantly, her works give Swedish literature unique mother figures.

Sara Lidman (b. 1923), in a more global sense, continues the Martinson tradition of writing about women, about society's underdogs and marginal types, as in *Bära mistel* (1960; To Carry) about a homosexual musician. Lidman, as did Lagerlöf, writes about atonement, guilt, and responsibility toward others. In her fiction from the 1970s and 1980s the author returns to her own province and in a language that rejuvenates Swedish prose sets out to write the history of the proletarian movement of northern Sweden in broad, epic narrative.

Kerstin Ekman (b. 1933) writes Sweden's most broad social epics with women in the central roles, as in *Häxringarna* (1974; Witches' Circles), *Springkällen* (1976; The Source), and *Änglahuset* (1979; House of Angels). Her novel *En stad av ljus* (1983; A City of Lights) is the study of a father–daughter relationship and the many shapes and forms love takes. Fredrika Bremer's father–daughter theme, combined with concerns with the relationship among language, self, and female sexuality, is still prominent in Swedish literature.

PAAL BJÖRBY

T

TAIWAN. Women constitute half the 20 million people inhabiting a 240-mile-long Nationalist Chinese island off China's southeast coast. Long a frontier where Chinese immigrants fought with Aboriginal peoples for land, from 1895 to 1945 a Japanese colony, and, since the Nationalist takeover an arena of political-economic struggle between old residents and the "Mainlanders" who followed Chiang Kai-shek, Taiwan regained its prewar standard of living and began rapid industrialization in the early 1960s. Contemporary women's lives have been shaped by the patriarchal Confucian traditions of Chinese and Japanese states, by their important role in production for the international and domestic markets, and by a limited, but significant, repertory of women's cultural institutions.

Late imperial Chinese culture prescribed extreme subordination for women in the family, the polity, and the cosmos; foot-binding,* practiced in Taiwan until the Japanese forbade it, translated Confucian ideals of proper womanly conduct into physical reality by crippling the majority of little girls. The Nationalist state, which still conducts sacrifices annually to honor five concubines who committed suicide rather than risk rape, continues to base its official morality on the Confucian tradition (Diamond). Women in positions of real political power in Taiwan are rare, children technically "belong" to their fathers in cases of divorce, and, by custom, only sons inherit family property. Women's access to political, economic, and ideological power remains correspondingly limited (Chiang and Ku).

However, Japanese and Nationalist policy countercurrents broadened women's opportunities, particularly through education, with the Nationalists continuing and expanding the Japanese pattern of schooling for both genders. By 1970, most children entered junior middle school, and now almost as many girls as boys complete senior middle school. Many women hold respected, if poorly paid, jobs as schoolteachers, accountants, and clerical workers. Some college graduates have better-paying and more prestigious work, notably in education and government service. Higher education in Taiwan is seen as a mixed blessing for women, however, for men and their parents generally prefer brides whose accomplishments will not outshine those of their husbands.

In the past century, Taiwan's labor has become increasingly integrated into the world economic system. Women tea pickers created prosperity in the late nineteenth century, pioneer schoolgirls found niches in Japanese social and economic development, and young factory women now power the post-1960s export boom (Kung; Arrigo). Between job entry in their middle teens and marriage in their middle 20s, women manufacture and assemble most of the clothing and electronic products for which Taiwan is famous and on which domestic and multinational profits largely depend. Officials boast of the docility and cheapness of their labor, guaranteeing these qualities through state-sanctioned patriarchy and through schooling that channels girls into unrewarding studies.

The expanding economy also relies heavily on the work of mothers, daughters, sisters, and wives in the petty capitalist sector that reproduces and socializes factory labor, supplies that labor with cheap consumer goods and services, and inexpensively subcontracts export production for large corporations. Family businesses, embedded in an informal economy of moneylending, reputational credit, and real estate manipulation, have been relatively open to women who have both business talent and a little capital of their own. Because many contemporary brides receive gifts of money and gold jewelry and have learned accounting at school and practical business management at home, married women often found small businesses that earn them increased income, prestige, and power. Their ventures range from elegant boutiques to day-care centers to noodle stands, some owned outright and others managed in partnership with husbands. For the majority of Taiwan's women, small enterprise offers more chance of achieving personal autonomy and a comfortable standard of living than do academic degrees. Business talent is welcomed by marital families, and working-class brides are still expected to join producer families' unpaid workforces (Hsiung).

In a culture dominated by patriarchal symbols and institutions, women's culture is nonetheless much in evidence in Taiwan, especially among farmers and other small business families. Informal groups of village and neighborhood women control and mediate social relations in their communities (Wolf), and women's choices about rearing, adopting, and marrying their children have long been crucial to the shaping of families. (Wolf and Huang).

Folk religion abounds with gender symbolism and public roles for working-class women. Female deities loom large; women meet informally at worship and formally to study ritual chants in temples; older women pilgrims energetically tour Taiwan's busy ceremonial circuit; and even patrilineal worship is largely enacted by women.

Folk religion supplies not only positive female images and occasions for sociability and self-cultivation but also ideological support for women who wish to withdraw from childbearing and sexual relations, as many do. A few women refuse marriage to enter Buddhist convents, while others move to vegetarianism and celibacy when they have borne enough children; sexual abstinence is essential to much folk religious practice. The nonreligious sometimes justify withdrawal from sexual relations not by ritual considerations but by the belief that a woman's children need her presence in order to sleep well.

Elite women have different options for self-expression. Narrow circles of female relatives and former classmates often dine together for fun and emotional support or broaden their networks through social and sports clubs. Many paint, write, perform, or absorb a literature emphasizing life's intimate relations. Women scholars research and promote feminist positions with increasing public and academic support.

Political activity for feminist goals was sharply limited by the martial law that governed Taiwan from 1945 to 1987. Under that law, feminist activist Hsiu-lien Liu was jailed for her participation in a major social protest in 1979. From the later 1970s to the 1990s, women have participated fully in the movement for political pluralism. Greater political engagement has enlarged the social role of women of all classes. With citizens now free to unite in pursuit of common goals, women are especially active in environmental, charitable, and social justice organizations. Taiwan's evolving feminism accords a large place to women as metaphoric "housewives" whose duties include social as well as domestic hygiene and as "mothers" who expect to nurture not only their own but society's children. Struggles for equal rights in the workplace ally with, but do not overshadow, those for healthy, secure families and communities.

References. Linda Arrigo, "Control of Women Workers in Taiwan," *Contemporary Marxism* 11 (1985): 77–95; Lan-hung Chiang and Mei-Chih Hsu, *Bibliography of Literature on Women in Taiwan, 1945–1985* (Taipei, Taiwan, 1985); Lan-hung Nora Chiang and Yenlin Ku, *Past and Current Status of Women in Taiwan* (Taipei, 1985); Norma Diamond, "Women under Kuomintang Rule: Variations on the Feminine Mystique," *Modern China* 1 (1975): 3–45; Ping-Chun Hsiung, *Living Rooms as Factories* (Philadelphia, 1996); Lydia Kung, *Women Factory Workers in Taiwan* (Ann Arbor, Mich., 1984); Arthur P. Wolf and Chieh-shan Huang, *Marriage and Adoption in China, 1845–1945* (Stanford, Calif., 1980); Margery Wolf, *Women and the Family in Rural Taiwan* (Stanford, Calif., 1972).

HILL GATES

TAOISM is the major religion native to China and holds women in high esteem. In comparison, Buddhism,* China's other major religion, looks down on women, and Confucianism,* China's traditional political ideology, limits them to a submissive role within the family. From the earliest times, Taoist theory attributed equal importance to the female and male principles of yin and yang. Early Taoist philosophy even glorifies the passive and responsive female principle. In the Taoist movements of the second century A.D. women held important civil and military leadership positions. But from antiquity until the present, the theoretical equality of male and female in Taoism has been eroding under the pressures of forces in Chinese society that tend to constrain and degrade women.

Taoism provides three roles for women: lay believer, religious professional, and divine woman (in ascending order of sanctity and honor). Boundaries between the three roles are not fixed but allow movement upward. Lay believers support the church with patronage and faith, without necessarily sacrificing family life. The religious, including nuns and female church officials, perform the liturgy on behalf of the community, administer the worldly institution of the church, study doctrine, meditate, propagate the faith, and carry on research in fields related to Taoist thought such as astronomy and alchemy. They usually leave household life to devote themselves exclusively to religion. Divine women, including both saints and goddesses, use their powers and virtues to save living beings, to lead, and to teach.

All three roles embody ideal paths or models. Laywomen exemplify the virtues of devotion, charity, good works, and proper conduct within the family. Church officials and nuns provide examples of knowledge, sanctity, wisdom, and skill, in addition to the virtues expected of lay devotees. The life of the religious professional always offered a path to education and independence. Female saints, human beings who achieved sanctity by following the paths of laywomen or religious professionals to perfection, provided models of hope and power for women in all walks of life. The goddesses, possessing special arts and powers beyond human capabilities, embody a host of transcendent characteristics. A goddess may be an awesome creatrix, a compassionate mother, a wise teacher, or a sensual mistress. Female Taoist deities express the desires and ideals of the people who pray to them.

Saints and goddesses captured the imagination of Taoist writers and the belief of the faithful. One important saint was Tanyangzi, a teenage girl mystic of the sixteenth century who collected a host of learned Confucian men as followers. The most important goddess was the Queen Mother of the West (of whom Tanyangzi believed herself an incarnation), the deity governing immortality and communication between the human and divine realms. The Queen Mother of the West, legend has it, was the lover and teacher of emperors.

The Taoist canon, the *Tao tsang*, contains many books describing the stories and contributions of great laywomen, religious professionals, and divine women. The canon also includes works on medicine, sexuality, ritual, and meditation for women. These valuable texts provide information about the social as well as religious history of women in China. They are just beginning to receive attention from modern Western and Asian scholars.

SUZANNE CAHILL

TEACHING as a profession opened its doors to women in the 1830s. The nation's growing systems of common schools needed teachers, and economic and social factors combined to produce a new philosophy that regarded women as the *natural* teachers of the young, extending into the public sphere the female domestic role of nurturing the young.

Public school teachers were needed to educate the children to become useful members of the democracy, and the nation recruited its young womanhood to answer this call to duty. The status of teaching was low when women first entered the arena. Men who stayed in education left the classroom for higher-paying, more prestigious administrative positions. By default the classroom became woman's domain; elementary school teaching, her territory.

After the Civil War, the crucial need for schoolteachers became even more pressing, and questions of the propriety of women working outside the domestic sphere became irrelevant. Black and white women went into the South with the zeal of missionaries to teach recently emancipated blacks; immigration into the urban areas of the East and settlement of the West contributed further to the expanding need for teachers. Through the 1870s and 1880s the proportion of women teachers rose in secondary education and administration as well as in elementary teaching. Concern seems to have developed only as people realized that women were monopolizing public secondary schools as they had already monopolized the elementary schools.

The need was so great that college-educated women and normal school graduates could fill only a small portion of the teaching positions available. Teacher training characteristically was included as part of secondary education curriculum in industrial institutes and high schools.

Teaching became a respectable stopgap for women before marriage* or a respectable career for the unmarried. After World War I, it became the democratic road to social mobility for daughters of the working class. Although women's salaries made it possible to be self-supporting, they were not sufficient to support a family or even a high standard of living for one. From the start women were hired because they worked cheaply. The taxpayers wanted and got a bargain. Men always were paid higher salaries because it was assumed they had families to support, but, in fact, the majority of female teachers historically supported other family members, even though they themselves were unmarried. Not until the 1970s did teacher organizations gain bargaining strength to bring salaries into parity.

Why were schoolteachers unmarried? Public opinion, more often than law, prohibited the hiring and retention of married teachers. School boards demanded that only single women be teachers, citing the argument that a working married woman deprived a theoretical male head of household of a potential job. Only in large city districts where teachers were granted tenure was it safe for a woman to marry. Married teachers were hired after World War I as an emergency measure and fired during the Great Depression. Until the post–World War II era, few teachers were married.

As a rule, city school districts pay better salaries and offer better chances for promotion, more attractive living conditions, and greater personal freedom than small towns and rural areas, where, traditionally, the teacher turnover rate is high as teachers move on to better pay and professional advancement or, in the past, to marriage.

Black women, like their white counterparts, have considered the vocation of teaching to be the logical public extension of their domestic roles as caretakers and teachers of children in the home. More to the point, because sexism* as well as racism limited employment opportunities of educated black women, teaching became the primary occupation for black as well as for white women, no matter what their professional training.

Reference. S. N. Kersey, *Classics in the Education of Girls and Women* (Metuchen, N.J., 1981).

CAROL O. PERKINS

TELEVISION is arguably the most complex and powerful medium through which women's experiences are depicted, influenced, framed, and potentially changed. As a vehicle for a wide variety of political and cultural expressions over a range of ideological positions, television offers images of gender, sexuality, family, romance, work, and public and private life that viewers consume from their own specific social positions.

From postwar discussions about where to put the television set itself to current arguments over the possible impact of the medium's depictions of violence and sexuality, television has always been considered in terms of its role in cultural life. Yet viewers have a more complicated relationship to the medium and its offerings than such debates may reveal. Like television itself, which simultaneously shapes and reflects the world around it, the audience both accepts and resists television's versions of reality. Although television has been the subject of controversy from its earliest days because of its potential to influence viewers' ideas about the social world, audience members do not sit passively before the set and absorb whatever they see. Instead, they take up programs in sometimes contradictory ways— becoming deeply involved in a soap opera story line about, for instance, interracial romance while also openly criticizing the program's depiction of that story's characters. Viewers' involvement may take many forms, from setting aside time to watch a specific show to participating in fan activities; and resistance can also come in a variety of guises, from talking back to the television set to organizing letter-writing campaigns or advertiser boycotts.

There are several different topics to consider when thinking about women's relationships to television. First, there is the historical fact of women's roles as both producers and consumers of television programming. Women have worked as actors, writers, directors, and so on since the medium's earliest days, which makes them a major focus for understanding the history of television both as an industry and as a cultural artifact. Figures such as comedians Lucille Ball, Mary Tyler Moore, and Roseanne, director Ida Lupino, series creators Agnes Nixon, Barbara Avedon and Barbara Corday, news anchor Barbara Walters, and network executive Jamie Tarses illustrate the range of women's contributions to the development of television.

Equally important are women's roles as consumers of that same programming, viewers whose tastes and reactions must be taken seriously and who therefore occupy positions of considerable power in shaping television's content. The emphasis on ratings also makes them valuable objects of manipulation to commercial networks and stations, where advertising (and therefore programming) targets women as potential purchasers of the products being promoted. This last fact is especially important in U.S. television, where, despite the existence of officially noncommercial public television, commercial sponsorship or corporate underwriting supports nearly all network, independent, and cable programming. The recognition that adult women control considerable spending power makes them extremely valuable to advertisers, who are therefore eager to sponsor programs that appeal to their target markets. (This commercial interest explains the existence of, for instance, CBS's famous Monday-night lineup of "women's" programming in the early 1980s, when series such as *Cagney and Lacey* and *Designing Women* aired opposite ABC's *Monday Night Football*.)

The characterization of the medium as a *domestic* one can also be very useful in understanding women's relationships to television. Part of the medium's power comes from the fact that television entertainment is consumed within the home, rather than existing, like theatrical films or stage productions, as a part of a more public sphere. Television is thus often seen as bringing the "outside" world into the home, an incursion that can be understood as either threatening the domestic sphere (by, for instance, giving children access to images of sexuality or violence) or as enlarging it (through high-culture offerings, educational or public-service programming, enlightened views of race, and so on). Television's domesticity also refers to the idea that programs and the habit of watching them are easily made part of the routines of daily life, and certain genres take pointed advantage of that fact. This coordination of daily life and television format is especially noteworthy in soap operas, which many critics recognize as a paradigm of commercial fictional programming as a whole. Soaps were originally designed to target women viewers whose constantly interrupted family responsibilities can make it difficult to follow a conventional linear narrative. The lengthy exposition, constant repetition, and elongated story lines of soaps are remarkably congenial to an audience attempting to watch the programs while also doing housework or child care, and the programs' daily telecast makes it easy to incorporate viewing into that domestic routine.

Specific programs and genres address issues of particular interest to women and may deal more broadly with questions of gender. For example, much of television's content is also profoundly domestic. Situation comedies have traditionally focused on family, whether defined in the familiar terms favored by domestic sitcoms from *I Love Lucy* to *The Cosby Show* or redefined as workplace "families" (e.g., *The Mary Tyler Moore Show*, *M*A*S*H*). Despite conservative critiques, network television remains moderately liberal, rather than radical, reinforcing more often than challenging traditional visions of gender and rarely dealing sympathetically with overtly feminist ideas. Yet television movies and series have sometimes taken more chances than mainstream theatrical films in exploring the changes in women's experiences over the decades, dealing directly, if briefly, with controversial topics such as abortion, racism, and domestic violence. Some series have presented explicit challenges to television's usual version of family life by recasting it in working-class terms (e.g., *Roseanne*) or by focusing on African American characters (with *Cosby* the most influential example). More recent challenges to sitcoms' long-standing view have included single mothers (*Murphy Brown*) and the incorporation of gay and lesbian characters as significant figures (most notably, *Ellen*).

Other genres designed explicitly to attract women viewers have long been framed largely in terms of domestic issues, and specific day-parts (e.g., daytime) are also often filled with programs meant to appeal mainly, although not exclusively, to women. Soap operas deal primarily with romance and kinship relations; magazine shows focus on domestic tasks and family life; daytime talk shows focus on the exigencies of personal relationships. The increasing practice of "narrowcasting," in which entire cable services are programmed to appeal to a specific demographic group, has also led to the development of Lifetime, a cable service that explicitly targets women viewers with original and syndicated series and movies.

Television's attention to the personal has become increasingly important even in genres that were once far more interested in the public sphere. Since the 1980s, prime-time genres that were originally built around stereotypically "male" interests and occupations, such as crime and even medical dramas, have been increasingly influenced by soap opera style and content. Thus, for example, police shows now habitually incorporate story lines about the officers' personal and romantic lives and may actually devote greater attention to those stories than to more traditional crime plots. The fact that men as well as women find these melodramatic tales compelling was proven by the success of dramas like *Hill Street Blues* and *L.A. Law* and of "prime-time soaps" such as *Dallas* and *Dynasty*, all of which also drew heavily on soap opera conventions such as open-ended episodes and multiple story lines.

Many scholars of television as a form of popular culture have analyzed women's particular viewing practices. Once again, much of this work has focused on soap opera audiences, who tend to maintain an extraordinary degree of loyalty to their favorite programs and whose daily habits seem especially compatible with the genre's structural constraints. Other researchers have studied the social uses women viewers make of the programs they watch, such as the common practice of using soaps or other melodramatic series as a way to bond in the workplace or to examine difficult or controversial topics. Still others have examined the influence of women who have organized letter-writing campaigns either to save (as in the case of *Cagney and Lacey*) or cancel (*Married . . . with Children*) programs, another demonstration of women's function as active viewers willing to make clear their stake in television's future.

As a major medium for the production and transmission of popular culture, television has both direct and indirect connections to other artifacts created and consumed by women. Specific TV genres such as daytime and prime-time soaps, for example, use many of the conventions of stage and film melodrama and often echo the themes explored in written forms such as romance or gothic novels, while daytime talk shows often bear a strong resemblance to the features commonly found in women's magazines. Series and television movies have been inspired by novels and feature films, while the tremendous success of the sitcom *Roseanne*, based on its star's stand-up comedy act, shows that far less traditional forms of women-oriented popular culture can also find their way into mainstream television. Finally, a variety of fan projects, from traditional fan clubs and conventions to 'zines and Internet newsgroups, have grown up around women's favorite television programs and genres, underlining the fact that, as viewers, women are not merely passive recipients but actively and productively engaged with what they see on the small screen.

References. Mary Ellen Brown, *Soap Opera and Women's Talk: The Pleasures of Resistance* (Thousand Oaks, Calif., 1994); Charlotte Brunsdon, *Screen Tastes: Soap Opera to Satellite Dishes* (New York, 1997); Julie D'Acci, *Defining Women: Television and the Case of Cagney and Lacey* (Chapel Hill, N.C., 1994); Tania Modleski, *Loving with a Vengeance: Mass-Produced Fantasies for Women* (New York, 1984); Laura Stempel Mumford, *Love and Ideology in the Afternoon: Soap*

Opera, Women, and Television Genre (Bloomington, Ind., 1995); Jane Shattuc, *The Talking Cure: TV Talk Shows and Women* (New York, 1997); Lynn Spigel, *Make Room for TV: Television and the Family Ideal in Postwar America* (Chicago, 1992).

LAURA STEMPEL MUMFORD

TEMPERANCE CRUSADE AND THE WOMEN'S CHRISTIAN TEMPERANCE UNION (WCTU) placed the initiative in American temperance reform in the hands of women for a quarter of a century and created a significant multidimensional movement for social reform. Furthermore, the activism of American temperance women launched a pioneering international organization, the World's WCTU (WWCTU), which united women across the world in struggle for change in women's status and other reforms.

Women formed a large part of the army of American temperance reform since its emergence as a mass movement in the 1820s, but until the 1870s the dry forces always fought under male leadership. During the winter of 1873–1874, tens of thousands of women in hundreds of small towns and cities across the Midwest and Northeast began to besiege local saloons and other liquor outlets. Their action was provoked by a spike in spirits consumption, an explosion in the retail liquor business, and the failure of local authorities to enforce liquor controls. Undeterred by frequent abuse in the newspapers and sometimes violent mob resistance, the crusaders marched peacefully from saloon to saloon, singing hymns to bolster their courage and offering prayers for the saloonkeepers' salvation. Their main object was to persuade liquor dealers to give up their business. A grassroots movement by the mothers, wives, and daughters of prosperous middle-class families, imbued with the spirit of Protestant evangelicalism, the crusaders portrayed the liquor traffic as a source of irresistible temptation, male drinkers as victims, and the drinker's female kin as the "chief sufferers" from men's intemperance. Men had further failed in their duty to protect women by allowing legal restrictions on liquor sales to lapse, leaving women, harmed by the effects of men's drinking, only the inadequate option of civil damage suits against dealers. Braving arrests and prosecutions as well as opposition in the streets, the crusaders, aided by the impact of a severe economic depression, brought about a significant reduction in the number of dealers, leaving many towns without liquor outlets for at least a short time.

The crusade represented the largest women's mass movement to that time in the United States, but its energies were locally focused and uncoordinated, making organization of a national movement in its wake difficult. The task was undertaken late in 1874 by a national convention in Cleveland of veteran women activists, which launched the WCTU under the leadership of Annie Turner Wittenmyer (1827–1900). During its first five years the WCTU grew slowly as a centrally directed organization focusing on temperance, but its strategy, structure, and size all changed radically when Frances E. Willard (1839–1898) became its president in 1879. Willard proposed a "Do Everything" policy under which the WCTU's interests and involvement expanded well beyond temperance and Prohibition to include a wide range of issues such as woman suffrage, trade unionism, peace, dress reform, sexual assault, prostitution, child care, and education. Each local society, however, was left free to pursue whichever of these reforms its members chose. This flexibility made the WCTU during the late nineteenth century an umbrella organization for a diverse set of activists. Their numbers and geographic scope grew after Willard and others conducted national organizing campaigns during the 1880s, so that by the end of that decade the adult membership stood at more than 150,000, in addition to girls and young women organized into a youth branch. The WCTU was the largest American women's organization of the nineteenth century.

WCTU activism tended to broaden the horizons of middle-class women and sometimes to radicalize them by exposing them to the plight of the working class. Willard persuaded the membership during the 1880s to endorse the Prohibition Party, which under Willard's prodding further expanded its focus beyond Prohibition and added radical planks to its platform. In 1892 she nearly brought the Prohibition Party into an alliance with the Populists, but she never convinced the WCTU to adopt her Christian socialist program. The achievements of the WCTU before Willard's death in 1898 were impressive, however, including state laws raising the age of consent and mandating temperance education, major contributions to state Prohibition and woman suffrage referenda, and construction in the Woman's Temple of a feminist architectural statement in the heart of Chicago's business district. Most important, the WCTU mobilized women, linked them together, and gave them a public—often political—role at a time when popular ideology and practice confined them to a passive role in the home. Not only did the WCTU bring women into public affairs, but it also encouraged them to question male power within the domestic sphere.

After Willard's death the WCTU continued its multifaceted program of activity, but under the leadership of presidents less creative than Willard it lost its innovative role within the Prohibition movement. Prohibition leadership passed to the Anti-Saloon League, a male-dominated pressure group narrowly focused upon gaining Prohibition through primarily political means. By the time national Prohibition came into effect in 1920, new cultural styles were already eroding the WCTU's base of support. Furthermore, the WCTU's sponsorship of Prohibition gave it a defensive and reactionary public image, and Prohibition's repeal in 1933 sealed the organization's loss of cultural authority.

A consequential, but often neglected, achievement of Willard's leadership was the founding in 1884 of the WWCTU, the first international organization of women. Based on already existing WCTUs in the United States and Canada as well as the British Women's Temperance Association, the WWCTU spread through the indefatigable organizing of temperance missionaries whose travels spanned the globe. By the 1920s the organization claimed 40 national affiliates and a following of more than 1 million women. Through its active life, from the 1890s through the 1920s, the WWCTU took part in crusades against prostitution and international trade in hallucinogenic drugs and for peace, woman's rights, and Prohibition. Through the WWCTU, women in many societies developed a wider and more international perspective. This effect was limited, however, since the WWCTU had a significant presence only in countries within the Anglo-American sphere of influence. Furthermore, injunctions to international sisterhood and cultural adaptation were often undercut by attitudes of Anglo-American cultural superiority. In addition, both the American WCTU and the WWCTU were committed to Prohibition as the only solution for intemperance, while temperance workers in some other societies found moral suasion aimed toward achieving moderate drinking habits a more appropriate strategy. As Victorian culture crumbled during the 1920s, and national Prohibition was repealed in the United States, the appeal of women's temperance reform waned. The temperate ideal for which the WCTU fought, however, long outlasted the heyday of the organization. That ideal in altered form inspired the next wave of women's temperance activism when Mothers Against Drunk Driving arose in the 1980s.

References. Jack S. Blocker, Jr., *"Give to the Winds Thy Fears": The Women's Temperance Crusade, 1873–1874* (Westport, Conn., 1985); Ruth Bordin, *Woman and Temperance: The Quest for Power and Liberty, 1873–1900* (Philadelphia, 1981); Ruth Bordin, *Frances Willard: A Biography* (Chapel Hill, N.C., 1986); Sharon Anne Cook, *"Through Sunshine and Shadow": The Woman's Christian Temperance Union, Evangelicalism, and Reform in Ontario, 1874–1930* (Montreal and Kingston, Calif., 1995); Barbara Leslie Epstein, *The Politics of Domesticity: Women, Evangelism, and Temperance in Nineteenth-Century America* (Middletown, Conn., 1981); Ian Tyrrell, *Woman's World/Woman's Empire: The Woman's Christian Temperance Union in International Perspective, 1880–1930* (Chapel Hill, N.C., 1991).

JACK S. BLOCKER, JR.

THEOLOGY, FEMINIST. Feminist theology is the critical, constructive, and creative discussion of established forms of religion from a perspective that advocates the liberation of women from the patriarchal structures the major world religions in their traditional expressions often support and embody. Feminist theology takes its starting point from the fact that women have, to a major extent, not actively participated either in formal theology or as authorized agents of religious life. Women's contributions to theology and religious leadership have traditionally been excluded from the canons of relevant and normative writings, and religious movements that allowed for women's leadership have often been declared heretical by mainstream religion. Feminist theologians seek to recover the voices of women in the religious traditions to which they belong, to critically evaluate their own religious traditions with regard to their value and validity for women, and to find constructive reconceptualizations of Christian theology and praxis that allow for women to be fully authoritative. While feminist movements also exist in other world religions such as Judaism and Islam, this entry remains restricted to Christian feminist theology.

Feminist theologians suggest a critical rereading of the existing canon of theological tradition. They also advocate the expansion of the canon of those religious texts and experiences considered relevant to achieve the public representation of women as well as the expression of women's spirituality in theology. They set out to develop a critique of the core religious symbols of Christianity such as Christ, the Trinity, and Mary as well as of the major texts within both the Christian and Hebrew traditions. Particular expressions of core symbols, such as the use of male God-language, are identified as metaphorical and therefore open to transformation. They also seek to point out how some aspects of Christian theology have, in the past, been instrumental in the oppression and marginalization of women and their sexuality. Prominent examples are Rosemary Radford Ruether's discussion of the centrality and the impact of Christology for women and the discussion of Mariology as the expression of an essentially disembodied female symbol, constructed by celibate male theologians to repress and exclude women's bodies and sexuality. Feminist theologians argue for a critique and reconceptualization of traditional religious symbols and for a retrospective addition of women's traditions into what religion understands as its heritage. This necessitates the retrieval of women as agents and authors in the history of the church and its tradition.

Among the predecessors of feminist theologians are the women participating in the life of early Christian communities such as Montanist prophetesses; female medieval mystics such as Julian of Norwich and Hildegard of Bingen; women leaders within the Quaker movement; and authors like Elizabeth Cady Stanton, compiler of *The Women's Bible*, one of the earliest works of women's biblical criticism. The contemporary movement of feminist theology began after the Second Vatican Council, in response to both the council's neglect to address the issue of women's role in the "church in the modern world" and the emerging women's liberation movement.

Feminist theologians argue that women's experiences have so far been neglected in the community's theological reflections and are not represented in different aspects of Christianity, such as spirituality, liturgy, and written and oral tradition. New ways of interpretation and new forms of religious life need to be developed that focus on women's experiences as vital sources of Christian traditions in past, present, and future.

In terms of method, feminist theologians have largely drawn on Latin American liberation theology, which identifies theology as critical reflection on the Bible in the light of the experience of the Christian community and the poor in particular. Feminist theology confronts the marginalization and oppression of women in both church and theological academe. This includes challenging dominant, male-centered methods of scholarship as well as the struggle for the ordination of women to the priesthood in all Christian churches. The latter is, however, not seen as a valid goal as long as it remains restricted to the mere inclusion of women into structures that remain unchanged and dominated by men and male power, but only if such ordination leads to the transformation of ecclesial structures. Christian churches must be modeled on feminist principles of equality, mutuality, and models of authority that arise in relation to particular functions for which women's as well as men's gifts may be equally relevant.

Feminist theologians are concerned not only with "religious matters" but with all issues relevant to women's lives. These include reproductive rights, poverty, and the well-being of lesbian as well as heterosexual women. Political concerns and theological debate, religious worship and societal issues are inseparable for feminist theologians who, as women, attempt to construct a just relationship among one another and with men. This follows from the significance attributed to women's bodies and women's sexuality in feminist theological reflections. Feminist theologians argue for an end to the oppression of women's sexuality as polluting and dangerous, as expressed, for instance, in the Roman Catholic concept of the male priesthood and in the Orthodox churches' refusal to admit menstruating women to communion. Women's bodies are to be recovered as sources of holistic and liberating spirituality. Menstruation, childbirth, and menopause are to be recovered as vital aspects of women's spiritual experiences. Thus, an important aspect of feminist critiques of patriarchal religion is the rejection of a perception of the world and religious reality in dualistic structures. These ultimately reflect a male/female dualism in which the male represents the sacred and dominant, while the female expresses the inferior and carnal aspects of life, which need to be overcome.

Holistic feminist spirituality also includes an increasing concern for nonhuman creation. Human survival is being threatened by the destruction of the ecosystem they see as connected to the oppression of women by patriarchy. The political concerns of feminist theology and spirituality cannot remain restricted to humanity but have to take into account the connectedness and interdependence of the whole of nature, human and nonhuman.

Even though many feminist theologians work to reconceptualize Christianity in ways that are liberating for women, other feminists identify all forms of religion as ultimately patriarchal and instrumental in jeopardizing women's well-being and wholeness. The most famous among these post-Christian feminists is the philosopher and trained theologian Mary Daly, who sees her feminist philosophy of women's liberation as antireligion and "sisterhood" as "antichurch."

While feminist theology started out as a predominantly white academic North American movement, women of color and Hispanic women pointed out that feminist theologians had so far claimed to speak for all women. They began to argue that women's experience as a theological criterion, in fact, meant the experience of white, middle-class women, who simply ignored the experiences of other women and thereby contributed to the oppression of these women rather than to their liberation. As a consequence black women developed *womanist* theology, while Hispanic women expressed their spirituality as *mujerista* theology. In recent years feminist theology has become a much more international movement with both the publication of the works of Asian and Third World feminist theologians and the development of feminist theology in a European context.

Though the women's movement can be seen as one of the birthing factors of feminist theology, religious feminism has always been faced with a certain isolation in academic theology as well as in academic feminism. Feminist theologians are only beginning to enter into dialogue with other theologians and other feminists. Examples are the development of study programs such as the Center for Women's Studies in Religion at Harvard Divinity School or the recognition of feminist theology as an academic subject, as through the introduction of a chair in feminist theology in a Dutch university. Overcoming this double isolation to both feminism and theology might also result in an expansion of the scope of those aspects of women's religious experience studied by feminist theologians. Feminist theologians face the challenge to respond to the increasing influence of politically and religiously conservative movements that deny women their appeal for greater justice. They need to find a basis for dialogue among feminist theologians from different backgrounds as well as with feminists from other parts of the women's movement.

References. Luis K. Daly, *Feminist Theological Ethics. A Reader* (Westminster, U.K., 1994); Catherine Mowry LaCugna (ed.), *Freeing Theology. The Essentials of Theology in Feminist Perspective* (San Francisco, 1993); Ann Loades (ed.), *Feminist Theology—A Reader* (London, 1997); Rosemary Radford Ruether, *Sexism and God-Talk. Toward a Feminist Theology* (London, 1983); Letty M. Russell and J. Shannon Clarkson (eds.), *Dictionary of Feminist Theologies* (Louisville, Ky., 1996).

NATALIE KNÖDEL

THEOLOGY OF DOMINATION is the notion that women are inferior to men morally and intellectually and must be directed and controlled by them. The theology of domination is a recurring concept in all the religions of the modern world. The position is, at the same time, contrary to the major tenets of creation held by each of the major religions of the world as well. The resulting subjugation and limitation of the roles of women, however, not only bring into question the integrity of the various teachings of particular religious groups but have implications for the broader social order as well.

The teaching of major religions about women derive primarily from two facets of religious philosophy: first, from the definition of the creative process that serves to explain the origins of human life and, second, from the interpretation of the creation myths of each faith that present models of basic human relationships between the sexes. These two concepts are in tension with each other. The definition of the creative process identifies the manner and substance of creation. The creation myths, on the other hand, describe the roles and functions of the creatures of earth. From these two perspectives come the theological teachings about the nature and purpose of human life. From them also flow the structures, norms, and interpretations of human society.

In every major religion the act of creation is described as unitary and equal. The human being is determined to have emanated from a being of pure spirit, a coequal couple or a hermaphroditic being. In every instance, in other words, creation makes no distinction between males and females. Both males and females, it is taught, have been created from the same substance or same source, which is itself without weakness, separation, or inferiority. The creative source makes both females and males from the same creative principle. Based on this point of view, men and women must be equal, capable of like responses, and full partners in the human endeavor.

In creation myths, on the other hand, women fall prey to interpretations of blightedness: in the Hindu tradition, Father Heaven must control Mother Earth because she brings forth evil as well as good. Shiva must bring force to bear on Kali to deter her unrestraint from destroying the earth. Buddha's temptation is from the daughters of Mara—Pleasure, Pride, and Sensuality. Eve tempts Adam, and the human race loses privilege and primal happiness. The fact that Adam is no stronger than Eve in being able to understand or resist the demonic is ignored in the retelling. The fact that Kali's freedom is forever destroyed without real cause and despite the great good she has done for the human race is overlooked. The fact that Mara's daughters are temptations but not temptresses is given no notice in the analyses. On the contrary, the theological web begins to be spun that women are created by God as carnal or irrational creatures whose role by nature is sexual, whose purpose is secondary, whose value is limited, and whose presence is dangerous to the higher functioning of the men of the society. The foundation is laid for women to accept their own oppression as the price of their sanctification. Men, for instance, become the "heads" of the family; women are confined to the home; the way women dress becomes the explanation of why men rape; and since women are by nature incapable of more than physical service, public business and "important" matters become the province of men.

The justification for all forms of diminishment of women is now complete and the theology of domination thus becomes a tenet of faith. God, who made women equal to men on one level, does not mean for women to have the opportunity to live that equality out in ways open to men. The creation principle and the creation myth become the polar tensions in which women live their lives. The responsibilities they bear, on one hand, are canceled by the privileges they are denied, on the other.

The history of women, as a result, is one of historical and universal oppression, discrimination, and violence. In Buddhism, women who have led lives of total spiritual dedication are trained to take orders from the youngest of male monks. In Islam, women are required to veil their heads and cover their bodies to express their unworthiness and signal the fact that they belong to some man. In Hinduism, women are abandoned by their husbands for higher pursuits and larger dowries or held responsible for their deaths by virtue of a woman's bad karma. In Judaism, women are denied access to religious ritual and education. In Christianity until recently and in many sectors still, the legal rights of women have been equated with those of minor children; wife beating is protected as a domestic right, and even the spiritual life of women is dictated, directed, and controlled by the men of the faith.

The theology of domination says, in essence, that men and women are created out of the same substance but that men are superior; that God, in effect, made some humans more human than other humans; and that some people are in charge of other people and can do whatever is necessary to maintain this God-given right and responsibility. The social implications of such theology are serious. If God built inequality into the human race, then it is acceptable to argue that some races are unequal to other races. It is clear that the subjugation of whole peoples by another group is natural and even desirable. It is obvious that the use of force against other nations and cultures that are considered inferior can be justified and embarked on as a way of life. Even in democracies, some people may be denied the vote because they are inferior, untouchable, or unacceptable to those who have gained power, whether by force or by natural rights.

The theology of domination makes sexism, racism, and militarism of a piece. It brings into clear focus the role of religion in world order, development, and peace.

References. Mircea Eliade, *Patterns in Comparative Religion* (New York, 1965); Rosemary Radford Reuther (ed.), *Religion and Sexism* (New York, 1974); Peggy Reeves Sanday, *Female Power and Male Dominance* (New York, 1981); George Tavard, *Women in Christian Tradition* (South Bend, Ind., 1973).

JOAN D. CHITTISTER

TIBETAN WOMEN have, to a certain extent, enjoyed a higher status and more freedom than women in neighboring India and China. But their position has undergone changes during the course of history and varies according to class and region. In the earliest records (c. second century C.E.)

about proto-Tibetan tribes, Chinese historiographers described a "women's kingdom" in southeastern Tibet where the political power was in the hands of women, while men were subordinate warriors and servants, and ancient Greek legends (corroborated by Sanskrit sources) place another women's kingdom in the west of Tibet, the Amazons' kingdom, which Alexander the Great could not conquer. By the time the Tibetan people entered the era of recorded history (seventh century C.E.) these matriarchal empires had almost vanished but imprinted traces upon later developments. During the era of the Lha sa dynasty (seventh to ninth centuries), the mothers of the Tibetan emperors played a vital role in politics. Some empresses and princesses actively participated in government, and many were among the first Tibetans to be attracted to Buddhism, which was introduced from India by that time. The *History of the sBa Family* records that in the eighth century special Buddhist teachers were appointed to instruct aristocratic women in Buddhist tradition. The history of the later Tibetan principalities located in the border regions abound in stories of heroic women of the past and present (some actively involved in the resistance against the Chinese occupation in 1950), while the Lhasa nobility adopted, to some extent, the patriarchal system of neighboring countries.

The social organization of the ordinary Tibetan people was based on two conflicting systems of kinship structure: patrilineal lineages (clans) and extended families uniting members of the patrilineal clans and matrilineal kinship. As a general rule, marriages within one's clan were disapproved of, with the result that the wife normally belonged to a different clan from that of her husband and children. This implies that the boundaries of the clans, patrilineal as well as matrilineal, cut across those of the families. The mother's lineage was known as *sha* (flesh), and the father's as *rus* (bones). Certain social and religious responsibilities were confined to one or the other lineage, while others had to be taken over by the family as a whole regardless of the clan affiliation of its individual members.

Polygamous marriage systems existed side by side with monogamy. A system of fraternal polyandric marriage (i.e., a woman was married with two or more brothers of the same family) was mainly practiced by wealthy peasants who were under the authority of the Tibetan government and not under that of the nobility or the clergy. This form of marriage not only limited the growth of population, vital for surviving in a fragile ecological zone, but also was seen as giving a special status to the wife. She would be courted by several men and in charge of more "manpower," which translated into greater wealth. However, polyandry was not practiced by all Tibetans. Polygynic marriages occurred mainly among the nobility, sometimes in conjunction with polyandric marriages, resulting in a form of "group marriage." However, the most common form of marriage was monogamy. Divorce was frequent and could be initiated by either party. In such cases, the property was divided between husband and wife by taking into account what each had brought into the marriage. In general, the sons would then stay with their father and his family; the daughters, with their mother and her family, but there were many exceptions to this rule. Remarriage was the norm for both parties. In general laypeople would marry, but women as well as men could stay single without living a celibate life. Present Chinese research puts the number of unmarried Tibetan laywomen at 5 percent of the entire female population.

Women owned and operated businesses and inherited land and other assets. The short-distance market economy was almost exclusively in the hands of women, while the long-distance trading economy was a traditionally male territory. Women played a crucial role as mother, as pivot of the family, and as trustee of the material resources of the family, to which they equally contributed through their work. Division of labor was organized in accord with the difference in physical strength of man and woman and with the need to nurse babies and toddlers. Sexual contacts were not necessarily confined to married partners. Extramarital children resulting from such contacts were raised together with the other children. Women took the same liberties in having love affairs as men. Nuptial fidelity was nothing but a lofty ideal with little impact on the daily life of the people. Nineteenth-century Western travelers criticized the Tibetans for their laxity in moral matters. Despite fairly lax sexual morals, only male homosexuality was (silently) accepted as part of the monastic life, while female homosexuality, although existing particularly among the nobility, was harshly prosecuted.

Mahayana Buddhism, the dominant religion of the Tibetans, emphasizes female symbols (for instance, ultimate wisdom in the form of a goddess), considers women to be of equal spiritual potential, and asserts that designations like male or female are irrelevant with regard to the absolute reality (Buddha nature). Yet, the reality was ambiguous. There had always been fewer Buddhist nuns in Tibet than monks, and among the voluminous Buddhist literature very few works were ascribed to women. While the monks could engage either in scholastic studies or contemplative seclusion, nuns were excluded from the formal study of Buddhist philosophy but exceeded monks in Tantric practice. As exceptions some nuns became advisers to the nobility and cabinet ministers. Others were famous for their spiritual achievements; some—like Ma-gcig Lab-sgron (1044–1131)—founded distinctive traditions within the mainstream of Tibetan Buddhism. But Buddhism also preserved, to some extent, traces of male dominance customary in India and China when the Tibetans adopted this faith. For example, nuns were under the monks' supervision, and some literary works depicted women as a source of male temptation. Thus, there is a misogynist strand within Tibetan Buddhism when women are seen as obstructing the spiritual progress of men.

During the last decades most of the Tibetan people were confronted with modernity as mediated through contemporary Chinese culture. The results were often drastic changes affecting some sections of the population and some regions more than others. More than 100,000 Tibetans live now as refugees in India, and several thousand live in the Western world, where they are exposed to the current discussion of the role and place of women in the world. Among the exile communities in India, reforms of the educational system (in monasteries and convents) are on the way but are still in an experimental stage. Exiled Tibetan women only reluctantly follow the call for more participation in public life and for improving their education and pay, at most, only lip service to the ideals of feminism. Unlike many women of the People's Republic of China, large numbers of Tibetan women remain still in a traditional and often rural environment that precludes their participating in the process of modernization. Thus, today one meets many more well-educated young Tibetan men (often with degrees from prestigious Chinese universities) than women, although an increasing number of women try to break out from the confines of the past and take up a professional life.

References. Tsultrim Allione, *Women of Wisdom* (London, Boston, and Melbourne, 1984); José I. Cabezón, *Buddhism, Sexuality, and Gender* (Albany, N.Y., 1992); Jérome Edou, *Machig Labdrön and the Foundations of Chöd* (Ithaca, N.Y., 1996); Eva Neumaier-Dargyay, *The Sovereign All-Creating Mind: The Motherly Buddha. A Translation of the Kun byed rgyalpo'i mdo* (Albany, N.Y., 1992); Eva Neumaier-Dargyay, "Buddhist Thought from a Feminist Perspective," in M. Joy and E. K. Neumaier-Dargyay (eds.), *Gender, Genre and Religion: Feminist Reflections* (Waterloo, Ont., 1995), 145–170; Karma Lekshe Tsomo, *Sakyadhita, Daughters of the Buddha* (Ithaca, N.Y., 1988); Janice Willis, *Feminine Ground. Essays on Women and Tibet* (Ithaca, N.Y., 1989, 1995).

EVA NEUMAIER-DARGYAY

TITLE VII is that portion of the Civil Rights Act of 1964, as amended, that prohibits discrimination on the basis of race, color, sex, religion, or national origin. It covers *all* terms, conditions, and privileges of employment such as hiring, discharge, training, promotion, compensation, and fringe benefits. Sexual harassment* is considered to be a form of discrimination.* The law applies to virtually all public and private employers, including educational institutions and state and local governments, whether or not they receive any federal financial assistance. The law also states that the courts may "order such affirmative action as may be appropriate" in particular cases. This has included court-imposed quotas to correct the effects of past discrimination. Enforcement of Title VII has been influenced by the 1971 Supreme Court decision in the case of *Griggs v. Duke Power Company*, which determined that the existence of discrimination could be inferred not only through a demonstrated *intent* to discriminate but also through a review of the *consequences* of employment practices. The responsibility for enforcing Title VII rests with the Equal Employment Opportunity Commission (EEOC), which was created for that purpose.

DAYLE MANDELSON

TITLE IX, part of the Educational Amendments of 1972, prohibits sex discrimination* against students and employees in any educational program or activity receiving federal financial assistance. It affects virtually all public school systems and postsecondary educational institutions and has had its greatest impact on athletic programs. Title IX's employment provisions deal with employment criteria, recruitment and hiring, compensation, job classification and structure, leaves of absence and fringe benefits, and sex as a bona fide occupational qualification.* Other provisions affect admissions, financial aid, and academic programs. The law is enforced by the Department of Education. In 1984, the Supreme Court decision in the case of *Grove City College v. Bell* greatly narrowed the scope of Title IX by reducing its coverage from the whole educational institution receiving federal funds to the specific program or activity that has received the assistance. Congress' attempts to reinstate the original intent of Title IX were finally successful in 1988, when the Civil Rights Restoration Act was passed over a presidential veto.

DAYLE MANDELSON

TRAINING. *General training* is training in skills such as literacy, mathematics, typing, computer programming, and so on that enhance productivity in a wide variety of occupations. Because of its wide applicability, employers are reluctant to pay for it. Women's labor market skills tend to derive from general training.

Specific training is training that provides skills needed for work in a particular firm only, for example, an introduction to a firm's idiosyncratic bookkeeping system. Employers tend to pay for this but offer it only to those employees they expect to stay with the firm for a long time. Women tend to be excluded from this type of training and from the advancement within the firm that such training can promote.

SUSAN B. CARTER

TRANSSEXUALISM (also called sex reassignment) is the culmination of a series of professional procedures, both psychological and medical, designed to change the "gender identity," sex role, and anatomy of persons to conform them to the opposite sex. The word "transsexualism" did not become part of the English language until the 1950s, when it was used to define persons who had an overwhelming desire to change their sexual anatomy based on their claim to be members of the opposite sex. Thus, the popular definition of a transsexual, for example, is that of "a woman trapped in a man's body." The popular definition also highlights that more men desire and undergo sex reassignment than women. Although the exact ratios are disputed in the professional literature, the generally accepted ratio is 4:1.

Transsexual surgery has been possible since the early 1930s. The hormonal and surgical techniques, however, were not refined and made public until the 1950s, when Christine (formerly George) Jorgensen was transsexed in Denmark, and the event gained international publicity in 1953.

In the United States, Dr. Harry Benjamin is responsible for the initiation of transsexual surgery and research. A major expansion of this research and surgery took place in 1967 with the formal opening of the Johns Hopkins Gender Identity Clinic in Baltimore. The fact that a major medical institution with the prestige of Johns Hopkins had undertaken such controversial treatment and surgery catapulted transsexualism into the public and professional eye as a legitimate medical problem. However, as Johns Hopkins was the first major medical institution to perform the surgery in the United States, it was also the first to terminate its program in 1979— 12 years after it began.

A study conducted by Jon Meyer, psychiatrist and director of the Johns Hopkins sexual consultation program, found that there was no difference in long-term adjustment for individuals who undergo the surgery and those who do not. Using extensive follow-up evaluation of employment status, marital and cohabitation success, psychological and legal problems, Meyer's study concluded that transsexual surgery served "as a palliative measure [but] it does not cure what is essentially a psychiatric disturbance" (*The Johns Hopkins Medical Institutions News*).

Reports conflict about the actual number of transsexual operations that are performed in this country, as well as how many persons seek the surgery. In the absence of any national directory of transsexual applicants, data on patients for surgery are inconclusive.

For the male-to-constructed-female transsexual, primary surgery entails castration, penectomy, and vulvo-vaginal construction. Surgery for the female-to-constructed-male transsexual consists of bilateral mammectomy, hysterectomy, and salpingo-oophorectomy. These procedures may be followed by phalloplasty and the insertion of testicular prostheses. Because the technology of phallus construction is still quite primitive, most female-to-constructed-male transsexuals undergo mammectomy and hysterectomy. Secondary surgery, such as limb, eye, chin, and/or ear surgery, scar revision, and/or reduction of the Adam's apple, is often sought by transsexuals for aesthetic reasons and/or to correct real or felt complications. Many transsexuals, especially male-to-constructed-females, go to great lengths to adapt to the culturally prescribed body type of the opposite sex.

The medical odyssey of the transsexual does not begin or end with surgery, however, but rather with the administration of hormones. Exogenous estrogens, for example, decrease certain existing sex characteristics such as body hair and augment the development of breasts in men. The treatment of male transsexual candidates is almost totally dependent on estrogen to induce hormonal castration and feminization. Such treatment is long-term—in most cases, lifelong.

The causes of transsexualism have been debated in various circles. Most etiological theories fall into two camps—organic and psychogenic. Organic theories have emphasized neuroendocrine factors, while psychogenic etiologies have focused on imprinting, family conditioning (with an emphasis upon mother–son symbiosis), and/or separation anxiety. While organic and psychogenic explanations seek different causes, both utilize similar theoretical models—that is, both locate the cause of transsexualism within the individual and/or interpersonal matrix. In these etiological theories, social, political, and cultural causes tend to be relegated to a subsidiary or nonexistent role. For example, psychogenic theories measure a transsexual's adjustment or nonadjustment to the cultural identity and role of masculinity or femininity. They seldom locate the origins of transsexualism in a gender-defined society whose norms of masculinity and femininity generated the desire to be transsexed in the first place.

The diagnosis of transsexualism is problematic from many points of view. That it is subject to diagnosis is in itself an issue that follows upon its designation as legitimate medical territory. If transsexualism is a disease, then does the desire qualify as disease? As Thomas Szasz has asked, does the old person who wants to be young suffer from the "disease" of being a "transchronological," or does the poor person who wants to be rich suffer from the "disease" of being a "transeconomical"? Transsexualism is a self-diagnosis by definition. But it is a self-diagnosis that has become colonized by the medical model.

In the last century, more and more areas of life have come to be defined as medical and technical problems. Feminist critics contend that accepting transsexualism as a medical and therapeutic problem encourages persons to view other persons (especially children) who do not conform to stereotypical sex-role behavior as potential transsexuals. Thus, for example, for the boy who likes to play with dolls or the girl who wants to be a truck driver, these behaviors can be interpreted as transsexual behavior instead of as nonstereotypical behavior that reflects a protest against, or a discomfort with, sex roles.

Feminist critics also question the political and social shaping of masculine and feminine behavior that is an integral part of the treatment process. Persons wishing to change sex come to so-called gender identity clinics, as well as to private therapists, for counseling and ultimately for surgical referral. Most clinics require candidates for surgery to live out opposite-sex roles and stereotypically defined, opposite-sex behavior for periods of six months to two years. Thus, the role of these clinics and clinicians in reinforcing sex-role stereotypes is significant.

Transsexual surgery for persons wishing to change sex is controversial. There is a lack of well-controlled follow-up studies documenting the safety and effectiveness of the surgery itself. Surgery may confer the artifacts of outer and inner female organs, and it may alter the anatomical and hormonal sex of a person, but it cannot change the history of what it means to be born in a male or female body. Georges Burou, a Casablancan physician who has operated on over 700 American men who wanted to be women, has given this summary of his work: "I don't change men into women. I transform genitals into genitals that have a female aspect. All the rest is in the patient's mind" (*Time*, p. 64).

Feminist debates about transsexualism have been largely superseded by debates over transgender. The term "transgender" covers preoperative and postoperative transsexuals, persons who take long- or short-term hormones but do not continue with surgery; men who have undergone breast implants; transvestites; drag queens; cross-dressers; and some gays, lesbians, bisexuals, and heterosexuals who claim to challenge gender by assimilating aspects of masculine or feminine roles.

Feminist critics of transgenderism contend that in "transgressing" the stereotypes of masculine and feminine gender roles by assimilation, transgender is actually a strategy of preserving sex differences. Although mixed and matched in a supposedly gender-defiant way, transgender behavior adheres to many self-selected ingredients of these roles. Masculinity and femininity are seen as entities in themselves, to be preserved and grafted onto one another.

Critics point out that the transgender language, text, and posture of sexual rebellion are a new brand of sexual conformity. Transgenderism is the product of a historical period that confines any challenge to sex roles and gender definitions to assimilating these roles and definitions in another form. Transgender, they maintain, encourages a style rather than a politics of gender resistance in which an expressive individualism has taken the place of collective political challenges to power. Although provocative, the new transgender outlaw is the old/new gender conformist.

References. Richard Green and John Money (eds.), *Transsexualism and Sex Reassignment* (Baltimore, 1969); Sheila Jeffreys, *Lesbian Heresy: A Feminist Perspective on the Lesbian Sexual Revolution* (North Melbourne, Victoria, 1993); Thomas Kando, *Sex Change: The Achievement of Gender Identity among Feminized Transsexuals* (Springfield, Ill., 1973); Janice G. Raymond, *The Transsexual Empire: The Making of the She-Male*, reprinted with a new Introduction on transgender (New York, 1979, 1994); *The Johns Hopkins Medical Institutions News*, Press Release, August 13, 1979, 2; Judith Shapiro, "Transsexualism: Reflections on the Persistence of Gender and the Mutability of Sex," in Julia Epstein and Kristina Straub (eds.), *Bodyguards: The Cultural Politics of Gender Ambiguity* (New York, 1991), 248–279; Thomas Szasz, "Male and Female Created He Them," *The New York Times Book Review* (Review of Janice G. Raymond, *The Transsexual Empire*), June 10, 1979, 11, 39; *Time* (January 21, 1974): 64.

                                                    JANICE G. RAYMOND

TROUBADOUR LITERATURE is the poetry of Occitania (modern-day Provence in southern France) from the end of the eleventh century to the final decade of the thirteenth. Written in the medieval language of the region (*langue d'oc*), it was influenced by Arab sources, Ovid's love poetry, and contemporary vernacular verse but constituted essentially a new literature. Fittingly, the word "troubadour" means "finder" or "inventor" in Occitanian. Of the 400 known troubadours, 20 were women (the *trobairitz*).

With the exception of the earliest known troubadour, Guilhelm VII of Poitiers (1071–1127), the male troubadours were generally sedentary poets attached to a court. The songs they wrote were extremely formulaic, despite the inventive use of a limited number of figures of speech known as conceits or *topoi*.

Troubadour poetry gave rise to the conception of *fin' amors*, loosely translated as courtly love. *Fin' amors* was not an established system of rules for behavior but a mode of thought emanating from the literature itself. Within this courtly ethos, the usual roles of aristocratic men and women were reversed. In most cases, the troubadour addressed his poetry as a humble knight to the wife of his lord and, thus, to a woman of higher status than himself. He vowed eternal homage and obedience to this lady as his master (*midons*, literally "my lord"). Through his love, he hoped to ennoble himself to her level and, therefore, to that of his patron.

Unlike much medieval literature that regarded women as obsessively carnal, troubadour poetry venerated the lady as a sexual being. Although the love professed by the troubadour was rarely consummated, this consummation was the goal of each supplicant. Through the denial resulting from such frustrated desires, the troubadour hoped to better himself. In general, troubadours were without landholdings and came from a relatively new and fluid class of noble families. The courtly love ethic they developed negated the effects of birth and declared the troubadours the equals of their lords through the ennobling effects of their long-suffering love. In essence, the lady was the embodiment of the troubadour ideal and a passive means of offering homage to her husband.

Although we know little about the lives of the female troubadours, it is clear that all of them were from the aristocracy and, as such, the potential objects of troubadour veneration. Approximately one-third of them were patrons of the arts who had troubadours in their own courts, several were probably the sisters or cousins of male troubadours, and certainly all of them knew troubadours personally. Except for the relative autonomy of the medieval convent, which produced several great literary works by female authors (e.g., Hildegard of Bingen), Occitania was the only region during this period to generate such a flowering of female literature.

The twelfth century seems to have been a period of economic and political decline for aristocratic women in many regions of Europe. In contrast,

Occitania was a pocket of somewhat greater female power. One of the reasons for this difference may have been the legal system in southern France. Unlike other parts of Europe, Occitania retained vestiges of Visigothic law. As a result, unmarried daughters of the aristocracy could inherit equally with their brothers, and when these women married, they ceded only the use of their property (usufruct) to their husbands and retained ownership themselves. Since land was the basis of wealth and power during the Middle Ages, the legal system allowed Occitanian women of the aristocracy more power than their sisters had in other parts of Europe. In fact, by the beginning of the tenth century several important southern French fiefs were in the hands of women, including Montpellier, Nimes, Auvergne, Toulouse, Béziers, Périgord, Carcassonne, and Limousin. When the Crusades began (1095), aristocratic women in southern France consolidated their positions of power. Wives were left in charge of their husbands' lands, and many remained in power when their men fell in battle.

Trobairitz poetry reflects the contradictory situation of the powerful woman within a male-defined culture. The female troubadours were ladies who had stepped down from their pedestals. No longer the passive object of male paeans, these women took an active voice in the troubadour love relationship, thereby neutralizing their supposed domination as the arbiters of love. As a result, one common theme of *trobairitz* poetry was the desire to be acknowledged and to have a controlling voice in the courtship. With the reversal of male–female relationships in the poems, however, the analogy to the courtly system was seriously weakened. There was no idealization of the suitor and no prize to be gained by the *trobairitz*. In fact, the *topos* of *mezura* (patience, discretion) is practically absent from the women's poems, since the *trobairitz* continued to define themselves as the object of pursuit. This definition gave rise to such convoluted constructions as the countess of Dia's portrayal of her beloved as "he whom I most desire to have me."

In extending the limits of courtly love, the old *topoi* called into question many of the values upon which *fin' amors* was based. For instance, the female troubadours made liberal use of newly coined mercantile *topoi* such as *pretz* (value) and *merce* (grace, salary), which for their male counterparts implied a love relationship based on a means of exchange. However, lacking the usual connotation of vassalage implied in the male poems, what resulted was a concept of purely sexual power. Thus, in employing the conventional troubadour conceits in a different context, the *trobairitz* disrupted the poetic structure developed by their male counterparts.

The 20 known *trobairitz* were the countess of Dia, Tibors, Almucs de Castinau, Iseut de Capio, Azalais de Porcairages, Maria de Ventadorn, Alamanda, Garsenda, Isabella, Lombarda, Castelloza, Clara d'Anduza, Bieiris de Romans, Guillelma de Rosers, Domna H., Alais, Iselda, Carenza, Gaudairença, and Gormonda de Montpellier.

References. Joan M. Ferrante, *Woman as Image in Medieval Literature: From the Twelfth Century to Dante* (New York, 1975); Marianne Shapiro, "The Provençal *Trobairitz* and the Limits of Courtly Love," *Signs* 3 (1978): 560–571.

NANCY VEDDER-SHULTS

TURKEY, a republic since 1923, in 1926 replaced the Sharia, Muslim family law, with a civil code modeled on the Swiss, thus becoming the exception, a secular state in the Islamic world. Mustafa Kemal Ataturk's modernization and nationalization included the emancipation of women. When it was virtually impossible in the West, women were radio announcers, technicians, and university faculty. In 1934 there were 18 women in Parliament (4.6 percent), and in 1946, 44 percent of university faculty in the natural sciences were women. Although multiparty government decreased women's membership in Parliament in the 1940s, they continue to be well represented in professional and public life.

The reforms, however, affected only a small group of women. Turkey is a land of widely disparate conditions, from the modern, technology-based culture of the major cities to some cultures in eastern Turkey that are still tribal. While major cities contained a small class of highly educated professional women, the vast majority of women in rural Turkey continued to live lives little changed from the days of the Ottoman empire. In the traditional cultures local custom, not the civil code, controlled their lives. The reforms did not change classic patriarchal relationships, nor did they improve access to education or economic opportunity for women outside the urban elite.

After World War II the growth of capitalism, urbanization, and massive migration, both internal and external, brought rapid changes that were bound to affect the traditional norms of society. In the 1950s no more than a quarter of the population was urban; by 1995, it was 69 percent urban, with migration continuing. About 25 percent of the population is concentrated in the great metropolitan areas of Istanbul, Ankara, and Izmir.

In the serious economic downturn of the 1970s, tensions and turmoil mounted as rising left-wing radicalism brought a new radicalism of the Right, Islamic fundamentalism. Religious fundamentalism, a worldwide phenomenon of the 1970s, was considered such a threat to Turkey's secularized government that the military intervened in 1980. Although civilian government soon resumed, the country continued to be affected by unrest, ethnic warfare, and terrorism through the 1990s.

In the 1980s, as more conservative elements pushed for renewed emphasis on woman's role as wife and mother, the women's movement began actively working on women's issues, and the government began to take a serious interest in women's problems. As it attempted to restructure and to prepare for entry into the European Union, it ratified, with reservations, the Convention on the Elimination of All Forms of Discrimination against

Women (CEDAW) (1985), the Nairobi Forward-Looking Strategies Agreement (1990), and the European Union's Social Charter (1989); and women's issues were seriously addressed in the Sixth Five Year Plan (1990–1994). The feminist movement's success in organizing public opinion around important issues and the actions taken by the government and by nongovernmental organizations (NGOs) brought significant improvement to the status of women.

To comply with CEDAW, changes are needed in some sections of the civil code, criminal code, and labor laws. While the civil code was enlightened for its day, some articles have had negative effects on women, and labor legislation designed for women's protection in practice has helped to limit them to traditional and low-paying occupations. In 1993 a draft amendment to the civil code was submitted to Parliament. However, it had not, by mid-1997, been acted upon.

Nevertheless, Turkey, in general, remained faithful to its international commitments. By the early 1990s mechanisms existed within government ministries that could address women's issues, and these issues were kept on the national agenda. Among the serious problems addressed were the rapidly rising population, women's and children's health, low educational attainment among the population, but especially among women, and low female participation in the industrial labor force, in part, stemming from lack of education. Some progress was made in almost all areas, but increasing fundamentalist trends pose a threat to continuing progress.

Population and Health Issues. In Turkey the low average age of first marriage, particularly in rural areas, is slowly rising (from 17.6 in 1982 to 18.2 in 1988). The age difference between husband and wife at first marriage also narrowed, but there is an average six-year difference for women marrying at less than 20.

Between 1950 and 1965 the population expanded by about 150 percent. To attempt to curb the high fertility rate the government began in a small way in 1965 to spread modern contraceptive use. The program was expanded and was an important factor in lowering the fertility rate from 6.8 in 1960 to 2.7 in 1993. The widespread use of traditional, rather than modern, contraceptive means; the belief in the economic benefits of large families for agriculture; and cultural and traditional values have kept the fertility rate high in certain regions—it was a reported 4.99 in Eastern Turkey in 1988. Even with reduced fertility, the decline in infant mortality (from 165 per 1,000 live births in 1965 to 52.6 by 1988) and other health improvements have kept the population growth rate over 2 percent.

Turkey's population (62,032,000 in 1995) is 49 percent female. The excessive male population seems primarily a result of high maternal mortality. Although declining since 1960, in 1981 it was 132 per 100,000 women. (Maternal mortality rates in industrialized countries range from 5 to 15.)

In 1981 it was estimated that the maternal mortality in eastern Turkey was as high as 284.

Leading causes of the high rate of maternal mortality include early and frequent pregnancies, lack of prenatal care, ignorance of personal hygiene, and, especially in rural areas where anemia is common, lack of medical attention (35 percent of births are without attendant health personnel). Goals for the year 2000 include bringing the population growth rate below 2 percent, increasing prenatal care and providing health personnel at all deliveries, and reducing maternal, infant, and child mortality rates by set amounts.

Economic. Although, in 1990, some 60 percent of the population was urban, 77 percent of the women in the labor force were in agriculture (and 80.4 percent of them were unpaid family members). In 1994 the rural female labor force participation (LFP) rate was 43.7 percent; the urban, 16.2 percent. As the urban population climbed, female LFP declined, from 70 percent in 1955 to 33 percent in 1990. Women moving into urban areas may not find work outside the home because of limited opportunities for female employment, lack of education, or social constraints—allowing women to work not on the family farm but among strangers is unacceptable to many. Actually, however, the 16.2 percent urban LFP is understated because it does not include informal sector employment. In the *gecekondu*, the shantytowns that surround major cities, women, who retain strong ties to their home villages, have devised many strategies for earning income.

Women's urban employment is concentrated in unskilled or semiskilled, intensely sex-segregated jobs closely related to their traditional duties. Eighty percent of women work in textiles and food services; 80 percent of these workers are in the lower ranks. Discriminatory protective legislation, poor education, and lack of consideration of the needs of women in development programs have all contributed to keeping women from attaining the skills needed for modern sector employment. In 1990 two-thirds of illiterate workers were women, and only 5 percent of rural women workers had more than a primary education.

Agricultural extension and research delivery systems focused exclusively on male activities until women's issues became a concern in the late 1980s. The Ministry of Agriculture launched a program (1990–1994) to develop new ways for extension to reach women. One was a pilot program to retrain home economists as extension agents to assist women farmers. Rural development projects since 1990 have included a women's component in their design.

The government has introduced several small credit programs designed to encourage and support small-scale businesses. One of these, the Family Credit Program, gave 80 percent of its loans to women involved in handicrafts in the home. Although government incentives are pretty well confined to women's businesses in traditional fields, NGO foundations have offered limited cash and in-kind credit programs in nontraditional agricultural activities.

Education. Since the 1970s efforts to erase illiteracy and reduce the gender gap in education have made significant progress. Although still very high in eastern and southeastern Anatolia, the illiteracy rate for women overall fell from 69 percent in 1970 to 29 percent in 1992 (men's illiteracy rate fell to 8 percent).

Nearly as many girls attend primary school (grades 1–5) as boys, but girls' attendance declines with the increasing grade level: in 1991–1992, for middle school (grades 6–8) it was 47.7 percent to 71.3 percent for boys; for secondary school, 31.1 percent to 47.3 percent.

Secondary education has two tracks, general and vocational-technical. More girls enter vocational schools, which are highly sex-segregated. About one-third are girls' schools, originally started to attract girls because in some regions parents will not send adolescent daughters to coeducational schools. The courses focus on traditional occupations such as textiles, ceramics, food processing, and hairdressing, have little potential for career growth, and do not teach the skills needed for self-employment or business management. About a quarter of the schools are gender-neutral, giving courses in commercial and tourism training. The enrollment is about one-third girls. The rest are boys' schools. Today either sex may attend any of the schools, but boys make up less than 1 percent of enrollment in the girls' schools, and girls are about 6 percent of enrollment in boys' schools. Private, religious-based secondary schools, where the emphasis is on traditional roles, are becoming increasingly popular.

In higher education 33.1 percent of the students are women. There has been a marked increase in the number of women entering the nontraditional fields of commerce and business administration. Enrollments are also high in engineering, but most of the women are enrolled in the architectural and urban planning programs rather than in the more technical fields. The percentage of women university faculty is above the world average. In 1991–1992, 28.2 percent of the lecturers and 20.4 percent of the professors were women (in Sweden women hold 20 percent of lectureships and 7 percent of professorships). They are basically absent from university administration, however.

The government that took control in 1991 made some very positive steps, including creating a separate Ministry of State for Women, and a women's movement crusade against violence led to the creation of some shelters and hostels in urban areas. In 1993 Tansu Ciller became the first woman prime minister, but her government fell in 1995 amid charges of corruption. New elections were followed by several short-lived governments, including the one led by the Islamist Welfare (*Refah*) Party (June 1996–June 1997). When this entry was written, the fate of women's gains in the 1990s and the possibilities for continuing improvements were unclear.

U

UKRAINE, a country of 50 million, became independent of the USSR in 1991. Although, through its turbulent history, it enjoyed only brief periods of unity and independence, starting in the 1880s, Ukrainian women established similar community organizations in all of the European states in which they lived—the Russian and Austrian empires and, after their disintegration in 1917, in Poland, Romania, Czechoslovakia, and, in different guise, the Soviet Union. They united all classes, stressed self-help programs rather than philanthropic ones, and provided women with practical information. While participating in the international women's movement, especially to call attention to the discrimination against their conationals, most did not consider themselves feminists. Their interest in a feminist agenda grew only after the organization they established was challenged. Ukrainian women's organizations foreshadow those in colonial states where national discrimination seems more obvious than sexual discrimination.

Natalia Ozarkevych Kobrynska (1855–1921) pioneered the first community organization of women in western Ukraine in 1884. In 1887, together with Olha Drahomaniv Kosach (better known as Olena Pchilka [1849–1930]), a writer from eastern Ukraine, she coedited *The First Wreath*, which stresses women's solidarity in both empires.

When Austria fell, and the Russian tsar was overthrown at the end of World War I, women participated in all political movements and in all governments of Ukrainians. The government that finally won in Kiev joined the Union of the Soviet Socialist Republics, which was established in 1922. Since the Ukrainian Bolsheviks did not recognize the particular needs of Ukrainian women and did not use local women to organize its women's sections, there was greater opposition to Bolshevik policies among Ukrainian women than in Russia proper. Except for the period between 1924 and 1926 (when Maria Levchenko, a Ukrainian communist, headed the Women's Section of the Party of Ukraine), Moscow, not Ukraine, exercised full control over the policy toward women. During the collectivization in 1927, especially in the first stages of the famine of 1933, peasant women led the opposition to the dispossession of the peasants. In 1930, the separate women's sections in the communist parties that had been established to mobilize the women for work in society were disbanded. The official decision was made that the women's issue in the Soviet Union had been solved. There was no women's organization in the Soviet Union from 1930 until 1945, when a government-sponsored women's organization was established to enable Soviet women to participate at international women's gatherings. In January 1987, a separate organization of Ukrainian women was founded in Kiev.

In the western Ukrainian territories, which were under Polish, Czechoslovak, and Romanian control in the interwar years, women established mass independent women's organizations that developed programs for women and by women to modernize the villages. The movement grew because women saw the advantages that the organization offered their families. They perceived the family not as a barrier to women's freedom but as a bastion against the encroachments of the state. This practical community feminism ended for the Ukrainians with the invasion of the Nazi Germans from the west and the Soviet Russians from the east. Both of these states had specific policies for women that were not determined by the women.

The communist regime left an ambivalent legacy for women. On one hand, the regime provided formal gender equality, an assured representation in the governmental assemblies for women (granted, largely pro forma but gender-integrated), and the expectation and need to work for pay. On the other hand, centralized planning with no input of women, low standard of living with few household amenities, the economic necessity of working outside the home with little attempt to spread the burdens of housework, and a politically oppressive regime that infringed upon the legal, national, and human rights of the population proved the expectation of gender equality false. The reality of the communist political system negated woman's rights in practice, even beyond the violation of basic human rights. Ukrainian women had national as well as political reasons to resent the party's manipulation of women. Communist women's activists were used to subvert the integrity of local communities and to promote policies of cultural Russification. Yet the erosion of Soviet totalitarianism in the former USSR also generated a distrust of women, women leaders, and feminism, which in public consciousness was linked to leftist ideologies. Today, many women in the Ukraine feel that the feminists' insistence on equality of women was as responsible as Marxism for the double burden of work heaped upon them. (Because the communist regime in its propaganda stressed the achievements of women in the USSR, established a quota of women's seats in local and state legislatures, and eliminated restrictions on women's work, many contemporary Ukrainians equate women's rights with communist exploitation of the individual, thus discrediting any attempt at women's rights. Furthermore, feminization of low-paying professions, the preponderance of women in labor-intensive physical work, and a more direct exposure to idealized middle-class dreams of wives comfortably supported by loving husbands have also contributed to giving any aspect of feminism or women's rights a bad or, at best, a questionable reputation.)

Women's distrust of the communist system was evident in the inability of the official Soviet women's organizations to restructure themselves during the period of perestroika. In the Ukraine, the creation of a separate women's council in 1989 was already a concession to local pressure, although there is no evidence to suggest that the party in power was aware of the historical antecedents of the Ukrainian council of women.

In the last years of the existence of the USSR, women's organizations outside the control of the party mounted mass demonstrations that challenged the Soviet political system. The Ukrainian Committee of Mothers of Soldiers, an organization founded in 1989 to ameliorate conditions in the military service (especially onerous in the unpopular war in Afghanistan and in using recruits to clean up the nuclear waste at Chernobyl), popularized the idea that a smaller state could be more responsive to the needs of their population than the vast USSR. Other women's organizations drew upon some historical precedent. The Women's Community (Zhinocha Hromada) seeks to ensure that women be included in the political reform. The independent Women's Union (Soiuz Ukrainok), the heir to the democratic traditions of the Women's Union, strives to be a middle-class volunteer organization. All in all, there are about 40 different women's organizations.

The discrepancy between the de facto and de jure position of women is both glaring and recognized. The high level of professional education of women is offset by the low numbers of women in higher responsible positions. None hold major elective or appointed political positions. Only 3 percent of deputies in Parliament are women, although women constitute 55 percent of the population. Feminization of low-paying professions, a phenomenon of the Soviet period, continues. Women continue to constitute 38 percent of low-paying transport workers and to be engaged in heavy labor.

The government and the political parties formed in the Ukraine in the 1990s are primarily interested in vouchsafing human rights, establishing a rule of law, creating conditions for economic development based on private property, and preventing the amassing of power by any one single structure or individual. Women's rights are assumed as a given, and few political parties mention issues relating specifically to women. Few women have tried to organize political parties. Olha Horyn, a political activist from western Ukraine, organized a Christian Women's Party in 1991, but it was never able to gather much momentum and simply disintegrated. A welcome development that marked an increasingly serious approach to women's issues was the holding of the first parliamentary hearings in the Ukraine on the status of women in July 1995. The First International Conference on Women in State Building, held May 28–30, 1993, organized by the Women's Community, should also be mentioned. Much of its agenda served as the basis for preparations for the parliamentary hearings. Conference resolutions drew on the Ukraine's commitment to enforce provisions of the United Nations Document to End Discrimination of Women that the Soviet Ukraine signed after the Nairobi Conference in 1985 to vouchsafe equality of women. The women also moved into the language of modernity, asking for the drafting of gender-related legislation and demanding that measures be taken to combat covert discrimination, create conditions that would make sexual harassment difficult and eventually illegal, and support the creation of women's studies centers at institutions of higher learning.

The largest and most popular of the Ukrainian women's journals, the monthly magazine formerly published as *Soviet Woman (Radians'ka Zhinka)* has become, under the able leadership of Lidia Mazur, simply *Woman (Zhinka)*. Most women's organizations publish more modest newspapers, and there have been interesting ventures into glossy, upscale women's magazines. Of these *Eve (Ieva)*, edited by Iryna Danilevska, is the most interesting one.

There are also a very small, moderate feminist movement and some public discussion of women's issues. Especially significant are practical attempts to address the educational needs of girls, including the introduction of boarding schools with a demanding curriculum. Religion and tradition, as rallying cries for women, draw their contemporary popularity from the persecution of religion and the attempt of the Soviet government to extirpate local culture. Some women find solace in religion and ethnography, especially rediscovering old songs, rituals, food, clothing. Others cluster in religiously oriented societies. Organized religions draw the women into public activity for faith and good works. Obviously, sometimes such organizations view woman's role in the family as limited to raising children while being supported by a husband who will care for her. In 1992 the first International Women's Club of Kiev, composed of non-Ukrainian women working and living in Kiev, which serves as a monthly meeting ground for professional women and those in the diplomatic community, was established. Nongovernmental organizations in the Ukraine are breaking the isolation of Ukrainian women by moving quickly into participation within the international context.

Ukrainian women immigrants to the United States and Canada established their own organizations in the major industrial cities, and by the 1920s they created a central women's organization, the Ukrainian National

Women's League of America. In the 1920s and 1930s it supported labor unions and collected funds to relieve poverty in the home country; in the 1950s it became largely cultural and philanthropic.

References. Martha Bohachevsky-Chomiak, *Feminists despite Themselves: Women in Ukrainian Community life, 1884–1939* (Edmonton, Alberta, Canada, 1987); Rosalind Marsh (ed.), *Women in Russia and Ukraine* (Cambridge, U.K., 1996); Frances Swyripa, *Wedded to the Cause: Ukrainian-Canadian Women and Ethnic Identity* (Toronto, 1993).

MARTHA BOHACHEVSKY-CHOMIAK

UNEMPLOYMENT of women is a relatively new concern with serious implications for equity and feminist goals.

According to the official definition, a person is *unemployed* if he or she is looking for work but is unable to find a job. The official *unemployment rate*, based on a survey that is published monthly by the Bureau of Labor Statistics, is the total number of unemployed persons during a survey week relative to the entire labor force of employed and unemployed persons. For instance, if 95 people are employed, and 5 are unemployed, the labor force consists of 100 people and the unemployment rate is 5 percent. Unemployment rates are computed for various demographic groups, and it is possible to examine gender differences in unemployment.

It is important to recognize that the official concept of unemployment in the United States as well as in virtually every other country applies only to work in *paid* employment. "Employment" refers to paid work, and "unemployed" persons are seeking paid work. People who perform unpaid work at home or volunteer work and who are not seeking paid employment are neither "employed" nor "unemployed." Despite the fact that unpaid activities are both useful and time-consuming, for all practical purposes, they are ignored in our economic statistics. Like many other aspects of our economic life and social relations, unemployment has been defined from a male perspective. Until relatively recently, work in paid employment has been predominantly a male activity, while most women, especially married women, worked at home and were neglected in the official unemployment statistics.

The increasing participation of women in paid employment has raised questions regarding the interpretation of women's unemployment. Should women who formerly "worked" as full-time homemakers be counted as unemployed just because they now declare themselves "looking for work"? During the 1970s, as homemakers began entering the labor force in increasing numbers, many observers contended that the attendant rise in the unemployment rate was an illusion. Had these women continued in their former roles as homemakers, they would not be included in the unemployment count, and hence the national unemployment rate would not be so high. Some people suggested that women's unemployment should not be included in the official figure, and press releases began to emphasize the unemployment rate for married men as well as the overall rate, the rate for married men being considerably lower. Others suggested a "weighted rate" in which women's unemployment should receive a lesser weight than men's. By the mid-1970s, the whole question of how to treat women's unemployment in a period of rapid transition in women's work roles became a major national controversy in which policymakers took advantage of the issue to divert attention from the deflationary economic policies that were the major cause of high unemployment in those years. A distinguished national commission was established to consider the issue and, after lengthy hearings and debates, disbanded with no major recommendations.

One reason that women's unemployment was controversial during this time was that women experienced higher unemployment rates than men, and this, in turn, increased the national rate above historic levels as more women entered the labor force. During the 1970s the unemployment rate for adult women averaged 6.0 percent, compared with 4.5 percent for adult men. The higher rate for women was partly related to their new entry into the workforce, but it also resulted from the fact that they received less on-the-job training than men and were often the last hired and first fired.

Beginning in the 1980s, as women's participation in the paid labor force continued to climb, the picture began to change dramatically. Sizable job losses occurred in many goods-producing industries traditionally dominated by men, due to the expansion of world trade, shifts in demand, and other factors. Between 1979 and 1994, there was a loss of nearly 2 million jobs in the male-dominated manufacturing sector, while an increase of 20 million jobs occurred over the same period in the female-dominated sectors of wholesale and retail trade and the services.

Not only did this structural shift in the composition of available jobs displace more men than women, but the cyclical nature of manufacturing employment created more job loss for men than for women in periods of recession. Thus, the disadvantage of recent labor force entry and relative inexperience became offset by women's relative employment in cyclically stable sectors of the economy where job growth was occurring. Since the mid-1980s, unemployment rates for adult males and females have been roughly the same at cyclical peaks, with male unemployment rising above that of women in periods of recession. This phenomenon is creating new tensions between men and women, especially in two-earner families where the male loses his job, and the woman keeps hers.

It should be noted, however, that although the occupational segregation of women in service and trade jobs has resulted in more stable employment for women on average than for male workers, wage rates are much lower in these jobs, perpetuating a substantial pay gap between men and women workers. A worker in a low-paying job is not considered unemployed, even though the job may not fully utilize her skills or pay a decent wage.

While the controversy just described focused on measurement of unemployment, another issue centers on the extent to which unemployment is as serious a problem for women as it is for men. This view reflects the ambivalence many people still feel about women as breadwinners and the reality that for women there are always socially acceptable "job opportunities" in the home. An extreme position would hold that economic independence for women has undermined the traditional family and that if family resources are inadequate, ways should be found to supplement the income of the male breadwinner rather than promote employment opportunities for women.

In the past, many women relied on their husbands for both financial support and social status. Today this is no longer the case. However romantic the appeal of the traditional family with a single male breadwinner, only about a quarter of Americans today live in such families. Most families are dependent, at least in part, on a woman's earnings, and many are supported entirely by women. Moreover, with the current high divorce rate, a paid job becomes a kind of "divorce insurance" for those women who are married to relatively affluent husbands. Paradoxically, women who maintain families and who presumably have the greatest financial need have much higher unemployment rates than other women, while married men have much lower rates than other men. This suggests that family responsibilities improve men's labor market prospects but are a negative element for women workers.

Even apart from financial considerations, a paid job provides an independent source of social status for women. For those women in our society trying to achieve independence along many lines—economic, social, psychological, emotional—a job in the paid labor market is an important first step. To be unemployed is to be seeking this opportunity. Certainly, the ramifications of women's unemployment are different from men's in this regard—men are not newly seeking economic independence, and men's unemployment is a threat to their established dominance rather than a barrier to independence. Yet as an equity issue, women's unemployment has serious consequences. Like most issues relating to women, the debate over women's unemployment is largely a debate over women's changing roles. Those who wish to minimize the significance of women's unemployment are simply reflecting the view that "a woman's place is in the home."

Reference. Francine D. Blau and Marianne A. Ferber, *The Economics of Women, Men, and Work* (Englewood Cliffs, N.J., 1986), ch. 9.

NANCY S. BARRETT

UNION FRANÇAISE POUR LE SUFFRAGE DES FEMMES (UFSF) was the principal woman suffrage organization in France from 1909 to 1940 and the French affiliate of the International Woman Suffrage Alliance (IWSA).

Moderate, middle-class feminists founded the UFSF following a national congress in Paris in 1908. Their purpose was to give French suffragism a broader, more national base than Hubertine Auclert's pioneering (and militant) society, Suffrage des femmes.* The leaders in creating the UFSF were Jane Misme, the moderate feminist editor of *La Française*, and Jeanne Schmahl, a feminist who had previously devoted herself to the passage of a Married Women's Property Act in France (1907).

Schmahl outlined the characteristics of the UFSF in a series of articles in *La Française* in early 1909. It was to be a moderate society, exclusively devoted to winning the vote and carefully adhering to legal tactics. Three hundred women joined in the initial meeting of February 1909, and the UFSF was formally accepted as the representative of French suffragism at the IWSA congress in London two months later.

Under the leadership of Cécile Brunschwicg as secretary-general, the UFSF rapidly grew into a national society. Relying on a series of provincial lecture tours and the organizational efforts of local feminist schoolteachers, Brunschwicg expanded the UFSF to 12,000 members in 1914, with chapters in 75 departments of France.

Brunschwicg directed a strategy of collaboration with the parliamentary advocates of woman suffrage, most notable of whom was Ferdinand Buisson, the author of the Buisson Report (1909). She also accepted a program of gradual enfranchisement, beginning with local suffrage only. Brunschwicg and Misme deplored all militant demonstrations and participated in the great "Condorcet Demonstration" of 1914 (5,000 marchers) with reluctance.

During World War I, the UFSF suspended its suffragist activities and rallied to support the government. At the end of the war the leadership of the UFSF was convinced that the government would reward women for their war effort by giving them the vote. The French Chamber of Deputies adopted a women's suffrage bill in 1919, but the French Senate defeated it in 1922 and blocked it at every subsequent introduction.

Under the continuing leadership of Brunschwicg, the UFSF grew rapidly after 1922, surpassing 100,000 members in 1928. The shock of the senatorial rebuff induced the UFSF to consider more militant suffragism, and it briefly collaborated with the militant efforts of Louise Weiss. Brunschwicg generally adhered to the union's traditional moderation, however, and continued collaboration with parliamentary suffragists. This led to her appointment by Premier Léon Blum as undersecretary for national education in the Popular Front government of 1936, making her (with Irène Joliot-Curie and Suzane Lacore) one of the first woman to sit in a French cabinet.

The Blum government also supported the UFSF with a suffrage bill in 1936, but the conservative Senate again blocked it. The UFSF collapsed during World War II. Brunschwicg did not reestablish the union after the war because General Charles de Gaulle granted women's suffrage in 1944.

References. Steven C. Hause with Anne R. Kenney, *Women's Suffrage and Social Politics in the French Third Republic* (Princeton, 1984); James F. McMillan, *Housewife or Harlot: The Place of Women in French Society, 1870–1940* (New York, 1981).

STEVEN C. HAUSE

UNION OF SOVIET SOCIALIST REPUBLICS (1917–1991). Soviet women experienced lives of more promise and possibility than their predecessors, although communism promised more than it ultimately could deliver. After three years of world war, it was women who precipitated the revolution in Russia in February 1917, rioting over bread to feed their families. When revolution came again in October 1917, the communists under V. I. Lenin (1917–1924) declared that they would end Russia's involvement in World War I and grant the peasants the land they had taken from the nobility over the past year. But the communists promised much more than that. They pledged to establish a new, egalitarian society in which everyone who worked would have equal rights under the law and the opportunity to develop individual potential to contribute to society.

According to communist doctrine, women were equal to men. This conception was very different from the one that had prevailed in Russian culture and law up to the revolution. Although women's social position and their legal rights had been steadily improving for centuries, they still experienced severe disadvantages. An old peasant proverb declared that "a hen is not a bird, and a woman is not a person," an attitude that persisted long after the revolution in 1917. Because Russian women worked for a fraction of the wages men received, factory owners before the revolution preferred hiring women, and the numbers of women in the labor force steadily grew. Despite this, women workers as such had little representation either in politics or in the trade unions that were formed after the first revolution in 1905.

Soon after the revolution, the Communist Party granted women full citizenship. Discrimination officially was based not on sex but on social class. The government introduced laws that made divorce easier and legalized abortion. Wives were no longer obliged to accompany their husbands in a change of domicile, thereby increasing women's freedom of movement. In addition, a separate section of the party was established to address women's problems and attract women to the party. This was called the Zhenskii Otdel, or Zhenotdel.*

The work of the Zhenotdel was hampered from the beginning by the low level of priority it occupied within the Communist Party and by the low numbers of female party members. Even by 1922, only 8 percent of party members were female, and these occupied positions of lesser authority, with a few notable exceptions. Nadezhda Krupskaya, Lenin's wife, was an active revolutionary and a party leader in culture and education. Alexandra Kollontai was the only woman to be elected to the party's Central Committee and served as an ambassador to Norway and Sweden. However, she fell out of favor with the party and Lenin for her liberal views about sexuality and feminism and for her support for the Worker's Opposition group, which challenged the party's authority in 1921.

During the 1920s there was evidence that change was slowly taking place. Women were becoming increasingly involved in the political process, winning election to local soviets or councils, and taking part in Congresses of Worker and Peasant Women. By 1927, women constituted 12 percent of the Communist Party. However, social unrest had been mounting, caused primarily by increasing unemployment, which struck women workers particularly hard, and social dislocation from years of war, revolution, and famine. In 1928, in a desperate effort to gain control of the country, Joseph Stalin (1924–1953) approved the collectivization of agriculture and the First Five-Year Plan to industrialize the country at an accelerated pace. These decisions were to have profound effects on the lives of Soviet women. Massive industrialization required a huge pool of labor, and as a result, by 1937 women constituted over 40 percent of all industrial workers and 82 percent of all newly hired workers. Another result of the government's efforts to gain control was that the Zhenotdel was formally abolished in 1930. It had been a vehicle through which women's feminist consciousness had been raised and through which they could agitate for their own distinct needs. The party had always discouraged factionalism and now formally put it to rest. The Zhenotdel was revived only in the 1960s as the Zhensoviet.

The industrialization of the Soviet Union benefited women by drawing them into the workforce in huge numbers, but it did little to lighten their burden. Soviet industrialization was concentrated in heavy industry and military strength. This meant that consumer goods and services assumed a low priority, and the amenities of existence enjoyed by Western industrialized nations remained underdeveloped in the Soviet Union. This affected women most of all. They continued to shoulder the burden of domestic work in addition to work outside the home, where they performed on a par with men for less status and pay as before. In addition, during the 1930s the government reversed measures meant to liberate women. By restricting divorce and abortion and encouraging procreation, Stalinists hoped to promote the stability of the family and society. In contrast to the 1920s, housework was now viewed as "socially useful labor." Moreover, many women became heads of households due to a persistent deficit of males, lost to successive waves of war, collectivization, and purges. By 1959, almost one-third of Soviet households were headed by women. Burdened by domestic responsibilities, child care, and work outside the home, most Soviet women were hampered in their efforts for self-improvement by a simple lack of time for education and professional growth.

The extraordinary burdens placed upon Soviet women eventually began to tell in statistical terms. By the 1960s, the birthrate was falling in European Russia, causing concern among demographers and politicians. Some commentators advised encouraging higher fertility rates through easing economic and other burdens on families. Others suggested that simply redistributing domestic chores evenly between women and men would solve the problem. However, there was evidence of a popular reaction against the "masculinization of women" and of deep-seated opposition to a lack of differentiation in male and female roles. Even Soviet feminism sought equality of opportunity in education and work for women but supported maintaining women's traditional social roles. Women and men alike mourned women's loss of femininity and insisted on the importance of supporting women's maternal role. In the last decades of Soviet power, therefore, to satisfy an ideological commitment to women's equality, policymakers stressed growth in the consumer sector, rather than challenge to the Soviet family's traditional structure.

Nevertheless, after years of economic stagnation under Leonid Brezhnev (1964–1982), the "women's question" seemed scarcely closer to solution. Despite the fact that in the late 1960s Brezhnev had officially declared the question "unsolved" and thus open to discussion and amelioration, women's double burden of domestic and outside work was not lessened by any monumental shifts in terms of either consumer convenience or gender sensibilities. Moreover, although by 1970 women constituted 51 percent of the industrial labor force and 40 percent of rural workers, their jobs continued to be concentrated in the lowest-paid and least-skilled positions. In politics, women were still absent from top positions. Therefore, when Mikhail Gorbachev (1985–1991) came to power in the mid-1980s, declaring the beginning of a radical effort to decentralize and restructure the Soviet economy called perestroika, many women became his strongest supporters. Gorbachev was considered the most sensitive leader since Lenin to the concerns of Soviet women, and his economic reforms promised unprecedented growth in the consumer and service sectors of the economy, which would benefit women foremost. Many women believed that a more efficient economy would finally allow them time to fulfill their maternal aspirations with some measure of material comfort and security, whether through the earnings of their husbands or through full salaries for part-time work in a rationalized production system.

These hopes were not realized. In the wake of perestroika there were economic, social, and political changes that, if anything, seemed to make Soviet women's lives harder. Rapidly rising unemployment and chronic food shortages affected women disproportionately. Women seemed to be shut out of new groupings and parties forming in a newly democratic political atmosphere. The glasnost or openness in the Soviet media that accompanied economic and political reform both advanced and reversed progress on women's issues. Glasnost allowed discussion on such issues as prostitution, the lack of contraception choices, and the terrible conditions at abortion clinics. But the media also began to blame women for a whole range of social ills, presumably because they had been found lacking in their roles as caretakers of the family and society.

The changes that Gorbachev had accelerated in the 1980s created a juggernaut that could not be stopped. In 1991, the Soviet Union was formally dissolved. Whether the situation of Soviet women will change in the post-Soviet era depends, as it always did in the past, on general economic, political, and social conditions throughout the former Soviet Union.

References. Dorothy Atkinson, Alexander Dallin, and Gail Warshovsky Lapidus (eds.), *Women in Russia* (Stanford, Calif., 1977); Mary Buckley (ed.), *Soviet Social Scientists Talking: An Official Debate about Women* (Hampshire, U.K., 1986); Mary Buckley (ed.), *Perestroika and Soviet Women* (Cambridge, U.K., 1992); Francine du Plessix Gray, *Soviet Women: Walking the Tightrope* (New York, 1989).

ELIZABETH A. HARRY

UNITED NATIONS DECADE FOR WOMEN is the years from 1975 to 1985, designated by the United Nations (UN) to be devoted to the advancement of women at the national, regional, and international levels and to the pursuit of equality between men and women in law and practice. Three conferences were held during the decade to raise awareness of the special concerns and contributions of women: the Mexico City Conference in 1975, commemorating International Women's Year and the start of the decade; the Copenhagen Conference in 1980, to review the progress of the first half of the decade; and the Nairobi Conference in 1985, to assess the accomplishments of the decade and plan for the future. Each of these conferences, which were attended by formal governmental representatives, produced a plan for programs aimed at advancing the status of women at all levels and drawing attention to the linkages between the status of women within separate nation-states and within the global political and economic system. Nongovernmental organizations held a parallel set of meetings at each conference, giving an even larger number of women an opportunity to come together and exchange ideas. Workshops for training and developing strategies to address the obstacles to women's advancement were also included at these nongovernmental meetings.

The decade adopted three broad themes—equality, development, and peace. Addressing the theme of equality, the Commission on the Status of Women drafted the Convention on the Elimination of All Forms of Discrimination against Women,* which came into force in 1981 and provided for a Committee on the Elimination of Discrimination against Women to monitor the implementation of the treaty. The second theme, development, emphasized the need to increase the role of women in development decision making. Of the many programs planned, the Voluntary Fund for the United Nations Decade for Women was one of the most important. Created in 1976, the fund concentrates on grassroots projects, giving priority to those aiding poor rural and urban women. With similar purpose, the UN established the International Research and Training Institute for the Advancement of Women, a center to share information and to coordinate the use of the limited resources available for development projects aimed at women. One of the institute's main goals is the improvement of statistics on the status of women, especially providing information that would aid in incorporating women into development planning. Probably the most controversial theme was peace. Efforts to address the plight of Palestinian women and women living under apartheid disrupted the 1980 conference. In order to promote consensus at the 1985 conference, these political issues were minimized in the final program for future action.

The decade also recognized three subthemes: health, education, and employment. Under these themes attention was focused on the role of women as health care providers; access to family planning and maternal and child care; traditional and contemporary violence against women; discrimination against girls and women in education; sex-role stereotyping; and unpaid and underpaid women's work. Principles and programs for all the decade themes and subthemes were addressed in a summary document, the *Forward Looking Strategies*, which provides recommendations for national and international action (see Joanne Sandler).

In 1995, commemorating the 20 years since the beginning of the UN Decade for Women, there was a conference in Beijing, China. Prior to the formal United Nations meeting, an International Forum was held in a small town outside Beijing. Workshops, panels, speakers, and displays were offered to a gathering of over 20,000 women from national and international nongovernmental organizations. Despite major obstacles presented by the host government, the forum demonstrated the continuing growth and strengthening of the global women's movement since the Mexico City meeting. The formal UN Conference adopted a resolution urging universal ratification of the Convention on the Elimination of All Forms of Discrimination against Women.

The decade led to the creation of new programs and the redefinition and redirection of existing ones and began a transnational movement for change that has legitimated women's claim for political, economic, and social power commensurate with their dedication, service, and contributions.

References. Rebecca J. Cook (ed.), *Human Rights of Women: National and International Perspectives* (Philadelphia, 1995); Natalie Hevener Kaufman, *International Law and the Status of Women* (Boulder, Colo., 1983); Joanne Sandler, *It's Our Move Now: A Community Action Guide to the U.N. Nairobi Forward Look-*

ing Strategies for the Advancement of Women (New York, 1989). United Nations, *The United Nations and the Advancement of Women* (New York, 1996); Andrea Wolper and Julie Peters (eds.), *Women's Rights/Human Rights: An Agenda for Change* (London, 1995).

NATALIE HEVENER KAUFMAN

U.S. SANITARY COMMISSION (1861–1865), a government-sanctioned, privately run relief organization, is not often associated with the American Red Cross. Clara Barton is given most of the credit for beginning the Red Cross, an organization she began in response to the carnage she saw working as a nurse during the U.S. Civil War. Yet the U.S. Sanitary Commission (USSC) was on the battlefields of Gettysburg and Antietam with Barton during the war and deserves to share some of that honor. The USSC organized and distributed supplies and provided medical care to soldiers and other victims of the war. Like the Red Cross today, the USSC relied on private donations, a small corps of paid professionals, and vast resources of voluntary labor. Years before the organizational meetings of the International Red Cross took place in Geneva and well before Barton became interested in initiating a domestic branch of the humanitarian relief organization, women and men worked together to create an extensive civilian relief operation that helped save the lives of soldiers and war refugees in the most destructive war in U.S. history.

In 1861, when the war broke out, most Americans were caught by surprise. Few had expected that the differences between the North and South would be resolved through war, and when the fighting began, the American public was shocked to learn how ill prepared the U.S. army was to care for wounded and ill soldiers. Everywhere, women organized into soldiers aid societies and collected food, clothing, and medical supplies for the soldiers. Others boarded trains to Washington, D.C., where they hoped to find work as nurses. Nineteenth-century gender ideology encouraged all women to think of themselves as their families' nurses, so many were convinced that they could use these domestic skills to help the soldiers who were so far from home. As in previous wars, women supplied the troops with uniforms and cared for the men when they passed through town. Traditionally, women held bazaars and staged local fairs to encourage enlistment and to raise money to outfit the soldiers and support their families during their absence. To a small group of women living in the North, though, it became clear that this war would require a more systematic approach than previous wars had demanded.

Dr. Elizabeth Blackwell, the first American woman to graduate from medical school, was the first to recognize the potential of harnessing the energy of these early, localized efforts to an organized system of relief. Blackwell's original plan had two facets: centralizing scattered local supply efforts and training a select group of women as professional nurses. With direct access to military intelligence, Blackwell believed she and a group of well-connected women and men could mobilize local women's groups to systematically provide for the changing needs of the soldiers. In an extended war fought in various environments at once, soldiers' needs would vary and would surely test the limits of the army's supply and medical capacities. Blackwell and her friend Florence Nightingale had long debated the potential of turning nursing into a medical profession for women. Whereas the Crimean War provided Nightingale with the opportunity to begin training women nurses in Great Britain, the Civil War seemed the perfect occasion for Blackwell to propose the idea to the U.S. government.

Unwilling to allow the reality of women's exclusion from political decision making to delay her plans, Blackwell enlisted the support of a group of New York doctors and philanthropists to bring her plan to President Lincoln. In Washington, the men joined forces with Dorothea Dix, a well-known advocate for the mentally ill, who had similar aims, and together they convinced the president to approve of the creation of the USSC. As the plan was eventually executed, neither Blackwell nor Dix played a very visible role in the USSC's administration. Their influence, however, continued to motivate the many women who came to work for the USSC as officers of supply, local canvassing agents, and nurses, and the traditions of women's community reform work determined the shape of the organization's supply efforts.

Blackwell and her sister Emily trained more than 100 women nurses, who went on to work in field hospitals and army camps throughout the war. (Several of Blackwell's students began one of the first nurse training programs in the country at Bellevue Hospital in New York City after the war.) Dix was actively involved in the placement of nurses and oversaw many of Blackwell's trainees. Through the dedication and commitment of a group of young women in Elizabeth Blackwell's circle of influence, women's soldiers' aid societies were organized into an effective national supply network that provided critical support to the army throughout the war. Kept informed of military operations, local women's organizations were able to fulfill—even anticipate—the changing needs of the army. In this way, local women focused their supply efforts on the needs of the army at large rather than expending all their energy sending food and clothing to individual soldiers and local regiments, with whom communication was often difficult.

The USSC offered many women the opportunity of working for a national organization for the first time. In the mid-nineteenth century, women's lives were shaped by familial connection and community-based benevolence. After working for the USSC, women became involved in reform work that took them outside their homes and connected them to women in other towns and states. The experience of working with other women at the USSC's branches of supply helped women recognize the potential of gender-specific organization. Women who had enjoyed the camaraderie of their work for the USSC and had found the connection to a national organization with a political agenda empowering joined the temperance crusade after the war. Others became interested in more overtly feminist initiatives and led the resurgence of suffrage activism in the postwar years.

References. Rejean Attie, " 'A Swindling Concern': The USSC and the Northern Female Public, 1861–1865," Ph.D. diss., Columbia University, 1987; Judith Ann Giesberg, " 'The Truest Patriots': The United States Sanitary Commission and Women's Reform in Transition," Ph.D. diss., Boston College, 1997; Kristie Ross, " 'Women Are Needed Here': Northern Protestant Women as Nurses during the Civil War, 1861–1865," Ph.D. diss., Columbia University, 1993.

JUDITH ANN GIESBERG

UTERINE PROLAPSIS is a condition in which the uterus drops out of its normal position. The ligaments that hold the uterus in place may be weakened during childbirth by lacerations or "overstretching." Not until years later, however, when estrogen levels have dropped after menopause,* do the weakened supports shrink or atrophy, causing the uterus to fall.

In some cases the uterus falls backward into the vaginal canal (retrodisplacement). In other cases, the uterus goes partially or wholly through the vaginal canal, bringing the vagina in upon itself. In second-degree prolapse, the cervix extends partially or completely through the vaginal opening. In a complete prolapse, the uterus itself extends outside the vagina. Prolapse of the bladder, urethra, and rectum often accompanies the more severe degrees of prolapse. Retrodisplacement may not need treatment. Second-degree prolapse may be corrected by surgery, but hysterectomy is usual for complete prolapse and is often chosen in second-degree prolapse as well.

UTOPIAN SOCIALIST MOVEMENTS focused on the emancipation of women and workers. In these movements, which reached their peak of popularity in the 1830s and 1840s in Western Europe and the United States, lie the origins of modern feminism as well as modern social democratic and communist movements. The most popular and influential were the Owenites in England and the Saint-Simonians and the Fourierists in France; all, however, crossed the Atlantic and had numerous followers in the United States. Similarly, their message was carried across Europe to Russia and across the Mediterranean to Egypt. Their message survives today on Israeli kibbutzim.*

At the end of the 1820s some of these movement ideologues first used the word "socialist" to distinguish themselves from radical democrats of the French Revolutionary era. Early socialists criticized the revolution because of its association with violence and terror, a consequence, they maintained, of the revolution's encouragement of selfish individualism. Democratic radicals were criticized for focusing too narrowly on such "political" questions as the form of the regime (whether it was a monarchy or a republic, or who had the right to vote or to govern). In contrast, socialists would create a new social order by better regulating relations among the classes, particularly employers and workers, and between women and men. Their strategy for social change was to create alternative communities where "association" or cooperation, rather than some supposedly enlightened self-interest, would prevail, and where the absolute rights of private ownership would yield to the "social good," being either collectively owned or at least subject to public regulation. Moreover, by constructing these alternative communities, utopians would not only create cooperative social structures but also provide a peaceful means for change in contrast to revolutionary means. The New World Order or New Moral World (both terms were used by all these utopians) would be constructed alongside the old, and people, merely by observing the far preferable utopian life, would be won over to join with utopians and create more of these alternative communities.

Utopians differed not only from "political" radicals of the revolutionary era but also from earlier feminist writers of the seventeenth and eighteenth centuries and from feminist activists of the revolutionary period who had focused on the individual rights of citizenship, including political rights. Utopians thought these concerns were too narrowly individualistic; in contrast, they would focus on new ways of organizing both production and enduring social networks (e.g., intimacy, sexuality, and reproduction) to ensure sexual equality and sexual liberation.

Utopians' language and mode of analysis also differed from those of earlier feminists. They were Romantics rather than Enlightenment rationalists. They extolled feminine difference rather than the universality or sameness of women's and men's natures. Unlike more traditional Romantics, however, they did not argue that women's "different" nature required their confinement to domestic concerns. On the contrary, women's very difference from men became the basis of arguments favoring their inclusion in the governance of the New Moral World.

Charles Fourier was the first of the utopian socialist feminists. Writing in the first decade of the nineteenth century, he envisioned an ultimate stage of human progress whereby women and men would be equal and equally free and productive. A unique education system would scrupulously treat girls and boys alike. Fourier even demanded that the two sexes dress the same in recognition of the variety of ways that socialization may affect equality. In his utopia, Harmony, women would not be excluded from any social or economic function, "not even from medicine or teaching," nor from his corps of professors, the expected leaders of his community.

Fourier proposed the organization of new communities ("phalansteries") based on associations that would organize production, households, house-keeping, and even sexual experience in new ways. All work would be col-lectivized. Because Fourier viewed the work of the home, including both the socialization of children and housekeeping tasks, as productive work, it also would be collectivized. He held that isolated households and per-manent marriages enslaved both women and men. Love alone should bind couples, and their union should last only so long as their "passionate" attraction joined them.

Although Fourier worked in isolation for most of his life, the utopian socialist movements, whose developments he so significantly shaped, be-came immensely popular in the 1830s. Their work was mainly propagan-distic, and hundreds of people reportedly attended their lectures in cities throughout Europe and the United States. In Paris, in the early 1830s, Saint-Simonians lectured daily to hundreds of interested women and men of the working and middle classes. In London, at the same time, Owenites lectured three times a week. Owenite "stipendiary lecturers" and Saint-Simonian "missionaries" fanned out to other cities throughout England and France and to other countries as well. Significant numbers of women were active as speakers, organizers, and directors of the movements' many pro-jects; countless numbers of other women heard their lectures and read their propaganda literature.

Not all their work was propagandistic, however; utopians did actually establish some alternative communities. Owenites set up 7 such commu-nities in England between 1821 and 1845 and about 15 in the United States. (New Harmony in Indiana was probably the most famous Owenite community in the United States.) Saint-Simonians established several col-lective *maisons de famille* (family houses), each directed by one male and one female (a "brother" and a "sister"), in Paris in the early 1830s, and those who lived together pooled their financial resources. Meals were col-lectively prepared and served for an even larger group of adherents. "As-sociationists" (as the followers of Fourier began calling themselves in the late 1830s) set up 1 community in France, in Guise (construction began in 1859), and over 30 such communities in the United States between 1840 and 1860. (Brook Farm in Massachusetts was probably the most famous of the U.S. Associationist communities.)

Most communities were short-lived, however. Soon, beginning in the 1850s, the utopian strategy would be supplanted by more "scientific" forms of socialism that placed their faith for revolution in class struggle and the ultimate victory of the proletariat. Voices proclaiming concern for both workers' emancipation and women's emancipation were nearly drowned out. That class struggle and sex struggle were once united in utopian so-cialism was nearly forgotten. In the 1830s and 1840s, however, utopian socialists envisioned the transformation of all aspects of social life, not just economic and political relations. For them, a new relationship between women and men figured as prominently as a new relationship between workers and capitalists.

References. Jonathan Beecher, *Charles Fourier: The Visionary and His World* (Berkeley, Calif., 1986); Robert B. Calisle, *The Proffered Crown: Saint-Simonianism and the Doctrine of Hope* (Baltimore, 1987); Susan K. Grogan, *French Socialism and Sexual Difference* (New York, 1992); Claire Goldberg Moses, *French Feminism in the Nineteenth Century* (Albany, N.Y., 1984); Claire Goldberg Moses and Leslie Wahl Rabine, *Feminism, Socialism, and French Romanticism* (Bloomington, Ind., 1993); Barbara Taylor, *Eve and the New Jerusalem: Socialism and Feminism in the Nineteenth Century* (New York, 1983).

CLAIRE GOLDBERG MOSES

UTOPIAS, EUROPEAN. A utopia is an imaginary society, either an imaginary "good place" or "no place". More imaginary societies have been written about by twentieth-century women authors of the United States than by women in Britain or Europe. Yet the imaginary society has existed in European literature written by women at least since the fifteenth century, when Christine de Pizan, the first European woman to earn her living by her pen, wrote her *Cité des dames*, an account of a city occupied by women of virtue. An answer to Jean de Meung's attack on women in his *Roman de la rose, Cité* was Christine's contribution to the *querelle des femmes** of the late Middle Ages.

In 1611 in England, Emilia Lanier (or Aemilia Lanyer) published a book of poetry entitled *Salve Deus Rex Judaeorum*. The third part of this three-part volume contains dedicatory poems to titled ladies noted for their learning, a religious poem including a spirited defense of women, and one of the first country house poems in English literature: a description of a lost female paradise of tranquil happiness.

Three eighteenth-century English women authors, Mary Astell, Sarah Robinson Scott, and Clara Reeve, wrote descriptions of all-women societies that provided education and useful occupation, primarily for unmarried gentlewomen. Astell's *A Serious Proposal to the Ladies for the Advancement of Their True and Greatest Interests* (1694, 1697) presents a plan for an all-woman religious and educational community. Scott's *A Description of Millenium Hall, and the Country Adjacent* (1762) describes an estate owned and managed by women, and Reeve's *Plans of Education* (1792) presents a plan for women's education.

A number of futuristic, nineteenth-century British novels by men deal with women's lives, and a few anonymous (thus, possibly by women) books describe positive utopias in which women have achieved equality. *New Amazonia: A Foretaste of the Future*, published by Mrs. George Corbett in 1889, presents an Ireland revitalized by women's rule.

Twentieth-century European dystopias by men have most often focused upon technology and totalitarianism, attacking both fascist and socialist states (Aldous Huxley's *Brave New World*, George Orwell's *1984*, Henri Barbusse's *We [Nous Autres]*). In contrast, twentieth-century utopias by women have shown more interest in challenging gender roles. Some see gender as a societal construct; others see it in essentialist terms. *A Woman's Utopia* (1931) falls into the antisocialist category. Published under the pseudonym of "A Daughter of Eve," it attacks socialism and advocates a meritocracy of talent. *My Own Utopia*, by Elizabeth Mann Borghese (1961), constructs gender as a status unrelated to biological sex (children are genderless, all adults become "women" upon maturity, and a smaller number become "men" in later life). In Mary Gentle's *Golden Witchbreed* (1983) biological gender is not established until maturity, and no social gender roles exist. Among Doris Lessing's several novels of speculative fiction, her *The Marriages between Zones Three, Four, and Five* suggests men's and women's values are essential and immutable; the allegory attempts a "marriage" between them.

Monique Wittig's *Les Guérilières* (1969) has had great impact on the international women's movement. An account of a women's revolution, Wittig's novel deliberately subverts expectations about language and structure, as does another French feminist utopia, *Archaos ou le jardin étincelant* (1972) by Christiane Rochefort. Many of the new French feminist theorists have used language in new and subversive ways: Hélène Cixous in "La rire de la méduse" (The Laugh of the Medusa) and Julia Kristeva in *Des chinoises* (About Chinese Women) describe women's possible futures. A French Canadian poet, Nicole Brossard, describes women loving women in a transformed, utopian New York City in *Amantes* (1980; English trans., *Lovhers*, 1986). A satire from Norway, Gerd Brantenberg's *Egalia's Daughters*, subverts gender roles by reversing them.

In summary, although French feminist authors, influenced by structuralist and poststructuralist theory, have produced some of the most daring nonfiction works about the future and in spite of the works by Brantenburg and Lessing, Britain and Europe have not yet seen a flowering of speculative fiction by and about women like what has occurred in the United States.

References. Elaine Marks and Isabelle de Courtivron (eds.), *New French Feminisms: An Anthology* (New York, 1981); Lyman Tower Sargent, "Women in Utopia," *Comparative Literature Studies* 10 (1973): 302–316; Barbara Brandon Schnorrenberg, "A Paradise Like Eve's," *Women's Studies* 9 (1982): 263–273.

CHARLENE BALL

UTOPIAS, U.S. are works depicting imaginary societies: as *eutopia*, conditions for women are better than the author's world; as *dystopia*, they are worse; or as *satiric* utopia, inversion discredits women's conditions. Various utopian strategies appear: description of an ideal society, a dream of an alternative world, a voyage to an exotic land or distant planet, a romance of a frontier community, time travel to an ideal future, or a satiric dialogue exposing contemporary inequities.

Several contrasts emerge within utopian writing by U.S. women from the first known example in 1836, "Three Hundred Years Hence," by Mary Griffith, to the upsurge of the 1970s and 1980s. First, whereas earlier writers were more likely to conceptualize utopia as static, an already perfected community, writers of the last decades locate utopia in a process of becoming: the nineteenth-century utopias are closer to blueprints; those since 1960 show values in the process of being realized in action. A second contrast concerns the understanding of freedom. Up until about 1960, freedom for women in utopia has appeared as freedom *from*—especially marital or familial strictures. From the 1970s, freedom has meant autonomy—freedom *to* pursue self-defined goals and fulfill potential, with support coming less often from a heterosexual family than from a women's community. Third, location has varied. In keeping with the literary realism of the late 1800s, utopias, too, were likely to be set in the then-contemporary United States. Now, with women's utopias often exhibiting characteristics of New Wave science fiction, a common setting is a distant future on a distant planet.

Production has varied. Up to 1870 might be called a latency period, with slightly more than one utopia appearing each decade. Thereafter, three periods emerge. The output of the first period—from 1870 to 1920, the year women received the vote—averaged somewhat more than one utopia each year. This increase coincided with a large outpouring of utopian writing by U.S. men as well. Charlotte Perkins Gilman's *Herland* (1915) is the important work from this period. Between 1921 and 1960, few utopias appeared—about one every other year. Postsuffrage complacency, depression blues, and World War II mobilization turned energies elsewhere. The transitional 1960s returned to almost one utopia a year, but since then the output has averaged nearly two a year. Significant works from this period are *The Female Man* (1975) by Joanna Russ, *A Weave of Women* (1978) by E. M. Broner, *The Wanderground* (1979) by Sally Gearhart, and *Woman on the Edge of Time* (1976) by Marge Piercy.

The utopias of each period exhibit characteristics of the historical context: the suffrage movement, an interim, quieter period, and the recent feminist movement. The period from 1836 to 1920 stresses such solutions for reducing men's control over women's labor and sexuality as paid work, education, suffrage, and cooperation. Paid work appears as a solution in many utopias by men as well as by women. Education appears more before than after the Civil War, when higher education for women became more accessible. Suffrage appears as a solution in less than a quarter of the utopias, a suggestion that mere votes would not lead to greatly improved lives for women. Cooperation appears as a solution in more than half the utopias (e.g., shared house- or child-tending or whole-scale communitarian experiment). Though few of the cooperative solutions imagined have come to pass, the problems they were designed to solve are currently receiving widespread study. Though not blueprints, these utopias were harbingers. Their nowhere of actual place became a somewhere of inner vision, a predictor of the strongly spiritual dimension of current utopias.

During the period from 1920 to 1960, few utopias were feminist—only 6 of 27 by women, and of these, half make sex women's central concern. Of the three that permit women broadly human needs, one makes happiness central, another critiques free love as simply another deception foisted upon women, while the third posits a war-free world where love is neither exclusive nor possessive.

Since the 1960s, a decade of cultural transition, a new paradigm of values has emerged from feminist utopias. This paradigm includes not mere acceptance but also nurturance of diversity and nonviolence as a solution to resolving resultant differences. Three value clusters exist—the communitarian, the ecological, and the spiritual. The first cluster stresses the interrelatedness of all people—the notion of a global village, where villagers must be aware of the impact upon each other of their choices and behavior, where family members must permit the needs of each member to be met. Half of recent feminist utopias are all-female societies, validating and explicating women's experience and knowledge. The second cluster, the ecological, focuses upon our human impact upon animals, landscapes, natural resources, and outer space. Finally, spiritual values receive stress: utopia becomes a healing state of mind where readers may retreat for renewal and empowerment, a *Gedankenexperiment* (thought-experiment). Two utopias of the 1980s stress language as creating and transmitting culture, a mechanism like religion that binds society together: Suzette Haden Elgin, *Native Tongue* (1984) and *A Dictionary and Grammar of Láadan* (1985); and Ursula Le Guin, *Always Coming Home* (1986). Utopias of the 1990s in Marge Piercy's *He, She and It* (1991) and Octavia Butler's *Parable of the Sower* (1994) include more diversified populations than previously.

References. Frances Bartkowski, *Feminist Utopias* (Lincoln, Nebr., 1989); Carol Farley Kessler (ed.), *Daring to Dream: Utopian Fiction by United States Women before 1950* (bib. to 1988) (Syracuse, N.Y., 1995); Darby Lewes, *Dream Revisionaries: Gender and Genre in Women's Utopian Fiction 1870–1920* (Tuscaloosa, Ala., 1995).

CAROL FARLEY KESSLER

V

VAGINITIS, inflammation of the vagina, is so common that it is said that every woman has the irritation at some time in her life. Problems with vaginitis are most likely to occur, however, in women who are sexually active with men, who have multiple (three or more) partners, who are pregnant or using oral contraceptives, or whose vaginas respond with symptoms to stress and nutritional imbalance. After menopause* women who do not respond sexually on a regular basis either by masturbating or interacting with others are at greater risk of vaginal symptoms resulting from diminished estrogen.

Vaginitis in women who are premenopausal is most likely caused by bacteria (often Gardnerella vaginalis or associated anaerobic bacteria), Candida albicans (yeast), or Trichomonal vaginitis (trich), a one-celled organism. Distinguishing among the causes of vaginitis is possible only by microscopic examination of vaginal secretions and is sometimes definitive. Treatment with over-the-counter or nonprescription medications is not usually helpful, as such medication may merely suppress symptoms temporarily. Treatment with herbal remedies may better control early symptoms. If these fail, medical treatment may be sought.

Difficulties with vaginal irritation may begin with an increase in vaginal secretions and a change in color from clear or white to yellowish, greenish, brownish, or clear with shreds of mucus. The secretions may cause inflammation and irritation of the vaginal opening, labia, and perineal area as well as the urethra, where passage of urine will sometimes be painful. (It is helpful to differentiate this irritation of the external genitals by the passage of urine from the internal irritation of the urethra or even the bladder, which is likely due to a urinary problem.)

Other changes in vaginal health indicators may include a stronger scent, which may result from an increase in quantity of secretions or may be characteristically "fishy," a sign not found in yeast overgrowth. Itching of the vaginal area may range from vague uneasiness to intense misery. Sexual interactions, especially vaginal sex, may be uncomfortable or painful.

Bacteria is a common cause of vaginitis and is treatable with oral antibiotics. When a woman is diagnosed with a bacterial vaginal infection, sexual interactions should be modified to minimize transmission, and oral sex avoided until antibiotic therapy is completed. Condoms should be used in sexual interactions with men during the course of treatment. The man should be tested for the presence of a bacterial infection and treated if indicated. Bacteria can be transmitted to female sexual partners and may or may not cause infection.

Yeast "infections" (actually an overgrowth of a fungus that is commonly present in the vagina) are most commonly characterized by vaginal secretions that clump and are therefore described as "cottage cheese–like" with an earthy scent. Yeast is most amenable to changes in lifestyle such as reducing refined sugar intake, increasing intake of lactobacillus (in milk and yogurt), soothing baths, and nonirritating sexual response that increases circulation to the genital area. Yeast overgrowth that does not respond to these interventions can be treated with an antifungal preparation such as Nystatin.

Yeast overgrowth can cause irritation of the penis in male sexual partners, and the male may need treatment if the woman continues to have yeast infections. Women may transmit yeast to female sexual partners. This may or may not result in symptoms in the partner. Yeast may cause a condition of the mouth and throat called thrush; therefore, oral sex should be avoided while yeast or other vaginal symptoms persist. Infants may develop thrush (which is also treatable with an antifungal preparation) if the mother has an active yeast infection during birthing. Yeast is more commonly transmitted from infected mother to infant due to poor hand washing. To prevent recurrence, medication must be used for its full course of treatment, not just until symptoms subside.

Trichomonal infections are less common but may be persistent and be harbored by a male sex partner who has no symptoms. Trich is usually treated with metronidazole (Flagyl), a controversial drug that cannot be used in pregnancy. Home remedies are less effective but are a possible alternative. One folk remedy is the use of a garlic suppository.

Some aspects of a woman's lifestyle may inadvertently promote the likelihood of developing vaginitis. Eating a diet high in refined sugar, using antibiotics such as tetracycline, wearing nylon underwear or tight-fitting restrictive clothing, and using tampons or toilet tissue infused with perfume inhibit the body's ability to maintain a balance in the vagina and to resist infection.

General health measures such as a balanced diet, adequate sleep, exercise, and avoidance of debilitating stress levels help to reduce problems with vaginitis.

ELAINE WHEELER

VARIABILITY HYPOTHESIS. Developed in the late nineteenth century, the hypothesis asserts that males are more likely than females to vary from the norm in both physical and mental traits. Variability was defined most often in terms of range of ability or incidence of abnormality. The variability hypothesis provided a way of explaining sex-related differences in social and intellectual achievements after the doctrine of generalized female inferiority was no longer tenable.

The variability hypothesis is noteworthy for three reasons. (1) It gained popularity among scientists largely because of an overextension of Darwinian theory by a zealous popularizer, Havelock Ellis. (2) It became an issue as much because of personal interests of scientists as because of its compatibility with the zeitgeist. (3) Early feminist researchers were largely responsible for its eventual decline.

The idea that the sexes might differ in their tendency to vary was introduced by Charles Darwin in 1868. Darwin invoked the idea of greater male variability in an attempt to explain the elaborate nature of male secondary sex characteristics in many species. Like most other nineteenth-century scientists, Darwin considered female mental inferiority a fact of nature.

Evolutionary theorists considered variation the driving force of evolution. Greatness, whether of an individual or a society, was achieved through deviation from the norm.

Havelock Ellis suggested that sex differences in physical variation might be accompanied by sex differences in mental variation. In the first edition of *Man and Woman* (London, 1894), he devoted an entire chapter to the variability hypothesis. He argued that both physical and mental abnormalities are indicators of variability and that both are more frequently observed in males. As regards mental abilities he asserted that both retardation and genius are more frequent among males than females.

Ellis used as proof of male mental variability statistics from homes for the "mentally defective," which housed many more males than females. His evidence of the greater frequency of male genius was the overwhelming preponderance of men of eminence. He reasoned that men are more likely to achieve fame, fortune, and professional prestige and that an innate difference in variability must therefore exist.

His major critic was the biometrician Karl Pearson, who himself regarded male intellectual superiority a kind of male secondary sex characteristic.

Ellis' ideas had a major impact on the generation of male psychologists then developing the first tests of mental ability. By 1903 one of them (J. McK. Cattell) asserted the sex difference a truism: "The distribution of women is represented by a narrower bell-shaped curve." That is, the population of males is described by a broader range of ability; the population of females clusters more about the average. For some scientists, the idea that females would be unlikely to excel suggested that it was unnecessary to provide them with opportunities to do so.

At about the same time the first wave of female Ph.D. psychologists were commencing their careers. Helen B. Thompson (Wolley) published her doctoral dissertation, *The Mental Traits of Sex* (Chicago, 1903), and reported finding no differences in variability. Mary Whiton Calkins (later the first female president of the American Psychological Association) carried on a lively debate in the journals with one of the more vociferous proponents of the hypothesis, Joseph Jastrow. The most active feminist critic and the one who ultimately had the greatest impact was Leta Stetter Hollingworth, the doctoral student of a nationally known and respected educational psychologist who was also a prominent advocate of the variability hypothesis (E. L. Thorndike).

Hollingworth approached the question of variability from several different research angles. She demonstrated the inconsistency among the various statistical techniques purporting to demonstrate a sex difference. Then, in an effort to isolate innate variations she examined the length and weight of a large group of newborns and found no sex difference in physical variability. As for variations in intellect, Hollingworth argued that low-IQ women would be more capable of finding work or support outside an institutional setting (e.g., via housework* or prostitution*) and so should be underrepresented among the institutionalized. She further argued that the limitations circumscribing women's social role accounted for the rarity of women's public achievement. Because women's role was defined in terms of housekeeping and child rearing, "channels where eminence is impossible," and because of the constraints that the female role placed on women's education and employment, there was simply no valid way to compare the ability of women with that of men, who "have followed the greatest possible range of occupations, and have at the same time procreated unhindered" (524, 526).

During World War I, the mental testing movement rapidly became more technically sophisticated. The issue of sex differences* in variability became just one of many dimensions on which the sexes were contrasted and probably would have faded into obscurity except for the work of psychologist Lewis Terman. He began a longitudinal study of children with very high IQ in the 1920s. The highest-scoring child in his sample was female, but the ratio greatly favored males. Terman concluded that there was merit in the variability hypothesis after all, and a new round of scientific debate was initiated. Later in his career Terman reversed himself and attributed the apparent rarity of female genius to "motivational causes and limited opportunity" rather than inherent intellectual limitations.

Even in the past two decades one finds occasional scholarly speculation as to the merits of the hypothesis. Notably absent is the notion of complementarity of the sexes, which provided the framework and justification for the hypothesis originally. The variability hypothesis is treated today as a statistical question rather than a justification for limiting opportunities for girls and women.

References. Leta Stetter Hollingworth, "Variability as Related to Sex Differences in Achievement," *American Journal of Sociology* 19 (1914): 510–530; S. A. Shields, "Ms. Pilgrim's Progress: The Contributions of Leta Stetter Hollingworth to the Psychology of Women," *American Psychologist* 30 (1975): 854–857; S. A. Shields, "The Variability Hypothesis: The History of a Biological Model of Sex Differences in Intelligence," *Signs* 7 (1982): 769–797.

STEPHANIE A. SHIELDS

VEIL was first required for women by law during the Middle Assyrian period. Between the fifteenth and eleventh centuries B.C.E., the code of laws known as the Middle Assyrian Law Code was promulgated. As important and far-reaching in their effect as the Code Hammurabi (c. 1750 B.C.E.), they contain examples of early attempts to regulate and control the activities of women in Mesopotamia. The law regarding the veiling of women, MAL 40, reads:

Neither [wives] of [seigniors] nor [widows] nor [Assyrian women] who go out on the street may have their heads uncovered. The daughters of a seignior . . . whether it is a shawl or a robe or [a mantle], must veil themselves. . . . [W]hen they go out on the street alone, they must veil themselves. A concubine who goes out on the street with her mistress must veil herself. A sacred prostitute whom a man married must veil herself on the street, but one whom a man did not marry must have her head uncovered on the street; she must not veil herself. A harlot must not veil herself; her head must be uncovered. (trans. James Pritchard)

The implications of this law are several and great, and the effects of the law remain with us today, not only in the most obvious of cases, such as the wearing of the *chador* in Islamic nations, but also in the distinction between the woman who is "respectable" and the woman who is "not respectable."

A "respectable woman" is defined for the first time through MAL 40. She is a woman who can be identified as the property of an Assyrian nobleman—wife, widow, or daughter. The secondary wife, or concubine, is also defined as respectable when she appears in public with the first wife, her mistress. A slave woman, on the other hand, must not veil herself, nor must a prostitute. These women, if they wear a veil, are subject, under this law, to severe punishment and mutilation. Women are thus classified by law according to their sexual activities. Women who are servants to a man and who otherwise see to his sexual needs or are under his protection are veiled. These women are marked off, in essence, as "private property."

Women who are not in this position—slave women, freeborn concubines, commercial and sacred prostitutes—are unveiled; in other words, they are "public property." Of equal note is the fact that a man who failed to report the violation of the veiling law was also severely punished and disfigured.

Such a law served to lower the social standing of certain groups of women and define them purely on the basis of their relationship (or lack of relationship) to men of the upper class. This is particularly striking in the case of sacred prostitutes, who, as priestesses representing various goddesses, had heretofore been fairly autonomous, independent, and respected. An unveiled woman henceforth would be viewed de facto as a commercial prostitute; furthermore, the public nature of the punishment and its severity mark the importance of MAL 40 as an early sign of the open intervention of the state into the realm of private sexual conduct. In this way, the limited privileges of upper-class women, symbolized by the mark of the "good woman," the veil, were kept separate from the economic and sexual oppression of lower-class women, which acted as a powerful force to divide women from one another. With MAL 40, the state assumed control of female sexuality. This essential feature of patriarchal power was first institutionalized in Mesopotamia during the second millennium B.C.E.

References. G. R. Driver and John C. Miles, *The Middle Assyrian Laws* (Oxford, England, 1935); Gerda Lerner, *The Creation of Patriarchy* (Oxford, England, 1986); J. B. Pritchard, *Ancient Near Eastern Texts Relating to the Old Testament*, 2d ed. (Princeton, 1955).

KRISTINA M. PASSMAN

VEIL. Political Use of the veil has emerged recently in many parts of the Middle East and North Africa. Controversies over women's dress are not unique to the Muslim world, but the new veiling movements are an especially intriguing example of symbolic politics. The *hijab*, or covered dress, offers a new public voice for many Muslim women caught in a web of crosscutting global, class, and gender inequalities. It expresses and alleviates women's concerns about the direction of change in a world moving between tradition and modernity.

To understand what the new veiling means, it is important to consider the links between veiling and Islam and the politics of traditional veiling. Often viewed as an Islamic dictate, veiling actually began before Islam and was an established custom in the tribes of the Arabian peninsula. The Koran advocates covering the hair, shoulders, and upper arms and secluding oneself from inappropriate viewers. This advice refers, however, to the wives of the Prophet, who were the religious and social elite and often in the public eye. The implications for ordinary women are unclear and have been interpreted in a wide variety of ways.

The focus on women's dress indicates a cultural concern with modesty and family honor. But veils or covered dress vary throughout the Middle

East and North Africa from heavy gowns to gauzy scarves draped loosely over the hair. Face veils may or may not be part of the attire. Further, veils may signify social, economic, and nationalistic, as well as gender, messages. For example, veiling may emphasize relations of familiarity and distance within kinship bonds. Women draw their covering dress closer around them or cover their face when in the presence of strangers and leave their face uncovered in front of male relatives. As many families move from villages to cities, veiling may be extended as women encounter strangers more frequently. Veiling may be tied to class; while less possible for poor women who labor in the fields, veiling may increase in the middle or upper classes and express the luxury of this higher status. Veiling may present statements about religious affiliation or cultural authenticity. Veils may function as a symbolic code, indicating marital status, education, or village origin. Subtle changes in how the veil is worn, the materials it is made from, or small decorations let women change the message the outfit sends. Veiling has traditionally formed part of the symbolic politics of these communities, expressing negotiations over women's role and family standing.

The recent history of veiling in Cairo, Egypt, can illustrate the politics of the new veiling movements. In 1923, Hoda Shaarawi, an upper-class woman involved in the national struggle against British occupation, launched a movement to abandon the face veil. This movement was successful among upper-class women, and until recently upper-middle and upper-class women in Cairo have worn modest versions of Western dress. Lower-class and rural women continued to wear their various traditional outfits, long, colorful, printed dresses covered by a black outer garment and head scarf (their dress never included a face covering). Yet since the 1970s a new form of dress has emerged, and many middle- and upper-class women have reveiled, or, more accurately, they have adopted new versions of covered dress, different from the dress their grandmothers wore or the dress lower-class women still wear and ranging from fashionable turbans and silky gowns to austere head-to-toe coverings.

The most interesting thing about this new veiling is its emergence as a women's movement, a voluntary veiling initiated and promoted by women. Not confined to Cairo, this new veiling has appeared throughout the Muslim world, although its exact meaning varies according to local context. It has been used within political disputes, as in the revolution in Iran in 1979, when the *chador* was used in public demonstrations to signal disaffection with the Westernization of the shah's repressive regime; to signal membership in Islamist groups, as in the universities in Egypt in the late 1970s; or to signal nationalist sentiment, as in the Palestinian struggle. The *muhaggaba*, or covered woman, is a new phenomenon and a political force in the Muslim world today. But why do women find the new veils an appealing political gesture?

Returning to Cairo, we can examine the politics in more detail. Cairo has grown from 2 to 12 million people in recent decades, swelled by rural families in search of work and a modern life. These families form the lower-middle class and live in cramped apartments of two tiny rooms for 8–10 people. The fathers work as mechanics or small shop keepers or do construction, often away in richer parts of the Arab world, while the mothers are housewives who raise ducks or sew for extra income. These families benefited from social programs of the Nasser era (1960s) providing for free education for the children and guaranteed jobs in the government bureaucracy for graduates of high school. In the 1980s many of these young women, educated and working outside the home, embraced the new veiling, abandoning the Western dress of the middle class and putting on the long dresses and head scarves of the covered woman. Why would these modernizing women be the ones embracing a return to the veil? The new veiling seems to be an expression of a double bind these women are experiencing, a symbolic "accommodating protest" rather than reactionary behavior. It involves a creative struggle over women's identity in a changing society, an attempt to deal positively with the dilemmas of transition from tradition to some form of modernity.

Change is viewed by these women as positive but involving difficult sacrifices of traditional customs and opportunities. The key change for these women is the move from household work to working outside the home in government offices. Women argue that there is a conflict between household and workplace; it is impossible to perform the job of wife and mother well while working outside the home. Yet the economic reality of this class pressures women to work, as their income is required to pay rent and other essential costs; inflation eats up their gains.

Additionally, an ideology of ambition pressures women, pushing the values of solidifying their middle-class status through women's second incomes. Yet, a gender ideology argues that women belong in the home, where their nature is fulfilled by caring for the family and managing household resources and finances. Economic and gender pressures are in conflict, producing a tension for women. They are pushed into work yet compromised in their primary role as wife and mother when they do. Caught in this double bind, women lose respect and resources, especially since, in this cultural context, family is highly valued, and women's traditional role as wife and mother is very respected. In this context women have started to wear the new veils. They say the dress bridges the gap between wife/mother and worker, allowing women to retain the new opportunity of mobility and working outside the home but stressing that women should be respected and valued for this decision. The new veils carve out a new identity and new opportunities in a changing Cairo. Women are rejecting both a return to tradition and a Westernized modernity and deciding instead for a new way to be the modern Muslim woman. These new veils function as a political protest, accommodating by using a traditional symbol, yet definitely pressing new demands. Voluntary veiling offers an impressive example of imaginative political voice outside the realm of obvious political struggles but, for this very reason, an intriguing example of women's politics.

References: Fadwa El-Guindi, "Veiling Infitah with Muslim Ethic," *Social Problems* 28, 4 (1981); Arlene MacLeod, *Accommodating Protest: Working Women, the New Veiling, and Change in Cairo* (New York, 1991); Guity Nashat (ed.), *Women and Revolution in Iran* (Boulder, Colo., 1983); Sherifa Zuhur, *Revealing Reveiling: Islamist Gender Ideology in Contemporary Egypt* (Albany, 1992).

ARLENE ELOWE MACLEOD

VICTIMIZATION OF WOMEN is the practice of visiting abuse—physical, psychological, and/or sexual—upon women and then blaming the women for being abused. Women have come to internalize the blame. A typical reaction of a man to an unprovoked attack might be: "Why did he do that to me?" The typical reaction of a woman: "What did I do that he did that to me?"

VICTIMS OF CRIME. An important source of information on the victimization of women, the National Crime Victimization Survey (NCVS), has been collecting data on victimization since 1973. The NCVS gathers data for victims 12 years of age and older, by sex of victim, for four interpersonal crimes—rape, robbery, assault, and personal larceny (purse snatching/pocket picking). The data reported here, for 1993, reflect the recent redesign of the survey, which now reports more accurately both sexual assault and crimes among nonstrangers—offense types that affect women more than men. Important patterns include the following:

Amount and Type of Crime. For every 1,000 females age 12 or over, there were 44.9 victimizations. This compares to a rate of 63.2 for males. Crimes of theft (purse snatching/pocket picking) were slightly higher for females (2.6 per 1,000) than males (2.3 per 1,000). Comparative rates for crimes of violence were 42.3 for women and 60.9 for men. Of the female victimizations, 62 percent were simple assaults, 19 percent were aggravated assaults, 9 percent were robberies, and 9.6 percent were rapes or other sexual assaults. In comparison, for men 58 percent of violent victimizations were simple assaults, 27 percent were aggravated assaults, 14 percent were robberies, and less than 1 percent were rapes or sexual assaults.

Strangers versus Nonstrangers. About 62 percent of women's violent victimizations were at the hands of nonstrangers. This compares to 36 percent for men. Robberies against women were most likely to be committed by strangers (66.8 percent of the victimizations were by strangers), followed by aggravated assaults (50.4 percent), simple assaults (31.1 percent), and rape (25.8 percent). Generally rates of violent victimization increase as social distance increases, with the exception that "well-known" offenders are more frequent than casual acquaintances. For women, the rate of stranger violence is 14.8 per 1,000 women, well-known offenders 12.3 per 1,000, relatives 7.5 per 1,000, and casual acquaintances 6.5 per 1,000. While male and female risks are similar for well-known and casual acquaintance victimizations, there are strong differences in the other two categories. Men's victimization rate from strangers is 36.3, while women's is only 14.8—reflecting, most probably, the greater tendency of men to interact with strangers. Victimizations by relatives affect women much more strongly than men, with the male rate at 2 per 1,000, while the female rate is 7.5 per 1,000—almost 4 times as high as for men. Thus, stranger victimizations for men are 18 times the amount of relative victimizations, while for women stranger victimizations are only 1.9 times as high as victimizations by relatives.

In summary, women's experience of criminal victimization is an experience of danger from intimates and an experience marked strongly by sexual and simple assaults, most usually committed by men. This contrasts strongly with men's experience of violence, which is most often at the hands of strangers of the same sex.

Injuries. Women are more likely than men to be injured in the course of their victimizations. In robberies, 30.2 percent of female victims sustain injuries, as compared to 27.8 percent of male robbery victims. In assault 27.3 percent of women victims are injured, compared to 19.6 percent of male victims.

Age, Race, and Socioeconomic Status (SES). Generally, the older women are, the safer they are. Victimization peaks in the late teens (ages 16–19), where rates are 97.9 per 1,000, and drops off to 85.4 per 1,000 for 20–24-year-olds, after which there are more dramatic drops for each age category (age 25–34 = 47.6, age 35–49 = 38.9, age 50–64 = 12.6, over 65 = 5.2). This is true for all crimes, and rates decline for men as well as women. Differences in race/ethnicity most probably reflect SES differences and are as follows. For robbery and aggravated assault, black women are more at risk than white women, and Hispanic women are more at risk than non-Hispanics. However, risks of rape and simple assault do not vary widely by race/ethnicity. This pattern reflects the fact that the latter offenses are likely to be committed by intimates, while robbery and aggravated assault are more frequently stranger crimes and are thus sensitive to poverty. The very poor (those with incomes below $7,500) have quite high rates of violent crime, and increases in income cause these rates to decline dramatically; those with incomes of $7,500 to $14,000 have only 64 percent the rate of the poorest group. Again the pattern emerges that simple assault and rape/sexual assault are not so impacted by income. Except for the very poor and the wealthy rates are not very different for these two offenses, though they are for robbery and aggravated assault.

Marital Status. Married persons are less at risk than are divorced/singles for both men and women, but this is much more pronounced for women.

Divorced/single women have a total victimization rate 4 times that of married women (81.4 versus 20); whereas for men the rate is only 2.4 times as high (72.4 versus 30.1). The most dramatic differences are for rape, where divorced/single women have a rape rate 9 times as high as married women. As poverty influences stranger victimization very strongly, these differences most probably reflect the greater economic vulnerability of divorced/single women as compared to their male counterparts.

Sex of Household Head. Because female-headed households are poorer than male-headed households, we would expect the victimization rates of their inhabitants to be higher. However, there are pronounced sexual differences, even accounting for this. Children living in female-headed households have higher rates of victimization than do those living in male-headed households. But while men are safer in male-headed households if they live with others rather than alone (rates are 34.1 versus 68.6 per 1,000), women are safer in female-headed households if they live *alone* rather than with others (rates are 34.1 for females living alone in female-headed households and 59 for females living with others in female-headed households). Thus, men living alone in male-headed households have twice the rate of men living with others in male-headed households, while in female-headed households women living alone have half the rate of women living with others in such households.

Crimes Not Measured by the NCVS. Homicide data are not collected by the NCVS. Federal Bureau of Investigation (FBI) data (Uniform Crime Reports, annually) on homicide show that though men are much more likely to be victims of murder than are women (in 1994 there were 17,309 male victims and 4,739 female victims), virtually all of the female homicide victims were killed by men. In 1994, of all single offender–single victim homicides where data on sex of both were known, 66 percent of homicides were male offender–male victim, 23 percent were male offender–female victim, 8.8 percent were female offender–male victim, and only 2.5 percent were female offender–female victim. Too, research demonstrates that many homicides of men by women are victim-precipitated—that is, the relationship was one with a long history of wife battery. Among all female murder victims in 1994, 28 percent were killed by husbands or boyfriends, while only 3 percent of male victims were killed by wives or girlfriends. Nineteen percent of male victims were killed in the course of other felonies, while only 14 percent of female victims were so killed. But among felony-type murders, 14 percent of female victims were killed in sexual crimes—rape, prostitution, or other sexual offenses—while among men the percentage is below 1. Thus, the pattern seen in nonlethal personal victimizations is reflected again in murder—women are more likely to be assaulted by intimates, by the opposite sex, and in sexual circumstances than are men.

Sex Differences in Victimization. Some of the sex difference in victimization is explained by women's lesser economic power than men's. Victimization rates are higher for those who are poorer because poor persons have less capacity to protect themselves from stranger criminals (through living in "safe" neighborhoods, household safety devices, fewer public interactions, etc.) However, as we have observed, rape and simple assault (much of which, for women, is probably wife battery) are not sensitive to poverty.

The greater part of the sex difference in criminal victimization is accounted for by the fact that sex is an organizing principle—a principle of hierarchy. The sexual crimes of rape and wife battery, as well as pornography and sexual harassment, arise because, in giving men as a class power over women as a class, power is sexualized, and sex is politicized; that is, this hierarchy not only gives men power over women but produces sexual power—power that emerges when a sexual relationship emerges.

Thus, even if women gain more economic power, unless the hierarchy formed by sexual power is reduced or eliminated, we cannot expect the pronounced differences in criminal victimization to disappear. Conversely, to the extent that sexual crimes against women reinforce or even create men's power over women, as these crimes decline, woman's power, including her economic power, will increase.

NANCI KOSER WILSON

VINDICATION OF THE RIGHTS OF WOMAN, A, is a feminist work written by Mary Wollstonecraft and published by the radical printer Joseph Johnson in 1792. Wollstonecraft advocates, in opposition to a host of male "authorities," that women be treated as rational human beings who can contribute to society; she calls for the establishment of national coeducational day schools to train both boys and girls in mutual respect so that they can overcome the conventional sexual roles of male gallantry and female coquettishness. *Vindication* was generally well received in 1792 as a treatise on education, although most reviewers ignored its more subversive and revolutionary implications. When Wollstonecraft's husband, William Godwin, published *Memoirs of the Author of a Vindication of the Rights of Woman* (1798), revealing such details as Wollstonecraft's illegitimate child by Gilbert Imlay, attacks against the author and the book began. *Vindication* has been reissued and reread since the 1960s and is regarded as anticipating many arguments of the current feminist movement.

The radicalism of *Vindication* stems not so much from Wollstonecraft's explicit argument in which she relies on the Enlightenment faith in God-given human reason and perfectability but rather from her constant mode of establishing by analogy the relationship between the political and the domestic spheres. In so doing, Wollstonecraft uses the rhetoric of rights—the rhetoric of the French Revolution and its sympathizers. She constantly opposes blind obedience to authority, claiming that "liberty is the mother of virtue" and that one can exercise one's duties only if one has basic human rights. She rejects distinctions based on wealth and power in all institutions of society: royalty, aristocracy, military, church, and marriage. Wollstonecraft's analogies and her frequent, questioning use of such ideologically loaded words as tyranny, slavery, rank, privilege, and authority subvert the power structure of the male-dominated family and the society of which it is a microcosm.

In arguing against the view of woman as ornament and possession for man, Wollstonecraft explicity attacks the view of women in several literary works and in the work of popular male conduct-book writers of the day. Although she takes on John Milton's depiction of Eve and alludes to many of the eighteenth-century satirists, especially Alexander Pope, Wollstonecraft focuses her attack on Jean-Jacques Rousseau and his creation of an "ideal" woman, Sophia, in *Emile* (1762). She particularly objects to Rousseau's depiction of feminine weakness and passivity as sexually appealing to men. Wollstonecraft also points out the hypocrisy of a culture that values women only for beauty and pleasure but at the same time condemns women for caring only for vanity, fashion, and trivia.

Wollstonecraft implicates both men and women in the perpetuation of the status quo. Women, she argues, accept their outward powerlessness within society because they can use their sexual power to attain "illicit sway" over men, thus getting what they want through manipulation and deceit. Men who value women not as rational beings but as objects of pleasure and amusement allow themselves to be manipulated as long as their desires are fulfilled. Marriage in such circumstances is for Wollstonecraft a form of legal prostitution because a relationship that is not based on mutual respect and esteem is essentially opportunistic and predatory. Wollstonecraft calls for a rethinking of the domestic economy and sexual relationships in order to give both male and female equal responsibility and control. But she fundamentally supports the family unit, and although she hints at possible professions for women (e.g., in the fields of politics and medicine), she essentially sees the ideal woman as fulfilling her "station" as wife and mother.

In order to bring about reform, Wollstonecraft calls for a rethinking of the educational process to include rigorous mental and physical exercise for both sexes. She proposes that boys and girls be educated together during the day and that children return to their families in the evening. She sees the social interaction among children as essential to their forming enlightened views of male–female relationships and the day-school concept (as opposed to boarding schools) as reinforcing the importance and integrity of the family unit in human development. Wollstonecraft sees the role of the schools as training students to think rather than simply to recite facts by rote. Thus, she implies that an open system of education is essential to human freedom. Because Wollstonecraft does not extend her discussion beyond elementary education, we do not know what she envisioned beyond the early years. However, given the centrality of education in her dream to reform human relationships and society, higher education for all capable men and women, regardless of social class, would be a logical extension.

Impressive as the *Vindication* is as a feminist document, it does have flaws. Wollstonecraft articulates her ideas forcefully, but her structure is unnecessarily repetitious. Her desire to demonstrate the inherent rationality of women also, perhaps, leads her to understate the reality of female sexual passion. Nonetheless, despite flaws in the structure or unresolved tension in the ideas, the *Vindication* remains a forceful statement of woman's rights within the context of essential human rights and responsibilities.

References. R. N. Janes, "On the Reception of Mary Wollstonecraft's *Vindication of the Rights of Woman*," *Journal of the History of Ideas* 39 (1978): 293–302; Mary Poovey, *The Proper Lady and the Woman Writer* (Chicago, 1984); Carol H. Poston (ed.), *A Vindication of the Rights of Woman* [Norton Critical Edition] (New York, 1988); Ralph M. Wardle, *Mary Wollstonecraft: A Critical Biography* (Lincoln, Nebr., 1966).

JUDITH W. PAGE

W

WAGE GAP is the difference between the average wages of men and women full-time workers. Occupational segregation,* whether brought about by tradition, socialization, or discrimination,* has kept most women crowded into a limited number of occupations and kept the pay for those occupations low. Women college graduates earn less than male high school graduates. Black men earn less than white men, white women earn less than black men, and black women earn less than white women. During the 1980s, women's comparative earnings fell to an average of 59¢ for every dollar earned by men, then rose again. By 1986 women's earnings averaged 64¢ to the men's dollar; in 1988, it was 70¢.

WAGON TRAINS were a primary means for transporting women and men emigrants to the West during the mid-nineteenth century. Between 1840 and 1866 the Oregon–California trail was a primary route of travel for westering Americans. Stretching for over 2,000 miles from departure points along the Missouri River, along the Platte River, through the South Pass of the Rockies, and through the deserts of the Far West, the trail carried approximately 350,000 people to their destinations in California, Oregon, and Utah. It is unclear how many of the migrants were women. Although the years 1849 and 1850 were marked by the large numbers of single men traveling the trail to the California gold fields, by 1853, 35 percent of the emigrants were women and children, according to the emigrant registers at Fort Kearney and Fort Laramie. This remained the standard percentage throughout the 1850s. Travelers' experiences on the trail varied over time. Emigrants before 1850 could not count on much aid or support once they departed the states (roughly contiguous with the Missouri River); after 1850, forts, ferries, and other forms of traveler's aid proliferated, making the journey somewhat easier. Each individual emigrant's experience differed, however, as it was shaped by conditions unique to his or her own journey. The trip took an average of four and a half months. Midwesterners were the primary users of the trail because of their proximity to Missouri River departure points, and emigrants from Missouri predominated.

The overlanders, realizing that their travels were a historically important development, chronicled the details of their experiences in diaries and letters. More than 800 diaries of trail travels are extant; many were written by women and provide a revealing look at nineteenth-century women at a key juncture in their lives. These diaries describe their work, which consisted of domestic chores of the trail—cooking, washing, and child care—all shaped by the rigors of travel. They gathered buffalo chips to use for fuel and wild foods from the prairie to supplement their monotonous diet of bacon, beans, bread, and coffee, while struggling to maintain minimum standards of cleanliness and keep their children safe in the face of prairie and desert dangers. Migrant women also performed typically male tasks like driving wagons and herding stock and pitched in during times of emergency to work with men for the safety of all. Women also served as nurses to the ill and injured. Because diseases like cholera and accidents with guns and stock stalked the trail, they were often occupied as caretakers of the sick and dying.

Many women were pregnant on the journey, and it was not uncommon for births to occur along the trail. Women took charge of these events as well, although pregnant women rarely wrote about their health or the details of their deliveries in their diaries. Nineteenth-century reticence held sway over this important part of woman's sphere. Perhaps because nineteenth-century women were the keepers of home and hearth and nurtured family relationships, they tended to note deaths in a personal and detailed fashion. The trail diaries often describe deaths in camp or along the trail, revealing the high cost that westering carried. With monotonous regularity, women also chronicled the vital elements of wagon travel—feed and forage, fuel, and water.

Historians disagree about the meaning of the trail experience for women. Some believe that most women were unwilling participants in the adventure; that they had no interest in the potential economic advancement that a move might bring and instead mourned the loss of home, family, and friends, resenting their husbands for forcing them to leave. Other historians, while recognizing that most women held to their social ties more dearly than did their men, think that most were able to adjust to the move and that many quickly rebuilt the emotional ties and social institutions that they had left behind.

References. Kenneth L. Holmes, *Covered Wagon Women: Diaries and Letters from the Western Trails*, 14 vols. (Spokane, Wash., 1983–1997); Lillian Schlissel, *Women's Diaries on the Westward Journey* (New York, 1992); John Unruh, *The*

Plains Across: The Overland Emigrants and the Trans-Mississippi West, 1840–60 (Urbana, Ill., 1979).

PAULA M. NELSON

WEIR MITCHELL REST CURE was a famous and widely imitated medical treatment of the late nineteenth century. As with many physicians of his day, Silas Weir Mitchell (1829–1914), a neurologist, sought a somatic cause for various expressions of nervousness, collectively diagnosed in the late nineteenth century as "neurasthenia," which meant literally "nervous exhaustion." He found his cause in anemia but also recognized that a stressful environment, be it a competitive business world or busy household, could exacerbate the condition. His solution was a "rest cure," which removed the patient from her or his anxiety-producing surroundings and placed her or him on a rigorous regimen of total bed rest for six to eight weeks, controlled diet, and massage, with eventual mild exercise. In his book *Fat and Blood*, Mitchell described his treatment thus:

At first . . . I do not permit the patient to sit up or to sew or write or read. The only action allowed is that needed to clean the teeth. In some instances I have not permitted the patient to turn over without aid. . . . In all cases of weakness, treated by rest, I insist that the meats shall be cut up, so as to make it easier for the patient to feed herself.

This treatment, based on Mitchell's work with nerve-damaged soldiers in the Civil War and first documented as a treatment for neurasthenia in 1873, was a welcome and insightful change from existing interventive treatments, notably bleeding, surgery, and electrical shock. Mitchell, already a noted researcher in immunology, was also forward-thinking in his recognition that "women's work" in the home was emotionally and physically demanding and that husbands were often insensitive to their wives' needs. His sympathy for women probably makes it no accident that the majority of his patients came to be women of the upper and upper-middle classes: for many of whom neurasthenia had become a status "illness."

Mitchell, however, was also a product of Victorian morality. Although he supported higher (even medical) education for women, he believed woman's "natural" role to be that of wife and mother. These views, plus the limits of his predominantly somatic approach to psychology, caused problems for women whose conditions were rooted in the roles they were expected to fulfill or who had more complex conditions than anemia. For those who did not respond to his regimen, Mitchell described the rest cure as punishment for "willful" or "foolish" women: protective seclusion became isolation and rest became enforced inactivity. His description of the physician's complete control over his patient, effective as it was with many frightened and invalid women, also rests uncomfortably with our current preference for a more egalitarian relationship between physician and patient. "Wise women," wrote Mitchell in *Doctor and Patient*, choose their "doctors and trust them. The wisest ask the fewest questions."

Although many women complained of the philosophy and method of Mitchell's rest cure, many more praised the treatment and idolized its creator. Truly, many women were (at least temporarily) restored to active and happy lives by the Weir Mitchell rest cure. At its peak, the rest cure was practiced widely throughout the United States and Western Europe, but with the rise of psychoanalysis (which, in fact, initially drew some of its practices from Mitchell), Mitchell's therapy, or modified versions of it, fell into disuse by the middle to late 1930s.

References. Silas Weir Mitchell, *Fat and Blood, and How to Make Them* (Philadelphia, 1877); Silas Weir Mitchell, *Doctor and Patient* (Philadelphia, 1888); Suzanne Poirier, "The Weir Mitchell Rest Cure: Doctors and Patients," *Women's Studies* 10 (1983): 15–40; Barbara Sicherman, "The Uses of Diagnosis: Doctors, Patients, and Neurasthenia," *Journal of the History of Medicine and the Allied Sciences* 32 (1977): 33–54.

SUZANNE POIRIER

WELFARE. In the minds of the public, welfare and the AFDC (Aid to Families with Dependent Children) program are synonymous. Not that AFDC is our nation's only welfare program. It is one of 70 programs financed by the federal and state governments that deliver cash and in-kind benefits to the poor (Levitan). Nor can it claim to be either the largest or most costly of welfare programs. In 1994, AFDC with 13.7 million recipients ranked third behind Medicaid (36.3 million) and Food Stamps (26.9 million) in the size of its average monthly caseload, and it tied for third with the Food Stamps in terms of total outlays ($22.8 billion) behind Medicaid ($159.5 billion) and Supplemental Security Income program ($27.6 billion) (U.S. Bureau of the Census). Moreover, 20 percent of AFDC families are not headed by single mothers but by two parents or grandparents (U.S. House of Representatives). Nevertheless, abetted by media coverage, the mention of welfare normally conjures up images of poor single mothers and their children.

The focus on single mothers and their children intensified when the Clinton administration promised to "end welfare as we know it." This promise was fulfilled when the 104th Congress passed the Personal Responsibility and Work Opportunity Act of 1996 (P.L. 104–193), which abolishes AFDC and with it, 60 years of entitlement of poor families to federal assistance. Under the law, AFDC is replaced by the Temporary Assistance to Needy Families program, or TANF, as it is popularly known, which authorizes individual state programs of assistance with mandated work requirements, family caps on benefits, and lifetime limits on the duration of receipt. Federal funds are allocated as block grants rather than through an open-ended matching formula as under AFDC, and states may set an upper limit on their total expenditures in any one year. Assistance can be denied once this upper limit is met.

Undeniably, single women face many difficulties in satisfying the dual demands of nurturing parent and breadwinner. One-half (50.3 percent) of such family units are officially poor (1994), the highest poverty rate for any demographic group (Baugher and Lamison-White). Making ends meet when the father of her children is absent has always presented special problems for some mothers. In contrast, society's attitude about the degree to which and how it should assist mothers in this challenge has fluctuated.

Historically, welfare has been available to those Americans considered to be the *deserving poor*, or persons who are poor through no fault of their own. Four demographic groups have been awarded this distinction: children, the aged, the blind, and the disabled. All others (nonaged adults) have been considered undeserving because it is assumed that they can provide for themselves by working, males and females alike. The poverty experienced by nonaged adults has often been viewed as the outcome of inherent character flaws: laziness, instability, dishonesty, and so on. Providing economic assistance to such persons has been regarded as tantamount to rewarding these character traits. Single mothers, as able-bodied, nonaged adults, have not been considered deserving of assistance to meet their individual needs (*Poverty among Plenty*).

When first established in 1935, the primary program of cash assistance for the nonaged, Aid to Dependent Children (ADC), provided aid to poor children living with no more than one parent. ADC benefits were paid to the custodial relative assuming financial responsibility for the children, most often the mother. The amount of the benefit reflected only the needs of the children present in the family. No provision was made for the adult relative until 1950, at which time Congress amended the law to increase family benefits to cover the essential needs of one needy relative with whom the dependent children were living. The change occurred only after Congress was convinced that it was necessary to meet the needs of the custodial relative in order to ensure that the children's benefits were not diverted to this purpose. The name of the program was simultaneously changed in most states to Aid to *Families* with Dependent Children (AFDC). AFDC was further liberalized in 1961 to allow the states the option of extending eligibility to two-parent families in which children were deprived of support as the result of the unemployment of one parent. Because this option was equated with assisting the undeserving poor, only 26 states chose to do so, and most two-parent families remained ineligible for AFDC benefits (U.S. House of Representatives).

During its early history, AFDC policies were influenced by the general belief that a single mother's place was in the home creating a nurturing environment for her children. As more mothers in two-parent families entered the paid labor force, AFDC also began to encourage the mothers of school-age children to train for, and find, work in the paid labor market. The official policies of the Johnson, Nixon, Ford, and Carter administrations mandated AFDC mothers to work their way off the welfare rolls by enrolling in job readiness, training, and placement programs. But these programs were not given serious financial support and placed less than 5 percent of AFDC mothers in jobs. More successful were policies that rewarded work with a gradual reduction in welfare benefits. In the determination of eligibility and benefits, mothers were allowed to deduct the cost of working (child care, transportation) and one-third of their earnings when reporting income (U.S. House of Representatives). Incentives took precedence over mandates in these latter policies. These policies encouraged mothers to meet their own needs through work. If they did so, the state would provide for their children. These policies' success is reflected in the fact that a third of the exits from AFDC were attributable to an increase in the mothers' earnings (Bane and Ellwood).

By the time Ronald Reagan entered the White House in 1981, the percentage of mothers in two-parent families who worked for pay had grown dramatically from 28 percent in 1960 to 54 percent (Baugher and Lamison-White). Public opinion regarding the propriety of mothers' working followed this trend. In this climate, policymakers began to argue that more should be done to increase the work hours and earnings of AFDC mothers. Led by Reagan, conservatives successfully passed legislation (Omnibus Reconciliation Act of 1981 or OBRA) that reduced welfare benefits one dollar for each dollar of earnings after four consecutive months of work. Mothers who had previously combined earnings and welfare faced significant reductions in income. Their options now appeared to be quitting their jobs because their effective wage rates were zero or leaving AFDC with the hope of earning more than the maximum benefits. To choose to stay at home meant certain poverty in all but three states where combined benefits from all programs raised recipients above the poverty line (U.S. House of Representatives). To choose work was to leave one's children to the care of another without any guarantee of bettering their economic situation.

OBRA also permitted states for the first time to require work as a condition of receiving benefits. Evaluation of these "workfare" programs revealed disappointing results. The most successful of them raised the earnings of participants by only $1,000 per year (measured two years after the end of the program). There is no evidence that they moved AFDC families out of poverty (Baugher and Lamison-White). Nevertheless, the Temporary Assistance to Needy Families program extends these work requirements to all states and in doing so eliminates the option of being a stay-at-home mom for poor single mothers needing assistance. The days when an "undeserving" mother can receive welfare benefits as the head of her family are a thing of the past. Benefits are payable only if the mother undertakes her parental responsibility to provide for her children through work. Further, children will receive no assistance if their mother does not work. It is as though children have joined the ranks of the undeserving by virtue of their association with their undeserving mothers.

References. M. J. Bane and D. T. Ellwood, "Slipping into and out of Poverty: The Dynamics of Spells," *Journal of Human Resources* 21 (1986): 1–23; E. Baugher and L. Lamison-White, U.S. Bureau of the Census, Current Population Reports, Series P60–194, *Poverty in the United States: 1995* (Washington, D.C., 1996); D. T. Ellwood, *Poor Support: Poverty in the American Family* (New York, 1988); I. Garfinkel and S. S. McLanahan, *Single Mothers and Their Children* (Washington, D.C., 1986); L. Gordon, *Pitied but Not Entitled: Single Mothers and the History of Welfare* (New York, 1994); M. B. Katz, *The Undeserving Poor: From the War on Poverty to the War on Welfare* (New York, 1989); S. A. Levitan, *Programs in Aid of the Poor*, 6th ed. (Baltimore, 1990); L. M. Mead, *The New Politics of Poverty* (New York, 1992); *Poverty among Plenty, The American Paradox*, Report for the President's Commission on Income Maintenance Programs (Washington, D.C., 1969); U.S. Bureau of the Census, *Statistical Abstract of the United States; 1995*, 115th ed. (Washington, D.C., 1995); U.S. House of Representatives, Committee on Ways and Means, *1990 Green Book* (Washington, D.C., 1990).

JENNIFER L. WARLICK

WESTWARD MOVEMENT. The meaning of the frontier experience for Americans has been a subject of heated debate since 1890, when Frederick Jackson Turner set the terms for the discussion in his famous essay "The Significance of the Frontier in American History." For Turner and his disciples, the economic and political opportunities presented by free lands to the west of settlement had shaped American institutions and character. Because these historians wrote before the advent of women's history or ethnic history, their work focuses on the white male experience. Today historians are working to discover a new multicultural, gender-conscious interpretation of the American West. It will not be easy to create such an interpretation because, for women, the American frontier experience varied dramatically according to time, place, class, race or ethnic background, religion, stage in the life cycle, and individual circumstances such as personality type; good, bad, or no marriage; personal goals; and luck.

For Native American women the term "frontier" experience does not even apply, because they were not residing on a "frontier" but in traditional homelands. (See AMERICAN INDIAN AND ALASKAN NATIVE WOMEN.) In fact, many of the "new" western historians refuse to use the term "frontier" at all because of what they see as its traditional meaning, as Patricia Nelson Limerick put in her lectures, the place "where white people get scarce." A single overriding interpretation of such diversity may never be found.

It is possible, however, to make some broad generalizations. For Native American women, cultural precepts varied from tribe to tribe, but in most, women were the producers and processors of food and managed all the domestic work, broadly defined, while men engaged in warfare and the hunt. Native American women played an interesting role as cultural liaisons in the fur trade once Euro-Americans entered a region in search of furs. Some married non-Indian traders "in the custom of the country," processed the furs involved in international trade, and acted as mediators as two cultures met. They and their mixed-blood children became the foundation of blended communities in the West.

Perhaps the most common role for women in the West was that of producer and processor of food and other material goods for the support of the family. This is what women in agricultural societies did, and the frontiers east of the Mississippi, in Oregon, on the midwestern prairies, and on the Great Plains were primarily agricultural frontiers. Time and environment shaped women's duties on the various agricultural frontiers, however. Woodland pioneers in Ohio in 1800 were largely self-sufficient, producing their own food, clothing, furniture, and housewares from the wealth of the forest. The southern frontier expanded the slave system; white women produced and processed food or managed the enterprise according to class, while black slave women did fieldwork and household work according to the dictates of their masters. Great Plains homesteaders 80 years later depended, to some extent, on goods purchased from stores, including fabric, sugar, coffee, and canned goods; and their treeless, semiarid environment militated against domestic self-sufficiency, as did the increasing availability and variety of consumer goods. Because the Great Plains was settled by native-born whites and blacks and also by European immigrants, women's farm and home duties varied to some degree by cultural expectations.

Women in the West did more than work on family farms. After 1840, when teaching began to be defined as women's work, young women increasingly turned to schoolteaching, at least until they married. Domestic service on farms or in the growing towns also employed large numbers, as did other service establishments such as hotels and restaurants. Some women (their numbers are unknown) turned to prostitution to support themselves in towns that served miners or the cattle trade. Chinese *tongs*, or secret societies, imported Chinese women to serve as prostitutes for the large numbers of Chinese laborers working in the mines of the Far West. (For them, a move to the American frontier was a trip east, not west.) Married women on the mining frontier might take in boarders, bake bread, or do laundry for the single men in the mining towns. By the late nineteenth century, land rushes to unsettled Great Plains regions included single women who hoped to win homesteads. Approximately 7 to 10 percent of homesteaders between 1890 and 1920 were single women in pursuit of economic opportunity. As the larger society broadened the role of women, so, too, did the frontier offer expanded possibilities for women.

The arrival of women and children often symbolized the close of the frontier to the single men who inhabited it before their coming. It is true that along with women came organized social institutions such as churches, schools, and stable family life. Nineteenth-century middle-class ideals about separate spheres for men and women assigned women the tasks of domesticating, refining, and civilizing the frontier. Some followed these ideals with vigor and worked to create an ordered society that duplicated what had been left behind. Not all women were so inclined, however, and men also helped "civilize" the frontier through predominantly male institutions such as commercial clubs and political groups.

Historians disagree about the meaning of the frontier for women. Frederick Jackson Turner alleged that the frontier provided greater economic opportunity and freedom for men, although his conclusions are still fiercely debated. Historians of women have studied the issue primarily for white women; they disagree about the amount of economic opportunity and freedom the frontier provided for such women. Some argue that the frontier allowed women more opportunities for work in all areas, including nontraditional pursuits, and provided broader tolerance of nontraditional women. Others argue that the city and urban-industrial culture provided economic opportunity for women; the frontier, according to this view, was traditional and patriarchal, keeping women captive in a narrow, rural culture with limited opportunity of any kind. Most historians agree that many women participated in the social and cultural development of the West through their activities in churches, schools, and women's clubs; the issue for debate here has been whether there was any distinctive frontier component to this process or whether frontier women merely resumed the conventions of the settled world following a brief, but arduous, sojourn in the wilderness.

References. Susan Armitage and Elizabeth Jameson, *The Women's West* (Norman, Okla., 1987); Susan Armitage and Elizabeth Jameson, *Writing the Range: Race, Class, and Culture in the Women's West* (Norman, Okla., 1997); Kathleen Neils Conzen, "A Saga of Families," in Clyde Milner et al., *The Oxford History of the American West* (New York, 1994); Sarah Deutsch, *No Separate Refuge: Culture, Class and Gender on an Anglo-Hispanic Frontier in the American Southwest, 1880–1940* (New York, 1987); Lillian Schlissel, Vicki L. Ruiz, and Janice Monk, *Western Women: Their Land, Their Lives* (Albuquerque, 1988); Frederick Jackson Turner, *The Significance of the Frontier in American History* (Washington, D.C., 1894).

PAULA M. NELSON

WET-NURSING was breast-feeding the children of women who were unable or unwilling to do so themselves. Although little is known about wet-nursing outside Europe and the United States, its history goes back at least to the earliest civilizations, where patrician women often transferred the responsibility of nursing their children to slaves or, as was to become the custom in later centuries, hired women who made wet-nursing their profession.

Evidence remains sketchy, however, until the seventeenth century, when it developed into an active trade. Some wealthy women brought wet nurses into their homes to care for their infants under strict supervision. Here, nurses encountered restrictions on their social life and diet and were often held responsible for the overall health of the sucklings. The majority of urban women sent their infants to be nursed in the country, to be returned after weaning at approximately age 2. Many viewed wet-nursing as an alternative to rearing infants in crowded, disease-ridden cities and thought rural wet nurses to be the healthiest. Others disliked the disruption of their household by wet nurses, preferring a more distant arrangement.

In eighteenth-century France, wet-nursing reached its zenith; it became common for even working-class women to send children to nurse. A Wet-Nursing Bureau was established in Paris in 1769 in order to meet parents' specifications and to provide medical examinations and certifications of good character. As they were often unable to have direct contact with the nursing child, parents relied on intermediaries to bring them information and transport supplies and money to the nurse. The wet nurses, in turn, viewed the arrangement as a means of supporting their families and improving their living conditions.

Explanations for the prevalence of wet-nursing range from the economic to the cultural and medical. The inability of parents to provide for their families forced many urban women to enter the job market. Consequently, they could not nurse their babies. The eighteenth and nineteenth centuries also witnessed a growing belief in the value of infant life, and many believed the infant's chances of survival were greater if sent to the country. Moreover, wet-nursing was considered a better alternative to maternal breast-feeding than artificial methods or the use of animal milks.

By the late nineteenth century sending children out to nurse became less common as reformers described the evils associated with it: infant mortality rates for the wet nurses' children and the infants in their care were high. Thus, the practice became increasingly confined to the wealthy, who brought nurses into their homes.

Just as cultural, economic, medical, and technological factors contributed to the rise of wet-nursing, so these causes also played a part in its decline. In the late nineteenth century it became more fashionable for upper-class women to breast-feed. In addition, a substantial decrease in the number of women in the workforce meant that more women could nurse their own children. The advent of safer, more efficient means of infant feeding, including the baby bottle and safely prepared formulas, allowed for an alternative to wet-nursing. As a result, the practice of wet-nursing largely died out after World War I.

References. Valarie Fildes, *Wet Nursing from Antiquity to the Present* (Oxford, 1988); Janet Golden, *A Social History of Wet Nursing in America: From Breast to Bottle* (Cambridge, U.K., 1996); Mary Lindermann, "Love for Hire: The Regulation of the Wet-Nursing Business in Eighteenth-Century Hamburg," *Journal of Family History* 6 (1981): 379–395; David L. Ransel, *Mothers of Misery: Child Abandonment in Russia* (Princeton, 1988); Joan Sherwood, *Poverty in Eighteenth-Century Spain: The Women and Children of the Inclusa* (Toronto, 1988); George D. Sussman, *Selling Mother's Milk: The Wet-Nursing Business in France, 1715–1914* (Urbana, Ill., 1985).

JANET GOLDEN and VIRGINIA MONTIJO

WHITE SLAVERY is a Progressive Era term for the entrapment, transportation, and supply of women and girls for the purpose of prostitution; in a broader sense, it means forced prostitution.

The term "white slavery," which originally referred to the condition of exploited English female factory workers in the early industrial era, later became synonymous with the abduction of young girls for sexual enslavement. The late 1870s saw the beginning of an international movement against the coercive traffic in women. British antiprostitution crusader W. T. Stead roused Victorian society in the mid-1880s with reports of a procurement trade both in London and between England and the continent. Stead told stories of British girls being kidnapped and locked in Belgian brothels. In a series called "The Maiden Tribute of Modern Babylon," he narrated his deliberate purchase of a 13-year-old girl. Stead and his Social Purity forces pushed through legislation to raise the age of consent, and the worldwide furor they generated popularized the idea of the prostitute as a forced brothel dweller or street worker. (See SOCIAL PURITY MOVEMENT.)

From the end of the nineteenth century until the opening years of World War I, Britain and America spearheaded increasingly fervent antislavery campaigns. Evangelists and reformers lobbied for investigations of the alleged white slave traffic, particularly in immigrant women. Such agitation resulted in American adherence to an international white slave treaty as well as tougher legislation to prosecute panderers and close down red-light districts.

"Race" writers, concerned about black women's migration to northern cities, also cautioned against the bad influences and evil companions that might propel the unwary to prostitution. Yet, as the term "white slavery" suggests, reformers did not include black prostitutes among the coerced. In their assumption that forced prostitution was for white women what slavery had been for all blacks, they tended to overlook the rather racist implications of their own thinking.

By the early twentieth century, belief in the existence of white slavery was widespread, particularly in Progressive (1900–1917) America. Progressives believed in exposing and correcting social ills and urged the abolition of prostitution, which they viewed as the economic victimization of women. Whether prostitutes were abducted, manipulated, or, having more or less resorted to "the life," were exploited once in it, reformers tended to view them as white slaves.

Many Americans found an outlet for nativist and antiurban prejudices by viewing films or reading white slave tract accounts of country girls and sweatshop workers stalked by the Jewish or Italian "cadets" of vice organizations who drugged and imprisoned the hapless women in bordellos. Chicago prosecutor Clifford Roe's *The Great War on White Slavery* (1910) fueled fears of a network of slavers and titillated readers with veiled descriptions of the bewildered victim's experiences in the brothel. Aside from its erotic content, a tract like Roe's played on what historian Mark Thomas Connelly termed anxiety about the decline of "civilized morality" in the American city.

Agitation against white slavery resulted in the 1910 passage of the Mann Act to prevent the interstate transportation of women for immoral purposes. Over 1,000 slavers were prosecuted under the act. While investigators in the United States and abroad found no evidence of international syndicates or national networks, period documents demonstrate that procurers employed force or fraud to entice and retain women in the trade. Modern estimates, though, vary greatly. Some historians discount white slavery altogether; others claim that almost 10 percent of American prostitutes entered the trade as white slaves.

What seems more worth scrutiny is the period preference for viewing prostitution within a white slave context. Rather than dealing with the variety of reasons, many of them volitional, for women's entry into the trade, ideologues often reduced prostitution to the plight of the youthful innocent. The fate of the woman alone in the modern city was dire, argued these theorists; criticizing female autonomy was merely "protecting womanhood." White slave ideology thus reassured those who were disturbed by the new feminine movement toward independence outside the domestic sphere.

References. Edward J. Bristow, *Prostitution and Prejudice: The Jewish Fight against White Slavery, 1870–1939* (New York, 1983), Mark Thomas Connelly, *The Response to Prostitution in the Progressive Era* (Chapel Hill, N.C., 1980); Laura Hapke, *Girls Who Went Wrong: Prostitutes in American Fiction, 1885–1917* (Bowling Green, Ohio, 1989); Laura Hapke, "The Migration of Colored Girls from Virginia," *Hampton Negro Conference Bulletin* 1 (September 1995): 75–79; Ruth Rosen, *The Lost Sisterhood: Prostitution in America, 1900–1918* (Baltimore, 1982); Vice Commission of Chicago, *The Social Evil in Chicago: A Study of Existing Conditions, with Recommendations* (Chicago, 1911).

LAURA HAPKE

WIDOWHOOD, the role assumed by either marital partner upon the death of a spouse, affects all societies where marriage exists, creating individual and social problems that cut across national and cultural boundaries. Although almost half of all adults in the world have experienced or will experience widowhood, in most societies, in both the past and present, widowhood imposes more serious penalties on women than men. In contemporary society, especially in the West, where female life expectancy exceeds that of males, and monogamous marital traditions dictate that women marry men older than themselves, widowhood is increasingly concentrated among elderly women and persists far longer than in earlier times. That widowhood will be a prevalent and enlarging aspect of the human condition is ensured by the worldwide longevity revolution, in which the number of persons over 60 throughout the world will double by the year 2000.

Severing the marriage bond through widowhood (and to some extent, through divorce* or desertion) creates certain persistent problems whose resolution has differed according to historical time, place, and other variables. Widowhood alters and disrupts the configuration and functions of the family,* potentially depriving the surviving spouse of sexual consortium, companionship, and assistance in household duties and financial affairs. Frequently, it reduces the economic and social status of women and their families and often strains the societal fabric, which may be unable or unwilling to care for dependent, elderly widowed women or widows incapable of supporting themselves and minor children. Just as other single women may incur hostility and fear of those who are married, so, too, may the widow, who becomes an unattached sexual object and potential threat.

Yet unlike divorced women, widows, who become single involuntarily, must also contend with grief and bereavement, as well as with "role loss." One of the most stressful aspects of widowhood in the Western cultural tradition is the impact on the widow's identity of breaking the attachment to the deceased spouse as she makes the transition from being a wife to being a widow to somehow becoming an independent woman on her own. Because so much of a woman's status is intertwined with being married, widowhood creates a sense of loss that penetrates to the very soul of the individual. Nor is the society particularly sensitive to the widow's needs or helpful in supporting her adaptation to a new life.

On the other hand, it is also evident that in some non-Western cultures, where women's social and economic status is less contingent upon the marital relationship, the traumatic rupture of widowhood is mitigated. Further, even in the West, during different historical periods, legal statutes and practices in some instances have empowered widows, providing them with control over property and children that they lacked as married women. For some women who successfully cope with the transition through widowhood to attain an independent status, spousal loss provides an impetus to control their lives unavailable during marriage.

Despite the universality of widowhood, its impact on the individual woman and her ability to cope with it depend on variables that make the experience different for different women. These include (1) the *society itself*, which incorporates social class and cultural proscriptions and practices that influence both appropriate behavior for widows and older women and appropriate grief and mourning rituals; (2) *sex and age ratios* of the population, which affect opportunities for remarriage; (3) *the community* in which the widow lives, which determines the availability of support networks and economic opportunities, either through savings, pensions, government programs, or paid employment; (4) *family* and *the law*, which affect the nature of marriage and selection of mates, inheritance, and the rights of women to property; (5) *personal resources*, which include friends and neighbors, parents, children and kin, church and social groups, and fellow workers; and (6) the widow's own skills and psyche. Other factors involved in the adjustment to widowhood include age at marriage and at widowhood; circumstances surrounding the husband's death; economic status; the rights and duties of wives and widows in relation to kin and family; and historical context.

   More detailed knowledge and more comparative data on the way women in different societies during different time periods have responded to widowhood are needed to determine whether the many responses to widowhood reflect universal behavior or are culturally determined. While recognizing the difficulty of weighing the many factors affecting widows and their ability to cope with widowhood, the one factor that stands out above all others is financial security. Without the assurance of financial security or of knowing that she will be able to gain a living for herself and any minor children, the widow's ability to cope is seriously threatened.

   Reference. H. Z. Lopata, *Women as Widows: Support Systems* (New York, 1979).

ARLENE SCADRON

WITCHCRAFT is the belief, found in most, but not all, societies in the world, that humans can manipulate supernatural forces for their own purposes. In most non-Western cultures the power of witchcraft is itself morally neutral, useful for healing as well as harming, capable of bestowing blessings as well as curses. Nevertheless, it is widely feared as a means by which otherwise weak or powerless individuals satisfy their greed, lust, and vengefulness. While most societies believe that men as well as women can be witches, especially where witchcraft entails training in secret lore and bestows elite status, throughout the world the great majority of witches are women.

   At the level of popular culture, witchcraft beliefs within the Western tradition closely resemble beliefs in those African and Asian societies in which they are also widely held. They serve as an explanation for the misfortunes and disasters of everyday peasant experience (e.g., deaths or illnesses of humans or animals that do not appear to have natural causes), especially if there is plausibly someone in the village with whom one has had a specific quarrel or who has a general reputation for causing trouble through witchcraft.

There is abundant documentary, literary, and archaeological evidence that belief in witchcraft was nearly universal among all social classes in the ancient Greek, Roman, and Jewish civilizations. The triumph of Christianity had a paradoxical double effect, at least among the educated. On one hand, Christian doctrine emphasized, as Judaism had done, that witchcraft was wholly evil, a turning away from God for low and worldly purposes. Consistent with the early Christian stereotype of the female as spiritually inferior to the male, far more vulnerable to lusts and temptations, the church taught that women were far more likely than men to succumb to belief in, and practice of, witchcraft. On the other hand, the medieval church adopted Augustine's teaching that witchcraft was not real but rather a devilish illusion that served to tempt women and men into sin and damnation.

From a few scattered references, we can assume that among the European peasantry witchcraft beliefs (and practices) persisted essentially unchanged. Witchcraft, however, was a very minor concern for the religious and secular authorities during the High Middle Ages. They were much more worried about the heretical movements that emerged at the end of the twelfth century and spread through urban Europe, especially the Rhine Valley, northern Italy, and southern France. In combating the latter, the authorities portrayed heresy as the polar opposite of orthodoxy. It was claimed that the heretics met secretly, at night, for services of worship that were in reality obscene orgies of sexuality. Both ecclesiastical and secular courts also adapted from Roman legal practice the procedures of inquisitorial justice, by which they could circumvent the restraints and protections that the accused enjoyed in customary law. Women were prominent in the heretical movements, and this fact may have enforced the orthodox teaching that they were more prone than men to sin.

In the fifteenth century, popular and official concern about witchcraft intensified dramatically. Especially in the alpine regions of Germany, Italy, France, and Switzerland, there were trials of witches that anticipated features of the witch trials of the sixteenth and seventeenth centuries. For the first time, peasant witches were being hunted out and brought before ecclesiastical or secular courts. At their trials, traditional accusations of harming people, animals, and crops were amalgamated with accusations that derived both from the dark side of the popular folklore—baby-eating, night flying, and the like—and from the church's propaganda against heretics.

In 1486, two Dominican inquisitors at Cologne published a treatise called *Malleus maleficarum* (*The Hammer of Witches*), which synthesized much of the popular and learned opinion into the "new heresy" of witchcraft. The book was one of the earliest best-sellers of the new printing technology. Reprinted 14 more times before 1520, republished frequently during the period of the most intensive witch-hunting in the late sixteenth and early seventeenth centuries, its influence was considerable, although it is difficult to determine precisely what that influence was. Prefaced by a papal bull calling for inquisitorial proceedings against witches, the *Malleus* provided a tacit repudiation of the traditional theology, insisting instead that witches really were heretics who worshiped the Devil and had sexual intercourse with him. Moreover, the book was obsessively and perversely misogynistic, insisting on the inherent weakness and wickedness of women.

The Malleus was only one symptom of a gradual intensification of concern about witchcraft. While there were comparatively few witch trials in the 70 years after its first publication, the era also saw the printing of many sermons, pamphlets, and illustrated "devil books" that dwelt on Satan and the horrors that he was working in the world.

The new concern for witches was also incorporated into various statutes and legal codes, notably the *Carolina*, promulgated in 1532 by Charles V for the entire Holy Roman Empire. With the exception of areas where the new ideas of demonology failed to penetrate, the European regimes permitted the use of torture and the testimony of people like felons, spouses, and children, which was not allowed in other kinds of trials.

The height of prosecutions, the so-called witch craze, lasted for a century, from about 1560 to 1660. (See WITCHCRAFT CRAZE.) It was most severe in some of the petty states in southwestern Germany and in parts of present-day France and the Low Countries. At the other end of the scale were England, where Roman law never penetrated, and Italy and Spain, where the Roman Catholic Church still controlled witch-hunting procedures and after 1600 reaffirmed the traditional theological doubts about the reality of witchcraft.

Everywhere, witch trials were essentially a local phenomenon, with those accused and convicted being victims of village rivalries, feuds, and disputes that sometimes went back for generations. However, the witch-hunts were exacerbated by the religious rivalries of the sixteenth and seventeenth centuries and the warfare that was endemic to much of Europe in the period. But neither religion nor warfare explains why at least 80 percent of those executed were women.

Historians have recently pointed to three interrelated phenomena as having contributed significantly to women's being the victims of the witch-hunts. First, the witch stereotype as it had evolved was the virtual opposite of the male-created stereotype of femaleness. Those accused of witchcraft were routinely depicted by their accusers as being quarrelsome, independent, and unruly, and they were frequently economically marginal as well. Their accusers, very often also women, saw a threat in the witches and the anarchic freedom they represented.

Second, in both Catholic and Protestant states, the governments had taken over the supervision of morals that had formerly been the responsibility of the clergy. In much of Europe north of the Alps, this entailed prosecution of infanticide,* adultery,* sodomy, and bestiality as well as witchcraft, all of which were seen as threats to religion, the state, and the family.* The private and domestic nature of these offenses meant that women, formerly excluded from the courts, now appeared frequently, both as accused and as accusers.

Third, witchcraft was also a political crime. By giving their allegiance to the devil, witches challenged not only God but also the rulers who were his earthly representatives. The very disorderliness of the era led those in authority to become obsessive about the importance of order and thus to invest local outbreaks of witch fears and accusations, usually directed at marginal women within the villages, with cosmic political significance.

Early in the seventeenth century, officials in various parts of Europe began to have doubts about both the judicial procedures that had been introduced to root out witches and the demonological theories that justified them. Sometimes the excesses of the trials themselves led to questions about them; in addition, some writers began to reassert traditional doubts about the reality of witchcraft or else to inject a healthy skepticism as to the capacity of humans to know the minds of God and Satan as thoroughly as the demonologist claimed.

Ironically, two of the most extensive trials occurred late in the seventeenth century, in places that had formerly been largely immune to the worst excesses. In Sweden, the testimony of children led to a wave of trials that lasted for several years beginning in 1669. In the American colonies, where the pattern of witchcraft prosecutions had been virtually identical with that in England, with occasional trials on the traditional grounds of harming people or animals, claims by a group of adolescent girls in Salem Village, Massachusetts, that they had been possessed by evil spirits sent by witches led to over 100 arrests and 20 executions.

By 1700, prosecution for witchcraft had ended in most of the Western world. It was a more secular and a more pragmatic era, in which authorities no longer were determined to crush moral and religious deviance through inquisitions and prosecutions. Meanwhile, in the rural universe of the peasants, witch beliefs remained essentially what they had been for millennia. And so they remain today.

References. David Gentilcore, *From Bishop to Witch* (Manchester, U.K., and New York, 1992); J. Klaits, *Servants of Satan: The Age of the Witch Hunts* (Bloomington, Ind., 1985); C. Larner, *Witchcraft and Religion: The Politics of Popular Belief* (Oxford, 1984); Brian Levack (ed.), *Articles on Witchcraft, Magic and Demonology*, 12 vols. (New York, 1992).

CLARKE GARRETT

WITCHCRAFT. Contemporary (WICCA) is a revival, reinterpretation, and reinvigoration of traditional pagan religious practices. J. B. Russell points out that three discrete phenomena (simple sorcery, diabolic late medieval European witchcraft, and the pagan revival of the twentieth century) have each been labeled witchcraft. Contemporary American witches use the terms witchcraft and Wicca interchangeably to refer to a woman-centered, goddess-worshiping, nature-affirming, participative, this-worldly religion whose practitioners are initiated into the religion by legitimate Wiccan priests and priestesses. By using the term "witchcraft," they stress the connections between contemporary Wicca and earlier, including pre-Christian, practitioners of witchcraft (see Murray). Some estimate that the United States holds 100,000 practicing initiated witches, alongside as many as 500,000 American participants in pagan ceremonies, in radical faery practices, and in other activities akin to witchcraft (Melton).

Wicca is a goddess-centered religion. While witches affirm that the divine itself may transcend issues of gender or sex, they cite the goddess as the primordial metaphor for apprehending the divine. That is, the divine is made present and available to experience through the goddess. For women and men striving to develop models of divinity that support newer gender roles, "Goddess symbolism is spiritually uplifting, for it legitimates female power . . . in contrast with the usual images . . . of women as . . . seductive or sinful" (Roof, 143). A component of the metaphor of the divine as female is the goddess' multiplicity. The goddess shows herself through an almost limitless array of faces: as maid, mother, crone, and so forth.

Further, the goddess hallows and brings into the center of religious sensibility women and women's experiences. As many feminist Christian thinkers have pointed out, the maleness of the Christian god has marginalized and devalued women; God the Father and God the Son have told women that their primary religious roles are always subordinate to those of men. The goddess, on the other hand, valorizes women. With the goddess, women's concerns and experiences throughout the life cycle and in their many roles find an echo and an affirmation in the divine. Further, the goddess' many faces present her moving through the life cycle, rather than being caught static in any one role. The goddess enters puberty and menarche; she ages, and she grieves. The goddess' multiplicity not only valorizes women but also affirms women's physicality, their sensuality, their sexuality. Through the goddess, women's bodies are hallowed and brought into the center of religious experience, not—as in the Christian myth—as the site of sin ("through Eve all have sinned") but rather as the locus of celebration and as vehicles and agencies of the divine.

For Wiccans, the divine always presents itself through images of balance and harmony. Although Wicca is goddess-centered, the multiple quality of the divine is also experienced through male guises. Alongside the goddess is the god. The central act in Wiccan ritual is the divine marriage between the goddess and the god, the conjunction of the chalice and the sword. In this *hierogamos*, the divine female and the divine male act both together and discretely.

Witches affirm a radically immanent divine at one with nature and the world. The radical immanence of the goddess has two important consequences. On one hand, witches assert the holiness of nature. Ecological concerns come naturally to witches. Nature is neither a chaotic force to be tamed nor a morally neutral field on which humans play or over which they are given dominion. Rather, nature is the divine, and we and nature are one. Wicca here is similar to many Native American religions that see the earth itself as holy, as the mother of us all. Like ecologists, witches understand that to love your mother is to love the earth, that care for the earth is care for the self and for the divine.

On the other hand, since the divine is immanent in human lives and bodies, witches are held strongly responsible. Wiccan ethics are the ethics of responsibility, rather than an ethics of sin or guilt. Witches hold that an individual's acts are hers alone; acts have consequences, and individuals alone are held to account for their acts and their consequences. Actions then are not judged against some universal abstract standard but against their consequences. The Wiccan notion of ethics is summed up in the "Wiccan Rede." The Rede is a set of instructions, a knitting together of the sense of Wicca, and a warning. According to the Rede, "An ye harm none, do what ye will" (Scarboro, Campbell, and Stave, 47). With the caution that the witch must do no harm, the Rede asserts that the only limit to a witch's possibility is her will.

A witch's will is expressed in magic. Magic, in Wiccan belief, is the action of one's will on self, others, and the world. Magic is the bringing into effect of ends willed or intended by the witch. Many witches compare magic to effective prayers: one asks appropriately, and that sought occurs. For witches, magic includes a meditative element whereby the witch brings herself into alignment with the principles undergirding the cosmos. When one is aligned—when one lives responsibly—good things happen to one. "That," according to many Witches, "is magic" (Scarboro et al., 47).

Witchcraft is celebrated in participative religious rituals. Every initiated witch is priestess or priest of Wicca with immediate and effective connections to the divine, without the need for any intermediaries. Everyone in circle—a Wiccan ritual or religious enactment—joins in the activity: all initiates participate in creating the sacred space for the ritual; everyone participates in the chants, the dance, the ceremony of cakes and wine, the greeting and farewell to the spirits attending, and so on.

Wicca is a religion characterized by theological openness. Witches talk about Wicca as *one* path, among many, to the goddess or to religious truth. They ask of seekers, "Does this path work for you? Is it the right path?" "If not," they continue, "find one that does work for you." Witches are also open to theological or spiritual truths within other religious traditions. For example, the Hindu notion of karma has been easily, almost seamlessly, grafted onto the Wiccan notion of ethical responsibility.

As a religion, witchcraft affirms the lives that its practitioners act out in their everyday surroundings, seeing those lives, in all their particularities and differences, as parts of a cosmic whole. Wicca assures the witch that she participates fully and wholly in cosmic processes and affirms that the self is captain of its own journey, responsible to its actions and to the meaning that undergirds the universe. Wicca underscores individual connectedness and value in the face of a world increasingly fragmented and perplexing, but a connectedness within a community of fellow witches who live willfully and responsibly in a reenchanted world.

References J. G. Melton, "Modern Alternative Religions in the West," in J. Hinnels (ed.), *A Handbook of Living Religions* (London, 1984), 455–474; M. Murray, *The Witchcult in Western Europe* (New York, 1953); W. C. Roof, *A Generation of Seekers: The Spiritual Journeys of the Baby Boom Generation* (San Francisco, 1993); J. B. Russell, "Witchcraft," in Mircea Eliade (ed.), *Encyclopedia of Religion*, vol. 15 (New York, 1987), 415–423; A. Scarboro, N. Campbell, and S. Stave, *Living Witchcraft: A Contemporary American Coven* (Westport, Conn., 1994).

ALLEN SCARBORO

WITCHCRAFT CRAZE was the outbreak of witchcraft accusations that swept through early modern Europe. Official sanction of witch-hunting encouraged thousands of witch trials between 1450 and 1700, leading to the executions of between 60,000 and 100,000. Though the statistics varied from region to region, about 80 percent of those accused and 85 percent of those executed were women.

Despite a strong belief in magic and the stereotype of the solitary old woman as witch in the Middle Ages, there were relatively few arrests until the fifteenth century. Many of the accusations made against women as witches were similar to those earlier used against Jews, homosexuals, and heretics. In 1484 Innocent VIII issued a papal bull affirming the Church's opposition to all forms of witchcraft. This bull was in support of the Dominicans Heinrich Kramer and Jacob Sprenger, who published the authoritative witch-hunter's manual, the *Malleus Maleficarum* (Hammer of the Witches) two years later, in 1486. *The Malleus* went through at least 30 editions by the middle of the seventeenth century and identified women as the chief practitioners of witchcraft; it also detailed the legal procedures to prosecute them.

The witch craze was particularly virulent in the French–Swiss borderlines, the Hapsburg Netherlands, Germany, and the Basque country. It was also severe in Scotland but less so in England, where torture per se was not allowed. The victim of the witch-hunts was often a poor, elderly, single woman living on the margins of society; however, young women as well as old, men, and children were also victims.

Acceptable evidence of witchcraft included (1) mischief following anger, (2) witch marks, (3) familiars, (4) specters, (5) the water test, and (6) confessions. If a poor woman muttered at her neighbors, and subsequently their barn burned down or their cow dried up, this was evidence of witchcraft. Prosecutors searched the accused for witch marks, which they claimed the devil used to sign his pact. Any mole, wart, or other irregularity, particularly likely as the woman aged, could be judged a witch mark. If the woman had a cat, dog, or other domestic animal, people might call it her familiar, a demon in animal form, which was allegedly fed by nursing on her witch mark, the "witch's tit." Many believed that witches could travel through the air and pass through barriers to inflict injury as spirits or specters. Spectral evidence was difficult to refute, since a witch could send out her spirit to do mischief even though seemingly at home or even visible in court. The accused witch was often "swum." Tied up and thrown in the "pure" substance of water, if she floated, she was rejected; if she sank and thus demonstrated her innocence, she might well also drown. Torture was sometimes used; many women under duress confessed and named others, perpetuating the trials.

Historians have offered a variety of explanations for the witch craze. In the fifteenth, sixteenth, and seventeenth centuries, enormous social, economic, political, and cultural changes were occurring. Many people felt adrift as the Reformation shook the foundations of faith. Witch-hunting grew out of fear of heresy, and religious wars bred a climate of fear and hate. Reformers emphasized that the devil was active in the world; combined with the misogynous stereotype of women as carnal and weak, myths of the witches' sabbat, the mass orgy, and devil worship easily caught hold. Powerful men were responsible for local incidents of hundreds of witch burnings. Crop failures, disease, and war increased poverty and the numbers of women living alone. At the same time, attitudes were changing about community or individual responsibility for the poor. As a result, single women were an alien, marginalized element in the society. The stereotype of the witch, once established, created its own folklore.

By the middle of the seventeenth century, however, the witch craze began to lose its force. The educated elite, including court officials, began to question the execution of people for supernatural crimes. The French Parliament refused to accept evidence procured with torture. But once the belief in witchcraft had been sanctioned, it was difficult to destroy. Even after governments repealed laws against witchcraft, the belief was still strong in the countryside. Though the executions died out, the stereotype of the witch continues today.

References. Anne Llewellyn Barstow, *Witchcraze: A New History of the European Witch Hunts* (San Francisco, 1994); Joseph Klaits, *Servants of Satan* (Bloomington, Ind., 1985); Brian Levack, *The Witch-Hunt in Early Modern Europe*, 2d ed. (New York, 1995); Deborah Willis, *Malevolent Nurture: Witch-Hunting and Maternal Power in Early Modern England* (Ithaca, N.Y., 1995).

CAROLE LEVIN and ELAINE KRUSE

WOMAN IN THE NINETEENTH CENTURY is a treatise written by Margaret Fuller that inspired the 1848 Declaration of Sentiments in Seneca Falls, New York, and served as the intellectual foundation of the subsequent American feminist movement.

The eldest child of a Harvard-educated lawyer who for a time served as a representative to the U.S. Congress and the state legislature, Fuller was born in 1810 in Cambridgeport, Massachusetts. While her mother was engaged in housework and raising younger children, her father—an independent-minded thinker who was acquainted with Mary Wollstonecraft's educational views—tutored her in a rigorous classical education. It was, however, the consequences of his death in 1835 that educated her as to the economic disadvantages women face. The control of her father's diminished estate was turned over to a narrow-minded uncle. The financial reverses suffered by her family showed her that options were limited even for a woman of Boston's intellectual, elite class. Inevitably, she tried schoolteaching but soon turned her energy to "nontraditional" students. She originated "Conversations," seminars that many women from the Boston establishment paid to attend. These formed a nucleus for many of the ideas she later developed in *Woman*.

At this time, Fuller belonged to the transcendentalist literary and intellectual coterie that flourished under the aegis of Ralph Waldo Emerson, and for two years she edited its journal, the *Dial*. In addition to translating German writers, in 1844 Fuller published *Summer on the Lakes*, an account of a westward journey in which she demonstrates her concern for the environment, the Native Americans, and pioneer women. The success of *Summer* brought her a chance to work as a feature writer for the *New York Tribune* shortly before *Woman* appeared in print. Publication of *Woman* brought her national and international celebrity and notoriety. Her *Tribune* articles concerning literary and social criticism continued to stir controversy; as a result, when she left for Europe in 1846, she was able to sell articles to Horace Greeley's *Tribune* as its foreign correspondent. In England, France, and Italy, she became more radical politically. Her diverse dispatches reflected her concern with poverty and women's "survival" problems, and her contacts with Giuseppe Mazzini, George Sand, Thomas Carlyle, and Adam Mickiewicz. By the time she reached Italy she took as her lover a young Italian nobleman, Marchese Giovanni Angelo Ossoli. After their son was born, she joined the revolutionaries who overthrew papal political control of Rome and established the Roman Republic during the wave of revolutions that swept Europe in 1848. She organized nursing services while Ossoli fought in the front lines. When the republic fell, the couple fled with their child for the United States. The family was lost at sea when their ship foundered during a storm.

Even before her untimely death, the treatment accorded to Fuller by the Establishment followed the familiar patriarchal practice of attacking those who threaten its power. When *Woman* was first published, she was snidely criticized for being "an old maid." When she took a lover, she became a "fallen woman." Instead of dealing with her dissident ideas, opponents attacked her personally. They castigated her sexuality, her appearance, her personality, and, most damaging of all, her writing ability. In the *Memoirs of Margaret Fuller Ossoli* (1852), "friends," including Emerson, stressed that her "pen was a non-conductor." Hence, to this day academic critics repeat this misrepresentation from the *Memoirs* instead of reading Fuller's work and acknowledging her genius.

Published in 1845, *Woman in the Nineteenth Century* is a feminist manifesto in which Fuller demanded total equality and freedom for women: "We would have every arbitrary barrier thrown down. We would have every path open to woman as freely as to man."

Woman is written in the organic style characteristic of the American transcendentalists. Its structure is cyclical, its prophetic tone optimistic, and its erudition impressive. *Woman*'s philosophic framework is predicated on universals: that a spiritual wellspring exists, as do principles of good and evil. Nevertheless, when Fuller argues the mundane questions of a woman's life, she is uncompromising. She asserts that a woman must be self-reliant and not expect help from men and instead posits the concept of sisterhood—women must help each other, including prostitutes.

To show the capabilities of women, she includes a vast catalog from mythology, folklore, the Bible, poetry, fiction, and history and also from her own day to prove that "no age was left entirely without a witness of the equality of the sexes in function, duty and hope." Eventually, in her search for the feminine principle, she delves back in time to the prototype Earth Spirit. She believes that woman's psychic power and intuition are no more valued in her time than in Cassandra's.

In *Woman* Fuller demonstrates a remarkable psychological acumen with which she confronts issues still completely relevant today. She suggests the androgynous nature of sexuality, that "there is no wholly masculine man, no purely feminine woman," and asks that there be an end to sexual stereotyping and to the sexual double standard. *Woman* explores issues raised in modern women's studies and consciousness-raising* groups, such as the image of woman in literature and mythic study. Its most famous plea is that all jobs be open to women, even that of sea captain.

Her utopian vision that a just society is possible is an affirmation of human possibility, a hortatory call to women and men to recognize their interdependence and to grow spiritually.

Lamenting Margaret Fuller's death, leaders at the first national woman's rights convention in 1850 said they had hoped she would have been their leader and that she had vindicated their right to think.

References. Joseph Jay Deiss, *The Roman Years of Margaret Fuller* (New York, 1969); Marie Mitchell Olesen Urbanski, *Margaret Fuller's Woman in the Nineteenth Century: A Literary Study of Form and Content, of Sources and Influences* (Westport, Conn., 1980).

MARIE MITCHELL OLESEN URBANSKI

WOMAN SUFFRAGE MOVEMENT (U.S.) was a social and political reform movement that sought the right to vote for women. The first demand for woman suffrage in the United States occurred at the Seneca Falls woman's rights convention of 1848. For the next 20 years, woman suffrage was demanded by a broadly radical woman's rights movement seeking female emancipation. In 1869, two national woman suffrage organizations were established to pursue female enfranchisement. After two decades of hard work and meager results, these organizations merged in 1890. In the twentieth century, a more narrowly specialized woman suffrage movement acquired a new momentum, achieved victories in several states, enjoyed a more hospitable reform climate, and capitalized on opportunities with a new strategic sophistication. The result was passage (1919) and ratification (1920) of the Nineteenth Amendment to the U.S. Constitution, which granted women the right to vote.

Before the Civil War, woman suffrage was an integral part of the reform agenda of the woman's rights movement, which primarily consisted of women who had been active in the abolitionist movement and detected parallels between the enslavement of blacks and the subordination of women. (See ABOLITIONISM and WOMAN'S RIGHTS MOVEMENT.) After the Civil War, the Republican Party and the abolitionist movement sought a series of constitutional amendments to outlaw slavery, extend civil rights, and enfranchise blacks. Many woman's rights activists felt this was an appropriate moment to enfranchise women as well, and they called on Republican abolitionists to recognize the justice of woman suffrage as well as the support many women had provided the abolitionist cause. The Republican response was that it was the "Negro's hour": that the needs of black slaves had a historical priority over the needs of white women and that the effort to grant rights to blacks should not be jeopardized by a simultaneous effort to enfranchise women. Woman's rights activists were especially dismayed to learn that the Fourteenth Amendment supported by Republican abolitionists to enfranchise black men would introduce the term "male" into the Constitution for the first time, thereby necessitating an additional constitutional amendment to enfranchise women. These events caused a schism in the woman's rights movement; some individuals (including Lucy Stone and Henry Blackwell) reluctantly agreed with the "Negro's hour" position, while others (including Elizabeth Cady Stanton and

Susan B. Anthony) adamantly opposed proposals to enfranchise blacks without simultaneously enfranchising women.

In May 1869, Stanton and Anthony definitively broke with Republican abolitionists and established the National Woman Suffrage Association (NWSA). In November 1869, Stone and Blackwell founded the American Woman Suffrage Association (AWSA). For the next 21 years, these two organizations operated as rivals in the woman suffrage movement until lack of success helped promote a merger between them. Beyond differing attitudes to Republican abolitionists, there were ideological, strategic, and personality differences that nurtured the split. Under Stanton and Anthony's leadership, NWSA retained a broad and radical posture toward women's emancipation and consciously linked the demand for suffrage with other grievances. Under Stone and Blackwell's leadership, AWSA adopted a narrow and moderate posture and sought woman suffrage as a single-issue demand. In strategic terms, NWSA favored a federal strategy of amending the U.S. Constitution, which, though difficult to achieve, would enfranchise all women simultaneously. AWSA favored a state strategy that would win suffrage in a number of states and ultimately create sufficient momentum to produce a federal amendment as the logical culmination of piecemeal gains in various states.

Both organizations labored hard through the 1870s and 1880s with relatively little success. The only places where women could vote at this time were the territories of Wyoming (which granted woman suffrage in 1869) and Utah (which did so in 1870). In other locations, women occasionally won limited forms of suffrage that allowed them to vote for school board officers, local budget propositions, and the like. In all these cases, the rationale behind woman suffrage was not female emancipation but rather territorial consolidation, party expediency, or social control—in short, women were granted limited suffrage when it served larger, partisan, nonfeminist interests. In 1878 a modicum of success appeared on the national level when Senator A. A. Sargent of California introduced what came to be known as the Anthony Amendment into Congress; it read, "The right of citizens of the United States to vote shall not be denied or abridged by the United States or by any state on account of sex." In 1882, both houses appointed committees on woman suffrage, which reported favorably. The Senate committee did so again in 1884 and 1886, and the bill reached the floor of the Senate in 1887 only to be defeated by a substantial margin. The state strategy proved no more successful in this period as a number of referenda in several states went down to defeat. In light of these defeats and at the urging of Lucy Stone's daughter Alice Stone Blackwell, the two suffrage organizations merged in 1890 to form the National American Woman Suffrage Association (NAWSA).

The 1890s brought some successes on the state level. Wyoming was admitted into the Union with woman suffrage in its constitution, becoming the first state to permit women to vote. Suffrage forces won victories in Colorado in 1893 and in Idaho in 1896, when Utah was also admitted into the Union with woman suffrage. These successes provided no lasting momentum to suffrage forces, however, as no new states were won for another 14 years. In the interim, NAWSA was plagued by strategic and ideological disputes. The organization vacillated on the issue of federal versus state strategies, and it accommodated itself to the racism of southern suffragists whose determination to maintain white supremacy dominated their approach to female enfranchisement. Soon after the merger, the narrow and moderate orientation of the former American association came to predominate over the former national association's broadly radical posture, and NAWSA thereby entered the twentieth century as a specialized, single-issue movement. If NAWSA fared poorly in this period, other events around the turn of the century set the stage for more successful efforts after 1910.

Throughout the nineteenth century, the suffrage movement had been based on appeals to justice and equality and had drawn its support almost exclusively from middle-class women. As the movement entered the twentieth century, it added new pro-suffrage arguments and appealed to a broader range of women. Newer pro-suffrage ideology was exemplified by municipal housekeeping arguments that claimed that in a rapidly urbanizing society, women required municipal suffrage simply to meet their traditional obligations of protecting the health and welfare of their families. The broader constituency of the movement was evident in the participation of women from all social classes. On one hand, the movement recruited working-class women through the Women's Trade Union League and the settlement house movement.* On the other hand, upper-class women became involved as part of the Progressive Era mobilization for various reforms. (See PROGRESSIVE MOVEMENT.) As it entered the twentieth century, then, the movement was constructing a specialized, cross-class, multiconstituency alliance that would ultimately contribute to a more successful fight for the vote.

From 1910 to 1914, carefully orchestrated campaigns won the vote in Arizona, California, Illinois, Kansas, Montana, Nevada, Oregon, and Washington. More ominous, however, was the fact that a seeming victory in Michigan was reversed by ballot tampering and that liquor and brewing interests were mobilizing a nationwide antisuffrage campaign. These events intensified the debate over federal versus state strategies, particularly when the Shafroth–Palmer resolution introduced into Congress promised to make state referenda easier to place on the ballot. As NAWSA became immobilized by strategic disputes, a NAWSA committee called the Congressional Union split from the larger group, became an independent organization under the same name, and dedicated itself to winning woman suffrage through an amendment to the U.S. Constitution. This organization was instrumental in reintroducing the Anthony Amendment into Congress in 1914. Late in 1915, NAWSA urged Carrie Chapman Catt to reclaim the presidency of the organization and use her widely respected organizational abilities to lead NAWSA out of its impasse.

Catt accepted the challenge and drafted a "Winning Plan," which identified states most likely to grant suffrage, specified ways to increase pressure on Congress, and anticipated the ratification struggle that would have to follow congressional approval of any suffrage amendment. As NAWSA directed its resources to the most promising state campaigns, the Congressional Union initiated more militant tactics to pressure national politicians. On the eve of U.S. entry into World War I, pickets from this organization appeared at the White House demanding the vote for women.

In 1917, Catt's plan produced state victories in Arkansas, Indiana, Michigan, Nebraska, New York, North Dakota, and Rhode Island. These victories provided new leverage to the cause, and this leverage translated into a major victory in the House of Representatives, which passed the Anthony Amendment by the required two-thirds majority on January 10, 1918. The Senate rejected the measure, however, and suffragists had to wait a bit longer for the goal they had sought so long. In the interim, Iowa, Maine, Minnesota, Missouri, Ohio, Oklahoma, South Dakota, and Wisconsin passed suffrage amendments. The newly seated Sixty-Sixth Congress proved more hospitable: the House passed the measure by a large margin on May 20, 1919, and the Senate followed suit on June 4. After a dramatic, 15-month campaign, the Nineteenth Amendment was ratified by the required number of states and adopted on August 26, 1920.

The length of the suffrage campaign may be attributed to women's institutional powerlessness in American politics, to extensive indifference in the general populace, and to specific oppositional forces. Among the latter, liquor and brewing interests fearful of female voters provided considerable financial backing to antisuffrage groups and sometimes used corrupt tactics to defeat woman suffrage measures. In addition, southern states were uniformly antisuffrage, fearing it would enfranchise black as well as white women and establish a principle of federal regulation of voting rights that would jeopardize white supremacy. Institutional powerlessness, generalized indifference, and specific opponents thereby made the suffrage campaign a long and difficult one.

The ultimate success of the campaign may likewise be attributed to general and specific factors. In general, suffrage victories became more likely in a climate of reform such as the Progressive Era. When combined with the political realignments prompted by U.S. participation in World War I and women's contributions to that effort, favorable circumstances materialized for the suffrage campaign. Equally important, the movement's hard work and strategic sophistication allowed it to take advantage of these favorable circumstances. By the 1910s, the movement had carefully constructed a specialized, cross-class, multiconstituency alliance comprising a broad base of support that could at last exert legislative pressure. Guided by Catt's careful leadership and prodded by the Congressional Union's militant agitation, the suffrage movement brought a 72-year effort to win woman suffrage to a successful conclusion.

References. Steven M. Buechler, *The Transformation of the Woman Suffrage Movement* (New Brunswick, N.J., 1986); Ellen DuBois, *Feminism and Suffrage* (Ithaca, N.Y., 1978); Eleanor Flexner, *Century of Struggle: The Woman's Rights Movement in the United States* (Cambridge, Mass., 1959; repr. Cambridge, Mass., 1975); Aileen Kraditor, *The Ideas of the Woman Suffrage Movement, 1890–1920* (New York, 1965).

STEVEN M. BUECHLER

WOMANIST, WOMANISM, WOMANISH are terms associated with varied conditions of black womankind. Particularly characteristic of gender-role traits and practices of African American women, these terms are applicable to all women of African descent. Alice Walker originally introduced the term "womanist," yet the ideals behind it have a long-standing significance in black culture. Long before Sojourner Truth's query "Ain't I a woman?" and continuing through contemporary African women's writing, womanism has import.

"Womanism," as conventionally employed in black culture, can refer to gender traits or can identify social/political consciousness. Womanism represents an expectation and experience of female knowledge, competence, and responsibilities that are beyond those associated either with youth or with the gender traits traditionally assigned females in Western culture. Its characterization of women as audacious as well as capable contrasts with the image of females under partriarchy* as submissive and inferior. It is significant to note that while black males, regardless of their ages, have been stereotypically addressed as "boys," black females were supposedly denigrated by being referred to as "women" rather than "ladies." However, the connotations of "women" within the black community have become positive ones, asserting and affirming the value in females of adult qualities such as ability, independence, creativity, loving, and strength.

"Womanish," then, represents an attitude or orientation toward life of strong-willed, opinionated self-confidence. Within black communities, even young girls are referred to as womanish, that is, behaving like, or assuming the responsibilities and prerogatives of, older, adult females. In fact, black females necessarily assume adult roles and develop a maturity at very young ages.

The form "womanist" identifies someone with a respect for, an appreciation of, and a reliance upon the capabilities of women. A womanist is decidedly pro-woman: an advocate of women's interests, equity, and enrichment within familial, community, religious, educational, economic, political, and social relationships and institutions. This advocacy and activism include an array of matrifocal endeavors, both homosocial and homosexual. Yet as Alice Walker and Chikwenye Okonjo Ogunyemi observe, a womanist is not a female separatist. The concerns of the womanist perspective are the survival, affirmation, and empowerment of all persons, male and female. Womanism encompasses a black feminism and has also been applied generally to feminists of color. Yet, as Walker asserts, given the complexity and dynamism of black women's lives, womanism has a greater scope and intensity than feminism.* (See BLACK WOMEN AND FEMINISM.) A womanist is spirited and spiritual, determined and decisive, committed to struggle and convinced of victory. A womanist acknowledges the particulist experiences and cultural heritage of black women, resists systems of domination, and insists on the liberty and self-determination of all people.

References. P. Giddings, *When and Where I Enter: The Impact of Black Women on Race and Sex in America* (New York, 1984); J. Ladner, *Tomorrow's Tomorrow: The Black Woman* (Garden City, N.Y., 1971); Alice Walker, *In Search of Our Mother's Gardens: Womanist Prose* (San Diego, 1983); Alice Walker and Chikwenye Okonjo Ogunyemi, "Womanism: The Dynamics of the Contemporary Black Female Novel in English," *Signs* 11 (1985): 63–80.

DEBORAH K. KING

WOMAN'S CLUB MOVEMENT often refers to the burst of voluntary associations that American women formed in the years between the Civil War and the Great Depression. In cities and towns throughout the nation, middle-class, leisured, and frequently, but not exclusively, white women established special-interest organizations devoted to social, educational, and civic purposes. Forming the backbone of the Progressive reform movement at the turn of the century, the groups succeeded in identifying social problems, especially those relating to women and children; researching them; and defining and implementing solutions by lobbying legislators, publicizing issues, and raising funds. Among the largest and most influential national groups, with local and regional branches, were the General Federation of Women's Clubs, the Women's Christian Temperance Union, the National Association of Colored Women, and the Association of Collegiate Alumnae—later, the American Association of University Women. Smaller groups like the Daughters of the American Revolution, the Drama League of America, the National Federation of Music Clubs, and myriad political study groups and philanthropic associations were no less effective in providing members with skills, sociability, self-development, and community projects. Throughout the nineteenth century, members faced criticism for their public life in clubs and the public voice they raised, which challenged the traditional notion that "women's place is in the home." The earliest women to achieve public office often found their support among sister clubwomen.

The origins of the women's club movement lay in the literary and civic clubs that formed the General Federation of Women's Clubs (GFWC) in 1890. Inspired by the two groups founded in 1868, Sorosis in New York City and the New England Woman's Club in Boston, thousands of women's clubs emerged throughout the nation. By 1890, many of them became federated. Despite the exclusive membership policies in many of the clubs, by 1910 over 1 million dues-paying women were addressing ambitious programs for "Municipal Housekeeping" through their art, civics, civil service reform, conservation, education, household economy, industrial and social conditions, public health, legislation, and literature and library extension departments; at local meetings; in annual, statewide conferences; and in national GFWC biennial conventions. Although the federation did not endorse woman suffrage until 1914, its history is the story of efforts on behalf of woman's rights issues, such as higher salaries for teachers, the hiring of police matrons, and improved education for children via vocational training, public libraries, well-equipped classrooms, parks, and playgrounds. During World War I, the clubs were important forces in mobilizing women for patriotic service. The 1920s, when membership peaked, was an era of lavish clubhouse building. Almost 2,000 GFWC member clubs purchased clubhouses, and, in 1922, a national headquarters was established at 1734 N Street NW in Washington, D.C. The General Federation of Women's Clubs, which still exists today, is steadily expanding its archives for researchers.

References. Karen J. Blair, *The Clubwoman as Feminist: True Womanhood Redefined, 1868–1914* (New York, 1980); Karen J. Blair, *The Torchbearers: Women's Amateur Arts Associations in America, 1890–1930* (Bloomington, Ind., 1994); Jane Cunningham Croly, *The History of the Woman's Club Movement in America* (New York, 1898); Cynthia Neverdon-Morton, *Afro-American Women of the South and the Advancement of the Race, 1895–1925* (Knoxville, 1989); Anne Firor Scott, *Natural Allies: Women's Associations in American History* (Urbana, Ill., 1992).

KAREN J. BLAIR

WOMAN'S RIGHTS MOVEMENT (1848–1861) officially began in the United States at the Seneca Falls convention in July 1848. This meeting was the product of a reunion of two women who had conceived the idea in 1840. In that year Elizabeth Cady Stanton and Lucretia Mott met at the World Antislavery Convention* in London and shared their indignation at the exclusion of women delegates from the deliberations. (See WORLD'S ANTI-SLAVERY CONVENTION OF 1840.) Over the course of many conversations during their stay in London, Mott, the respected Quaker abolitionist, inspired the younger Stanton with a vision of the possibilities inherent in women's talent and intellect. Before parting company, the two women vowed to hold a convention dedicated to an inquiry into women's status once they returned to the United States.

A combination of circumstances—family responsibilities, geography, and other commitments—prevented the fruition of this promise until the summer of 1848, when Mott was visiting her sister Martha Wright in the vicinity of Stanton's home in Seneca Falls, New York. When the two friends met, they resurrected their plans and began preparations for a woman's rights convention. Taking advantage of prevailing circumstances, including the nearby meeting of Hicksite Quakers, they announced the convention with only one week's notice.

With so little time available, the five women planning the convention, Mott, Stanton, Wright, and Jane Hunt and Mary McClintock, friends of Wright and Mott, urgently needed a document setting forth the philosophy and goals of the meeting. Casting about for an appropriate guide, they chose the Declaration of Independence. The resulting Declaration of Sentiments substituted the words "all men" for "King George" as the source of the injustices imposed upon women. Stanton undertook the further task of writing a series of resolutions to be considered by the convention. The 13 resolutions were primarily statements of general principles about the equality of men and women and the right of women to full partnership in all human enterprise. The most specific resolution called on women to secure to themselves the elective franchise.

On the first day of the convention the organizers were so overwhelmed by the numbers in attendance and the novelty of the enterprise that each refused to preside. That duty fell instead to Mott's husband, James. The women recovered their aplomb sufficiently to give speeches and participate actively in the proceedings that first day. The primary agenda item on the second day of the convention was consideration of the 13 resolutions. All were adopted unanimously except the suffrage resolution, which created a stir of controversy. Only the combined arguments of Stanton and abolitionist Frederick Douglass won slim approval for the resolution. At the conclusion of the convention, over 100 men and women signed the Declaration of Sentiments and the resolutions.

Two weeks after the meeting at Seneca Falls, by prior agreement, a second convention was held in Rochester, New York. This time a woman presided, although that fact created some initial consternation among many of the participants, including Stanton and Mott. The Declaration of Sentiments from the Seneca Falls meeting was read and adopted, as was a series of resolutions, the first of which called for women's right to the elective franchise. For the next one and a half years there were no further meetings. In 1850, local meetings were held in Ohio and Pennsylvania, and the first national convention met in Worcester, Massachusetts. The large turnout at the Worcester meeting—over 1,000 people—indicated that the momentum had not died in the interval since Rochester.

For the next decade, national conventions met each year (except 1857), and local meetings were held in Ohio, Pennsylvania, New York, Massachusetts, and Indiana. Woman's rights advocates did more than just attend meetings during these years, however. They also submitted suffrage petitions to legislatures, wrote numerous articles about their cause, addressed temperance and antislavery meetings on behalf of woman's rights, and in general kept their cause in the public's eye. Significant new recruits joined the movement during this period, including Susan B. Anthony, Lucy Stone, Antoinette Brown, and Sojourner Truth.

In addition to these varied activities, the development of the woman's rights movement in the 1850s rested on the creation of an ideology from which specific issues emerged and the evolution of a network of women who could translate the issues into an agenda for action. From earlier reform efforts, such as temperance, moral reform, and abolition, woman's rights advocates had inherited a general reform ideology based on a belief in republican virtues, the perfectability of society, the force of moral imperatives, and the merits of collective action. Women's involvement in these early reform crusades had also taught them the limits imposed on them by gender. But women who sought to champion the woman's rights cause found that they had no comprehensive, systematic analysis of women's status—the rights to which women were entitled, the wrongs from which they suffered, and the changes necessary to remedy the latter and obtain the former. Thus, the ideology was born of necessity, created through discourse among, and reflection by, the early activists.

The most significant of the theorists of a woman's rights ideology was Elizabeth Cady Stanton. Following her role at Seneca Falls and Rochester, Stanton received numerous requests to address woman's rights meetings and other audiences and to defend the women's cause in the press. As a result, she was compelled to expand the analysis of women's status contained in the Declaration of Sentiments. Because Stanton, like so many of the woman's rights pioneers, was involved in the abolitionist cause, it was natural that she would draw a parallel between the subordinate status of women and that of slaves, as Sarah and Angelina Grimké had done a decade earlier. Because of her ties to the political abolitionists, who emphasized the primacy of political solutions, Stanton insisted that enfranchisement was a necessary first step in women's emancipation.

Stanton did not confine her analysis, however, to the realm of voting rights. In a view shared with other prominent woman's rights advocates, including Stone, Mott, and Anthony, she identified the root of women's oppression as the prevailing concept of separate spheres for men and women. According to this concept, men rightfully held sway in the public sphere, while women were to confine their concerns and influence to the domestic sphere. Stanton attacked the sphere concept for its constraining influence on the development of women's full potential as human beings. She argued that societal adherence to separate spheres had led to women's dependent position in the marriage relation: deprived of an education and legally unable to control their wages or property, women were unable to be full partners in marriage. Even worse, as far as Stanton was concerned, unfair divorce laws held women in virtual bondage in marriage, regardless of the nature of the individual marriage relationship. Eventually, the issues of marriage and divorce would become paramount in Stanton's ideology and would provide both motivation and ammunition for her arguments in support of woman suffrage, coeducation, married women's property rights, divorce reforms, and employment opportunities for women.

Although Stanton was the most outspoken and articulate theoretician of the infant woman's rights movement, her family responsibilities circumscribed her participation during the 1850s, confining her, for the most part, to the written word. The activities necessary to keep the movement alive were carried out by the more visible national leaders such as Anthony, Mott, and Stone. Their participation in other reform movements had given these women the skills and confidence necessary to mount an independent reform movement on their own behalf. Together they and their counterparts in the states formed an essential network, a woman's rights sisterhood, which organized meetings, spoke to numerous gatherings, raised money, and recruited new women to the cause.

The role of these early leaders is illustrated by Anthony's petition to the New York state legislature in 1854. The petition called for the granting to women of control of their earnings, guardianship of children in the event of a divorce, and the right to vote. In its support, Anthony organized a drive that collected 6,000 signatures, and Stanton, in one of her rare public appearances during the decade, addressed the legislature. When the legislators failed to act favorably on the petition, Anthony set out on a one-woman tour of the state to gather more signatures. In 1855, when the petition was again submitted, the legislators responded even less favorably, treating the whole enterprise as a joke. The effort had not been a total loss, however: the woman's rights movement had made significant gains in new recruits, more publicity, and the emergence of its organizational genius— Anthony. Indeed, the close working relationship and friendship of Anthony, the tactician, and Stanton, the theorist, combined the two elements that were so critical to the pre–Civil War movement.

In spite of this activity, woman's rights in the 1850s did not become a large, effective, grassroots movement. This was due, in part, to internal obstacles, the most significant of which was the absence of a national organization to provide consistent leadership. Woman's rights advocates had deliberately eschewed formal structure in favor of an ever-changing executive committee that was incapable of long-range planning and coordination. Of the two best-known pioneers of the movement, furthermore, Stanton was tied to her home by an ever-increasing family, and Mott, although elected permanent president of the national convention in 1854, refused the mantle of leadership. The lack of specific remedies for the injustices enumerated by woman's rights advocates also acted as a hindrance. The two most common calls for action—suffrage and married women's property rights—had not yet attracted wide acceptance among American women and were therefore not sufficient for a grassroots movement.

The external obstacles were also important, however, because they contributed to the internal difficulties. The outstanding obstacle was the impact of developments in the antislavery movement during the 1850s. As abolition became an increasingly volatile topic during the decade, many woman's rights activists, who had prior allegiance to the antislavery cause, devoted most of their time and energy to abolitionism. The woman's rights movement ended its first stage with the last national convention in 1861. The outbreak of the Civil War disrupted the momentum of the movement; when the war was over, and activities resumed, the movement had been altered significantly. The unity of the prewar era became a victim of Reconstruction politics, and the sweeping vision of Stanton was abandoned by many woman's rights advocates in favor of a narrower focus on woman suffrage.

The early phase of the movement did, however, provide the essential groundwork for the future. The ideology, the recruits, and the early leaders would play important roles in the woman suffrage movement. The public had become aware of the issue of woman's rights, and the novelty of public women had been at least partially overcome. Finally, the woman's rights pioneers left a heritage of activism and feminism that inspired later generations of women in their quest for equal rights.

References. Kathleen L. Barry, *Susan B. Anthony—A Biography: A Singular Feminist* (New York, 1988); Ellen DuBois, *Feminism and Suffrage: The Emergence of an Independent Women's Movement in America, 1848–1869* (Ithaca, N.Y., 1978); Eleanor Flexnor, *Century of Struggle: The Woman's Rights Movement in the United States* (Cambridge, Mass., 1959); Elisabeth Griffith, *In Her Own Right: The Life of Elizabeth Cady Stanton* (New York, 1984).

FRANCES S. HENSLEY

WOMEN AND ECONOMICS is a bible of the early feminist movement written by American author Charlotte Perkins Gilman and published in 1898. The book was translated into at least six languages, including German and Japanese, and went through more than half a dozen printings. The *Nation* regarded *Women and Economics* as "the most significant utterance on the subject [of women] since Mill's *Subjection of Women*" (1869). Gilman won instant notoriety with the book and was hailed as the "most original and challenging mind which the [women's] movement produced" by Carrie Chapman Catt, the suffragist organizer. Although Gilman went on to publish several other books, none were more successful than *Women and Economics*; such works as *The Home: Its Work and Influence* (1903), *Human Work* (1904), and *The Man-Made World or Our Andro-*

centric Culture (1911) seem merely to expand on ideas already explored in *Women and Economics*.

Gilman's purpose in writing *Women and Economics* is suggested by the book's subtitle, *A Study of the Economic Relation between Men and Women as a Factor in Social Evolution*. Gilman, a true daughter of the nineteenth century and of Charles Darwin's ideas, believed in the inevitability of such evolution; as she writes in *Women and Economics*, "The laws of social evolution do not wait for our recognition or acceptance: they go straight on" (ch. 8). However, she saw in the economic relation between men and women (a relation that she termed "sexuo-economic") a source of evil and a hindrance to the "calm, slow, friendly forces of evolution" (ch. 15). It was this relation that she attacked in *Women and Economics* and that she sought to change through her life and her work.

Unlike the turn-of-the-century suffragists, Gilman did not see attainment of the right to vote as the key to women's emancipation. She believed that what women needed was to be freed from a false economic position in which there was no relation maintained between what they produced and what they consumed. Gilman raised the question of how women were to achieve full equality in a modern industrial society, and, in attempting to answer it, she ultimately envisioned a radical reordering of the economic structure of society.

Her vision was shaped by some of the main intellectual currents of the nineteenth century, including utilitarianism, socialism, Darwinism, and the Victorian gospel of progress. More immediate influences were Edward Bellamy's utopian novel *Looking Backward* (1888) and Lester Ward's article "Our Better Halves" (1898). Bellamy's work encouraged her belief in socialism, a belief that remained strong throughout her life. *Women and Economics* repeatedly asserts the importance of the group over the individual and notes that excessive individualism, promoted and maintained by sexuoeconomic relations, leads to greed, which, in turn, hurts society. Ward's article posited the biological supremacy of the female sex and suggested a gynecocentric theory of human development that saw the elevation of woman as essential to the further evolution of humankind. It is this latter premise that Gilman developed throughout *Women and Economics*.

Gilman argued that as long as women remain economically dependent on men, women's economic status will be tied to their sex relation; that is, their relation to men will continue to be defined by the one "commodity" that women own outright—their sex. Echoing Mary Wollstonecraft in her work *A Vindication of the Rights of Woman** (1792), Gilman noted that women's education taught them solely how to snare husbands. The mercenary marriage was seen as a natural consequence of women's economic dependence, and society's growth was ultimately retarded by the continuing dependence of half of its members. Gilman envisioned a new marriage based on companionship rather than profit. However, before such marriages could occur, women had to be freed from the confining strictures of their prescribed roles inside the home.

Gilman attacked Victorian matriolatry and the traditional ideas of the sanctity of motherhood, home, and family. Her idea was not to eliminate these institutions but to make them more efficient. *Women and Economics* anticipates the professionalization of domestic work, which would free women to find work of their own choice outside the home. Day-care centers are explored as a practical alternative to an enforced and prolonged maternity that isolates both mother and child within the individual home to their mutual disadvantage. While Gilman recognized society's attachment to traditional views of motherhood, home, and family, views steeped in sentiment, she greatly overestimated society's willingness to change these institutions once their obvious "inefficiencies" had been pointed out.

Finally, *Women and Economics* was most successful in capturing and exploring a phenomenon already well under way at the beginning of the twentieth century—the growing economic independence of women. Gilman firmly wedded this phenomenon to the concept of social evolution, and, decrying the "moral miscegenation" of the "diverse souls" of men and women, which was caused by their still unequal economic relation, she defined progress in terms of women's economic freedom and continuing entrance into society's workplace.

References. Carl N. Degler, "Charlotte Perkins Gilman on the Theory and Practice of Feminism," in Jean E. Friedman and William G. Slade (eds.), *Our American Sisters: Women in American Life and Thought* (Boston, 1973), 197–218; Mary A. Hill, *Charlotte Perkins Gilman: The Making of a Radical Feminist, 1860–1896* (Philadelphia, 1980); Gary Scharnhorst, *Charlotte Perkins Gilman: A Bibliography* (Metuchen, N.J., 1975).

VICTORIA C. DUCKWORTH

WOMEN'S COLLEGES are higher educational institutions for women, first founded during the nineteenth century and designed to provide women with a four-year course of study, usually leading to the bachelor's degree. According to data compiled by the Women's College Coalition in 1987, there are 98 women's colleges in the United States, including 30 Roman Catholic institutions. Women's colleges constitute approximately 4 percent of all U.S. higher educational institutions and currently educate about 2 percent of the total number of women undergraduates in the United States. Unlike coeducational institutions, the leadership of women's colleges is predominantly female: in 1980, 67 percent of all women's college presidents were women. Geographically, women's colleges are heavily concentrated in the East, with the Mid-Atlantic states accounting for 39 percent, New England 32 percent, the Midwest 14 percent, the South 12 percent, and the West 3 percent.

While recent trends show an 8 percent annual increase in applications to women's colleges, both the number of women's institutions and current enrollments represent a sharp decline since 1960, when 298 women's colleges existed, and approximately 9 percent of all women students attended single-sex colleges. This decline is attributable, in part, to the closing of some women's colleges, but more importantly, it reflects a larger pattern of growth in number and size of coeducational institutions since World War II. All but two traditionally all-male colleges (Morehouse and Hampden-Sydney) have become coeducational since the 1960s, and a number of women's colleges (including Vassar, Goucher, and, most recently, Wheaton) now admit men. Historically, the largest absolute number of women's college students was 106,000 in 1940, while the percentage of women enrolled in women's colleges has declined steadily since at least 1870, when it is estimated that 59 percent of all women students attended women's colleges. This last percentage had dropped to 30 percent by 1890 and continued to fall steadily during each decade of the twentieth century.

This pattern of decline, however, obfuscates the significance of women's colleges in the growth of American women's intellectual status over the past two centuries. Growing out of the female academies that began to flourish during the last quarter of the eighteenth century and the subsequent antebellum seminary movement, women's colleges represented an important new educational opportunity for nineteenth-century women and served, moreover, as a highly visible symbol of women's intellectual equality with men. Access to higher education was a central goal of the nineteenth-century women's movement, and men's exclusion of women from American colleges was incorporated by the Seneca Falls Convention in 1848 as a grievance in the *Declaration of Sentiments*, which observed: "He [man] has denied her [woman] the facilities for obtaining a thorough education, all colleges being closed against her."

By 1848, when the *Declaration of Sentiments* was framed, a number of female academies, seminaries, and colleges were, in fact, providing collegiate-level education to women, but their offerings often were not perceived to be as rigorous as those demanded by the leading men's colleges. A few coeducational colleges also had been founded, but women often were relegated to "ladies' courses" or other second-class programs. Oberlin, founded in 1833 as a coeducational preparatory and collegiate institution, had begun in 1837 to admit women to the regular degree program and had awarded the baccalaureate degree to a woman for the first time in 1841. A number of state universities began to admit women to some programs in the 1850s and 1860s. Still, it was not until the founding of degree-granting women's colleges modeled after the elite eastern men's colleges that the concept of women's intellectual equality and right to rigorous intellectual training was articulated as an institutional rationale. The early coeducational colleges and state universities, in most cases, admitted women in response to financial exigencies, and the institutional justification for educating women most often was to provide "helpmates" to the male ministers the colleges were training or to prepare some women to teach in the common schools. Women's intellectual ambitions and abilities rarely were discussed, and coeducational institutions often reduced or eliminated access for women to their programs when improved finances permitted. The women's colleges, on the other hand, represented women's education as a primary mission, and they served as a challenge to critics to justify the continued exclusion of women from the full privileges of higher education nationwide.

Arguments against the education of women beyond the secondary level held sway throughout the nineteenth century and, changing in form somewhat over the years, continued to condition beliefs about women's intellectual abilities well into the twentieth century. It was these denials of women's mental capacities that the nineteenth-century women's colleges (and some earlier academies) set out to disprove. Critics claimed that advanced education would "unfit" women for "the duties of their station," particularly their obligations as wives and mothers. It was argued that "man loves a learned scholar, but not a learned wife," that women's character would be "hardened" and "deformed" by a college education, and that the stress of intellectual activity not only would "unsex" women but actually would harm their reproductive organs and render them infertile. Women's intellectual capabilities were denied throughout the century by prominent educational spokesmen such as President Charles W. Eliot of Harvard University, who argued in 1873 that "women differ more from men than men differ from each other" and that "there is a fundamental pervading difference between all men and all women which extends to their minds quite as much as to their bodies" (Address to the Social Science Convention, Boston, May 14, 1873). Eliot and others argued that women therefore should be educated differently than men, and the theories and prescriptions for such distinctive educations ran the gamut from minor curricular alterations, such as the substitution of French for Greek, to elaborate regimens such as those proposed by Dr. Edward H. Clarke in 1873, which supposed women unable to accomplish mental tasks during certain phases of the menstrual cycle (and only moderately able to function at other times).

In spite of such objections, women's colleges increasingly began to upgrade their curricula to conform to the requirements of comparable men's colleges. Elmira College, founded in 1855, compared favorably in both its admissions standards and course requirements to neighboring men's colleges except for the level of Latin required for admission and the exclusion of Greek grammar as a prerequisite. Vassar College (1865) required both Greek and Latin on a par with the elite men's colleges for admission to its classical program, but in deference to the poor preparation of many girls it also provided a scientific course that did not require Greek or advanced

Latin. Smith College (1875) generally is credited with being the first women's college with both admission requirements and a course of study identical to those of the best men's colleges. Smith modeled its four-year program (as did Wellesley, which also opened in 1875) after the Amherst and Harvard curricula. Smith's admissions requirements were identical to those at Harvard, and Wellesley (which initially did not require Greek) matched the Harvard admissions requirements in 1881. These women's colleges insisted that women could meet the academic demands required of men, and the successes of their early generations of students provided substantial evidence that critics of women's higher education were wrong in their predictions.

The women's colleges continued to be attacked, however, as America moved into the twentieth century and as the number of women college students increased. Charges of "race suicide" were levied against women college graduates who had shown themselves less likely to marry than American women in general. (That the male graduates of Harvard and Yale also married at a lower rate than men in the general population during the late nineteenth and early twentieth centuries was deemed less alarming.) Attacks on women's colleges were particularly harsh, in part, because of the colleges' visibility as symbols of women's educational attainments and also because their alumnae represented a certain educational and social elite. The social activism of many women's college students and faculty was condemned by conservative critics, as was the pacifism that grew on women's college campuses prior to America's involvement in World War I. During the 1920s and 1930s, women's colleges faced a new assault as communities of women were charged with being "unnatural" or "sexually deviant" by Freudian critics, and public fears and prejudice against lesbianism found a convenient and symbolically powerful target in the women's colleges—a dynamic that has continued to the present. In defending their institutions against such attacks, therefore, women's college supporters historically have served as the defenders of women's education in general, and the importance of women's colleges as a social institution in American life has been much greater than the number of graduates would suggest. As the number of women's colleges has decreased, moreover, women have lost access to leadership positions as presidents, deans, and tenured faculty; women students, in turn, have lost highly distinguished role models.

Since the early 1970s, women's colleges have played a complex role in the contemporary women's movement. Criticized by many for lagging behind many coeducational institutions in adopting women's studies courses and programs, the women's colleges have responded to newly articulated feminist goals in diverse ways, reflecting differences in their institutional histories, religious affiliations, and economic needs. A number of women's colleges (most recently, Mount Holyoke and Spelman) have renewed their commitment to feminist goals by appointing women to the presidency after decades of male leadership. The elite eastern women's colleges, which provided the first generations of college-trained women with new opportunities for advanced study and professional employment, have been in the forefront of curricular and pedagogical innovation since the 1970s as they have reexamined their programs and practices in the light of feminist theory and goals. Other women's colleges across the country have reformulated their traditional commitment to women's education by promoting both women's studies on campus and an array of professional internship and training programs for women in the larger community. In spite of their differing perspectives, most feminist observers and educational scholars agree that it is important to preserve these women's institutions and that women's colleges continue to serve as a symbol of women's intellectual worth.

References. Sally Schwager, "Educating Women in America," *Signs* 12 (1987); Barbara Miller Solomon, *In the Company of Educated Women* (New Haven, Conn., 1985); Thomas Woody, *A History of Women's Education in the United States*, 2 vols. (New York, 1929).

SALLY SCHWAGER

WOMEN'S WORK is a major focus of concern and study among feminists. By the 1980s well over two-fifths of the labor force were female, more than two-thirds of all women 18 to 64 were employed, and, despite increased representation of women in the labor force and in some male-dominated jobs, over half of all men and women were employed in jobs where at least 80 percent of the workers are of the same sex. Further, it has been predicted that women will continue to work in largely low-paying, sex-segregated jobs in the future. Also, despite important changes, for women of color* occupational race segregation persists.

One consequence of interdisciplinary feminist scholarship has been the expansion of the term "women's work" to include all work women do: domestic labor, child care, and sexual services in the home, as well as wage work in the labor market. Sociology has made important contributions to this endeavor, and both major perspectives in sociology—mainstream and critical—have been significantly affected by feminist scholarship on women's work.

Mainstream sociology traditionally studied women only within the family until the early 1970s, when the focus shifted to include women in the paid labor force. Then, from the study of those factors that affected the individual woman (e.g., education, occupational training, sex-role attitudes, etc.) attention moved to the institutional and structural forces in the economic sector that affected women's occupational position, especially the highly sex-segregated nature of the labor market itself.

Despite serious problems in their theoretical categories and conceptualizations (e.g., although realizing its importance, sociologists were unable to incorporate women's unwaged domestic labor into their analyses of wage work) the mainstream schools contributed two essential features to the study of women and work: first, they helped to demystify and challenge many erroneous assumptions about women in paid employment and in the home, and, second, they provided a rich and varied base of empirical data on women in the contemporary labor market.

The best known of the critical or radical perspectives in sociology is the Marxist. Although its traditional focus on labor market activities excludes the relationship between home and work, Marxist theory has been important in helping shape an understanding of the complexity of the economy and, within it, women's lives and work. Marxist study of monopoly capitalism provided a basis for understanding (1) the development of markets that create new types of low-paying, low-status jobs, (2) the processes by which more skilled jobs are broken down into less desirable, more segmented parts and thereby "deskilled," and (3) the processes by which a sex-segregated or sex-segmented labor market develops. These insights help explain the increasing inclusion of women into the labor force in precisely these low-status, low-waged, often deskilled and sex-segregated jobs in an increasingly service-oriented society. The 1990s made us acutely aware of the globalization of labor and its impact on women's work in newer and more difficult ways—including in the service sector.

As Marxist scholars developed the implications of monopoly capitalism for the jobs people held, feminist scholars in the critical tradition began arguing for the essential connection between women's domestic and market labor. Marxist feminists argued that the capitalist mode of production* must be understood as a dual system of production that includes domestic unwaged labor as well as wage labor. The unpaid work women do in the home is basic to the reproduction of wage workers (the maintenance and continuation of the labor force) and the production of profits in the labor market. Without it, profits are not possible.

Radical feminists, anticapitalist but not Marxist, argued that the way to end economic class exploitation was to eliminate the primary class exploitation—the domination of women by men, or patriarchy*—on which capitalism rested (in contradistinction to the Marxist feminist position that the primary class exploitation is based on capitalist control over the means of production). Motherhood and housewifery were considered the quintessential patriarchal institutions on which all else rested, including wage labor–capitalist relations. Thus, radical feminism* argued for directing women's struggles explicitly against male domination, not class society.

The third group of critical feminists, socialist feminists, took what they considered best from the other traditions, reformulating certain questions and raising new ones to try to bring the analysis of women in late twentieth-century patriarchal capitalism to a new level.

Like Marxist feminists, socialist feminists assume that class relations, in particular capitalism and its construction of women's position in the home, are major causes of the problems faced by women in the labor market today. Thus, because women's domestic labor is unwaged and assumed to be "taken care of" by the men's paid labor in the market, when women enter the labor market, they are generally paid as "secondary" workers at wages far lower than men's. (Earnings of fully employed women average about 60 percent of those of fully employed men.) This is true for single women and even more tragically for women heads of households.

Like radical feminists, socialist feminists believe that an analysis of women's problems requires an understanding of the complex effects of the social relations of patriarchy. Thus, socialist feminists link radical feminism with Marxism. They argue that capitalist and patriarchal relations operate in both the home and the market, on both material (economic) and ideological (cultural) levels. Only by seeing this dynamic and dialectic system of patriarchal and capitalist relations is it possible to understand women's poor position in the labor market today.

Socialist feminists contribute four key points to the analysis of women's work. (1) Not only is women's home activity economically useful and essential to capitalism, it is also economically beneficial to men; for example, men, relieved of most of the unwaged labor in the home, are available for the more stable, higher-waged, better protected male-dominated jobs in the market. (2) All work women do is the material base of their oppression in society—in the market, the home, and the community. This work includes such tasks as child care,* cooking, cleaning, shopping, sewing, ego building, sexual servicing, typing, nursing, and so on—both for wages and as unwaged labor in the home. (3) Patriarchal relations operate in the home, and they are a major feature of the capitalist labor market as well. This helps explain why women are exploited in the market and why they are forced into seeking the home as their primary responsibility even when they are wage earners themselves. (4) Not only the social class system but the entire sexual division of labor, both between and within the home and the market, must be eliminated or transformed for the exploitation of women to cease. It is both cause and effect of the social relations of patriarchy and of capitalism in contemporary society.

Many socialist feminists have argued that socialist feminist theory must be transformed by the insights gained from women of color. Perhaps one of the major contributions to the study of women and work was made in the 1990s by black feminist scholars who argued for an explication of the complexly interrelated "gender/race/class dynamic" and how it impacted on the work of all people: men and women; employed and unemployed; rich and poor; black, white, Latino, Asian. This approach has led to a better understanding of broader material and historical forces on women's labor as well as the tensions and alliances between more and less privileged women as well as between men and women—both inside and outside the labor force. The study of women and work is enhanced by each new challenge.

References. Theresa Amott and Julie Matthaei, *Race, Gender and Work: A Multicultural Economic History of Women in the United States* (Boston, 1991); Rose Brewer, "Theorizing Race, Class, and Gender: The New Scholarship of Black Feminist Intellectuals and Black Women's Labor," in S. M. James and A.P.A. Busia (eds.), *Theorizing Black Feminism* (New York: 1993); Barbara Reskin and Patricia Roos, *Job Queues, Gender Queues: Explaining Women's Inroads into Male Occupations* (Philadelphia, 1990); Natalie J. Sokoloff, *Between Money and Love: The Dialectics of Women's Home and Market Work* (New York, 1980); Natalie J. Sokoloff, *Black Women and White Women in the Professions: Occupational Segregation by Race and Gender, 1960–1980* (New York, 1992).

NATALIE J. SOKOLOFF

WORKER MILITANCY. For most ordinary women, the decision to participate in collective protest revolves around a complex set of ideas and images that delineates the boundaries of what a woman should be. Whether banding together with neighbors and kin to protest the rising cost of food or joining with fellow workers to resist wage cuts and line speedups, female militants accentuate the profound connections between the kinds of gender expectations and self-images endorsed by a particular community and radical forms of protest. Informed by race, ethnicity, and class, notions about what women do shape female militancy and provide both motive force and direction to female acts of resistance. Consequently, the history of female militancy calls into question not only the reliability of traditional narratives that have viewed women as predominantly passive members of the working class but also "notions of fixity" that have represented as self-evident and natural categories of gender and sexual hierarchies.

In no way was this more evident than in the militant conflicts that characterized the industrial workforce in nineteenth-century New England. As the first mass recruits to the new industrial order, Yankee women were challenged in the factories of Lowell, Lawrence, Dover, Fall River, Pawtucket, and elsewhere to make their way not only as members of a new and uncertain labor force but as women members. The interconnections of sex and power within the mills were frequently evoked as "turnouts" brought to the surface the tensions between male management and female operatives. Attacking striking women as "amazons," "saucy girls," and "hoydenish" women, mill managers promoted a rhetoric of gender deviance that encoded female protest as unnatural, unfeminine, and, in general, beyond the bounds of respectable womanhood.

Reinforced by the sexual division of labor, cultural stereotypes about men and women simultaneously provided employers with the means to achieve a sexually segregated labor force. Sex labeling—the assigning of characteristics of gender—worked not only to assert control over both wages (by consigning women to low-paying "light" jobs based on real or imagined physical differences from men) and the labor force (by using female employment as a possible threat to male job security) but to promote separate male and female work cultures that further accentuated sexual differences in leisure-time and after-hours activities.

Nevertheless, while gender ideology militated against female militancy and collective action (especially among homeworkers, who tended to be cut off from traditions of protest and isolated from their peers), situational factors as well as ethnic, racial, and regional influences frequently contributed to self-perceptions that undermined the dominant discourse. Less likely than men to participate in unions and establish lasting organizations, laboring women were nevertheless key participants in the process by which the working classes came to assess power relations and organize in opposition to them. Furthermore, once engaged in collective action, laboring women were frequently more militant than men, especially in textile, garment, and mining communities where strikes tended to be an affair of the "tribe." Situated in a position to experience the interpenetration of the marketplace and the home place, laboring women in these communities were less apt than male workers to understand their lives as divided into separate spheres of a public workplace and a private home place. This was especially the case in strikes involving large numbers of immigrant women such as in Lawrence, Massachusetts, in 1912; the Lower East Side of New York City in 1909; or Tampa, Florida, in the late nineteenth and early twentieth centuries. Here issues of the shop floor merged with the home and the community as women fought for what is now described as "quality of life" issues such as health care, clean water, decent housing, and a safer environment.

Rigid divisions of labor and strong traditions of mutuality and reciprocity also combined to ignite disparate members of the community, forging a solidarity that frequently cut across categories of ownership. Furthermore, in communities where people are mobilized as neighbors and kin rather than as individual workers, non–wage-earning women proved equally committed to collective struggle. Joining strikers as "Breadgivers," that is, as negotiators of familial welfare and sustainers of life, unpaid housewives provided essential support, organizing soup kitchens, distributing information, maintaining strike discipline in both the household and the neighborhood, and caring for the children of striking workers.

For women wage earners in general, family relationships were especially critical in overcoming obstacles to labor activism. Young, unmarried women living with parents, for example, were less likely to engage in collective struggles than self-supporting women or wives living with husbands. At times, however, the working environment provided opportunities to overcome barriers to militancy. Boardinghouses, workstations, lunchrooms, and after-hours spots provided an autonomous space where young women could come together, not necessarily as wives and daughters but rather as fellow workers with common needs and mutual concerns.

For the most part, however, analyses of female activists that have explored household economy, marital status, and family type underscore the importance of familial relationships for female participation in labor activism. Two factors play especially critical roles: the degree to which women supported themselves and others, as opposed to depending on others, especially fathers and brothers; and the nature and length of a woman's participation in the labor force. Consequently, female wage earners who provided for dependents along with self-supporting women and wives living with husbands were more likely than young, unmarried women to participate in labor activism. This group also provided much of the leadership in labor conflicts, especially in textile manufacturing, shoe production, and tobacco factories, where strong traditions of female wage labor and associational lives encouraged solidarity and enabled women to assume activist roles in union drives and organizational activities.

Understanding female participation in worker militancy, therefore, means exploring topics once considered peripheral to labor history, including not only the family and household structure but also the inner world of female friendships, sexuality, and both gender formation and identity. More important, perhaps, the exploration of female militancy has posed new questions about the relationship between the construction of gender and the formation of power. Seldom peripheral to class politics, gender ideology was often the central terrain upon which power was both exercised and contested.

References. Ardis Cameron, *Radicals of the Worst Sort: Laboring Women in Lawrence, Massachusetts, 1860–1912* (Urbana, Ill., 1993); Nancy Hewitt, " 'The Voice of Virile Labor': Labor Militancy, Community Solidarity, and Gender Identity among Tampa's Latin Workers, 1880–1921," in Ava Baron (ed.), *Work Engendered: Toward a New History of American Labor* (Ithaca, N.Y., 1991); Alice Kessler-Harris, *Out to Work: A History of Wage-Earning Women in the United States* (New York, 1982); Ruth Milkman (ed.), *Women, Work, and Protest: A Century of Women's Labor History* (Urbana, Ill., 1985); Vicki Ruiz, *Cannery Women, Cannery Lives: Mexican Women, Unionization, and the California Food Processing Industry* (Albuquerque, c. 1987); Carole Turbin, *Working Women of Collar City: Gender, Class, and Community in Troy, New York, 1864–86* (Urbana, Ill., c. 1992).

ARDIS CAMERON

WORKINGWOMEN are women who labor in the home, the community, and the workplace. They contribute to the social reproduction of themselves and their families, but they may also do volunteer work and help build communities. Increasingly, they work for wages in formal labor markets nationally and internationally.

Women work, the world over. This is a feature of women's gender heritage that transcends national, ethnic, and ideological lines. However, not all women globally are involved in the same work, nor is their work valued equally. They share in common work in the domestic sphere,* which includes housework,* child care,* and socialization. In some parts of the world there is still a fairly close connection between work within the home and the economics of production. For example, black South African women in rural bantustans are a necessary adjunct to the system of labor migration that involves men in industrial work far removed from the area. The women toil and plant and carve out a meager living for their families. Under these circumstances, men are paid a single man's wage, even though impoverished families remain behind and in need of their economic contributions. Black South African women must support a community of old people and children largely through their own labor.

In the case of the United States, the growing number of women working for pay is one of the significant transformations in the American labor force. In addition, work within the home and voluntarism are essential elements in profiling American workingwomen. In the past 20 years, the transformation of women's work in these two spheres is noteworthy largely because of the growing number of women working for wages. Women's wage labor has put stress on the volunteer system and the child care system because both depend on unpaid female labor.

The most frequent adjustment to these changes is a greater workload for women. In fact, women in the United States are increasingly dual workers. They work a double day: first for pay, then as workers for the social reproduction of themselves and their families. This means that child care, cooking, cleaning, the emotional and physical support of husbands, children, and other kin, as well as wage work, are part of their workday. They share this situation in common with many women around the world, as other American women now join the large number of black American women who have always worked inside and outside the home.

Given women's importance as domestic laborers, analyzing reproduction as well as production is part of any satisfactory explanation of workingwomen. Furthermore, given the idea that domestic labor is work, some feminists have advocated wages for housework. Yet housework is only one aspect of women's labor within the home. Nurturing, birth, and socialization are also part of the workday. The major point, however, is that workingwomen span both unpaid and paid labor domains.

A second critical area to consider in discussing workingwomen is women as community builders and as volunteers. Women work within their communities. They work with children, old people, and the differently abled. They work in hospitals, churches, halfway houses, and associations. Women type, canvass, run offices, and help elect politicians. They work in all these spheres but not for pay. Increasingly, scholars are looking at volunteer work as essential to the maintenance and social reproduction of the community. Although this work is not given value in the traditional calculus of monetary reward as the measure of worth, women and their unpaid labor are the significant dimension in much of the community building of this country. As more women are bound to the double duty of paid labor and unpaid household labor, the issue of collective community responsibility must be addressed.

A third consideration is that the traditional conceptualization of workingwomen refers to those who work for pay. The phenomenon of large numbers of American women in the labor force has been called a revolution by some scholars. Even so, workingwomen in the United States are plagued by sex-segregated occupations, low pay, limited job mobility, and flat wage-earnings profile curves. Nonetheless, women continue to enter the labor force in growing numbers, and, increasingly, there is some occupational diversity.

Unfortunately, the media image of today's workingwoman is misleading. She is portrayed invariably as a young, successful, white, female professional. This is a woman not plagued by double duty, child care woes, sex discrimination,* or harassment on the job, or so goes the media hype. In reality, the picture is quite different. American workingwomen are likely to have children, be in their 30s, and not work in a high-paying profession, according to Mary Frank Fox and Sharlene Hesse-Biber (97). They go on to say that "she works, for example, in the typing pool of a large corporation, on the assembly line of a manufacturing firm, or she is a file clerk in an insurance company." She is also likely to provide a service: sell clothes, fix hair, prepare food. In many instances she is likely to be a part-time worker, and often this is not by choice. Part-time work means even lower pay, fewer chances for occupational mobility, and no job benefits. Women accept part-time work most often because there is no affordable child care or no full-time work for them. This is especially true for black women (Malveaux, 116).

If the profile of American workingwomen is translated statistically, it means that by the 1980s more than half of all women over the age of 16 were working outside the home. Elliot Currie and Jerome H. Skolnick point out that "since the 1950s, the labor force participation of married women with no children under 18 has risen by a little more than half, that of women with children aged 6 to 17 has more than doubled, and that of women with children under 6 nearly quadrupled. By 1982, 55 percent of children under 18 had mothers in the labor force, as did fully 46 percent of preschool age children, up from 12 percent in 1950" (based on statistics published by the U.S. Department of Labor, Women's Bureau, 1982, 1–2). Since 1982 the figures are even more dramatic for women with young children. In March 1987, 52 percent of mothers with children 1 year old and younger were in the labor force, and about 60 percent of mothers whose youngest child was between the age of 1 and 6 were in the labor force.

Workingwomen's labor force participation rates vary to some extent by race and ethnicity. Somewhat higher proportions of black women and somewhat lower proportions of Hispanic women are in the labor force than are white women. Black, Filipino, and Chinese women work more than other women of color (Almquist). Black, married women are most likely to be juggling the triple load of housework, volunteerism, and formal wage work. Yet even with high levels of labor force participation, black women cluster at the lower occupational levels. Their salaries lag behind those of white men, black men, and white workingwomen.

A final consideration regarding workingwomen is public policy. Policy changes regarding women, family, and work have been slow to keep pace with the shifting profile of American workingwomen. Their child care needs, health care concerns, and work/family responsibilities have not been clearly addressed in public policy initiatives. Moreover, American private employers have been slow to respond to workingwomen's issues. There is too little quality child care, too little flexible work time, and too little shared responsibility. Since most women are working because of economic need, policies that confront and incorporate women's dual role should be on the agenda. Of the industrial nations, the United States has been slowest in creating national policy initiatives along these lines: maternity leaves, flextime, shared child care, full employment. These issues will not disappear, given the large and growing number of workingwomen in this country.

In sum, women are workers. They work within the home, within the community, and within the labor market. Given this, public policymakers nationally and internationally will increasingly have to take into consideration the intersection of community, home, and wage labor in forging policies for workingwomen.

References. E. M. Almquist, *Minorities, Gender, and Work* (Lexington, Mass., 1979); Elliot Currie and Jerome H. Skolnick, *America's Problems* (Boston, 1984); Mary Frank Fox and Sharlene Hesse-Biber, *Women at Work* (Palo Alto, Calif., 1984); J. Malveaux, "Economics and You," *Essence* (November 1987).

ROSE M. BREWER

WORLD WAR I had a dramatic impact on American women, who participated widely in the war effort and took advantage of the wartime expansion of economic and political opportunity. However, these changes proved short-lived, and, in the long run, the war had only a minor effect on the lives of American women.

Women made significant contributions to the war effort. Even before Congress declared war in April 1917, several women's groups, such as the

Women's Section of the Navy League, advocated military preparedness. After U.S. intervention, women contributed to the war energetically. The National League of Women's Services and the Women's Committee of the Council of National Defense organized female volunteers all over the country to do necessary work such as knitting clothing and rolling bandages. Women enlisted in relief activities for servicemen, operating canteens and collecting and distributing food and clothing. They also played an important role in selling Liberty Bonds and war stamps, and, through the American Woman's Land Army, provided badly needed agricultural labor. For the first time, women entered the armed forces, not only as nurses but also as regular enlisted personnel. Over 12,000 women served in the navy, and 305 in the marines, freeing male clerical workers for military assignment. But after the war women were disenrolled, and the armed services once more became a male preserve.

Women eagerly took advantage of the new and better job opportunities available to them after business and government suffered wartime labor shortages. Those employed before the war were the primary beneficiaries, moving up into skilled jobs, but new workers also profited from expansion and a new flexibility in employment. White women workers gained access to high-paying, traditionally male jobs in hitherto inaccessible places such as machine shops, steel and chemical factories, airplane plants, and shipyards. Black women, especially those moving into northern cities at this time, also experienced better job opportunities, particularly in positions vacated by white women, such as clerical and government jobs, but they had little access to better-paying industrial jobs.

Discrimination against female workers remained the norm during the war years despite militancy among women workers, efforts on their behalf by women's organizations, and some governmental concern for the rights of female employees. The exigencies of a wartime economy did not abolish sex segregation, low and unequal wages, or hostility from male workers. After the war, women workers chose to stay in the workforce, but what they had gained was lost as men returned from war to claim their good jobs and high pay. In the 1920s, white women wage earners were concentrated in low-paying clerical, business, and service jobs, and black women were predominantly in domestic, laundry, and agricultural work.

War proved an important factor in women's struggle for the vote, facilitating passage of the suffrage amendment to the Constitution. When the war began, a revitalized women's movement was actively campaigning for suffrage, for which women had been struggling for more than 60 years. Suffragists took advantage of wartime to advance the cause of the vote. The National American Woman Suffrage Association, claiming almost 2 million members, conspicuously supported the prosecution of the war; its spokeswomen emphasized women's partnership and cooperation in the war effort, participating in war bond drives, stressing women's patriotism, and repudiating the militant tactics of the National Woman's Party (NWP), the other major suffrage organization. Concurrently, NWP leaders refused to subordinate the campaign for suffrage to the war effort. NWP picketers at the White House criticized President Woodrow Wilson, focusing attention and controversy on their activities. Exploiting Wilson's ideological justification for the war, suffragists stressed the contradictions between a "war for democracy" in Europe and the disfranchisement of women at home. In 1918 Wilson finally endorsed woman suffrage, noting women's "service and sacrifice" in the war effort and describing the vote for women as "vitally essential to the successful prosecution of the great war of humanity in which we are engaged."

A small, but vocal, group of women opposed the war. In 1915, prominent activists organized the Woman's Peace party (WPP) to denounce the war, promote mediation of the fighting in Europe, and, failing that, oppose U.S. intervention. Claiming that women have a special propensity for peace, the WPP linked the increase of feminine influence in public life through the vote with the end of wars and the extension of social justice. The involvement of many WPP women with reform and socialist movements and the continued opposition by some NWP members to the war after U.S. intervention led many people to associate suffragism and feminism with pacifism and radicalism.

Although the war was an important factor in American women's achievement of the franchise, it also stopped the momentum of a widespread reform movement in the United States, a movement in which women had played a vital role. Moreover, in the aftermath of war, reaction against reform as well as radicalism ushered in a new era and a new resistance to change for women.

JUDITH PAPACHRISTOU

WORLD WAR II. Nothing symbolized American women's experiences during World War II more than "Rosie the Riveter," the propaganda symbol for the women defense workers who put aside conventional work and family responsibilities in service to national priorities. A strong, patriotic woman comfortable with technology and able to negotiate her way in the previously male stronghold of heavy industrial work, "Rosie" signified the enormous importance of domestic production to the success of a nation engaged in modern war and the general priority accorded military activities over civilian needs.

In some ways, women's wartime experiences mirrored those symbolized by "Rosie." During the war years the American economy operated on a more nearly equal basis in regard to women than at any time before or since, primarily because the range of jobs open to women expanded dramatically. Many new categories opened up for women, especially in aircraft production, munitions, and shipbuilding, providing them with enormously improved opportunities to develop new skills in new areas, to receive much higher wages and greater benefits coverage than they had before the war, and to increase their power as workers through unionization. Because many women now worked in industrial and technical jobs previously open only to men, their success in these fields threatened to undermine many of the stereotypes that had been used to relegate women to a small number of low-paying job categories and, often, to justify their subordination outside the workplace. Moreover, women's access to jobs that paid well challenged the economic basis of men's power within the family and the society.

As a result of increased opportunities, the female labor force expanded in an unprecedented fashion, growing from 13 million workers in 1941 to 19 million in late 1943. Moreover, the wartime economy attracted especially large numbers of women who were married, had children, and were over age 35. These women found themselves working long hours on the job, coping with shortages and inconveniences occasioned by the war, and shouldering the major responsibility for child care and housework. Employers and public policymakers, however, concentrated on luring women into defense industries rather than on improving their status on the job or accommodating their work and family roles. They expected working-women to assume a disproportionate share of the burden of change so that men on the home front (especially husbands) and politics could function as "normally" as possible.

Despite the image of workplace integration promoted by "Rosie," historical evidence indicates that employers sought to maintain gender segregation as fully as possible through the spatial segregation of women and the designation of particular categories of manufacturing work, usually denoted with the titles "helper" or "assistant," for women. Moreover, the rapid increase in the numbers of women in clerical jobs during the war indicated the continuing vitality of long-term economic trends even in a defense-bloated economy. Once the war had ended, discrimination against women by employers, unions, and government ensured the return of "Rosie" to traditional "women's" work.

The meanings of the wartime experiences of American women were often contradictory. Some opinion makers sought to contain the threat implicit in women's new experiences through negative depictions of workingwomen as "unfeminine" and damaging to family life. Although present throughout the war years, such themes dramatically accelerated in 1944 and 1945, when the impending removal of many women from their jobs necessitated a justification. Building on wartime attempts to secure women's conformity to many conventional expectations regarding dress, domestic values, and sexual conduct, postwar propaganda emphasized that a satisfactory postwar readjustment required women's return to a deferential domesticity.

Despite the postwar reaction, some of the changes generated by the war years persisted and even accelerated in the ensuing decades. The entry of wives and mothers into paid employment has been an enduring attribute of postwar America, but it was not immediately accompanied by any radical shift in consciousness or in institutional arrangements to accommodate and advance these changes. Many of the married women employed during the war, however, did report that their experiences heightened their self-esteem and made them more assertive in their marriages, especially with regard to money matters. The trends accelerated by the war have served as a precondition for more recent changes in women's status and roles, including the rise of feminism, more positive and egalitarian views of women's abilities and their entitlements in a democratic society, greater equality under the law, and enhanced family power.

References. K. Anderson, *Wartime Women: Sex Roles, Family Relations, and the Status of Women during World War II* (Westport, Conn., 1981); S. Hartmann, *American Women in the 1940s: The Home Front and Beyond* (Boston, 1982).

KAREN ANDERSON

WORLD'S ANTI-SLAVERY CONVENTION OF 1840 was a gathering in London of leading abolitionists from throughout the Western world to chart the future course of antislavery. Among the American delegations were eight women from radical, Garrisonian bodies in Massachusetts and Philadelphia. Strong opposition from most of the male delegates met their proposed inclusion. Moderate abolitionists from both America and England argued that "English custom and usage" would be outraged by women's equal participation and that the convention had to focus its efforts on antislavery, to the exclusion of extraneous issues. Debate on the convention's first day centered on this controversy. With only a few men willing to champion their cause, the crucial vote went against the American women, and they were excluded from participation.

American and British women shared a sense of humiliation suffered at the hands of men and met over the next weeks to discuss their common grievances and hopes for the future. During this time, the American women delegates established strong and lasting friendships with their British sisters, which would prove of great importance as the drive for woman's rights progressed in the transatlantic community. Convention events also demonstrated to "delegate" Lucretia Mott and observer Elizabeth Cady Stanton that they could not rely on men to fight for women's equality, and they resolved to hold a Women's Rights Convention upon their return to America (held eight years later at Seneca Falls). The sense of cause and resolve, strengthened by the events of the convention, would lead to greater independence from men within the antislavery crusade and ultimately to a woman's rights movement* entirely distinct from the antislavery crusade.

KAREN I. HALBERSLEBEN

Y

YIN AND YANG are (along with the Five Phases) primary generating forces in traditional Chinese cosmology. They are mentioned in early classical texts (especially the *Book of Changes*) but find their fullest expression during the Han dynasty (206 B.C.–A.D. 220). Yin–yang and the Five Phase (or Five Element) theory exist within a system of correlative thinking and provide a model for interpreting change. Each of the Five Phases implies a color, a direction, an animal, and a time period and gives way to the next phase in a prescribed manner.

Yin and yang exist within this framework of correspondences. Yin is associated with the earth, the passive, the dark, and the feminine; yang is associated with the sun, the active, the light, and the masculine. Yin–yang theory distinguishes the two principles and, equally significant, asserts the necessity of the interaction between them. Thus, gender distinctions are built into the most fundamental cosmological categories. As yin and yang have their separate spheres, so do male and female. Yin and yang are complementary, with each necessary to the completion of the other. However, especially in the writings of later theorists, yang came to be seen as the dominant of the two forces. Hence, a cosmological theory that could be used to assert a complementary scheme of gender interactions was also used as a justification for male dominance.

Reference. Alison H. Black, "Gender and Cosmology in Chinese Correlative Thinking," in Caroline Bynum, Stevan Harrell, and Paula Richman (eds.), *Gender and Religion: On the Complexity of Symbols* (Boston, 1986).

ANN WALTNER

Z

ZHENOTDEL is the women's section or department (*zhenskii otdel*) of the Central Committee Secretariat of the Soviet Communist Party. Founded in 1919, its first and most prominent directors were Inessa Armand (1919–1920) and Alexandra Kollontai (1920–1922). The purpose of the Zhenotdel was to mobilize women in support of the Bolshevik regime and, secondarily, to involve women in their own emancipation.

From its central office in Moscow and through a network of local zhenotdels, the women's section, inter alia, campaigned against prostitution, attempted to liberate Muslim women from forced seclusion and subservience, established 18 women's journals, and organized construction of communal facilities in order to free women from nonproductive labor. Its principal technique for politicizing women was the use of delegates' assemblies composed of women factory workers and peasants. Delegates were chosen by their peers and exposed to lectures, literacy classes, and political discussions. Some of them became paid interns who then spent several months working in public agencies.

The problems of the women's section were legion. In Central Asia, numerous acts of violence against Muslim women who had forsaken the veil forced Zhenotdel organizers to moderate their efforts. Most Zhenotdel programs far outstripped its limited funds and staff. Unable to deliver on promises to its constituency—few day-care centers, for example, were actually built—the women's section gradually experienced a decline in authority. Politically, the leaders of Zhenotdel wielded little influence on party policies. More important, many male Bolsheviks were overtly hostile to the section, feeling that it smacked of female separatism and bourgeois feminism.

Despite its limitations, the Zhenotdel did manage to raise the consciousness of Russian women and to bring an increasing number of them into government and party organizations. Nonetheless, the section was abolished in 1930 during Joseph Stalin's reorganization of the Secretariat. Its demise brought an end to all specific efforts to emancipate women or increase their autonomy; women's issues were to be subsumed under the broader concerns of industrialization and collectivization.

References. Gail Lapidus, *Women in Soviet Society* (Berkeley, Calif., 1978); Richard Stites, *The Women's Liberation Movement in Russia: Feminism, Nihilism, and Bolshevism, 1860–1930* (Princeton, 1978).

REVA P. GREENBURG

Selected Bibliography

A limited number of bibliographic references are included in many of the articles in the encyclopedia. Listed below are additional works which may prove useful as a starting point for study.

Andersen, Margaret L. *Thinking about Women: Sociological Perspectives on Sex and Gender.* 3rd ed. New York: Macmillan, 1933.

Anderson, Jack. *Ballet and Modern Dance: A Concise History.* Princeton, N.J.: Princeton Book Co., 1986.

Baer, Judith A. *Women in American Law: The Struggle Toward Equality from the New Deal to the Present.* New York: Holmes and Meier, 1991.

Balsdon, J. P. V. D. *Roman Women: Their History and Habits.* Westport, Conn.: Greenwood Press, 1962.

Bergmann, Barbara R. *Economic Emergence of Women.* New York: Basic Books, 1986.

Blau, Francine D., and Marianne A. Ferber. *The Economics of Women, Men and Work.* 2d ed. New York: Prentice-Hall, 1992.

Bleier, Ruth, ed. *Feminist Approaches to Science.* New York: Pergamon, 1986.

Boles, Janet K., and Diane Long Hoeveler. *From the Goddess to the Glass Ceiling: A Dictionary of Feminism.* Lanham, Md.: Madison Books, 1996.

Boston Women's Health Book Collective. *The New Our Bodies, Ourselves: A Book by and for Women.* New York: Simon and Schuster, 1992.

Bowers, Jane, and Judith Tick, eds. *Women Making Music: The Western Art Tradition, 1150–1950.* Urbana: University of Illinois Press, 1986.

Boxer, Marilyn J., and Jean H. Quataert, eds. *Connecting Spheres: Women in the Western World, 1500 to the Present.* New York: Oxford University Press, 1987.

Bridenthal, Renate, Claudia Koonz, and Susan Stuard, eds. *Becoming Visible: Women in European History.* 2d ed. Boston: Houghton Mifflin, 1987.

Buhle, Mari Jo, and Paul Buhle, eds. *The Concise History of Woman Suffrage: Selections from the Classic Work of Stanton, Anthony, Gage, and Harper.* Urbana: University of Illinois Press, 1978.

Bullwinkle, Davis A. *Women of Northern, Western and Central Africa: A Bibliography, 1976–1985*. Westport, Conn.: Greenwood Press, 1989.

Byrne, Pamela R. and Suzanne R. Ontiveros, eds. *Women in the Third World: A Historical Bibliography* (Research Guides Series No. 15). Santa Barbara, Calif.: ABC-Clio, 1985.

Chung Sei-wha, ed. *Challenges for Women: Women's Studies in Korea*. Trans. Shin Chang-hyun et al. Seoul, Korea: Ewha Women's University Press, 1986.

Cohen, Aaron I. *International Encyclopedia of Women Composers*. New York: R. R. Bowker, 1981.

Daly, Mary, and Jane Caputi. *Webster's First Intergalactic Wichedary of the English Language*. San Francisco, Calif.: Harper & Row, 1987.

Daniel, Robert L. *American Women in the Twentieth Century: The Festival of Life*. San Diego, Calif.: Harcourt Brace Jovanovich, 1987.

Donovan, Josephine. *Feminist Theory: The Intellectual Traditions of American Feminism*. Expanded ed. New York: Ungar, 1992.

Dublin, Thomas, and Kathryn Sklar. *Women and Power in America*. Vols. 1 and 2. Englewood Cliffs, N.J.: Prentice-Hall, 1991.

Dubois, Ellen, and Vicki Ruiz, eds. *Unequal Sisters: A Multicultural Reader in U.S. Women's History*. New York: Routledge Press, 1994.

Dudley, Margot I., and Mary I. Edwards, eds. *The Cross-Cultural Study of Women*. New York: The Feminist Press, 1986.

Eisler, Riane. *The Chalice and the Blade: Our History and Our Future*. San Francisco, Calif.: Harper & Row, 1987.

Evans, Sara M. *Born for Liberty: A History of Women in America*. New York: Free Press, 1989.

Fausto-Sterling, Anne. *Myths of Gender: Biological Theories about Women and Men*. 2d ed. New York: Basic Books, 1992.

Fenton, Thomas P. and Mary J. Heffron. *Women in the Third World: A Directory of Resources*. Maryknoll, N.Y.: Orbis Books, 1987.

Fine, Elsa Honig. *Women and Art: A History of Women Painters and Sculptors from the Renaissance to the 20th Century*. Montclair, N.J.: Allanheld and Schram, 1978.

Flynn, Elizabeth A., and Patrocinio P. Schweichart, eds. *Gender and Reading: Essays on Readers, Texts and Contexts*. Baltimore, Md.: Johns Hopkins University Press, 1986.

Fox, Mary Frank, and Sharlene Hess-Biber. *Women at Work*. Palo Alto, Calif.: Mayfield Publishing Company, 1984.

Freeman, Jo, ed. *Women: A Feminist Perspective*. Mountain View, Calif.: Mayfield Publishing Company, 1995.

Gilbert, Sandra M., and Susan Gubar. *The Madwoman in the Attic*. New Haven, Conn.: Yale University Press, 1979.

———. *The Norton Anthology of Literature By Women: The Traditions in English*. 2d ed. New York: W. W. Norton & Company, 1966.

Gross, Rita M., and Nancy Auer Falk, eds. *Unspoken Worlds: Women's Religious Lives in Non-Western Cultures*. San Francisco, Calif.: Harper and Row, 1980.

Hahner, June E., ed. *Women in Latin American History*. Los Angeles: UCLA Latin American Center Publications, 1976.

Harding, Sandra, and Jean F. O'Barr, eds. *Sex and Scientific Inquiry*. Chicago: University of Chicago Press, 1987.

Harriman, Ann. *Women/Men/Management*. 2d ed. Westport, Conn.: Praeger, 1996.

Harris, Ann Sutherland, and Linda Nochlin. *Women Artists: 1559–1950*. New York: Alfred A. Knopf for the Los Angeles County Museum of Art, 1979.

Harrison, Cynthia A., ed. *Women in American History: A Bibliography*. 2 vols. Santa Barbara, Calif.: ABC-Clio Press, 1979.

Hellerstein, Erna O., Leslie P. Hume, and Karen M. Offen, eds. *Victorian Women*. Stanford, Calif.: Stanford University Press, 1981.

Hinding, Andrea, and Clarke A. Chambers. *Women's History Sources*. 2 vols. New York: Bowker, 1980.

Hoff, Joan. *Law, Gender and Injustice: A Legal History of U.S. Women*. New York: New York University Press, 1992.

Howell, Elizabeth, and Marjorie Bayer, eds. *Women and Mental Health*. New York: Basic Books, 1981.

Hrdy, Sarah B. *The Woman That Never Evolved*. Cambridge, Mass.: Harvard University Press, 1981.

Jagger, Alison, and Paula S. Rothenburg, eds. *Feminist Frameworks: Alternative Theoretical Accounts of the Relations between Men and Women*. New York: McGraw-Hill, 1993.

James, Edward T., Janet Wilson James, and Paul S. Boyer, eds. *Notable American Women: A Biographical Dictionary*, 3 vols. Cambridge, Mass.: Belknap Press, 1971.

Jones, Jacqueline. *Labor of Love, Labor of Sorrow: Black Women, Work, and Family, from Slavery to the Present*. New York: Basic Books, 1985.

Kerber, Linda K. *Women in the Republic: Intellect and Ideology in Revolutionary America*. Chapel Hill: University of North Carolina Press, 1980.

Kerber, Linda K., and Jane S. De Hart. *Women's America: Refocusing the Past*. 4th ed. New York: Oxford University Press, 1995.

Klein, Ethel. *Gender Politics*. Cambridge, Mass.: Harvard University Press, 1984.

Kraemer, Ross S. *Gender, Cult and Cosmology: Women's Religions among Pagans, Jews and Christians in the Graeco-Roman World*. New York: Oxford University Press.

———. *Maenads, Martyrs, Matrons, Monastics: A Sourcebook on Women's Religions in the Graeco-Roman World*. New York: Fortress Press, 1988.

Lablame, P. H., ed. *Beyond Their Sex: Learned Women of the European Past*. New York: New York University Press, 1980.

Lauter, Estella. *Women as Mythmakers: Poetry and Visual Art by Twentieth-Century Women*. Bloomington: University of Indiana Press, 1986.

Lefkowitz, Mary R., and Maureen B. Fant. *Women's Life in Greece and Rome: A Source Book in Translation*. Baltimore, Md.: Johns Hopkins Press, 1982.

Lerner, Gerda. *The Creation of Feminist Consciousness: From the Middle Ages to Eighteen-Seventy*. New York: Oxford University Press, 1993.

———. *The Creation of Patriarchy*. New York: Oxford University Press, 1986.

———. *Women and History*. 2 vols. New York: Oxford University Press, 1986–1993.

Loeb, Catherine R., Susan E. Searing, and Esther F. Steinman, with Meridith J.

Ross. *Women's Studies: A Core Bibliography*. Littleton, Colo.: Librarians Unlimited, 1979.

Mainieri, Lina. *American Women Writers, A Critical Reference Guide from Colonial Times to the Present*. 5 vols. New York: Ungar, 1972–1994.

Marting, Diane E., ed. *Women Writers of Spanish America: An Annotated Bio-Bibliographical Guide*. Westport, Conn.: Greenwood Press, 1987.

McDowell, Deborah E., ed. *"The Changing Same": Black Women's Literature, Criticism, and Theory*. Bloomington: Indiana University Press, 1995.

Meyer, Doris, and Margarita Fernandez Olmar, eds. *Contemporary Women Authors of Latin America*. 2 vols. Brooklyn: Brooklyn College Press, 1983.

Morgen, Sandra, ed. *Gender and Anthropology: Critical Reviews for Research and Teaching*. Washington, D.C.: American Anthropological Association, 1989.

Organization of American Historians. *Restoring Women to History: Teaching Packets for Integrating Women's History into Courses on Africa, Asia, Latin America, the Caribbean, and the Middle East*. Bloomington, Ind.: Organization of American Historians, 1988.

Ortner, Sherry B., and Harriet Whitehead. *Sexual Meanings: The Cultural Construction of Gender and Sexuality*. New York: Cambridge University Press, 1981.

Petteys, Chris. *Directory of Women Artists: An International Dictionary of Women Artists Born before 1900*. Boston: G. K. Hall, 1985.

Pomeroy, Sarah B. *Goddesses, Whores, Wives and Slaves: Women in Classical Antiquity*. New York: Schocken Books, 1975.

Powell, Gary. *Women and Men in Management*. 2d ed. Beverly Hills, Calif.: Sage, 1993.

Robertson, Priscilla. *An Experience of Women: Pattern and Change in Nineteenth-Century Europe*. Philadelphia: Temple University Press, 1982.

Ryan, Mary P. *Womanhood in America: From Colonial Times to the Present*. 3rd ed. New York: F. Watts, 1983.

Sapiro, Virginia. *Women in American Society*. Palo Alto, Calif.: Mayfield Publishing Company, 1994.

Sartori, Eva Martin, and Dorothy Wynne Zimmerman. *French Women Writers: A Bio-Bibliographical Source Book*. Westport, Conn.: Greenwood Press, 1991.

Searing, Susan E., with Rima D. Apple. *The History of Women and Science, Health, and Technology: A Bibliographic Guide to the Professions and the Disciplines* 2d ed. Madison: University of Wisconsin System Librarian, 1993.

Shephard, Bruce D., and Carroll A. Shephard. *The Complete Guide to Women's Health*. New York: Signet, 1985.

Showalter, Elaine. *A Literature of Their Own: British Women Novelists from Brontë to Lessing*. Princeton: Princeton University Press, 1977.

Sicherman, Barbara, and Carol Hurd Green, with Ilene Kantrov and Harriette Walker, eds. *Notable American Women: The Modern Period. A Biographical Dictionary*. Cambridge, Mass.: Belknap Press, 1980.

Sloane, Ethel. *Biology of Women*. 3rd ed. Albany, N.Y.: Delmar, 1993.

Smith, Bonnie G. *Changing Lives: Women in European History since 1700*. Lexington, Mass.: D.C. Heath, 1989.

Stichter, Sharon B., and Jane L. Parpart, eds. *Patriarchy and Class: African Women in the Home and the Workforce* (African Modernization and Development Series). Boulder, Colo.: Westview Press, 1988.

Stites, Richard. *The Women's Liberation Movement in Russia: Feminism, Nihilism, and Bolshevism, 1860–1930.* Princeton: Princeton University Press, 1978.

Stoner, K. Lynn. *Latinas of the Americas: A Source Book.* New York: Garland Press, 1989.

Stuard, Susan Mosher, ed. *Women in Medieval Society.* Philadelphia: University of Pennsylvania Press, 1976.

Tavris, Carol, ed. *Every Woman's Emotional Well-Being.* Garden City, N.Y.: Doubleday, 1986.

Vicinus, Martha, ed. *Suffer and Be Still.* Bloomington: University of Indiana Press, 1972.

Walker, Barbara G. *The Women's Encyclopedia of Myths and Secrets.* San Francisco, Calif.: Harper and Row, 1983.

Ware, Susan. *Modern American Women: A Documentary History.* New York: McGraw Hill, 1997.

Wei, Karen T. *Women in China: A Selected and Annotated Bibliography.* Westport, Conn.: Greenwood Press, 1984.

Wemple, Suzanne Ponay. *Women in Frankish Society: Marriage and the Cloister, 500 to 900.* Philadelphia: University of Pennsylvania Press, 1981.

Wilson, Katharina M. *An Encyclopedia of Continental Women Writers.* New York: Garland, 1991.

———. *Women Writers of the Renaissance and Reformation.* Athens: University of Georgia, 1987.

Woloch, Nancy. *Women and the American Experience.* 2d ed. New York: McGraw Hill, 1995.

Woods, Jean M., and Marie Furstenwald. *Women of the German-Speaking Lands: Learning, Literature and the Arts during the Seventeenth and Eighteenth Centuries, A Lexicon.* Stuttgart: Metzler, 1984.

Zophy, Angela Howard, with Frances M. Kavenek, eds. *Handbook of American Women's History.* New York: Garland Press, 1990.

Index

Abakanowicz, Magdalena, 494, 1277
Abbess, 905, 914, 915, 948, 1055. *See also* Nun
Abbey, 1266
Abbey, Elizabeth, 653
Abelard, Peter, 447–48
Abolitionism, 1–3, 1482, 1490, 1510. *See also* Slavery
Aborigine, 136, 139, 141
Abortion, 3–13; and activism, 1141–49; and Arab women, 101; and Canada, 198; and China, 235; and Denmark, 348; and East Africa, 29; and Federal Republic of Germany, 594; and femicide, 471; and France, 518, 530; and Germany, 586; and Greece, 611; and infanticide, 736; and Italy, 772, 773, 774; and Japan, 782; and law, 1142; and Medicaid, 1143; and midwives, 937, 939; and mortality, 1208–9; and National Organization for Women, 1143; and National Socialism, 589; and Norway, 999, 1000, 1001; and patriarchy, 1049; and Poland, 1098; and Portugal, 1125; and psychology, 1146; and Romania, 1222; and Sweden, 1386; and Third Republic, 534; and Tsarist Russia, 1243; and Union of Soviet Socialist Republics, 1431, 1432; and U.S. Supreme Court, 1383
Abortion clinic, 12
Absenteeism, 13–16
Abstract expressionism, 1036–37
Abuse: and battered women, 157–60, 188, 299, 381–82, 995; and divorce, 995; and masochism, 895; and mental illness, 931; and mentor, 933–34; and Norway, 1001; sexual, 272–73, 380, 381, 1307, 1376; spousal, 381–82, 778, 782; of substances, 1373–77
Abzug, Bella, 1062
Academia: and backlash, 150, 151; and feminism, 478, 479, 480–81; and feminist magazines, 877–78; and folklore, 508–9. *See also* Education
Academy of St. Luke, 536
Accommodation, 269–70
Achievement anxiety, 384
Achuch, Janet, 396
Acker, Kathryn, 1019
Acquired immunodeficiency syndrome. *See* AIDS
Activism: and abortion, 1141–49; and feminism, 477–78; and France, 1377; and French Revolution, 520, 521–22, 523; and grassroots organizing, 603–5; and Grimké, 861; and India, 710, 711, 712, 719, 724; and International Council of Women, 741–43; and Japan, 793; and Korea, 822; and Mexican Revolution, 935; and Nazis, 980; and progessive movement, 1149–51; and settlement house movement, 1287–89; and socialism, 1324–25; and Société des Républicaines Révolutionnaires, 1326–27; and Tsarist Russia, 1244; and women's colleges, 1497; and work, 1501–3; and World War I, 1507. *See also* Politics
Acts of Paul and Thecla, 1255

Drycupping, 5
Dryden, John, 692
Drysdale, George, 300, 301
Dual role, 407–8
Duchemin, Catherine, 536
Duff, Mary Ann, 403
Dulac, Germaine, 497
Duncan, Isadora, 331
Duncan, Sara Jeanette, 200
Dunn, Mary Chavelita (pseud. George Egerton), 991; *Keynotes,* 992
Dupin, Aurore, 545
Durán, María Angeles, 1340
Durand, Marguerite, 545
Duras, Claire de, 545
Duras, Marguerite, 546
Durga, 644
Durova, Nadezhda, 1247
Dutt, Toru, 726–27
Dyer, Mary, 271, 1199, 1200
Dysmenorrhea, 922, 923
Dystopia, 411–12

East Africa, 27–30
East Asia, 1197. *See also specific countries*
East Central European literature, 413–17
Eating, compulsive, 512, 513
Eating disorder, 17, 91–94, 384–85, 510–13
Eaton, Edith, 130
Eaton, Winnifred, 130
Ebner-Eschenbach, Marie von, 576
Ebtekar, Masumeh, 747
Eckenlied, 439
Eckhart, Meister, 965
Economy: and additional worker effect, 17; and Africa, 23, 24, 41–44; and Algeria, 72; and Central Africa, 26; and discouraged worker effect, 17; and domestic service, 377; and education, 422–27; and family, 454–57; and Gilman, 1492–94; and Greece, 612; and health, 628–30; and health movement, 635; and Hinduism, 646; and India, 715–17; and Indonesia, 730; and infanticide, 736, 737; and Iran, 744, 745; and kibbutz, 819–20; and Latin America, 841–42; and Middle Ages, 906–7, 908; and mode of production, 947; and Norway, 1000; and peasant society, 1063; and prostitution, 1156; and sexuality, 1305; and Spain, 1336; and West Africa, 38, 39–40
Ecuador, 838
Eddic poetry, 677

Edgell, Zee, *Beka Lamb,* 213
Edgeworth, Maria, 374, 375
Edgeworth, Mary, 888
Education, 418–28; and African American, 55, 56, 427; and African development, 43; and Algeria, 71, 72, 73; and American Revolution, 84; and American tribal peoples, 81; and ancient religion, 1190; and apartheid, 35–36; and Arab women, 101, 102–3; and architecture, 105–6, 106; and Argentina, 840; and art, 111–13, 1236; and Asian Americans, 128; and Australia, 138; and Bangladesh, 154; and Brazil, 176, 179; and Britain, 186–87, 188, 191, 192, 193; and British literature, 1081; and British Renaissance, 1264–65, 1266; and Canada, 200; and Central Africa, 26; and child care, 225; and China, 230, 232, 235, 236, 239, 241; and Chinese literature, 249; and class, 423, 424; and Confucianism, 295–96; and criminal justice, 316; and Cuba, 319–20; and Czech and Slovak Republics, 325, 326; and date rape, 338–39; and Denmark, 333; and development, 465; and differential socialization, 366; and discrimination, 368, 369–70; and displaced homemaker, 371; and double jeopardy, 386; and East Central European literature, 415; and economy, 422–25, 426–27; and Egypt, 428; and family, 426, 427; and Federal Republic of Germany, 593; and feminism, 482, 1064–66; and feminology, 490; and fertility, 224; and fiber art, 493; and Finland, 506; and France, 529, 530; and French art, 535–39; and gender role, 562–63; and German Democratic Republic, 590; and Germany, 578, 581; and Gilman, 1493; and Great Depression, 355; and Greece, 612; and health movement, 635; and Hinduism, 645, 646; and Holocaust, 652; and home, 426; and home economics, 656–57; and homelessness, 660; and human capital, 670; and immigration, 700; and India, 710, 711, 717, 722, 726; and Indonesia, 732; and industry, 426; and intelligence quotient, 740; and International Council of Women, 742; and Iran, 744, 745; and Italian art, 751; and Italian humanism, 1202; and Italian literature, 756; and Italy, 769, 771, 774; and Japan, 784, 785, 791, 793; and Jews, 808, 810; and judges, 813, 815; and Korea, 821;

Landon, Letitia Elizabeth, 1082, 1090
Landucci, Teresa Bandinetti, 756
Lane, Sara, 395
Lang, Helene, 581, 582
Langgässer, Elisabeth, 576
Language: and France, 530; and French
    feminism, 524–25, 527–28; and Japan,
    796; and Jews, 806; and Korea, 826; and
    mystics, 964; and patriarchy, 1049; and
    power, 1132; and science, 559; and semi-
    otics, 1283–87; and Woolf, 1011
Lanier, Emilia, 1441
Lansing, Sherry: *The Accused,* 502–3; *Fatal
    Attraction,* 503
Laos, 122, 125
Lara, Contessa, 758
Larcom, Lucy, 1092
Larkin, Alile Sharon, *A Different Image,*
    499
Larrocha, Alicia de, 289
Lars, Krystyna, 1107
Larsen, Nella, 51
Larsen, Wendy Wilder, 132
Lasker-Schüler, Else, 576
Lasson, Ann Margrethe, 333
Lathrop, Julia, 1150, 1288
Latina, 845–49
Latin America, 838–42, 889–91. *See also*
    Hispanic
Laurence, Margaret, 201
Law: and abortion, 1142; and Contagious
    Disease Acts, 183; and contraception,
    1142; and divorce, 371, 372, 373; and
    Egypt, 429; and equal employment op-
    portunity, 439–40; and European Union,
    443–44; and feminism, 1373; and
    Finland, 506; and German kingdoms, 572;
    and Greece, 610–11; and Hebrews, 636;
    and homelessness, 661; and homophobia,
    662; and homosexuality, 665; and immi-
    gration, 699–700; and incest, 701–4; and
    India, 713, 721; and Iran, 746; Islamic,
    747–50; and Italy, 760–62, 766; and Ja-
    pan, 778, 786–87; and Jews, 808, 812;
    and jurors, 816–17; and medieval peas-
    antry, 912; and midwives, 937; and por-
    nography, 1122; and Pro-Choice
    Movement, 1143–44; and Pro-Life Move-
    ment, 1146–47; and property, 184–85;
    and sex, 1383; and sexual harassment,
    1300–1301; and social feminism, 1320,
    1321; and Third Republic, 533–34; and

Tsarist Russia, 1242; and U.S. Supreme
    Court, 1380–84; and veil, 1449–50; and
    West Africa, 40; and witchcraft, 1474;
    and work, 1156–58. *See also* Crime; *spe-
    cific laws*
Lawrence, Susan. *See* Dana, Susan
    Lawrence
Lawson, Louisa, 141, 876
Lawyer, 813–16
Law-Yone, Wendy, 132
Lazarus, Emma, 1093
Leadership, and sports, 1362–63, 1364,
    1365
League of Sudanese Women, 32
Leah, 568
Learned helplessness, 353, 849–50
Learning, 555–57, 562–63. *See also* Cogni-
    tion; Education
Leavitt, Mary C., 793
Leduc, Violet, 855
Lee, Ann, 1195, 1310, 1311
Lee, Julia, 171
Lee, Laurie, 1086
Leeds, Deborah, 1322
Leffler, Anne C., 1388–89
Le Gallienne, Eva, 405
Leisure Time, 851–52
Lenin, V. I., 1431
Lenngren, Anna M., 1388
Lennox, Charlotte, *The Female Quixote,*
    1008
Leoba, 1266–67
Léon, Pauline, 1326
Leontion, 623
Lesbia, 1231
Lesbian, lesbianism, 852–60; and activism,
    554–55; and American Poetry, 1095; and
    bisexuality, 164–65; and *The Children's
    Hour,* 1078; and Denmark, 349–50; de-
    velopment of, 664–65; and drama, 406–7;
    and France, 519; and homophobia, 663;
    and literary criticism, 867; and maga-
    zines, 877; and Norway, 1001; and per-
    formance art, 1067; and sexuality, 1305;
    and sexually transmitted disease, 1309;
    and supermarket romance, 1378; and the-
    ory, 480; and women's colleges, 1497
Lesbiennes Radicales, 519
Leskova, Rebeka, 414
Lessing, Doris, 1442; *Children of Violence,*
    1013; *The Golden Notebook,* 926, 1013–
    14

and China, 228, 229, 230, 231, 233, 236–37, 238–39; and Code Napoléon, 515; and colonial America, 271, 273, 274; common law, 280; and communal property, 283–84; and concubine, 290–91; and Confucianism, 294, 295, 296; and Congress of Industrial Organization, 833; and contraception, 300; and coverture, 314; and crime, 1454–55; and Denmark, 346–47; and dependency, 350–51; and development, 466, 467; and displaced homemaker, 370; and divorce, 373; and domestic novel, 375, 377; and dower, 387; and dowry, 387–93; and dual-career, 407; and dual role, 408; and East Africa, 29; and education, 427; and Egypt, 429, 431; and endogamy, 434–35; and Enlightenment, 437; and exogamy, 434–35; and family, 453; and Federal Republic of Germany, 593; and femicide, 469–70; and foot-binding, 514; and France, 529; and French literature, 545–46; and gender role, 562; and German kingdoms, 573, 574; and Germany, 581, 585, 586; and gifts, 806; and Gilman, 1493–94; and Gouges, 344; and Great Depression, 355, 357; and Greece, 610, 611, 613; and Grimké, 861; and Hebrews, 637; and Hellenistic queens, 640; and Hinduism, 645, 646; and home economics, 656; and housewife, 667–68; and hypergamy, 675; and hypogamy, 675; and India, 706, 709, 713–15, 1153; and Indian devotional poetry, 728; and Indonesia, 732, 733; and infanticide, 736, 737; and Iran, 746–47; and Islamic law, 747–50; and Italy, 763, 766, 768, 769, 771, 774; and Japan, 778–79, 780, 781, 782, 785, 793; and Jews, 805, 806, 807, 808, 811; and kibbutz, 819; kinds of, 995; and Korea, 825–26; and labor force participation, 835; and Latin America, 841; and levirate, 862; and *Lienu Zhuan,* 864; and medieval nobility, 909, 910, 911; and medieval peasantry, 912–13; and medieval Spain, 1334, 1335; and Middle Ages, 906, 908, 1154; and military, 943, 944; and Mill, 1372; and Mormons, 950–52; and Ms. as title of address, 956; and Namibia, 37; and National Socialism, 588; and new woman, 991; and New Zealand, 993; and North Africa, 32, 33; and Nor-

way, 999; and Oneida, 1028; and organized labor, 831, 832, 834; and pastoral society, 1047; and patriarchy, 1049; and Philippines, 1070, 1071; and picture bride, 1074; and Pisanelli Code, 761; and Portugal, 1124; and poverty, 1127, 1129; and Pro-Choice Movement, 1141; and property, 891; and prostitution, 1151, 1153; and Reformation, 1154, 1186, 1187; and retirement, 1217; Roman, 1152–53; and Rome, 1224–25, 1229; and sati, 1258–59; and Saudi Arabia, 1260, 1262–63; and Social Security, 1323–24; and South Africa, 37; and Spain, 1337; and Spanish America, 1345; and Stanton, 1491; and status, 900–901; and Taiwan, 1394; and taxation, 892; and teaching, 1397, 1398; and Third Republic, 534; and Tibet, 1410–11; and Tsarist Russia, 1243, 1245; and Turkey, 1420; and *A Vindication of the Rights of Woman,* 1457; and West Africa, 40; and widow, 1471, 1472; and women's movement, 1491; and World War II, 1509. See also Concubine; Divorce; Dowry

Married Women's Property Act, 184, 192

Marsden, Dora, 876

Marsh, Ngaio, 362

Marshall, Paule, *Brown Girl, Brownstones,* 213

Martha, 689

Martin, Sara, 171

Martineau, Harriet, 1010; *Autobiography,* 144

Martín-Gaite, Carmen, 1342–43

Martini, Darnell, 504

Martins, Maria, 843

Martinson, Moa, 1390

Martyr, 626, 1254–56

Marx, Karl, 1030, 1031, 1211, 1324

Marxism: and British poetry, 1085; and Neolithic, 982; and socialist feminism, 1500; and work, 1499

Mary, 446–49; cult of, 889–91; and gnosticism, 597; and hagiography, 626; and medieval drama, 688, 689; and medieval nobility, 909; and spirituality, 1076; and Third Republic, 532

Mary Jacobi, 689

Mary Magdalene, 597, 689, 1153

Mary of Oignies, 117

Mary Salome, 689

and Reformation, 1187; and Social Purity, 1321–22; and veil, 1450; and Vietnam, 124, 125; and *A Vindication of the Rights of Woman*, 1457; and westward movement, 1466; and white slavery, 1469–70; and zhenotdel, 1513
Protective legislation, 1156–58
Protestantism, 18, 73
Proxemics, 996–97
Prudhomme, Pierre, 522
Przybyszewska, Stanisława, 1105–6
Psychanalyse et Politique, 517–18
Psychoanalysis, 1158–66
Psychology: and abortion, 1146; and divorce, 373; and femininity, 472–73; and menstruation, 925, 927–29; and occupational segregation, 1271–72; and self-fulfilling prophecy, 1282–83; and sex difference, 1291; and sexism, 1294–95; and sexuality, 1305; and substance abuse, 1374; and transexual, 1415, 1416
Puberty, 1166–70
Publication, 142, 1086, 1087–88, 1092
Public employee, 833–34
Public sphere, 455, 555, 1173; and American Poetry, 1095; and Athens, 1228; and Jews, 806, 812; and Korea, 825; and leisure time, 851; and magazines, 878; and Middle Ages, 907; and New Zealand, 993; and pastoral society, 1047; and peasant society, 1063; and prostitution, 1152; and Rome, 1228, 1229, 1233–36; and saints, 1253; and television, 1400–1401; and Third Republic, 533; and United States, 1112; and woman's club movement, 1487; and women's movement, 1490–91; and work, 1504–5
Puerto, Elvia Carrillo, 935
Puerto Rican American, 846
Puerto Rico, 838
Puget Sound Encampment, 1061
Pulci, Antonia Giannotti, 1203
þulur, 678
Purdah, 1173–75. *See also* Seclusion
Puritan, 271, 272, 1197–1201
Purity school, 991, 992
Pythia, 1192–93, 1196

Qing period, 238, 250
Qollahuaya people, 1195
Quaker, 271, 1195, 1199–1200, 1310
Queen, The, 880

Queen Mother of the West, 254, 1396
Queiroz, Carlotta Pereira de, 177
Queiroz, Rachel de, 180
Queler, Eve, 292–93
Querelle des femmes, 1177–78
Quickening, 7. *See also* Pregnancy
Quilt, 491–92, 494–95
Quilting, 45
Quiroga, Elena, 1342
Qui Ying, daughter of, 241

Rabbi, 805, 811
Rabbinic Judaism, 811–13
Rabenschlacht, Das, 439
Race: and comparable worth, 285; and crime, 1454; and Cuba, 320; and development, 466; and domestic service, 379; and double jeopardy, 385; and education, 423, 427; and Equal Rights Amendment, 442; and Great Depression, 356; and Latinos, 848; and management, 884, 885; and menarche, 1167; and poverty, 1129; and puberty, 1168; and rape, 460, 1181; and Spanish America, 1344, 1345, 1346; and sports, 1359, 1364–65; and wage gap, 1459; and white slavery, 1469; and women of color, 275; and work, 1506. *See also specfic groups*
Rachel, 567–68
Rachilde. *See* Eyméry, Marguerite
Racism: and African American, 52, 53, 54; and Aristotle, 108; and Asian Americans, 129, 130; and Chicana literature, 216; environmental, 206; and National Socialism, 589; and Southern Black Women's Network, 1331
Radcliffe, Ann, *The Mysteries of Udolpho*, 602–3
Radegundis, 572
Radius, Anna Zuccari, 758
Ragtime, 800
Rahab, 639
Rahbek, Karin Margrethe, 333
Rahelzeit, 1257
Raine, Kathleen, 1086
Rainer, Yvonne, 500
Rainey, Gertrude Pridgett, 170, 172
Rambert, Marie, 330
Rambouillet, Madame de, 543
Ramee, Marie Louise (pseud. Ouida), 1010
Ramos, Samuel, 873–74
Rankin, Jeanette, 1060, 1116

Consultants and Contributors

CONSULTANTS

SUSAN K. AHERN, Literature, Department of English, University of Houston-Downtown Houston, Texas

ROBIN L. BARTLETT, Economics, Denison University, Granville, Ohio

JANET K. BOLES, Political Science, Marquette University, Milwaukee, Wisconsin

MARILYN J. BOXER, Women's History, Department of History, San Francisco State University, San Francisco, California

JANE P. BRICKMAN, American History, Humanities Department, U.S. Merchant Marine Academy, Kings Point, New York

SUSAN B. CARTER, Economics, Smith College, Northampton, Massachusetts

MIRIAM COHEN, American History, Department of History, Vassar College, Poughkeepsie, New York

SUSAN G. COLE, Ancient History, formerly with Department of History, University of Illinois at Chicago, Chicago, Illinois

CAROL KLIMICK CYGANOWSKI, American Literature, Department of English and Communication, DePaul University, Chicago, Illinois

HELENE P. FOLEY, Classics, Department of Classics, Barnard College, Columbia University, New York, New York

GERALDINE FORBES, India, Department of History and Women's Studies, State University of New York at Oswego, Oswego, New York

RACHEL G. FUCHS, European History, Department of History, Arizona State University, Tempe, Arizona

DONNA R. GABACCIA, American History, University of North Carolina at Charlotte, Charlotte, North Carolina

MARILYN GOTTSCHALK, Fine Arts, Women's Studies Department, University of Wisconsin-Platteville, Platteville, Wisconsin

BEVERLY W. JONES, Black History, Department of History, North Carolina Central University, Durham, North Carolina

ROSS S. KRAEMER, Religion, formerly with Department of Religious Studies, Franklin and Marshall College, Lancaster, Pennsylvania

JUDITH LEAVITT, History of Medicine, University of Wisconsin-Madison, Madison, Wisconsin

CLAIRE GOLDBERG MOSES, European History, Department of Women's Studies, University of Maryland, College Park, Maryland

ILLENE NOPPE, Psychology, Department of Human Development/Psychology, University of Wisconsin-Green Bay, Green Bay, Wisconsin

MARY GOMEZ PARHAM, Iberian and Latin American History and Literature, University of Houston-Downtown, Houston, Texas

KRISTINA M. PASSMAN, Ancient History and Literature, Department of Foreign Languages and Classics, University of Maine, Orono, Maine

ANNIS PRATT, Literature, Department of English, University of Wisconsin-Madison, Madison, Wisconsin

BARBARA J. PRICE, Criminal Justice, Dean, Graduate Program, City University of New York, John Jay College of Criminal Justice, New York, New York

PATRICIA D. ROZEE, Psychology, Director of Women's Studies, California State University, Long Beach, California

ALLEN SCARBORO, Sociology, Department of Sociology, Augusta State University, Augusta, Georgia

BETH SCHNEIDER, Sociology, Department of Sociology, University of California at Santa Barbara, Santa Barbara, California

JANE SLAUGHTER, Twentieth-Century Europe, Department of History, University of New Mexico, Albuquerque, New Mexico

ETHEL SLOANE, Biology, Biosciences Department, University of Wisconsin-Milwaukee, Milwaukee, Wisconsin

GLORIA STEPHENSON, Women's Studies, University of Wisconsin-Platteville, Platteville, Wisconsin

ANN WALTNER, China and Japan, Department of History, University of Minnesota-Minneapolis, Minneapolis, Minnesota

MARIANNE WHATLEY, Curriculum and Instruction, University of Wisconsin-Madison, Madison, Wisconsin

ELAINE WHEELER, R.N., formerly with the Women's Studies Program, University of Wisconsin-Madison, Madison, Wisconsin and currently with Fox Lake Correctional Institution, Fox Lake, Wisconsin

CONTRIBUTORS

BARRY D. ADAM, Department of Sociology and Anthropology, University of Windsor, Windsor, Ontario, Canada

MARJORIE AGOSIN, Department of Spanish, Wellesley College, Wellesley, Massachusetts

SUSAN K. AHERN, Department of English, University of Houston-Downtown, Houston, Texas

LEILA AHMED, Department of Women's Studies, University of Massachusetts Amherst, Amherst, Massachusetts

MARGHERITA REPETTO ALAIA, Department of Italian, Columbia University, New York, New York

JILDA M. ALIOTTA, Department of Political Science, Miami University, Oxford, Ohio

JUDITH L. ALPERT, Department of Applied Psychology, New York University, New York, New York

BARBARA WATSON ANDAYA, Asian Studies Program, University of Hawaii at Manoa, Honolulu, Hawaii

KAREN ANDERSON, Department of History, University of Arizona, Tucson, Arizona

DEBRA D. ANDRIST, Modern and Classical Languages, University of St. Thomas, Houston, Texas

KATHRYN H. ANTHONY, Building Research Council, School of Architecture, University of Illinois at Urbana-Champaign, Champaign, Illinois

RIMA D. APPLE, School of Human Ecology and the Women's Studies Program, University of Wisconsin-Madison, Madison, Wisconsin

LYNNE S. ARNAULT, Philosophy Department, Le Moyne College, Syracuse, New York

KATHLEEN ASHLEY, Department of English, University of Southern Maine, Gorham, Maine

RICHARD D. ASHMORE, Department of Psychology, Rutgers University, New Brunswick, New Jersey

MARINA ASTMAN, Department of Russian, Barnard College of Columbia University, New York, New York

MAX AZICRI, Department of Political Science, Edinboro University of Pennsylvania, Edinboro, Pennsylvania

CHRISTINA L. BAKER, Department of English, University College of the University of Maine, Bangor, Maine

CHARLENE BALL, Department of English, Georgia Institute of Technology, Atlanta, Georgia

ELLEN M. BARRETT, Rev., New York, New York

NANCY S. BARRETT, Provost and Vice President for Academic Affairs, University of Alabama, Tuscaloosa, Alabama

ELIZABETH ANN BARTLETT, Department of Political Science, University of Minnesota-Duluth, Duluth, Minnesota

JUDITH R. BASKIN, Department of Judaic Studies, State University of New York at Albany, Albany, New York

SUSAN A. BASOW, Psychology Department, Lafayette College, Easton, Pennsylvania

PHYLLIS JO BAUNACH, Civil Division, Commercial Litigation Branch, U.S. Department of Justice, Washington, D.C.

TARCISIO BEAL, Departments of History, Religious Studies, and Peace and Justice Studies, Incarnate Work College, San Antonio, Texas

CHERYL BECKER, Health Sciences Libraries, University of Wisconsin-Madison, Madison, Wisconsin

MARY JANE BEECH, Department of History, Aurora University, Aurora, Illinois

MARIANNE BERARDI, Kansas City Art Institute, Kansas City, Missouri

BARBARA R. BERGMANN, Department of Economics, American University, Washington, D.C.

KATHRYN BERNHARDT, Department of History, Southern Methodist University, Dallas, Texas

MARY KAY BIAGGIO, School of Professional Psychology, Pacific University, Forest Grove, Oregon

PAAL BJÖRBY, Department of Scandinavian Studies, University of Oregon, Eugene, Oregon

KAREN J. BLAIR, Department of History, Central Washington University, Ellensburg, Washington

FRANCINE D. BLAU, Industrial and Labor Relations, Cornell University, Ithaca, New York

KATHLEEN M. BLEE, Department of Sociology, University of Kentucky, Lexington, Kentucky

MARY H. BLEWETT, Department of History, University of Massachusetts Lowell, Lowell, Massachusetts

JACK S. BLOCKER, JR., Department of History, Huron College, University of Western Ontario, London, Ontario, Canada

LAURA BOESCHEN, Health Services Center, University of Arizona, Tucson, Arizona

JANICE M. BOGSTAD, Chalmer Davee Library, University of Wisconsin-River Falls, River Falls, Wisconsin

MARTHA BOHACHEVSKY-CHOMIAK, National Endowment for the Humanities, Washington, D.C.

JANET K. BOLES, Department of Political Science, Marquette University, Milwaukee, Wisconsin

SUSAN BORDO, Department of Philosophy, University of Kentucky, Lexington, Kentucky

EDITH BORROFF, Department of Music, State University of New York at Binghamton, Binghamton, New York

BETSY BOWDEN, Department of English, Rutgers, The State University of New Jersey, Campus of Camden, Camden, New Jersey

JANE BOWERS, Department of Music, University of Wisconsin-Milwaukee, Milwaukee, Wisconsin

MARILYN J. BOXER, Vice President for Academic Affairs, San Francisco State University, San Francisco, California

DOROTHY H. BRACEY, Editor, Journal of Criminal Justice, John Jay College of Criminal Justice, City University of New York, New York

RITAMARY BRADLEY, Professor Emerita, Department of English, St. Ambrose College, Davenport, Iowa

ROSE M. BREWER, Department of Sociology, University of Minnesota, Minneapolis, Minnesota

HARRY BROD, Department of Philosophy, University of Delaware, Newark, Delaware

JEANNE BROOKS-GUNN, Center for Young Children and Families, Teachers College, Columbia University, New York, New York

VICTORIA BISSELL BROWN, Department of History, Grinnell College, Grinnell, Iowa

LAURIE BUCHANAN, formerly with Department of English, Illinois State University at Normal, Normal, Illinois

CHERYL BUCKLEY, Design History, Department of Historical and Critical Studies, University of Northumbria, Newcastle upon Tyne, U.K.

STEVEN M. BUECHLER, Department of Sociology, Mankato State University, Mankato, Minnesota

ELOISE A. BUKER, Political Science/Women's Studies, Denison University, Granville, Ohio

JANET M. BURKE, Phoenix, Arizona

ALYSON L. BURNS, Department of Psychology, University of California at Davis, Davis, California

AMY BUTLER, Freelance Writer, Washington, D.C.

ANTHONY R. CAGGIULA, Psychology, University of Pittsburgh, Pittsburgh, Pennsylvania

SUZANNE CAHILL, Program in Chinese Studies, University of California, San Diego, LaJolla, California

LESLIE J. CALMAN, Department of Political Science, Barnard College, Columbia University, New York, New York

ARDIS CAMERON, New England Studies, University of Southern Maine, Portland, Maine

ELIZABETH CARNEY, Department of History, Clemson University, Clemson, South Carolina

LUCY CARROLL, Department of History, Cambridge University, Cambridge, U.K.

SUSAN J. CARROLL, Egleton Institute for Politics, Rutgers University, New Brunswick, New Jersey

SUSAN B. CARTER, Department of Economics, Smith College, Northampton, Massachusetts

CHARLES E. CASE, Department of Sociology, Augusta College, Augusta, Georgia

JOHN CAVANAUGH-O'KEEFE, Human Life International, Front Royal, Virginia

ALICE YUN CHAI, Professor Emerita of Women's Studies, University of Hawaii at Manoa, Honolulu, Hawaii

DAVID A. CHERRY, formerly with Department of Classical Studies, University of Ottawa, Ottawa, Ontario, Canada

JOAN D. CHITTISTER, O.S.B., Mount Saint Benedict, Erie, Pennsylvania

GARNA L. CHRISTIAN, Department of Social Sciences, University of Houston-Downtown, Houston, Texas

CAROL A. CHRISTY, Department of Political Science, Ohio University-Lancaster, Lancaster, Ohio

PAULINE ROSE CLANCE, Department of Psychology, Georgia State University, Atlanta, Georgia

ELIZABETH A. CLARK, Department of Religion, Duke University, Durham, North Carolina

LINDA L. CLARK, Department of History, Millersville University, Millersville, Pennsylvania

ALBRECHT CLASSEN, Department of German Studies, University of Arizona, Tucson, Arizona

CATHERINE CLÉMENTIN-OJHA, Ecole française d'Extrême Orient, Paris, France

BARBARA EVANS CLEMENTS, Department of History, University of Akron, Akron, Ohio

MIRIAM COHEN, Department of History, Vassar College, Poughkeepsie, New York

JANE F. COLLIER, Department of Anthropology, Stanford University, Stanford, California

SUSAN P. CONNER, Department of History, Central Michigan University, Mount Pleasant, Michigan

JANE M. CONNOR, Communications Studies, State University of New York at Binghamton, Binghamton, New York

CONSTANCE A. COOK, Asian Studies, Department of Modern Foreign Languages, Lehigh University, Bethlehem, Pennsylvania

ELLEN PIEL COOK, Department of Educational Leadership, University of Cincinnati, Cincinnati, Ohio

GLORIA COWAN, Department of Psychology, California State University, San Bernardino, San Bernardino, California

JANE CRISLER, Dean, University of Wisconsin-Rock County, Janesville, Wisconsin

RALPH CROIZIER, Department of History, University of Victoria, Victoria, British Columbia, Canada

LEO C. CURRAN, Department of Classics, State University of New York at Buffalo, Buffalo, New York

CAROL KLIMICK CYGANOWSKI, Department of English, DePaul University, Chicago, Illinois

NANCY DATAN, late of Department of Human Development, University of Wisconsin-Green Bay, Green Bay, Wisconsin

LAURA NIESEN DE ABRUÑA, Department of English, Ithaca College, Ithaca, New York

ALEXANDER DE GRAND, Department of History, North Carolina State University, Raleigh, North Carolina

ADELAIDA LÓPEZ DE MARTÍNEZ, Department of Modern Languages, University of Nebraska, Lincoln, Nebraska

RIMA DE VALLBONNA, Professor Emerita of Spanish, University of St. Thomas, Houston, Texas

FRANCES K. DEL BOCA, Department of Psychiatry, University of Connecticut School of Medicine, Farmington, Connecticut

JANICE DELANEY, Library of Congress, Washington, D.C.

NEERA DESAI, Professor Emeritus, Women's Research Unit, SNDT Women's University, Bombay, India

NORMA DIAMOND, Department of Anthropology, University of Michigan, Ann Arbor, Michigan

DOMINGOS DE OLIVEIRA DIAS, late of Brown University, Providence, Rhode Island, and Braga, Portugal

SUSAN DICKMAN, United Faculty of Theology, Melbourne College of Divinity, Melbourne, Victoria, Australia

PETER M. DIMEGLIO, Department of History, University of Wisconsin-Platteville, Platteville, Wisconsin

KENNETH L. DION, Department of Psychology, University of Toronto, Toronto, Ontario, Canada

MARIA DITULLIO, Psychology Department, Le Moyne College, Syracuse, New York

JENIFER GRINDLE DOLDE, Curator, Delaware Agricultural Museum and Village, Dover, Delaware

JOSEPHINE DONOVAN, Department of English, University of Maine, Orono, Maine

LORAH DORN, Individual and Family Studies, Pennsylvania State University, University Park, Pennsylvania

VICTORIA C. DUCKWORTH, Department of English and Languages, San Jacinto College, Houston, Texas

RICHARD M. EATON, Department of Oriental Studies, University of Arizona, Tucson, Arizona

JACQUELYNNE S. ECCLES, Department of Psychology, University of Michigan, Ann Arbor, Michigan

WENDY R. EISNER, Paleoecologist and Archaeologist, Byrd Polar Research Center, Ohio State University, Columbus, Ohio

YAFFA ELIACH, Department of Judaic Studies, Brooklyn College, Brooklyn, New York

SHARON K. ELKINS, Department of Religion, Wellesley College, Wellesley, Massachusetts

STEVE L. ELLYSON, Department of Psychology, Youngstown State University, Youngstown, Ohio

PENELOPE J. ENGELBRECHT, formerly with Department of Women's Studies, DePaul University, Chicago, Illinois

DAGMAR A. E. ENGELS, German Historical Institute, London, England

PETER ERICKSON, Sterling and Francine Clark Art Institute, Williamstown, Massachusetts

VIRGINIA ESKIN, Concert Pianist, Boston, Massachusetts

CLAIRE ETAUGH, Dean, College of Liberal Arts and Sciences, Bradley University, Peoria, Illinois

MARK I. EVANS, Department of Pediatrics, Hutzel Hospital, Wayne State University, Detroit, Michigan

SARA M. EVANS, Department of History, University of Minnesota-Minneapolis, Minneapolis, Minnesota

WENDY J. EVANS, Division of Reproductive Genetics, Hutzel Hospital, Wayne State University, Detroit, Michigan

JUDITH EZEKIEL, Women's History and American Studies, University of Nancy II, Nancy, France

NANCY ELLEN AUER FALK, Department of Religion, Western Michigan University, Kalamazoo, Michigan

ETELA FARKÁŠOVÁ, Philosophy, Bratislava, Slovak

CLAIRE R. FARRER, Department of Anthropology, California State University, Chico, Chico, California

REZA FAZEL, Department of Anthropology, University of Massachusetts-Boston Harbor, Boston, Massachusetts

CLARICE FEINMAN, Professor Emeritus, Department of Law and Justice, Trenton State College, Trenton, New Jersey

SHELLEY FELDMAN, South Asia Program, Cornell University, Ithaca, New York

MARIANNE A. FERBER, Department of Economics, University of Illinois at Urbana-Champaign, Urbana, Illinois

KATHY E. FERGUSON, Department of Political Science, University of Hawaii at Manoa, Honolulu, Hawaii

NONA FIENBERG, Department of English, Keene State University, Keene, New Hampshire

RUTH FIRESTONE, Department of Foreign Languages, Fort Hays State University, Hays, Kansas

KATHY FLETCHER, Department of Theatre and Drama, Indiana University at Bloomington, Bloomington, Indiana

MARLEEN B. FLORY, Classics, Department of Religion, Gustavus Adolphus College, Saint Peter, Minnesota

IRIS G. FODOR, Department of Psychology and Women's Studies, New York University, New York, New York

GERALDINE FORBES, Department of History, State University of New York at Oswego, Oswego, New York

ALICIA FOSTER, London, United Kingdom

RITA JACKAWAY FREEDMAN, Private Clinical Practice, Scarsdale, New York

LUCY M. FREIBERT, Professor Emerita of English, University of Louisville, Louisville, Kentucky

VALERIE FRENCH, Department of History, American University, Washington, D.C.

IRENE H. FRIEZE, Psychology, University of Pittsburgh, Pittsburgh, Pennsylvania

RACHEL G. FUCHS, Department of History, Arizona State University, Tempe, Arizona

DONNA R. GABACCIA, Department of History, University of North Carolina at Charlotte, Charlotte, North Carolina

CAROLE GANIM, former Director, New Mexico Academic Centers, Chapman University, Albuquerque, New Mexico

FRANCES GARB, Biology, University of Wisconsin-Stout, Menomonie, Wisconsin

ALMA M. GARCÍA, Departments of Anthropology and Sociology and of Ethnic Studies, Santa Clara University, Santa Clara, California

CLARKE GARRETT, Department of History, Dickinson College, Carlisle, Pennsylvania

HILL GATES, Department of Anthropology, Stanford University, Stanford, California

JULIA M. GERGITS, Department of English, Youngstown State University, Youngstown, Ohio

MARY GIBSON, Department of History, City University of New York, John Jay College of Criminal Justice, New York, New York

MARY ELLIS GIBSON, Department of English, University of North Carolina at Greensboro, Greensboro, North Carolina

JUDITH ANN GIESBERG, doctoral student, Department of History, Boston College, Chestnut Hill, Massachusetts

JANET N. GOLD, Department of Spanish and Classics, University of New Hampshire, Durham, New Hampshire

JANET GOLDEN, Bala Cynwyd, Pennsylvania

PAM E. GOLDMAN, Independent Scholar, Lexington, Kentucky

CLIA M. GOODWIN, Independent Scholar, Dover, New Hampshire

REBECCA L. GOOLSBY, Department of Anthropology, Alaskan Pacific University, Anchorage, Alaska

KAREN GOULD, Department of Romance Languages, Bowling Green University, Bowling Green, Ohio

JULIA A. GRABER, Center for Young Children and Families and the Adolescent Study Program, Teachers College, Columbia University, New York, New York

JEAN GRANT, Imprint Memoirs, Lawrence, Kansas

NANCY GRAY, formerly with Department of English, California State Polytechnic University, Pomona, California

REVA P. GREENBURG, Department of History, University of Rhode Island, College of Continuing Education, Providence, Rhode Island

MAURINE WEINER GREENWALD, Department of History, University of Pittsburgh, Pittsburgh, Pennsylvania

BEVERLY GRIER, Department of Government, Clark University, Worcester, Massachusetts

ROBERT L. GRISWOLD, Department of History, University of Oklahoma, Norman, Oklahoma

JUDITH EVANS GRUBBS, formerly with Department of Classics, Stanford University, Stanford, California

ELLEN GRUENBAUM, School of Social Sciences, California State University Fresno, Fresno, California

KOLLEEN M. GUY, Division of Behavioral and Cultural Sciences, University of Texas at San Antonio, San Antonio, Texas

JAHYUN KIM HABOUSH, Center for East Asian and Pacific Studies, University of Illinois at Urbana-Champaign, Urbana, Illinois

NAN HACKETT, English Department, Concordia College, St. Paul, Minnesota

JUNE E. HAHNER, Department of History, State University of New York at Albany, Albany, New York

KAREN I. HALBERSLEBEN, Executive Assistant to the President, State University of New York at Oswego, Oswego, New York

LAURA HAPKE, Department of English, Pace University, New York, New York

JON HARNED, Department of English, University of Houston-Downtown, Houston, Texas

ELIZABETH A. HARRY, St. Paul, Minnesota

STEVEN C. HAUSE, Department of History, University of Missouri-St. Louis, St. Louis, Missouri

MELISSA HAUSSMAN, Department of Government, Suffolk University, Boston, Massachusetts

SUSAN E. HAWKINS, Department of English, Oakland University, Rochester, Michigan

BARBARA J. HAYLER, Criminal Justice Program, University of Illinois at Springfield, Springfield, Illinois

ESTHER HEFFERNAN, Department of Sociology, Edgewood College, Madison, Wisconsin

NANCY G. HELLER, Fine Arts, Georgetown University, Washington, D.C.

FRANCES S. HENSLEY, Department of History, Marshall University, Huntington, West Virginia

MELISSA HENSLEY, St. Louis, Missouri

GREGORY M. HEREK, formerly with Department of Psychology, City University of New York, New York

CAROLIVIA HERRON, formerly with Department of Afro-American Studies and Comparative Studies, Harvard University, Cambridge, Massachusetts

SUSANNAH HESCHEL, Jewish Studies, Department of Religion, Case Western Reserve University, Cleveland, Ohio

KATHLEEN HICKOK, Department of English, Iowa State University, Ames, Iowa

ANNE S. HIGHAM, Norfolk, Virginia

MARJORIE HONIG, Department of Economics, City University of New York, Hunter College, New York, New York

SHARON SHIH-JIUAN HOU, Department of Modern Languages and Literatures, Pomona College, Claremont, California

ANGELA HOWARD, Department of History, University of Houston–Clear Lake, Houston, Texas

FAITH INGWERSEN, Scandinavian Studies, University of Wisconsin-Madison, Madison, Wisconsin

LORNA IRVINE, Department of English, George Mason University, Fairfax, Virginia

JOAN IVERSEN, Professor Emeritus of History, State University of New York at Oneonta, Oneonta, New York

NAOMI JACOBS, Department of English, University of Maine, Orono, Maine

TOMÁS JIMÉNEZ, Department of Sociology, Santa Clara University, Santa Clara, California

MARK P. JOHNSON, Division of Reproductive Genetics, Hutzel Hospital, Wayne State University, Detroit, Michigan

PENELOPE D. JOHNSON, Department of History, New York University, New York, New York

BEVERLY W. JONES, Department of History, North Carolina Central University, Durham, North Carolina

KATHLEEN B. JONES, Department of Women's Studies, San Diego State University, San Diego, California

LESLEY ANN JONES, Department of Women's Studies, Stanford University, Stanford, California

BRIGITTE JORDAN, Institute for Research on Learning, Palo Alto, California

NATALIE BOYMEL KAMPEN, Department of Women's Studies, Barnard College, Columbia University, New York, New York

MARION A. KAPLAN, Professor, Department of History, City University of New York, Queens College, Flushing, New York

MARGARET FOEGEN KARSTEN, Department of Business and Accounting and Extended Degree Program, University of Wisconsin-Platteville, Platteville, Wisconsin

NATALIE HEVENER KAUFMAN, Department of Government, Institute for Families in Society, University of South Carolina, Columbia, South Carolina

DOROTHY KAUFMANN, Department of Foreign Languages, Clark University, Worcester, Massachusetts

M. THERESA KELLEHER, Department of Religion and Asian Studies, Manhattanville College, Purchase, New York

EVELYN FOX KELLER, Program in Science, Technology, and Society, Massachusetts Institute of Technology, Cambridge, Massachusetts

LYNN KELLER, Department of English, University of Wisconsin-Madison, Madison, Wisconsin

CAROL FARLEY KESSLER, Department of English and American Studies, Pennsylvania State University, Delaware County Campus, Media, Pennsylvania

LOUISE H. KIDDER, Department of Psychology, Temple University, Philadelphia, Pennsylvania

DEBORAH K. KING, Department of Sociology, Dartmouth College, Hanover, New Hampshire

DIANE KIRKBY, Department of History, La Trobe University, Bundoora, Victoria, Australia

JEAN KITTRELL, Department of English Language and Literature, Southern Illinois University at Edwardsville, Edwardsville, Illinois

ALISON KLAIRMONT-LINGO, University of California at Berkeley, Berkeley, California

GAIL KLIGMAN, Professor, Department of Sociology, University of California at Los Angeles, Los Angeles, California

NATALIE KNÖDEL, Department of Theology, University of Durham, Durham DHI 3RS U.K.

MARY P. KOSS, Department of Family and Community Medicine, Health Services Center, University of Arizona, Tucson, Arizona

ROSS S. KRAEMER, formerly with Department of Religious Studies, Franklin and Marshall College, Lancaster, Pennsylvania

DIANE KRAVETZ, School of Social Work, University of Wisconsin-Madison, Madison, Wisconsin

HELGA KRESS, Department of Literature, University of Iceland, Reykjavik, Iceland

AMELIA HOWE KRITZER, Department of Theater and Drama, University of Wisconsin-Madison, Madison, Wisconsin

ELAINE KRUSE, Department of History, Nebraska Wesleyan University, Lincoln, Nebraska

MARIANNE LAFRANCE, Director, Women's Studies, Boston College, Chestnut Hill, Massachusetts

C. S. LAKSHMI, Department of Psychology, Bombay, India

KAREN C. LANG, Department of Religious Studies, University of Virginia, Charlottesville, Virginia

MELISSA LATIMER, Department of Sociology, University of West Virginia, Morgantown, West Virginia

ALYCE LAVIOLETTE, Department of Psychology, California State University, Long Beach, Long Beach, California

MARNIA LAZREG, Department of Women's Studies, City University of New York, Hunter College, New York, New York

LAIFONG LEUNG, Department of East Asian Studies, University of Alberta, Edmonton, Alberta, Canada

CAROLE LEVIN, Department of History, University of Nebraska, Lincoln, Nebraska

JOAN H. LEVIN, Department of Italian, Vassar College, Poughkeepsie, New York

ELLEN LEWIN, San Francisco, California

BRIGITTE LHOMOND, Sociology, Centre National de la Recherche Scientifique and Centre Lyonnais d'Etudes Feministes, University of Lyon, Lyon, France

NAOMI LINDSTROM, Department of Spanish and Portuguese, Institute of Latin American Studies, University of Texas at Austin, Austin, Texas

AMY LING, Professor of English, Director of Asian American Studies Program, University of Wisconsin-Madison, Madison, Wisconsin

MARY LOU LOCKE, formerly with Department of History, University of California at San Diego, San Diego, California

SHARON LOCY, Department of English, Loyola Marymount University, Los Angeles, California

MARIAN LOWE, Department of Chemistry, Boston University, Boston, Massachusetts

MARY JANE LUPTON, Department of English, Morgan State University, Baltimore, Maryland

WENONAH L. LYON, Center for Social Anthropology and Computing, Department of Anthropology, University of Kent at Canterbury, Canterbury, U.K.

ARLENE ELOWE MACLEOD, Department of Political Science, Bates College, Lewiston, Maine

SUZANNE H. MACRAE, Department of English, University of Arkansas, Fayetteville, Arkansas

FRANCES G. MALINO, Jewish Studies and Department of History, Wellesley College, Wellesley, Massachusetts

DAYLE MANDELSON, Associate Professor of Economics, University of Wisconsin-Stout, Menomonie, Wisconsin

HARRIET MARGOLIS, Department of Theater and Film, Victoria University of Wellington, Wellington, New Zealand

NANCY F. MARINO, formerly with Department of Hispanic and Classical Languages, University of Houston, Houston, Texas

ELIZABETH WARREN MARKSON, Socio-Medical Sciences and Community Medicine, Boston University, Boston, Massachusetts

SUSAN E. MARSHALL, Department of Sociology, University of Texas-Austin, Austin, Texas

ELAINE MARTIN, Department of Political Science, Eastern Michigan University, Ypsilanti, Michigan

MARYLOU MARTIN, Department of Foreign Languages, Hendrix College, Conway, Arkansas

ANTONIO H. MARTÍNEZ, Department of Modern Languages, University of Nebraska, Lincoln, Nebraska

SUSAN MATISOFF, Department of Asian Languages, Stanford University, Stanford, California

E. ANN MATTER, Department of Religious Studies, University of Pennsylvania, Philadelphia, Pennsylvania

NAN L. MAXWELL, Department of Economics and Executive Director of Human Investment Research and Education, California State University, Hayward, Hayward, California

TRACY McCABE, formerly with Department of Afro-American Studies, University of Wisconsin-Madison, Madison, Wisconsin

FLORENCE E. McCARTHY, Philosophy and Social Sciences, Columbia University Teachers College, New York, New York

NELLIE McKAY, Department of Afro-American Studies, University of Wisconsin-Madison, Madison, Wisconsin

PENELOPE A. McLORG, doctoral student, Department of Anthropology, Southern Illinois University at Carbondale, Carbondale, Illinois

BEATRICE MEDICINE, Department of Anthropology, California State University, Northridge, Northridge, California

MARTHA T. MEDNICK, Professor Emeritus, Department of Psychology, Howard University, Washington, D.C.

ELIZABETH A. MEESE, Department of English, University of Alabama, Tuscaloosa, Alabama

JANE MEYER, Department of Exercise and Sport Science, University of Wisconsin-LaCrosse, LaCrosse, Wisconsin

BARBARA D. MILLER, Metropolitan Studies Program, Maxwell School, Syracuse University, Syracuse, New York

KAREN S. MITCHELL, Department of Communications, University of Northern Iowa, Cedar Falls, Iowa

WENDY MITCHINSON, Department of History, University of Waterloo, Waterloo, Ontario, Canada

AMALIA MONDRÍQUEZ, Department of Foreign Languages, Incarnate Word College, San Antonio, Texas

VIRGINIA MONTIJO, Acquisitions Editor, William and Mary Press, Williamsburg, Virginia

JILL G. MORAWSKI, Psychological Laboratory, Wesleyan University, Middletown, Connecticut

CLAIRE GOLDBERG MOSES, Department of Women's Studies, University of Maryland, College Park, Maryland

PRABHATI MUKHERJEE, Professor Emeritus, Indian Institute of Advanced Studies, Simla, India

LAURA STEMPEL MUMFORD, Writer–Independent Scholar, Madison, Wisconsin

RUTH NADELHAFT, University of Maine at Bangor, Bangor, Maine

MARGIT NAGY, Department of History, Our Lady of the Lake University of San Antonio, San Antonio, Texas

MEI T. NAKANO, Sabastopol, California

VASUDHA NARAYANAN, Department of Religion, University of Florida, Gainesville, Florida

GUITY NASHAT, Department of History, University of Illinois at Chicago, Chicago, Illinois

BARBARA J. NELSON, Vice President, Radcliffe College, Cambridge, Massachusetts

PAULA M. NELSON, Department of History, University of Wisconsin-Platteville, Platteville, Wisconsin

SARAH M. NELSON, Professor and Chair, Department of Anthropology, University of Denver, Denver, Colorado

BETTY A. NESVOLD, late of the Department of Political Science, California State University, San Diego, San Diego, California

EVA NEUMAIER-DARGYAY, Comparative Studies in Literature, Film, and Religion, University of Alberta, Edmonton, Alberta, Canada

BARBARA NEWMAN, Departments of English and Religion, Northwestern University, Evanston, Illinois

E. V. NIEMEYER, JR., International Office (retired), University of Texas at Austin, Austin, Texas

USHA NILSSON, Department of South Asian Studies, University of Wisconsin-Madison, Madison, Wisconsin

SHARON H. NOLTE, late of DePaul University, Greencastle, Indiana, and Sterling, Illinois

ILLENE NOPPE, Department of Human Development/Psychology, University of Wisconsin–Green Bay, Green Bay, Wisconsin

JILL NORGREN, Department of Government, City College of New York, John Jay College of Criminal Justice, New York, New York

MARY KAY NORSENG, Scandinavian Section, University of California at Los Angeles, Los Angeles, California

CHRISTINE OBBO, Department of Anthropology, Wayne State University, Detroit, Michigan

MAUREEN O'TOOLE, Independent Practice, Atlanta, Georgia

DOROTHY PAGE, Department of History, University of Otago, Dunedin, New Zealand

JUDITH W. PAGE, Department of English, Millsaps College, Jackson, Mississippi

IRÈNE PAGÈS, French Studies, University of Guelph, Guelph, Ontario, Canada

VIVIAN GUSSIN PALEY, Department of Education, University of Chicago, Chicago, Illinois

MICHAL PALGI, Institute for the Research and Study of the Kibbutz and the Cooperative Idea, Haifa University, Haifa, Israel

MICHELE A. PALUDI, Consultant in Sexual Harassments, Schenectady, New York

JUDITH PAPACHRISTOU, Department of History, Sarah Lawrence College, Bronxville, New York

LYNN PARINGER, Associate Dean of Business and Economics, California State University at Hayward, Hayward, California

JANE L. PARPART, Department of History, Dalhousie University, Halifax, Nova Scotia, Canada

BARBARA A. PARSONS, Department of Philosophy, University of Wisconsin-Platteville, Platteville, Wisconsin

KRISTINA M. PASSMAN, Department of Foreign Languages and Classics, University of Maine, Orono, Maine

KATHY PEISS, Department of History, University of Massachusetts Amherst, Amherst, Massachusetts

J. BERNARDO PÉREZ, Department of Spanish, Portuguese and Classics, Rice University, Houston, Texas

CAROL O. PERKINS, Women's Studies Department, California State University, San Diego, San Diego, California

PHEME PERKINS, Department of Theology, Boston College, Chestnut Hill, Massachusetts

ANNE C. PETERSEN, Individual and Family Studies, Pennsylvania State University-University Park Campus, University Park, Pennsylvania

ELIZABETH PETROFF, Department of Comparative Literature, University of Massachusetts Amherst, Amherst, Massachusetts

DIANNE M. PINDERHUGHES, Department of Political Science, University of Illinois at Urbana-Champaign, Urbana, Illinois

SUZANNE POIRIER, Department of Medical Education, College of Medicine, University of Illinois at Chicago, Chicago, Illinois

CYRENA N. PONDROM, Department of English, University of Wisconsin-Madison, Madison, Wisconsin

ANNIS PRATT, Department of English, University of Wisconsin-Madison, Madison, Wisconsin

EDITH E. PROSS, Professor Emeritus, College of Humanities, Houston Baptist University, Houston, Texas

NICOLE HAHN RAFTER, Northeastern University, College of Criminal Justice, Boston, Massachusetts

BARBARA N. RAMUSACK, Department of History, University of Cincinnati, Cincinnati, Ohio

SITA RANCHOD-NILSSON, Director of International Studies Program, Denison University, Granville, Ohio

AMY J. RANSOM, Department of Foreign Languages, University of Montevallo, Montevallo, Alabama

JANICE G. RAYMOND, Department of Women's Studies, University of Massachusetts Amherst, Amherst, Massachusetts

SHERRY L. REAMES, Department of English, University of Wisconsin-Madison, Madison, Wisconsin

WILLIAM A. REESE II, Department of Sociology, Augusta College, Augusta, Georgia

MARIE STEPHEN REGES, late Professor Emeritus, Edgewood College, Madison, Wisconsin

SUSAN REVERBY, Department of Women's Studies, Wellesley College, Wellesley, Massachusetts

BETSY COGGER REZELMAN, Department of Fine Arts, St. Lawrence University, Canton, New York

SUE TOLLESON RINEHART, Department of Political Science, Texas Technological University, Lubbock, Texas

BETTE B. ROBERTS, Department of English, Westfield State College, Westfield, Massachusetts

JENNIFER ROBERTSON, Department of Anthropology, University of Michigan, Ann Arbor, Michigan

SYLVIA ROBERTSON, Women and Children in Crisis, Inc., Bartlesville, Oklahoma

GAY ROBINS, Associate Professor of Ancient Egyptian Art, Art History Department, Emory University, Atlanta, Georgia

PAUL S. ROPP, Department of History, Clark University, Worcester, Massachusetts

ROBERT ROSENTHAL, Department of Psychology, Harvard University, Cambridge, Massachusetts

ELYCE J. ROTELLA, Department of Economics, University of Indiana, Bloomington, Indiana

JACQUELINE A. ROUSE, Department of History, Morehouse College, Georgia State University, Atlanta, Georgia

KUMKUM ROY, Satyawati Co-educational College, University of Delhi, New Delhi, India

PATRICIA D. ROZEE, Department of Psychology and Director of Women's Studies, California State University, Long Beach, Long Beach, California

NORMA L. RUDINSKY, Professor Emeritus, Department of English, Oregon State University, Corvallis, Oregon

DIANA E. H. RUSSELL, Department of Sociology, Mills College, Berkeley, California

RINALDINA RUSSELL, Professor, Department of European Languages Second Literature, City University of New York, Queens College, Flushing, New York

UTE MARGARETE SAINE, Modern and Classical Languages, Chapman University, Orange, California

WENDY SARVASY, Department of Political Science, California State University Hayward, Hayward, California

ARLENE SCADRON, Media Communications, Pima County Community College, Tucson, Arizona

ALLEN SCARBORO, Department of Sociology, Augusta State University, Augusta, Georgia

CHERYL B. SCARBORO, Department of Education, Voorhees College, Denmark, South Carolina

JO O'BRIEN SCHAEFER, Department of English, University of Pittsburgh, Pittsburgh, Pennsylvania

BETH E. SCHNEIDER, Department of Sociology, University of California at Santa Barbara, Santa Barbara, California

MARY ANNE SCHOFIELD, formerly with Department of English, St. Bonaventure University, St. Bonaventure, New York

JANE TIBBETTS SCHULENBURG, Department of Liberal Studies, University of Wisconsin-Madison, Madison, Wisconsin

SALLY SCHWAGER, Director, Women's History Institute, Harvard Graduate School of Education, Cambridge, Massachusetts

PAULA SCHWARTZ, Department of French, Middlebury College, Middlebury, Vermont

ANN SEIDMAN, School of Law, Boston University, Boston, Massachusetts

CAROL A. SENF, Department of English, Georgia Institute of Technology, Atlanta, Georgia

MARY LYNDON SHANLEY, Department of Political Science, Vassar College, Poughkeepsie, New York

STEPHANIE A. SHIELDS, Department of Psychology and Director of Women's Studies, Pennsylvania State University, University Park, Pennsylvania

JODY L. SINDELAR, Departments of Epidemiology and Public Health, Yale School of Medicine, New Haven, Connecticut

MARILYN B. SKINNER, Department of Classics, University of Arizona, Tucson, Arizona

JANE SLAUGHTER, Department of History, University of New Mexico, Albuquerque, New Mexico

SARAH SLAVIN, Department of Political Science, State University of New York at Buffalo, Buffalo, New York

ELEANOR SMITH, Vice Provost, University of Cincinnati, Cincinnati, Ohio

NATALIE J. SOKOLOFF, formerly with Department of Sociology, City University of New York, New York

BARBARA SOMMER, Department of Psychology, University of California at Davis, Davis, California

KATHERINE ST. JOHN, Supervisor of Client Services, Women and Children in Crisis, Family Violence Intervention Project, Bartlesville, Oklahoma

SARAH STAGE, Department of Arts and Sciences, Arizona State University, Glendale, Arizona

EVA STIGERS STEHLE, Department of Classics, University of Maryland, College Park, Maryland

SUSAN A. STEPHENS, Department of Classics, Stanford University, Stanford, California

GLORIA STEPHENSON, Department of English, University of Wisconsin-Platteville, Platteville, Wisconsin

PHYLLIS H. STOCK-MORTON, Department of History, Seton Hall University, South Orange, New Jersey

MARY ROSE SULLIVAN, Professor Emeritus, Department of English, University of Colorado at Denver, Denver, Colorado

K. E. SUPRIYA, Communications, De Paul University, Chicago, Illinois

AMY SWERDLOW, Professor Emeritus, History, Sarah Lawrence College, Bronxville, New York

NINA TASSI, Department of English, Morgan State University, Baltimore, Maryland

DIANE E. TAUB, Departments of Sociology and Psychology, Southern Illinois University at Carbondale, Carbondale, Illinois

CAROL TAVRIS, Social Psychologist and Writer, Los Angeles, California

KAREN J. TAYLOR, Department of History, College of Wooster, Wooster, Ohio

SUSAN L. TAYLOR, Department of English, University of Nevada-Las Vegas, Las Vegas, Nevada

URSZULA TEMPSKA, formerly with Department of English, College of Wooster, Wooster, Ohio

FREIDA HIGH TESFAGIORGIS, Department of Afro-American Studies, University of Wisconsin-Madison, Madison, Wisconsin

CAROL G. THOMAS, Department of History, University of Washington, Seattle, Washington

SUE THOMAS, Department of Government, Georgetown University, Washington, D.C.

ELIZABETH BOYD THOMPSON, Department of English, Purdue University, West Lafayette, Indiana

BURTON H. THROCKMORTON, JR., New Testament Language and Literature, Bangor Theological Seminary, Bangor, Maine

LEONORE TIEFER, Psychiatry, New York University School of Medicine and Albert Einstein College of Medicine, Bronx, New York

HELEN TIERNEY, late Professor Emerita of History, University of Wisconsin-Platteville, Platteville, Wisconsin

LASSE T. TIIHONEN, Department of Spanish and Portuguese, Baylor University, Waco, Texas

HITOMI TONOMURA, Department of History, University of Michigan, Ann Arbor, Michigan

JUDITH ANN TROLANDER, Department of History, University of Minnesota-Duluth, Duluth, Minnesota

JIU-HWA LO UPSHUR, Department of History and Philosophy, Eastern Michigan University, Ypsilanti, Michigan

MARIE MITCHELL OLESEN URBANSKI, Department of English, University of Maine, Orono, Maine

TOMÁS VALLEJOS, late of the Department of English, University of Houston-Downtown, Houston, Texas

ANNETTE VAN DYKE, Women's Studies Program and Individual Options Program, University of Illinois at Springfield, Springfield, Illinois

NANCY VEDDER-SHULTS, Madison, Wisconsin

VICTORIA V. VERNON, Department of Comparative Literatures, Hamilton College, Clinton, New York

PHYLLIS VINE, Freelance Writer, Hastings-on-Hudson, New York

OLGA VORONINA, Director, Moscow Center for Gender Studies, Moscow, Russia

CAROLE WADE, Department of Psychology, Dominican College of San Rafael, San Rafael, California

SUSAN S. WADLEY, Department of Anthropology, Syracuse University, Syracuse, New York

RONALD H. WAINSCOTT, Department of Theatre and Drama, Indiana University, Bloomington, Indiana

CHERYL WALKER, Department of English, Scripps College, Claremont, California

LYNN WALTER, Social Change and Development, University of Wisconsin-Green Bay, Green Bay, Wisconsin

ANN WALTNER, Department of History, University of Minnesota-Minneapolis, Minneapolis, Minnesota

JENNIFER L. WARLICK, Economics, University of Notre Dame, Notre Dame, Indiana

MARIA-BARBARA WATSON-FRANKE, Department of Women's Studies, California State University, San Diego, San Diego, California

ELIZABETH WEBBY, Australian Literature, University of Sydney, Sydney, Australia

MARSHA WEIDNER, Department of Art History, University of Kansas, Lawrence, Kansas

MARTA WEIGLE, Professor, Department of Anthropology, University of New Mexico, Albuquerque, New Mexico

CAROLYN M. WEST, Liberal Studies, University of Washington, Tacoma, Washington

ELAINE WHEELER, R.N., formerly with Women's Studies Program, University of Wisconsin-Madison, Madison, Wisconsin

ROBIN WHEELER, Performing Arts Consultant, Boston, Massachusetts

DINA WILKE, Data Specialist, Columbia Hospital Medical Library, Milwaukee, Wisconsin

JUANITA H. WILLIAMS, Professor Emeritus of Psychology, South Florida University, Tampa, Florida

MAYA BIJVOET WILLIAMSON, American University in Cairo, Cairo, Egypt

KATHARINA M. WILSON, Department of Comparative Literature, University of Georgia, Athens, Georgia

NANCI KOSER WILSON, Department of Criminology, Indiana University of Pennsylvania, Indiana, Pennsylvania

KAYE WINDER, Department of Fine Arts, University of Wisconsin-Platteville, Platteville, Wisconsin

KATHRYN WINZ, Department of Criminal Justice, University of Wisconsin-Platteville, Platteville, Wisconsin

SHARON L. WOLCHIK, Associate Dean, School of Public and International Affairs, George Washington University, Washington, D.C.

NANCY WOLOCH, Department of History, Barnard College, Columbia University, New York, New York

ANNE WOOLLETT, Department of Psychology, University of East London, London, U.K.

NANCY WORCESTER, Women's Studies Outreach, University of Wisconsin-Madison, Madison, Wisconsin

DIANE WORZALA, Department of Women's Studies, University of Wisconsin-Madison, Madison, Wisconsin

TOVA YEDLIN, Professor Emeritus of Slavic and East European Studies, University of Alberta, Edmonton, Alberta, Canada

MARY ANN ZETTELMAIER, Chesterton, Indiana

VIRPI ZUCK, Department of Germanic Languages and Literatures, University of Oregon, Eugene, Oregon

ISBN 0-313-31073-4

90000>

EAN

9 780313 310737

HARDCOVER BAR CODE